casseroles
slow cooker&soups

RDA ENTHUSIAST BRANDS, LLC
MILWAUKEE, WI

Taste of Home

Reader's digest

A TASTE OF HOME/READER'S DIGEST BOOK

©2015 RDA Enthusiast Brands, LLC, 1610 N. 2nd St., Suite 102, Milwaukee WI 53212-3906. All rights reserved.
Taste of Home and Reader's Digest are registered trademarks of The Reader's Digest Association, Inc.

EDITORIAL

Editor-in-Chief: Catherine Cassidy
Creative Director: Howard Greenberg
Editorial Operations Director: Kerri Balliet

Managing Editor, Print & Digital Books: Mark Hagen
Associate Creative Director: Edwin Robles Jr.

Editor: Amy Glander
Art Director: Maggie Conners
Layout Designer: Nancy Novak
Editorial Production Manager: Dena Ahlers
Copy Chief: Deb Warlaumont Mulvey
Copy Editors: Mary-Liz Shaw, Dulcie Shoener, Joanne Weintraub
Contributing Copy Editors: Steph Kilen, Valerie Phillips
Content Operations Manager: Colleen King
Content Operations Assistant: Shannon Stroud
Editorial Services Administrator: Marie Brannon

Food Editors: James Schend; Peggy Woodward, RD
Recipe Editors: Mary King; Jenni Sharp, RD; Irene Yeh

Test Kitchen & Food Styling Manager: Sarah Thompson
Test Cooks: Nicholas Iverson (lead), Matthew Hass, Lauren Knoelke
Food Stylists: Kathryn Conrad (senior), Leah Rekau, Shannon Roum
Prep Cooks: Megumi Garcia, Melissa Hansen, Bethany Van Jacobson, Sara Wirtz

Photography Director: Stephanie Marchese
Photographers: Dan Roberts, Jim Wieland
Photographer/Set Stylist: Grace Natoli Sheldon
Set Stylists: Stacey Genaw, Melissa Haberman, Dee Dee Jacq
Photo Studio Assistant: Ester Robards

Editorial Business Manager: Kristy Martin
Editorial Business Associate: Samantha Lea Stoeger

BUSINESS

General Manager, Taste of Home Cooking School: Erin Puariea
Executive Producer, Taste of Home Online Cooking School: Karen Berner

THE READER'S DIGEST ASSOCIATION, INC.

President and Chief Executive Officer: Bonnie Kintzer
Vice President, Chief Operating Officer, North America: Howard Halligan
Vice President, Enthusiast Brands, Books & Retail: Harold Clarke
Chief Marketing Officer: Leslie Dukker Doty
Vice President, Content Marketing & Operations: Diane Dragan
Senior Vice President, Global HR & Communications: Phyllis E. Gebhardt, SPHR
Vice President, Brand Marketing: Beth Gorry
Vice President, Chief Technology Officer: Aneel Tejwaney
Vice President, Consumer Marketing Planning: Jim Woods

For other Taste of Home books and products, visit us at **tasteofhome.com.**

For more Reader's Digest products and information, visit **rd.com** (in the United States) or **rd.ca** (in Canada).

International Standard Book Number: 978-1-61765-406-0
Library of Congress Control Number: 2014957263
3 5 7 9 10 8 6 4 2
Printed in China.

Cover Photographer: Dan Roberts
Set Stylist: Grace Natoli Sheldon
Food Stylist: Shannon Roum

Pictured on front cover: Lime Chicken Chili, page 304; Beer-Braised Roast with Root Vegetables, page 140; Simple Creamy Chicken Enchiladas, page 53.

Pictured on back cover: Broccoli-Ham Hot Dish, page 42; Beef Roast with Cranberry Gravy, page145; Hearty Hamburger Soup, page 232; Pink Grapefruit Cheesecake, page 219.
Spine: Individual Brunch Casseroles, page 15.

Pictured on page 1: Italian Breakfast Strata, page 20; Easy Beans & Potatoes with Bacon, page 201; Stuffing Dumpling Soup, page 252.

Contents

TURKEY & SPINACH STUFFING CASSEROLE / 65

Casseroles 101

HEARTY, COMFORTING ONE-DISH BAKES

GARDEN VEGGIE EGG BAKE / 16

Casserole, hot dish, potpie, strata, bake...no matter what you call it, it means convenient, comforting, home-cooked food. This book is brimming with **167** casserole recipes that are guaranteed to be delicious and satisfying.

WHY CASSEROLES ARE SO POPULAR:

- Many are convenient meals-in-one. Or just add a salad or vegetable, and dinner is ready!

- Cleanup is easy because everything bakes in one dish. You'll only have a few items to wash after dinner.

- You're free to do other things while it bakes.

- Many can be assembled one day, then refrigerated and baked the next day.

- Casseroles are great for large family gatherings and potlucks.

- Leftovers make a delicious lunch or quick dinner.

- Most reheat easily in the microwave.

- Full of flavor, casseroles make you feel warm and cozy.

The casseroles in this indispensible cookbook are sure to become some of your family's favorite dishes. You'll be sure to make them time and again!

Slow Cooker

EASY HOME-COOKED MEALS...READY WHEN *YOU* ARE!

101

ADVANTAGES OF SLOW COOKING:

CONVENIENCE. Slow cookers provide people with the ease of safely preparing meals while away from home. The appliances are readily available and budget-friendly.

HEALTH. As more people turn to more nutritious food choices to improve their health, slow cooking has gained popularity. Low-temperature cooking retains more vitamins in foods, and leaner cuts of meat become tender in the slow cooker without added fats. Lower-sodium and lower-fat versions of many canned goods are available, which can help you create even lighter, healthier meals. And, for many busy folks, knowing that a healthy meal is waiting at home helps them avoid the temptation of the drive-thru after work.

FINANCIAL SAVINGS. A slow cooker uses very little electricity because of its low wattage. For instance, it would cost roughly 21 cents to operate a slow cooker for a total of 10 hours. If you cook a pork roast for 2 hours in the oven instead of using the slow cooker for 10 hours, you'll spend $2.51 to operate an electric oven or $1.49 to operate a gas one. Also, slow cookers do not heat up the kitchen as ovens do, which saves on summertime cooling costs.

Try this: **Sweet Kahlua Coffee** on page 115.

Turn to your slow cooker for the best mix-it-and-forget-it convenience. With a slow cooker and these **209** recipes on hand, it's easy to put a hot, home-cooked meal on the table at the end of the day, even when you've been away.

MUSHROOM POT ROAST / 148

Slow Cooker 101 (*continued*)

know when it's
DONE!

→ # 145°F

- Medium-rare beef and lamb roasts
- Fish

→ # 160°F

- Medium beef and lamb roasts
- Pork
- Egg dishes

→ # 165°F

- Ground chicken and turkey

→ # 170°F

- Well-done beef and lamb roasts
- Chicken and turkey that is whole or in pieces

SLOW COOKING BASICS:

- Slow cooker models vary, but all of them usually have at least two settings, low (about 180°) and high (about 280°). Some models also have a keep-warm setting.

- The keep-warm setting is useful if you plan to use the slow cooker to serve hot foods while entertaining. Some slow cookers will automatically switch to a keep-warm setting after cooking. This provides added convenience and helps you avoid overcooking the food while you're away from home.

- We provide a range in cooking times to allow for variables such as meat thickness, whether the slow cooker is full and how hot the food should be when cooked. As you grow familiar with your slow cooker, you'll be able to judge which end of the range to use.

- New slow cookers heat up more quickly than older ones. If you have an older model and your recipe directs you to cook on low, try cooking on high for the first hour to ensure food safety.

- Slow cookers range in price from $20 to more than $200 and are available in sizes from 1½ to 7 quarts. Select one that fits your budget and choose a size appropriate for your family.

- To learn more about specific models, check online or in reputable consumer magazines for product reviews.

COOK TIMES:

Conventional Oven 15 to 30 minutes	Conventional Oven 35 to 45 minutes	Conventional Oven 50 minutes or more
Slow Cooker Low: 4 to 6 hours High: 1½ to 2 hours	**Slow Cooker** Low: 6 to 8 hours High: 3 to 4 hours	**Slow Cooker** Low: 8 to 10 hours High: 4 to 6 hours

TIPS FOR TASTY OUTCOMES

- Be sure the lid is secure over the ceramic insert, not tilted or askew. Steam during cooking creates a seal.

- Refrain from lifting the lid while using the slow cooker, unless the recipe instructs you to stir or add ingredients. The loss of steam each time you lift the lid can mean an extra 20 to 30 minutes of cooking time.

- Slow cooking may take longer at higher altitudes.

- When food is finished cooking, remove it from the slow cooker within an hour. Promptly refrigerate any leftovers.

- Use a slow cooker on a buffet table to keep soup, stew, savory dips or mashed potatoes hot.

- Heat cooked food on the stovetop or in the microwave and then put it into a slow cooker to keep it hot for serving. Do not reheat food in a slow cooker.

CLEANING TIPS:

1 Removable inserts make cleanup a breeze. Be sure to cool the insert before rinsing or cleaning with water to avoid cracking or warping. Do not immerse the metal base in water. Clean it with a damp sponge.

2 If the insert is dishwasher-safe, place it in the dishwasher. Otherwise, wash it in warm soapy water. Avoid using abrasive cleansers, as they may scratch the surface.

3 To remove mineral stains on a ceramic insert, fill the cooker with hot water and 1 cup of white vinegar; cover. Turn the heat to high for 2 hours, then empty. When cool, wash the insert with hot soapy water and a cloth or sponge. Rinse well and dry with a towel.

4 To remove water marks from a highly glazed ceramic insert, rub the surface with canola oil and allow to stand for 2 hours before washing with hot soapy water.

Soups 101

TAKE STOCK WITH THE BEST HOMEMADE SOUPS

Try this:
Chunky Chipotle Pork Chili
on page 307.

MAKEOVER CHEESY HAM 'N' POTATO SOUP / 243

Soups are versatile and can satisfy many menu-planning needs. Use a light broth or a cream-based soup as a first course. A full-bodied bean or a loaded chicken vegetable soup just needs a crisp salad or a hearty slice of bread to complete the meal. Or pair any one of these **139** soups with your favorite sandwich.

SOUPS, DEFINED:

BISQUE: A thick, rich pureed soup often made with seafood but may be made with poultry or vegetables.

BROTH: Made from simmering meats, poultry, fish or vegetables, broths have less body than stocks. The terms "broth" and "stock" may be used interchangeably for the recipes in this book.

CHILI: A hearty dish usually made with tomatoes and chili powder, but some chili dishes are white. The variations on chili seem endless. A chili can be mild or hot, have ground beef, stew meat, sausage, poultry or be meatless. It may have macaroni or spaghetti or no pasta at all.

CHOWDER: A chunky, thick, rich soup frequently made with seafood or vegetables, such as corn, but it can be made with other meat. Chowders have a milk or cream base and may be thickened with flour.

CONSOMME: A completely degreased, clarified stock. It has a rich flavor, and due to its high gelatin content, will set up when chilled.

CREAMED SOUPS: Pureed soups with a smooth, silky texture. The main flavor is frequently a single vegetable, such as asparagus or carrot. They may be thickened with flour or potatoes and can be made without cream.

GAZPACHO: An uncooked cold soup. The most common version uses tomatoes, cucumbers, sweet peppers, onion and garlic.

GUMBO: A hearty stew-like soup usually served with white rice that starts with a dark roux of flour and oil or butter. It may contain shellfish, chicken, sausage, ham, tomatoes, onions, garlic, sweet peppers and celery. In addition to the roux, okra is used as a thickening agent.

STOCKS: Usually made with meaty bones (possibly roasted), meat and vegetables. Stock should be clear, free of grease and have a subtle flavor.

ROASTED GARLIC BUTTERNUT SOUP / 265

Casseroles

GOLDEN, BUBBLY CASSEROLES ARE COMFORT FOOD AT ITS BEST. THEY'RE CONVENIENT, FREEZER-FRIENDLY AND MANY CAN BE ASSEMBLED THE NIGHT BEFORE.

ITALIAN BRUNCH BAKE
PAGE 13

CHICKEN MOLE CASSEROLE
PAGE 57

BROCCOLI AND CARROT CHEESE BAKE *PAGE 105*

EASY BREAKFAST STRATA

Apple-Raisin Baked Oatmeal

My kids love this baked oatmeal, especially with fun fruit variations on top. I love that it's economical and keeps them full.
—**CHRISTINA SMEAL** FAIRMONT, WV

PREP: 20 MIN. • **BAKE:** 35 MIN.
MAKES: 6 SERVINGS

- 3 cups old-fashioned oats
- ½ cup packed brown sugar
- 2 teaspoons baking powder
- 1½ teaspoons ground cinnamon
- ½ teaspoon salt
- ⅛ teaspoon ground nutmeg
- 2 eggs
- 2 cups fat-free milk
- 1 medium apple, chopped
- ⅓ cup raisins
- ⅓ cup chopped walnuts
    Additional fat-free milk, optional

1. Preheat oven to 350°. In a large bowl, combine first six ingredients. Whisk eggs and milk; stir into dry ingredients until blended. Let stand 5 minutes. Stir in the apple, raisins and walnuts.
2. Transfer to an 8-in.-square baking dish coated with cooking spray. Bake, uncovered, 35-40 minutes or until edges are lightly browned and a thermometer reads 160°. Serve with additional milk if desired.

**APPLE-RAISIN
BAKED OATMEAL**

Easy Breakfast Strata

This breakfast casserole lives up to its name. It's prepped the night before, so you don't have to deal with any fuss or dirty dishes first thing in the morning. It bakes up tender and golden and goes over well whenever I serve it.
—**DEBBIE JOHNSON** CENTERTOWN, MO

PREP: 20 MIN. + CHILLING • **BAKE:** 30 MIN.
MAKES: 12 SERVINGS

- 1 pound bulk pork sausage
- 1 large green pepper, chopped
- 1 medium onion, chopped
- 1 loaf (1 pound) herb or cheese bakery bread, cubed
- 1 cup (4 ounces) shredded cheddar cheese
- 6 eggs
- 2 cups 2% milk
- 1 teaspoon ground mustard

1. In a large skillet, cook sausage, pepper and onion over medium heat until meat is no longer pink; drain.
2. Place bread in a greased 13x9-in. baking dish. Top with sausage; sprinkle with cheese. In a large bowl, whisk eggs, milk and mustard. Pour over top. Cover and refrigerate overnight.
3. Remove from the refrigerator 30 minutes before baking. Preheat oven to 350°. Bake, uncovered, 30-35 minutes or until a knife inserted near the center comes out clean. Let stand 5 minutes before cutting.

The best part about this recipe is you can tailor it to the season and use whatever veggies and cheese you have on hand. I particularly love this in spring with fresh greens and asparagus.

—SHANNON KOENE BLACKSBURG, VA

FREEZE IT Bacon
Vegetable Quiche

PREP: 25 MIN. • **BAKE:** 30 MIN.
MAKES: 6 SERVINGS

- 1 **unbaked pastry shell (9 inches)**
- 1 **cup sliced fresh mushrooms**
- 1 **cup chopped fresh broccoli**
- ¾ **cup chopped sweet onion**
- 2½ **teaspoons olive oil**
- 2 **cups fresh baby spinach**
- 3 **eggs, lightly beaten**
- 1 **can (5 ounces) evaporated milk**
- 1 **tablespoon minced fresh rosemary or 1 teaspoon dried rosemary, crushed**
- ¼ **teaspoon salt**
- ¼ **teaspoon pepper**
- 1 **cup (4 ounces) shredded cheddar cheese**
- 6 **bacon strips, cooked and crumbled**
- ½ **cup crumbled tomato and basil feta cheese**

1. Preheat oven to 450°. Line unpricked pastry shell with a double thickness of heavy-duty foil. Bake 8 minutes. Remove foil; bake 5 minutes longer. Reduce oven to 375°.
2. Meanwhile, in a large skillet, saute mushrooms, broccoli and onion in oil until tender. Add the spinach; cook until wilted.
3. In a large bowl, whisk eggs, milk, rosemary, salt and pepper. Stir in vegetables, cheddar cheese and bacon. Pour mixture into crust. Sprinkle with feta cheese.
4. Cover edges loosely with foil. Bake 30-35 minutes or until a knife inserted near the center comes out clean. Let stand 5 minutes before cutting.

FREEZE OPTION *Cover and freeze unbaked quiche. To use, remove from freezer 30 minutes before baking (do not thaw). Preheat oven to 375°. Place quiche on a baking sheet; cover edges loosely with foil. Bake as directed, increasing time as necessary for a knife inserted near the center to come out clean.*

BACON VEGETABLE QUICHE

Prosciutto-Pesto Breakfast Strata

I'd never tasted prosciutto before I tried this recipe, and I was an instant die-hard fan! The layers of flavor in this dish make it well worth the time.

—VICKI ANDERSON FARMINGTON, MN

PREP: 25 MIN. + CHILLING • **COOK:** 50 MIN.
MAKES: 10 SERVINGS

- 2 cups 2% milk
- 1 cup white wine or chicken broth
- 35 slices French bread (½-inch thick)
- ¼ cup minced fresh basil
- ¼ cup minced fresh parsley
- 3 tablespoons olive oil
- ½ pound thinly sliced smoked Gouda cheese
- ½ pound thinly sliced prosciutto
- 3 medium tomatoes, thinly sliced
- ½ cup prepared pesto
- 4 eggs
- ½ cup heavy whipping cream
- ½ teaspoon salt
- ¼ teaspoon pepper

1. In a shallow bowl, combine milk and wine. Dip both sides of bread into milk mixture; squeeze gently to remove excess liquid. Layer bread slices in a greased 13x9-in. baking dish.
2. Sprinkle with basil and parsley; drizzle with oil. Layer with half of the cheese, half of the prosciutto and all of the tomatoes; drizzle with half of the pesto. Top with remaining cheese, prosciutto and pesto.
3. In a small bowl, whisk eggs, cream, salt and pepper until blended; pour over top. Refrigerate, covered, several hours or overnight.
4. Preheat oven to 350°. Remove strata from refrigerator while oven heats. Bake, uncovered, 50-60 minutes or until golden brown and a knife inserted near the center comes out clean. Let stand 5-10 minutes before serving.

Overnight Brunch Casserole

I love to cook for company and host brunches frequently. Standing out from most egg bakes, this casserole combines scrambled eggs and a cheese sauce that bake up into a rich and creamy dish.

—CANDY HESCH MOSINEE, WI

PREP: 30 MIN. + CHILLING
BAKE: 40 MIN. + STANDING
MAKES: 12 SERVINGS

- 3 tablespoons butter, divided
- 2 tablespoons all-purpose flour
- ½ teaspoon salt
- ⅛ teaspoon pepper
- 2 cups fat-free milk
- 5 slices reduced-fat process American cheese product, chopped
- 1½ cups sliced fresh mushrooms
- 2 green onions, finely chopped
- 1 cup cubed fully cooked ham
- 2 cups egg substitute
- 4 eggs

TOPPING
- 3 slices whole wheat bread, cubed
- 4 teaspoons butter, melted
- ⅛ teaspoon paprika

1. In a large saucepan, melt 2 tablespoons butter. Stir in flour, salt and pepper until smooth; gradually add milk. Bring to a boil; cook and stir 2 minutes or until slightly thickened. Stir in cheese until melted. Remove from heat.
2. In a large nonstick skillet, saute mushrooms and green onions in remaining butter until tender. Add ham; heat through. Whisk the egg substitute and eggs; add to skillet. Cook and stir until almost set. Stir in cheese sauce.
3. Transfer to a 13x9-in. baking dish coated with cooking spray. Toss bread cubes with butter. Arrange over egg mixture; sprinkle with paprika. Cover and refrigerate overnight.
4. Remove from the refrigerator 30 minutes before baking. Preheat oven to 350°. Bake, uncovered, 40-45 minutes or until a knife inserted near the center comes out clean. Let stand 10 minutes before cutting.

OVERNIGHT BRUNCH CASSEROLE

Sweet Orange Croissant Pudding

Time-crunched cooks are sure to appreciate the make-ahead convenience of this delightful dish. Feel free to replace the orange marmalade with any jam or jelly that suits your taste.

—MARY GABRIEL LAS VEGAS, NV

PREP: 15 MIN. + CHILLING
BAKE: 40 MIN. + COOLING
MAKES: 8 SERVINGS

- 4 croissants, split
- 1 cup orange marmalade, divided
- 3 eggs
- 1¼ cups milk
- 1 cup heavy whipping cream
- ½ cup sugar
- 1 teaspoon grated orange peel, optional
- ½ teaspoon almond extract

1. Spread each croissant bottom with 3 tablespoons marmalade; replace tops. Cut each croissant into five slices; place in a greased 11x7-in. baking dish.
2. In a large bowl, whisk eggs, milk, cream, sugar, orange peel if desired and extract; pour over croissants. Cover and refrigerate overnight.
3. Remove from refrigerator 30 minutes before baking. Preheat oven to 350°. Place dish in a larger baking dish. Fill larger dish with 1 in. of boiling water.
4. Bake, uncovered, 40-45 minutes or until a knife inserted near center comes out clean.
5. Remove pan from water bath; cool on a wire rack 10 minutes. Brush remaining marmalade over the top. Cut and serve warm.

ITALIAN BRUNCH BAKE

Italian Brunch Bake

This is a great overnight recipe to make when you have company coming over for brunch. I often make it during the holidays. When I wake up, all I have to do is pop it into the oven, and in no time, the troops are fed.

—VIVIAN TAYLOR MIDDLEBURG, FL

PREP: 30 MIN. + CHILLING
BAKE: 55 MIN. + STANDING
MAKES: 12 SERVINGS

- 1 pound bulk Italian sausage
- 1 pound baby portobello mushrooms, quartered
- 1 large onion, chopped
- 1 medium sweet red pepper, chopped
- 1 medium green pepper, chopped
- 2 garlic cloves, minced
- 2 packages (6 ounces each) fresh baby spinach
- 8 slices Italian bread (1-inch thick)
- 12 eggs
- 1 cup 2% milk
- 1 teaspoon Italian seasoning
- ½ teaspoon salt
- ½ teaspoon pepper
- ¼ teaspoon ground nutmeg
- 4 cups (16 ounces) shredded Italian cheese blend

1. In a large skillet, cook sausage, mushrooms, onion, peppers and garlic over medium heat until meat is no longer pink; drain and set aside.
2. In a large skillet coated with cooking spray, saute spinach until wilted. Place bread on a baking sheet. Broil 2-3 in. from heat for 1-2 minutes or until lightly browned. Transfer to a greased 13x9-in. baking dish.
3. In a large bowl, combine eggs, milk, Italian seasoning, salt, pepper and nutmeg. Layer sausage mixture and spinach over bread; pour egg mixture over top. Sprinkle with cheese; cover and refrigerate overnight.
4. Remove from refrigerator 30 minutes before baking. Preheat oven to 350°. Cover and bake for 50 minutes. Uncover; bake 5-10 minutes longer or until a knife inserted near the center comes out clean. Let stand 10 minutes before cutting.

SAUSAGE-POTATO BAKE

Sausage-Potato Bake

I not only make this casserole for breakfast, but sometimes for supper, too! To change it up a bit, you can substitute finely diced lean ham or crumbled turkey bacon for the sausage.

—RUTH RIGONI HURLEY, WI

PREP: 20 MIN. • **BAKE:** 55 MIN. + STANDING
MAKES: 6 SERVINGS

- ½ **pound bulk pork sausage**
- 3 **large potatoes, peeled and thinly sliced**
- ½ **teaspoon salt**
- ¼ **teaspoon pepper**
- 1 **jar (2 ounces) diced pimientos, drained**
- 3 **eggs, lightly beaten**
- 1 **cup 2% milk**
- 2 **tablespoons minced chives**
- ¾ **teaspoon dried thyme or oregano**
  Additional minced chives, optional

1. Preheat oven to 375°. In a large skillet, cook sausage over medium heat until no longer pink; drain.

2. Arrange half the potatoes in a greased 8-in.-square baking dish; sprinkle with salt, pepper and half the sausage. Layer with remaining potatoes and sausage; sprinkle with pimientos.

3. In a small bowl, whisk the eggs, milk, chives and thyme; pour over the pimientos.

4. Cover and bake 45-50 minutes or until a knife inserted near the center comes out clean. Uncover; bake 10 minutes longer or until lightly browned. Let stand 10 minutes before cutting. Sprinkle with additional chives if desired.

INDIVIDUAL BRUNCH CASSEROLES

Individual Brunch Casseroles

I created these fun individual breakfast cups one Sunday morning when I needed to use up some potatoes. They were a hit, and now our two daughters look forward to them.

—PEGGY MEADOR KELL, IL

PREP: 20 MIN. • **BAKE:** 25 MIN.
MAKES: 4 SERVINGS

- 3 **cups shredded uncooked potatoes**
- ¾ **cup diced onion**
- ½ **cup diced celery**
- ½ **cup diced green pepper**
- 2 **to 4 tablespoons canola oil**
- 4 **eggs**
- ½ **teaspoon salt**
- ¼ **teaspoon pepper**
- 1 **cup (4 ounces) shredded cheddar cheese**
- ½ **pound sliced bacon, cooked and crumbled**
- 1 **can (4 ounces) mushroom stems and pieces, drained**

1. Preheat oven to 350°. In a large skillet, saute potatoes, onion, celery and green pepper in 2 tablespoons oil until vegetables are crisp-tender. If necessary, add additional oil to prevent sticking. Remove from heat.

2. In a large bowl, whisk eggs, salt and pepper. Add cheese, bacon and mushrooms; mix well. Stir in potato mixture. Pour into four greased individual baking dishes.

3. Bake, uncovered, 25-35 minutes or until a knife inserted near the center comes out clean. Let stand 5 minutes before serving.

FREEZE IT Italian Quiches

This hearty dish tastes like pizza and can be enjoyed for breakfast as well as supper.

—BERNICE HANCOCK GREENVILLE, PA

PREP: 25 MIN. • **BAKE:** 35 MIN. + STANDING
MAKES: 2 QUICHES (6 SERVINGS EACH)

- 2 **unbaked pastry shells (9 inches)**
- 1 **pound bulk Italian sausage**
- 4 **cups (16 ounces) finely shredded part-skim mozzarella cheese**
- 1 **medium onion, thinly sliced**
- 1 **medium green pepper, thinly sliced**
- 1 **medium sweet red pepper, thinly sliced**
- 6 **eggs**
- 2 **cups milk**
- 1 **teaspoon minced garlic**
- ¼ **cup grated Parmesan cheese**

1. Preheat oven to 400°. Line unpricked pastry shells with a double thickness of heavy-duty foil. Bake for 4 minutes. Remove foil; bake 4 minutes longer. Remove from oven; leave oven on.

2. In a large skillet, cook sausage over medium heat until no longer pink; drain. Spoon sausage into pastry shells; sprinkle with mozzarella cheese. Top with onion and peppers. In a large bowl, whisk eggs, milk and garlic. Pour over peppers; sprinkle with Parmesan cheese.

3. Cover edges of quiches loosely with foil; place on a baking sheet. Bake at 400° for 35-40 minutes or until a knife inserted near the center comes out clean. Let stand for 10 minutes before cutting.

FREEZE OPTION *Cover and freeze unbaked quiches up to 3 months. To use, remove from the freezer 30 minutes before baking (do not thaw). Preheat oven to 400°. Cover edges of crust loosely with foil; place on a baking sheet. Bake 50-60 minutes or until a knife inserted near the center comes out clean. Let stand for 10 minutes before cutting.*

GARDEN VEGGIE EGG BAKE

Garden Veggie Egg Bake

Looking for a healthy way to start your day? Kids will actually enjoy eating their veggies when they're baked into this cheesy, nutrition-packed egg dish.

—JOANNE WILSON ROSELLE PARK, NJ

PREP: 20 MIN. • **BAKE:** 45 MIN. + STANDING
MAKES: 6 SERVINGS

- 5 **eggs**
- 2 **cups egg substitute**
- ½ **cup 2% cottage cheese**
- ⅓ **cup shredded pepper jack cheese**
- ⅓ **cup shredded cheddar cheese**
- ¼ **cup grated Romano cheese**
- ¼ **teaspoon pepper**
- ¼ **teaspoon hot pepper sauce**
- 1 **medium zucchini, chopped**
- 2 **cups fresh broccoli florets**
- 2 **cups coarsely chopped fresh spinach**
- ½ **cup shredded carrots**
- ½ **cup cherry tomatoes, quartered**

1. Preheat oven to 350°. In a large bowl, whisk eggs, egg substitute, cheeses, pepper and pepper sauce. Stir in the vegetables. Transfer to an 11x7-in. baking dish coated with cooking spray.

2. Bake, uncovered, 45-50 minutes or until a knife inserted near center comes out clean. Let stand 10 minutes before cutting.

ITALIAN QUICHES

Cinnamon Raisin Bake

This delightful dish, made with day-old raisin bread, is full of cinnamon flavor. I serve it for brunch with crispy sliced bacon and a colorful fruit compote.
—**BARBARA TRITCH** HOPE, ID

PREP: 20 MIN. + CHILLING • **BAKE:** 40 MIN.
MAKES: 4 SERVINGS

- ¼ **cup butter, softened**
- 3 **tablespoons ground cinnamon**
- 8 **slices day-old raisin bread**
- 4 **tablespoons brown sugar, divided**
- 6 **eggs, lightly beaten**
- 1½ **cups 2% milk**
- 3 **tablespoons maple syrup**
- 1 **teaspoon vanilla extract**
  Additional maple syrup

1. In a small bowl, combine butter and cinnamon; spread over one side of each slice of bread. Place four slices, buttered side up, in a greased 8-in.-square baking dish (trim bread to fit if necessary). Sprinkle with 2 tablespoons brown sugar. Repeat with remaining bread and brown sugar.
2. In a large bowl, whisk eggs, milk, syrup and vanilla; pour over bread. Cover and refrigerate overnight.
3. Remove from refrigerator 30 minutes before baking. Preheat oven to 350°. Bake, uncovered, 40-50 minutes or until a knife inserted near the center comes out clean. Serve with additional syrup.

DID YOU KNOW?

Prosciutto is a thinly sliced Italian-style ham that is salt-cured and air-dried for 10 months to 2 years. It is not smoked. It works well in casseroles, salads, pasta dishes and even as a topping on pizza.

Gruyere & Prosciutto Strata

Prosciutto, sweet onions and Gruyere cheese combine for a perfect make-ahead breakfast dish. I guarantee there won't be any leftovers.
—**PATTI LAVELL** ISLAMORADA, FL

PREP: 15 MIN. + CHILLING • **BAKE:** 35 MIN.
MAKES: 9 SERVINGS

- 2 **teaspoons canola oil**
- 4 **ounces thin slices prosciutto, chopped**
- 2 **large sweet onions, chopped (4 cups)**
- 1 **carton (8 ounces) egg substitute**
- 2½ **cups 2% milk**
- ¼ **teaspoon ground mustard**
- ⅛ **teaspoon pepper**
- 8 **cups cubed French bread**
- 1½ **cups (6 ounces) shredded Gruyere or Swiss cheese, divided**

1. In a large skillet, heat oil over medium-high heat. Add prosciutto; cook and stir until crisp. Remove from the pan with a slotted spoon. Add onions to the same pan; cook and stir until tender.
2. In a large bowl, whisk egg substitute, milk, mustard and pepper. Stir in bread and onions. Reserve 2 tablespoons cooked prosciutto for topping; stir remaining prosciutto into bread mixture.
3. Transfer half of the mixture to a greased 13x9-in. baking dish; sprinkle with half of the cheese. Top with remaining bread mixture. Separately cover and refrigerate strata and reserved prosciutto overnight.
4. Preheat oven to 350°. Remove strata from refrigerator while oven heats. Bake, uncovered, 20 minutes. Sprinkle with remaining cheese; top with reserved prosciutto. Bake 15-20 minutes longer or until a knife inserted near the center comes out clean. Let stand 5-10 minutes before serving.

GRUYERE & PROSCIUTTO STRATA

Vegetarian Egg Strata

I used to make this with turkey or chicken sausage, but adapted it for a vegetarian friend. It was a huge hit!

—**DANNA ROGERS** WESTPORT, CT

PREP: 25 MIN. + CHILLING
BAKE: 45 MIN. + STANDING
MAKES: 12 SERVINGS

- 1 **medium zucchini, finely chopped**
- 1 **medium sweet red pepper, finely chopped**
- 1 **cup sliced baby portobello mushrooms**
- 1 **medium red onion, finely chopped**
- 2 **teaspoons olive oil**
- 3 **garlic cloves, minced**
- 2 **teaspoons minced fresh thyme or ½ teaspoon dried thyme**
- ½ **teaspoon salt**
- ¼ **teaspoon pepper**
- 1 **loaf (1 pound) day-old French bread, cubed**
- 2 **packages (5.3 ounces each) fresh goat cheese, crumbled**
- 1¾ **cups grated Parmesan cheese**
- 6 **eggs, lightly beaten**
- 2 **cups fat-free milk**
- ¼ **teaspoon ground nutmeg**

1. In a large skillet, saute zucchini, red pepper, mushrooms and onion in oil until tender. Add garlic, thyme, salt and pepper; saute 1 minute longer.

2. In a 13x9-in. baking dish coated with cooking spray, layer half the bread cubes, zucchini mixture, goat cheese and Parmesan cheese. Repeat layers.

3. In a small bowl, whisk eggs, milk and nutmeg. Pour over top. Cover and refrigerate overnight.

4. Remove from the refrigerator 30 minutes before baking. Preheat oven to 350°. Bake, uncovered, 45-50 minutes or until a knife inserted near the center comes out clean. Let stand 10 minutes before cutting.

VEGETARIAN EGG STRATA

Mushroom-Artichoke Brunch Casserole

There's not much slicing or measuring required for this casserole, so it's a breeze to prep. It makes a delicious vegetarian egg bake, but you can also add a layer of little smoked sausages sliced lengthwise in half over the artichokes if you want a more substantial meal.

—SUZANNE FRANCIS MARYSVILLE, WA

PREP: 30 MIN. • **BAKE:** 40 MIN.
MAKES: 12 SERVINGS

- 3 **cups frozen shredded hash brown potatoes, thawed**
- 2 **tablespoons butter, melted, divided**
- ½ **teaspoon salt**
- 2½ **cups sliced fresh mushrooms**
- 1 **can (14 ounces) water-packed artichoke hearts, rinsed, drained and quartered**
- 3 **cups (12 ounces) shredded cheddar cheese**
- 12 **eggs**
- 1¾ **cups 2% milk**
- 1 **can (4 ounces) chopped green chilies, drained**

1. Preheat oven to 350°. Place potatoes in a greased 13x9-in. baking dish; drizzle with 1 tablespoon butter and sprinkle with salt. Bake 20-25 minutes or until lightly browned.

2. Meanwhile, in a small skillet, saute mushrooms in remaining butter until tender. Place artichokes on paper towels; pat dry. Sprinkle mushrooms, artichokes and cheese over the potatoes. In a large bowl, whisk the eggs, milk and green chilies; pour over cheese.

3. Bake, uncovered, 40-45 minutes or until a knife inserted near the center comes out clean. Let stand 5 minutes before serving.

Dulce de Leche French Toast Bake with Praline Topping

My overnight French toast has a rich flavor and a sweet and crunchy topping. It's perfect for fuss-free holiday breakfasts or when you're hosting overnight guests.

—ANNA STIGGER KATY, TX

PREP: 30 MIN. + CHILLING • **BAKE:** 40 MIN.
MAKES: 6 SERVINGS

- 8 **slices Texas toast**
- ⅓ **cup whipped cream cheese**
- ⅓ **cup dulce de leche**
- 3 **eggs**
- ½ **cup 2% milk**
- ½ **cup half-and-half cream**
- 3 **tablespoons sugar**
- 1½ **teaspoons vanilla extract**

TOPPING
- ½ **cup packed brown sugar**
- ¼ **cup butter, cubed**
- 1 **tablespoon corn syrup**
- ¾ **cup chopped pecans**

1. Preheat oven to 325°. Place Texas toast on an ungreased baking sheet. Bake 15-20 minutes or until light brown. Cool.

2. Arrange half of the toast in a single layer in a greased 8-in.-square baking dish, trimming to fit into dish if necessary. In a small bowl, mix cream cheese and dulce de leche; spread over toast. Top with remaining toast.

3. In a small bowl, whisk eggs, milk, cream, sugar and vanilla; pour over toast. Refrigerate, covered, overnight.

4. Preheat oven to 350°. Remove French toast from refrigerator while oven heats. In a small saucepan, combine brown sugar, butter and corn syrup; cook and stir over medium heat until sugar is dissolved. Stir in pecans; spread over top.

5. Bake, uncovered, 40-50 minutes or until puffed, golden and a knife inserted near the center comes out clean. Let stand 5-10 minutes before cutting.

DULCE DE LECHE
FRENCH TOAST BAKE
WITH PRALINE TOPPING

Italian Breakfast Strata

We used to raise our own chickens, so I always had plenty of eggs on hand for weekly brunch or supper dishes. This recipe is a combination of some of my favorite flavors and one my husband really enjoys. I freeze a pint jar or two of sliced chives from my garden during the summer months so we can enjoy them in recipes like this all year long.

—SUE GRONHOLZ BEAVER DAM, WI

PREP: 20 MIN. + CHILLING • **BAKE:** 45 MIN.
MAKES: 6 SERVINGS

- 4 slices sandwich bread, cubed
- ¼ cup coarsely chopped fresh basil
- ¼ cup soft sun-dried tomato halves (not packed in oil), finely chopped
- 6 bacon strips, cooked and crumbled
- 1 cup (4 ounces) shredded part-skim mozzarella cheese
- 6 eggs
- ⅔ cup 2% milk
- 1 garlic clove, minced
- ½ teaspoon salt
- ¼ teaspoon pepper
- 1 tablespoon minced chives

1. In a greased 8-in.-square baking dish, layer half of each of the following: bread, basil, tomatoes, bacon and cheese. Repeat layers.

2. In a small bowl, whisk eggs, milk, garlic, salt and pepper. Pour over layers. Refrigerate, covered, several hours or overnight.

3. Preheat oven to 350°. Remove casserole from refrigerator while oven heats. Bake, covered, 30 minutes. Uncover and bake 15-20 minutes longer or until puffed and golden and a knife inserted near the center comes out clean. Sprinkle with chives. Let stand 5-10 minutes before cutting.

Egg Biscuit Bake

Convenient refrigerated biscuits create a golden border around this all-in-one brunch dish. It's a variation of a simple egg-cheese combination my mother used to make.

—ALICE LE DUC CEDARBURG, WI

START TO FINISH: 30 MIN.
MAKES: 4-6 SERVINGS

- 1 can (5 ounces) evaporated milk
- 8 ounces process cheese (Velveeta), cubed
- 1 teaspoon prepared mustard
- ¾ cup cubed fully cooked ham
- ½ cup frozen peas
- 2 tablespoons butter
- 10 eggs, lightly beaten
- 1 tube (12 ounces) refrigerated buttermilk biscuits

1. Preheat oven to 375°. In a large saucepan, combine milk, cheese and mustard; cook over low heat until smooth, stirring constantly. Stir in ham and peas.

2. Melt butter in a large skillet; heat butter until hot. Add eggs; cook and stir over medium heat until eggs are completely set. Add cheese sauce and stir gently.

3. Spoon into an ungreased shallow 2-qt. baking dish. Separate biscuits and cut in half. Place with cut side down around outer edge of dish.

4. Bake, uncovered, 15-20 minutes or until a knife inserted near the center comes out clean and biscuits are golden brown.

EGG BISCUIT BAKE

ITALIAN BREAKFAST STRATA

Eggs Benedict Casserole

This breakfast bake is just as special and delicious as classic eggs Benedict, but even better for serving a crowd. Putting it together the night before makes morning cooking easier.

—**SANDIE HEINDEL** LIBERTY, MO

PREP: 25 MIN. + CHILLING • **BAKE:** 45 MIN.
MAKES: 12 SERVINGS (1⅔ CUPS SAUCE)

- 12 ounces Canadian bacon, chopped
- 6 English muffins, split and cut into 1-inch pieces
- 8 eggs
- 2 cups 2% milk
- 1 teaspoon onion powder
- ¼ teaspoon paprika

HOLLANDAISE SAUCE

- 4 egg yolks
- ½ cup heavy whipping cream
- 2 tablespoons lemon juice
- 1 teaspoon Dijon mustard
- ½ cup butter, melted

1. Place half of the Canadian bacon in a greased 3-qt. or 13x9-in. baking dish; top with English muffins and the remaining bacon. In a large bowl, whisk eggs, milk and onion powder; pour over top. Refrigerate, covered, overnight.

2. Preheat oven to 375°. Remove casserole from refrigerator while oven heats. Sprinkle top with paprika. Bake, covered, 35 minutes. Uncover; bake 10-15 minutes longer or until a knife inserted near the center comes out clean.

3. In top of a double boiler or a metal bowl over simmering water, whisk egg yolks, cream, lemon juice and mustard until blended; cook until mixture is just thick enough to coat a metal spoon and temperature reaches 160°, whisking constantly. Reduce heat to very low. Very slowly drizzle in warm melted butter, whisking constantly. Serve immediately with casserole.

Asparagus Phyllo Bake

I'm Greek, so phyllo dough was a staple in my house growing up. When asparagus is in season, I bring out the phyllo, butter it and start baking.

—**BONNIE GEAVARAS-BOOTZ** SCOTTSDALE, AZ

PREP: 25 MIN. • **BAKE:** 50 MIN.
MAKES: 12 SERVINGS

- 2 pounds fresh asparagus, trimmed and cut into 1-inch pieces
- 5 eggs, lightly beaten
- 1 carton (15 ounces) ricotta cheese
- 1 cup (4 ounces) shredded Swiss cheese
- 2 tablespoons grated Parmesan cheese
- 2 garlic cloves, minced
- ½ teaspoon salt
- ½ teaspoon grated lemon peel
- ½ teaspoon pepper
- ½ cup slivered almonds, toasted
- ¾ cup butter, melted
- 16 sheets phyllo dough (14x9 inches)

1. In a large saucepan, bring 8 cups water to a boil. Add asparagus; cook, uncovered, 30 seconds or just until asparagus turns bright green. Remove asparagus and immediately drop it into ice water. Drain and pat dry. In a large bowl, mix eggs, cheeses and seasonings; stir in almonds and the asparagus.

2. Preheat oven to 375°. Brush a 13x9-in. baking dish with some of the butter. Unroll phyllo dough. Layer eight sheets of phyllo in prepared dish, brushing each with butter. Keep remaining phyllo covered with plastic wrap and a damp towel to prevent it from drying out.

3. Spread ricotta mixture over phyllo layers. Top with remaining phyllo sheets, brushing each with butter. Cut into 12 rectangles. Bake 50-55 minutes or until golden brown.

NOTE *To toast nuts, spread in a 15x10x1-in. baking pan. Bake at 350° for 5-10 minutes or until lightly browned, stirring occasionally. Or, spread in a dry nonstick skillet and heat over low heat until lightly browned, stirring occasionally.*

ASPARAGUS PHYLLO BAKE

Cheese & Crab Brunch Bake

Here's an easy seafood casserole that can be prepped in 30 minutes, refrigerated overnight and baked the next morning.

—JOYCE CONWAY WESTERVILLE, OH

PREP: 30 MIN. + CHILLING • **BAKE:** 50 MIN.
MAKES: 12 SERVINGS

- 2 **tablespoons Dijon mustard**
- 6 **English muffins, split**
- 8 **ounces lump crabmeat, drained**
- 2 **tablespoons lemon juice**
- 2 **teaspoons grated lemon peel**
- 2 **cups (8 ounces) shredded white cheddar cheese**
- 12 **eggs**
- 1 **cup half-and-half cream**
- 1 **cup 2% milk**
- ½ **cup mayonnaise**
- 1 **teaspoon salt**
- ½ **teaspoon cayenne pepper**
- ½ **teaspoon pepper**
- 2 **cups (8 ounces) shredded Swiss cheese**
- 1 **cup grated Parmesan cheese**
- 4 **green onions, chopped**
- ¼ **cup finely chopped sweet red pepper**
- ¼ **cup finely chopped sweet yellow pepper**

1. Spread mustard over bottom half of muffins; place in a greased 13x9-in. baking dish. Top with crab, lemon juice and peel. Sprinkle with cheddar cheese. Top with muffin tops; set aside.
2. In a large bowl, whisk eggs, cream, milk, mayonnaise, salt, cayenne and pepper. Pour over muffins; sprinkle with Swiss cheese, Parmesan cheese, onions and peppers. Cover and refrigerate overnight.
3. Remove from refrigerator 30 minutes before baking. Preheat oven to 375°. Cover and bake 30 minutes. Uncover; bake 20-25 minutes longer or until set. Let stand 5 minutes before serving.

CHEESE & CRAB BRUNCH BAKE

Baked Eggs with Cheddar and Bacon

These little treats are simple to make and perfect for a special breakfast. They're also nice for a casual or late-night dinner. The smoky cheese and bacon elevate these egg cups to another level!

—**CATHERINE WILKINSON** DEWEY, AZ

START TO FINISH: 25 MIN.
MAKES: 2 SERVINGS

- 2 **eggs**
- 2 **tablespoons fat-free milk, divided**
- 1 **tablespoon shredded smoked cheddar cheese**
- 1 **teaspoon minced fresh parsley**
- ⅛ **teaspoon salt**
  Dash pepper
- 1 **bacon strip**

1. Preheat oven to 325°. Coat two 4-oz. ramekins with cooking spray; break an egg into each dish. Spoon 1 tablespoon milk over each egg. Combine cheese, parsley, salt and pepper; sprinkle over tops of ramekins.

2. Bake, uncovered, 12-15 minutes or until whites are completely set and yolks begin to thicken but are not firm.

3. Meanwhile, in a small skillet, cook bacon over medium heat until crisp. Remove to paper towels to drain. Crumble bacon and sprinkle over eggs.

Chorizo Tomato Strata

With chorizo sausage and Gruyere cheese, this oven-baked dish makes a satisfying morning meal. The seasonings blend to create a tantalizing flavor everyone at your table will remember.

—**DONNA COWLEY** DEKALB, IL

PREP: 25 MIN. • **BAKE:** 35 MIN. + STANDING
MAKES: 12 SERVINGS

- ½ **pound uncooked chorizo**
- 1 **cup (4 ounces) shredded Gruyere cheese, divided**
- ¼ **cup minced fresh cilantro**
- 1 **garlic clove, halved**
- 1 **loaf (½ pound) day-old French bread, cut into 1-inch slices**
- 2 **large tomatoes, sliced**
- 8 **eggs**
- 2 **cups milk**
- ¾ **teaspoon salt**
- ¾ **teaspoon pepper**
- ½ **teaspoon onion powder**
- ¼ **teaspoon crushed red pepper flakes**

1. Crumble chorizo into a small skillet; cook and stir over medium heat until fully cooked. Drain. Stir in ⅓ cup cheese and cilantro.

2. Preheat oven to 350°. Rub cut side of garlic clove over bread slices; discard garlic. Place bread in a greased 13x9-in. baking dish. Top with tomatoes, meat mixture and remaining cheese.

3. In a large bowl, whisk eggs, milk, salt, pepper, onion powder and pepper flakes. Pour over casserole.

4. Bake, uncovered, 35-45 minutes or until a knife inserted near the center comes out clean (cover loosely with foil if top browns too quickly). Let stand 10 minutes before cutting.

CHORIZO TOMATO STRATA

Burrito Lasagna

A friend showed me how to make stacked enchiladas years ago. I took it even further to create this filling casserole reminiscent of a Southwestern-style lasagna. Serve it with chips and salsa, Mexican corn and a refreshing dessert to round out the meal.
—DEANA BRIGGS MAUD, TX

PREP: 35 MIN. • **BAKE:** 30 MIN. + STANDING
MAKES: 12 SERVINGS

- 2 **pounds ground beef**
- 2 **cans (10 ounces each) enchilada sauce**
- 1 **envelope taco seasoning**
- 1 **tablespoon ground cumin**
- 1 **package (8.8 ounces) ready-to-serve Spanish rice**
- 12 **flour tortillas (8 inches), warmed**
- 1 **can (15 ounces) refried beans**
- 4 **cups (16 ounces) shredded Mexican cheese blend**
  Optional toppings: salsa, sliced avocado, shredded lettuce, taco sauce and/or sour cream

1. Preheat oven to 350°. In a large skillet, cook beef over medium heat until no longer pink; drain. Stir in enchilada sauce, taco seasoning and cumin; heat through.

2. Heat rice according to package directions. Spread each tortilla with about 2 tablespoonfuls beans. Spread 1 cup meat mixture into a greased 13x9-in. baking dish. Layer with 4 tortillas and a third of the rice, a third of the remaining meat mixture and a third of the cheese. Repeat layers. Top with remaining tortillas, rice and meat mixture (dish will be full).

3. Cover and bake 20 minutes. Sprinkle with remaining cheese. Uncover; bake 10-15 minutes longer or until cheese is melted. Let stand 10 minutes before serving. Serve with toppings of your choice.

BURRITO LASAGNA

⑤ INGREDIENTS Cheeseburger and Fries Casserole

Kids love this casserole; it combines two of their favorite fast foods. And I like that I can whip it up with just four ingredients.
—**KAREN OWEN** RISING SUN, IN

PREP: 10 MIN. • **BAKE:** 50 MIN.
MAKES: 6-8 SERVINGS

- 2 **pounds lean ground beef (90% lean)**
- 1 **can (10¾ ounces) condensed golden mushroom soup, undiluted**
- 1 **can (10¾ ounces) condensed cheddar cheese soup, undiluted**
- 1 **package (20 ounces) frozen crinkle-cut French fries**

1. Preheat oven to 350°. In a large skillet, cook beef over medium heat until no longer pink; drain. Stir in soups. Pour into a greased 13x9-in. baking dish.

2. Arrange French fries on top. Bake, uncovered, 50-55 minutes or until the fries are golden brown.

QUICK SHEPHERD'S PIE

CHEESEBURGER AND FRIES CASSEROLE

Shepherd's pie is great with leftover homemade mashed potatoes, but it's tasty with ready-made mashed potatoes from the grocery store, too.
—**JENNIFER EARLY** EAST LANSING, MI

⑤ INGREDIENTS Quick Shepherd's Pie

START TO FINISH: 20 MIN.
MAKES: 4 SERVINGS

- 1 **tub (24 ounces) refrigerated cheddar mashed potatoes**
- 1 **pound lean ground beef (90% lean)**
- 1 **envelope mushroom gravy mix**
- 1½ **cups frozen mixed vegetables**
- 1 **cup water**
- ⅛ **teaspoon pepper**

1. Heat potatoes according to package directions.

2. Meanwhile, in a large skillet, cook beef over medium heat for 6-8 minutes or until no longer pink, breaking into crumbles; drain. Stir in gravy mix. Add vegetables and water; bring to boil. Reduce heat; simmer until heated through, stirring occasionally. Transfer to a 9-in.-square baking pan.

3. Spread potatoes over top; sprinkle with pepper. Broil 4-6 in. from the heat for 10-15 minutes or until golden brown.

The Firehouse Special

Enjoy this versatile dish for breakfast, lunch or dinner. It's great served hot or cold, and it tastes even better the next day. It yields two casseroles so it's ideal for a crowd. Top with salsa or sour cream.

—DARRELL ALVORD BOISE, ID

PREP: 45 MIN. • **BAKE:** 55 MIN.
MAKES: 2 CASSEROLES (10 SERVINGS EACH)

- 2 cans (14½ ounces each) chicken broth
- 3 cups uncooked instant rice
- 4 tablespoons butter, divided
- 2 pounds ground beef
- 2 packages (12 ounces each) bulk spicy pork sausage
- 1 pound sliced fresh mushrooms
- 3 garlic cloves, minced
- 2 packages (10 ounces each) frozen chopped spinach, thawed and squeezed dry
- 2 cups (16 ounces) 4% cottage cheese
- 8 eggs, lightly beaten
- 1 envelope onion soup mix
- 1 envelope leek soup mix
- 2 teaspoons garlic powder
- 1 teaspoon Creole seasoning
- ¼ cup grated Parmesan cheese

1. Preheat oven to 350°. In a large saucepan, bring broth to a boil. Stir in rice; cover and remove from heat. Let stand 5 minutes. Stir in 2 tablespoons butter; set aside.

2. Meanwhile, in a large skillet, cook beef and sausage over medium heat until no longer pink; drain. Transfer to a large bowl.

3. In the same skillet, saute the mushrooms in remaining butter until tender. Add the garlic; cook 1 minute longer. Add to the meat mixture. Stir in the spinach, cottage cheese, eggs, soup mixes, garlic powder, Creole seasoning and reserved rice mixture.

4. Divide between two greased 13x9-in. baking dishes; sprinkle with cheese. Cover and bake 45 minutes. Uncover; bake 10-15 minutes longer or until heated through.

NOTE *The following spices may be substituted for 1 teaspoon Creole seasoning: ¼ teaspoon each salt, garlic powder and paprika; and a pinch each of dried thyme, ground cumin and cayenne pepper.*

Taco Noodle Dish

We were housebound during a snowstorm one winter, so I got creative and used ingredients I had on hand to come up with this hearty dinner.

—JUDY MUNGER WARREN, MN

PREP: 20 MIN. • **BAKE:** 10 MIN. + STANDING
MAKES: 8 SERVINGS

- 2 cups uncooked wide egg noodles
- 2 pounds ground beef
- 1 can (8 ounces) tomato sauce
- ½ cup water
- 1 can (4 ounces) chopped green chilies
- 1 envelope taco seasoning
- 1 teaspoon onion powder
- 1 teaspoon chili powder
- ½ teaspoon garlic powder
- 1 cup (4 ounces) shredded cheddar cheese
- 2 cups shredded lettuce
- 1 cup diced fresh tomatoes
- ⅓ cup sliced ripe olives, drained
- ½ cup taco sauce
- ½ cup sour cream

1. Preheat oven to 350°. Cook noodles according to package directions.

2. Meanwhile, in a large skillet, cook beef over medium heat until no longer pink; drain. Stir in tomato sauce, water, green chilies, taco seasoning, onion powder, chili powder and garlic powder. Bring to a boil. Reduce heat; simmer, uncovered, 5 minutes.

3. Drain noodles; place in a greased 11x7-in. baking dish. Spread with beef mixture; sprinkle with cheese. Bake, uncovered, 10-15 minutes or until cheese is melted. Let stand 10 minutes.

4. Top with lettuce, tomatoes, olives and taco sauce. Garnish with sour cream.

TACO NOODLE DISH

Creole Beef Casserole

My husband and I were each cooking something different one night and we combined them for this dish. The crushed cornflakes on top add a nice crunch.

—**NICKI AUSTIN** LAWRENCEVILLE, IL

PREP: 25 MIN. • **BAKE:** 40 MIN.
MAKES: 8 SERVINGS

- 2 cans (10¾ ounces each) condensed cream of chicken soup, undiluted
- 2 cups (16 ounces) sour cream
- 1 small onion, chopped
- ¼ teaspoon pepper
- 1 package (30 ounces) frozen shredded hash brown potatoes, thawed
- 2 cups (8 ounces) shredded cheddar cheese
- 1½ pounds ground beef
- 1 cup ketchup
- ¼ cup packed brown sugar
- 3 teaspoons Creole seasoning
- 1 teaspoon garlic salt
- 1 teaspoon dried oregano
- ¼ teaspoon cayenne pepper
- ¾ cup crushed cornflakes
- ¼ cup butter, melted

1. Preheat oven to 350°. In a large bowl, combine soup, sour cream, onion and pepper. Stir in potatoes and cheese; transfer to a greased 3-qt. baking dish.
2. In a large skillet, cook beef over medium heat until no longer pink; drain. Stir in ketchup, brown sugar and seasonings; spread over potatoes. Combine cornflakes and butter; sprinkle over top. Bake, uncovered, 40-45 minutes or until bubbly.
NOTE *The following spices may be substituted for 1 teaspoon Creole seasoning: ¼ teaspoon each salt, garlic powder and paprika; and a pinch each of dried thyme, ground cumin and cayenne pepper.*

CHILI MAC & CHEESE

Chili Mac & Cheese

The Southwestern flair of my comforting casserole gives it wide appeal. I think it's great because it's high on taste and low on the scale of difficulty—a delicious combo.

—**MARY AGUILAR** SHELBY, OH

PREP: 30 MIN. • **BAKE:** 20 MIN.
MAKES: 8 SERVINGS

- 2 packages (7¼ ounces each) macaroni and cheese dinner mix
- 2 pounds ground beef
- 1 small onion, chopped
- 1 can (14½ ounces) diced tomatoes, undrained
- 1 can (10 ounces) diced tomatoes and green chilies, undrained
- 1 can (8 ounces) tomato sauce
- 2 tablespoons chili powder
- 1 teaspoon garlic salt
- ½ teaspoon ground cumin
- ¼ teaspoon crushed red pepper flakes
- ¼ teaspoon pepper
- 2 cups (16 ounces) sour cream
- 1½ cups (6 ounces) shredded Mexican cheese blend, divided

1. Preheat oven to 350°. Set aside cheese packets from dinner mixes. In a large saucepan, bring 2 quarts water to a boil. Add macaroni; cook 8-10 minutes or until tender.
2. Meanwhile, in a Dutch oven, cook and stir beef and onion over medium heat 8-10 minutes or until beef is no longer pink; drain. Stir in tomatoes, tomatoes and green chilies, tomato sauce and seasonings. Drain macaroni; add to beef mixture. Stir in contents of cheese packets, sour cream and 1 cup cheese.
3. Transfer to a greased 13x9-in. baking dish; top with remaining cheese. Bake, uncovered, 20-25 minutes or until bubbly.

CORNED BEEF 'N' SAUERKRAUT BAKE

CORN CHIP BEEF CASSEROLE

Corned Beef 'n' Sauerkraut Bake

I love Reuben sandwiches, so this hot and hearty casserole really hits the spot. We especially like it with my husband's famous homemade sauerkraut.

—SUSAN STAHL DULUTH, MN

PREP: 10 MIN. • **BAKE:** 30 MIN.
MAKES: 6 SERVINGS

- 1¾ **cups sauerkraut, rinsed and well drained**
- ½ **pound thinly sliced deli corned beef, julienned**
- 2 **cups (8 ounces) shredded Swiss cheese**
- ¼ **cup Thousand Island salad dressing**
- 2 **medium tomatoes, thinly sliced**
- 6 **tablespoons butter, divided**
- 1 **cup coarsely crushed seasoned rye crackers**

1. Preheat oven to 400°. In a greased 1½-qt. baking dish, layer half the sauerkraut, corned beef and cheese.

Repeat layers. Drop salad dressing by teaspoonfuls over the cheese. Arrange tomato slices over the top; dot with 2 tablespoons butter.

2. In a small saucepan, melt remaining butter. Stir in crumbs; sprinkle over top of casserole. Bake, uncovered, 30-35 minutes or until heated through.

Corn Chip Beef Casserole

After my children left home, I found it difficult to whittle down meals for two, but I eventually succeeded, and this became one of our go-to recipes. You can easily freeze the extra portion if you're cooking for one.

—BARBARA BERNARD HOLYOKE, MA

PREP: 20 MIN. • **BAKE:** 15 MIN.
MAKES: 2 SERVINGS

- ½ **pound lean ground beef (90% lean)**
- ⅓ **cup finely chopped onion**
- ⅓ **cup thinly sliced celery**
- ⅓ **cup finely chopped green pepper**
- ¼ **teaspoon minced garlic**
- 1 **cup cooked brown rice**
- 1 **medium tomato, chopped**
- 1 **teaspoon lemon juice**
- ¼ **teaspoon salt**
- ¼ **teaspoon hot pepper sauce**
- ¼ **cup mayonnaise**
- ½ **to 1 cup corn chips, crushed**

1. Preheat oven to 350°. In a large skillet, cook beef, onion, celery and green pepper over medium heat until meat is no longer pink. Add garlic; cook 1 minute longer; drain. Stir in rice, tomato, lemon juice, salt and hot pepper sauce; heat through. Stir in mayonnaise.

2. Spoon into two 15-oz. baking dishes coated with cooking spray. Sprinkle with crushed corn chips. Bake, uncovered, 13-15 minutes or until heated through.

ITALIAN PASTA DISH

UNSTUFFED PEPPERS

Italian Pasta Dish

I love to make this whenever I need to bring a dish to pass. Fresh tomatoes add a nice touch that's missing from most other meat, pasta and tomato casseroles.

—KARLA JOHNSON EAST HELENA, MT

PREP: 40 MIN. • **BAKE:** 25 MIN.
MAKES: 8 SERVINGS

- 2 **pounds ground beef**
- 1 **large onion, chopped**
- 2 **garlic cloves, minced**
- 1 **jar (24 ounces) spaghetti sauce**
- 1 **can (14½ ounces) diced tomatoes, undrained**
- 1 **can (4 ounces) mushroom stems and pieces, drained**
- 1 **teaspoon Italian seasoning**
- 3 **cups uncooked medium pasta shells**
- 3 **plum tomatoes, sliced**
- ¾ **cup shredded provolone cheese**
- ¾ **cup shredded part-skim mozzarella cheese**

1. In a large skillet, cook beef and onion over medium heat until no longer pink. Add garlic; cook 1 minute longer. Drain. Stir in spaghetti sauce, diced tomatoes, mushrooms and Italian seasoning. Bring to a boil. Reduce heat; simmer, uncovered, 20 minutes.
2. Meanwhile, preheat oven to 350°. Cook pasta according to package directions; drain. Add to beef mixture and gently stir in tomatoes.
3. Transfer to an ungreased 13x9-in. baking dish. Sprinkle with cheeses. Cover and bake 25-30 minutes or until bubbly and heated through.

Unstuffed Peppers

If you like stuffed peppers, you'll love this quick and easy version. To speed up prep time, use 2 cups of leftover cooked rice if you have it on hand.

—BETH DEWYER DU BOIS, PA

START TO FINISH: 30 MIN.
MAKES: 6 SERVINGS

- 1 **cup uncooked instant rice**
- 1 **pound ground beef**
- 2 **medium green peppers, cut into 1-inch pieces**
- ½ **cup chopped onion**
- 1 **jar (26 ounces) marinara sauce**
- 1½ **teaspoons salt-free seasoning blend**
- ½ **cup shredded Italian cheese blend**
- ½ **cup seasoned bread crumbs**
- 1 **tablespoon olive oil**

1. Preheat oven to 350°. Cook rice according to package directions.
2. Meanwhile, in a large skillet, cook beef, green peppers and onion over medium-high heat until meat is no longer pink; drain. Stir in rice, marinara sauce and seasoning blend. Stir in cheese.
3. Transfer to a greased 2-qt. baking dish. Toss bread crumbs and oil; sprinkle over the top. Bake 8-10 minutes or until heated through and topping is golden brown.

RIGATONI ALFREDO

Rigatoni Alfredo

My kids love meatballs with rigatoni or spaghetti. The baked Alfredo cheese sauce in this recipe takes it over the top!
—**JENNIFER ROSS** CLINTON, OH

PREP: 1¼ HOURS • **BAKE:** 20 MIN.
MAKES: 6 SERVINGS

- 1 egg, lightly beaten
- ¾ cup seasoned bread crumbs
- ⅓ cup water
- ¼ cup grated Parmesan cheese
- 4½ teaspoons each minced fresh thyme, oregano and basil or 1½ teaspoons each dried thyme, oregano and basil
- 1½ teaspoons pepper
- ½ teaspoon salt
- 1½ pounds ground beef
- 1 tablespoon canola oil
- 1 small onion, chopped
- 3 garlic cloves, minced
- ⅓ cup dry red wine or beef broth
- 1 can (28 ounces) crushed tomatoes
- 1 tablespoon minced fresh parsley
- 12 ounces uncooked rigatoni or large tube pasta

ALFREDO TOPPING

- ¼ cup butter, cubed
- 2 tablespoons all-purpose flour
- 2 cups half-and-half cream
- 1 cup grated Parmesan cheese, divided
- 1 teaspoon minced fresh thyme or ¼ teaspoon dried thyme
- 1 teaspoon minced fresh oregano or ¼ teaspoon dried oregano

1. In a large bowl, combine egg, bread crumbs, water, cheese and seasonings. Crumble beef over mixture and mix well. Shape into 1½-in. balls. In a Dutch oven, brown meatballs in oil in batches; remove and keep warm.

2. Drain, reserving 1 tablespoon drippings. In drippings, saute onion until tender. Add garlic; cook 1 minute longer. Add wine; cook and stir 3 minutes.

3. Return meatballs to pan; stir in tomatoes and parsley. Bring to a boil. Reduce heat; cover and simmer 25-30 minutes or until meat is no longer pink.

4. Meanwhile, preheat oven to 400°. Cook rigatoni according to package directions.

5. For the Alfredo topping, in a small saucepan, melt butter. Stir in the flour until smooth; gradually add the cream. Bring to a boil; cook and stir 1-2 minutes or until thickened. Remove from the heat. Stir in ¾ cup Parmesan cheese.

6. Drain rigatoni; place in a large bowl. Add meatballs and sauce; stir to coat. Transfer to a greased 13x9-in. baking dish.

7. Top with Alfredo sauce; sprinkle with thyme, oregano and remaining Parmesan cheese. Bake, uncovered, 20-25 minutes or until bubbly.

Beefy Tomato Pasta

Sharing recipes with friends is a favorite pastime of mine, and I get many requests for this wonderful main dish. It's a fantastic way to use up leftover roasts.
—**TRUDY WILLIAMS** SHANNONVILLE, ON

PREP: 15 MIN. • **BAKE:** 20 MIN.
MAKES: 6-8 SERVINGS

- 1 large onion, chopped
- 1 tablespoon olive oil
- 2 cans (14½ ounces each) Italian diced tomatoes, undrained
- 1 can (8 ounces) tomato sauce
- 3 cups shredded fully cooked beef rump roast
- ¼ teaspoon salt
- ¼ teaspoon crushed red pepper flakes
- 4½ cups rigatoni or other large tube pasta, cooked and drained
- 2 cups (8 ounces) shredded mozzarella cheese
- 1 cup (4 ounces) shredded provolone cheese

1. Preheat oven to 400°. In a large saucepan, saute onion in oil until tender. Stir in tomatoes and tomato sauce. Bring to a boil. Reduce heat; cover and simmer 5 minutes. Stir in beef, salt and pepper flakes. Cover and simmer 5 minutes. Add pasta; toss to coat.

2. Transfer to a greased 13x9-in. baking dish. Sprinkle with cheeses. Bake, uncovered, 20-25 minutes or until cheese is melted.

Party Beef Hot Dish

Cozy up to this satisfying family favorite. Economical and delicious round steak gives it lots of stick-to-your ribs goodness.

—**KELLY HARDGRAVE** HARTMAN, AR

PREP: 30 MIN. • **BAKE:** 1¾ HOURS
MAKES: 6-8 SERVINGS

- 3 **tablespoons all-purpose flour**
- 1 **teaspoon salt-free seasoning blend**
- ½ **teaspoon pepper**
- 2 **pounds boneless round steak, cut into ½-inch cubes**
- 2 **tablespoons vegetable oil**
- 1 **cup water**
- ½ **cup low-sodium beef broth**
- 1 **garlic clove, minced**
- 1 **tablespoon dried minced onion**
- ½ **teaspoon dried thyme**
- ¼ **teaspoon dried rosemary, crushed**
- 2 **cups sliced fresh mushrooms**
- 2 **cups frozen peas, thawed**
- 3 **cups mashed potatoes (with added milk)**
- 1 **tablespoon butter, melted**
  Paprika

1. Preheat oven to 350°. In a large resealable plastic bag, combine flour, seasoning blend and pepper; add beef cubes and shake to coat. In a skillet over medium heat, brown beef in oil. Place beef and drippings in a greased shallow 2½-qt. baking dish.

2. To skillet, add water, broth, garlic, onion, thyme and rosemary; bring to a boil. Simmer, uncovered, 5 minutes; stir in mushrooms. Pour over meat; mix well.

3. Cover and bake 1½ to 1¾ hours or until beef is tender. Sprinkle peas over meat. Spread potatoes evenly over top. Brush with butter; sprinkle with paprika. Bake 15-20 minutes longer.

Hamburger Corn Bread Casserole

Welcome friends in from the cold with a hearty dish that all ages will love. A layer of corn bread makes this meal-in-one both filling and delicious!

—**KATHY GARRISON** FORT WORTH, TX

PREP: 25 MIN. • **BAKE:** 15 MIN.
MAKES: 6 SERVINGS

- 1 **pound lean ground beef (90% lean)**
- 1 **small onion, chopped**
- 1 **can (15 ounces) Ranch Style beans (pinto beans in seasoned tomato sauce)**
- 1 **can (14½ ounces) diced tomatoes, undrained**
- 1 **teaspoon chili powder**
- 1 **teaspoon Worcestershire sauce**

TOPPING
- ½ **cup all-purpose flour**
- ½ **cup cornmeal**
- 2 **tablespoons sugar**
- 2 **teaspoons baking powder**
- ¼ **teaspoon salt**
- 1 **egg, beaten**
- ½ **cup fat-free milk**
- 1 **tablespoon canola oil**

1. Preheat oven to 425°. In a large skillet, cook beef and onion over medium heat until meat is no longer pink; drain. Add beans, tomatoes, chili powder and Worcestershire sauce; bring to a boil. Reduce heat; simmer, uncovered, 5 minutes.

2. Transfer to an 11x7-in. baking dish coated with cooking spray. For topping, in a small bowl, combine flour, cornmeal, sugar, baking powder and salt. Combine egg, milk and oil; stir into dry ingredients just until moistened. Spoon over filling; gently spread to cover the top.

3. Bake, uncovered, 14-18 minutes or until filling is bubbly and a toothpick inserted into topping comes out clean. Let stand 5 minutes before cutting.

HAMBURGER CORN BREAD CASSEROLE

Church Supper Hot Dish

This recipe was in my mother's church cookbook, and now it's in my church cookbook! Apparently it was too good to miss a generation. I often make this dish to take to potlucks.

—NORMA TURNER HASLETT, MI

PREP: 40 MIN. • **BAKE:** 30 MIN.
MAKES: 8 SERVINGS

- 1 **pound ground beef**
- 2 **cups sliced peeled potatoes**
- 2 **cups finely chopped celery**
- ¾ **cup finely chopped carrots**
- ¼ **cup finely chopped green pepper**
- ¼ **cup finely chopped onion**
- 2 **tablespoons butter**
- 1 **cup water**
- 2 **cans (10¾ ounces each) condensed cream of mushroom soup, undiluted**
- 1 **can (5 ounces) chow mein noodles, divided**
- 1 **cup (4 ounces) shredded cheddar cheese**

1. Preheat oven to 350°. In a large skillet, cook the beef over medium heat until no longer pink; drain and set aside.

2. In same skillet, saute potatoes, celery, carrots, green pepper and onion in butter 5 minutes. Add water; cover and simmer 10 minutes or until vegetables are tender. Stir in soup and cooked ground beef until blended.

3. Sprinkle half of the chow mein noodles into a greased shallow 2-qt. baking dish. Spoon meat mixture over noodles. Cover and bake 20 minutes. Top with cheese and remaining noodles. Bake, uncovered, 10 minutes longer or until heated through.

CHURCH SUPPER HOT DISH

Lori's Marzetti Bake

I have 8 kids, so there were 10 of us in the house while they were growing up. For our large crew, a meal had to be delicious and make enough to feed us all. This hot dish was always a favorite, and now I serve it when my grandkids come to visit. I also take it to other parties and potlucks.

—**LORI SMITH** NEWARK, OH

PREP: 30 MIN. • **BAKE:** 35 MIN.
MAKES: 2 CASSEROLES (12 SERVINGS EACH)

- 2 **pounds ground beef**
- 1 **cup sliced fresh mushrooms**
- 1 **medium onion, finely chopped**
- ⅓ **cup chopped green pepper**
- 2 **garlic cloves, minced**
- 1 **teaspoon salt**
- ½ **teaspoon pepper**
- 3 **cans (15 ounces each) plus 1 can (8 ounces) tomato sauce**
- 1 **can (15 ounces) diced tomatoes, undrained**
- 2 **tablespoons brown sugar**
- 1 **package (16 ounces) egg noodles**
- 3 **cups (12 ounces) shredded cheddar cheese, divided**

1. Preheat oven to 400°. In a Dutch oven, cook the first seven ingredients over medium heat 8-10 minutes or until beef is no longer pink and vegetables are tender, breaking up beef into crumbles; drain. Stir in tomato sauce, tomatoes and brown sugar; bring to a boil. Reduce heat; simmer 10-15 minutes or until flavors are blended, stirring occasionally.
2. Meanwhile cook noodles according to package directions. Drain; add to sauce. Stir in 2 cups cheese. Transfer to two greased 11x7-in. baking dishes.
3. Cover with greased foil and bake 30-35 minutes or until heated through. Sprinkle with remaining cheese; bake, uncovered, 5 minutes longer or until cheese is melted.

SICILIAN SUPPER

Sicilian Supper

Ground beef, tomato and a tasty cream cheese sauce come together in this hot, hearty casserole. I recently took it to a banquet, and recipe requests came from every table.

—**GLORIA WARCZAK** CEDARBURG, WI

PREP: 30 MIN. • **BAKE:** 20 MIN.
MAKES: 4 SERVINGS

- 2 **cups uncooked egg noodles**
- 1 **pound ground beef**
- ½ **cup chopped onion**
- ¼ **cup chopped green pepper**
- 1 **can (6 ounces) tomato paste**
- ¾ **cup water**
- 1½ **teaspoons sugar, divided**
- ½ **teaspoon salt**
- ½ **teaspoon dried basil**
- ¼ **teaspoon garlic powder**
- ¼ **teaspoon chili powder**
- ¼ **teaspoon pepper, divided**
- 1 **tablespoon finely chopped green onion**
- 1 **tablespoon olive oil**
- 1 **package (8 ounces) cream cheese, cubed**
- ¾ **cup milk**
- ⅓ **cup plus 2 tablespoons grated Parmesan cheese, divided**

1. Preheat oven to 350°. Cook noodles according to package directions.
2. Meanwhile, in a large skillet, cook beef, onion and green pepper over medium heat until meat is no longer pink; drain. Stir in tomato paste, water, 1 teaspoon sugar, salt, basil, garlic powder, chili powder and ⅛ teaspoon pepper.
3. In a large saucepan, saute green onion in oil until tender. Add cream cheese and milk; stir until blended. Stir in ⅓ cup cheese, and remaining sugar and pepper. Drain noodles; stir into cheese mixture.
4. In a greased 8-in.-square baking dish, arrange alternate rows of beef and noodle mixtures. Sprinkle with remaining cheese. Cover and bake 20-25 minutes or until bubbly.

SHORT RIB COBBLER

1. Preheat oven to 350°. In a bowl, mix ½ cup flour, ¾ teaspoon salt and pepper. Dip short ribs in flour mixture to coat all sides; shake off excess.

2. In an ovenproof Dutch oven, heat 3 tablespoons oil over medium heat. Brown beef in batches. Remove from pan.

3. In same pan, heat remaining oil over medium heat. Add onion, chopped carrot and celery; cook and stir 2-3 minutes or until tender. Add garlic; cook 1 minute longer. Stir in tomato paste and remaining flour until blended. Gradually stir in stock and wine until smooth. Return beef to pan; stir in poultry seasoning, bay leaf and remaining salt. Bring to a boil.

4. Bake, covered, 1¾ hours. Stir in pearl onions and carrot pieces. Bake, covered, 30-45 minutes longer or until beef and onions are tender. Skim fat and remove bay leaf.

5. In a small bowl, combine biscuit mix and milk just until a soft dough forms. Drop by scant ¼ cupfuls over beef mixture. Bake, uncovered, 40-45 minutes longer or until topping is golden brown. Sprinkle with thyme.

Short Rib Cobbler

My family's love of beef stew and biscuits inspired me to create this savory dish. After years of making the two separately, I put the biscuits on top of the stew like a cobbler. This satisfying supper is as down-home as it gets.

—**JANINE TALLEY** ORLANDO, FL

PREP: 45 MIN. • **BAKE:** 3 HOURS
MAKES: 8 SERVINGS

- ½ **cup plus 3 tablespoons all-purpose flour, divided**
- 1¼ **teaspoons salt, divided**
- ½ **teaspoon pepper**
- 2 **pounds well-trimmed boneless beef short ribs, cut into 1½-in. pieces**
- 5 **tablespoons olive oil, divided**
- 1 **large onion, chopped**
- 1 **medium carrot, chopped**
- 1 **celery rib, chopped**
- 1 **garlic clove, minced**
- 2 **tablespoons tomato paste**
- 5 **cups beef stock**
- 1 **cup dry red wine or additional beef stock**
- 1 **teaspoon poultry seasoning**
- 1 **bay leaf**
- 1 **package (14 ounces) frozen pearl onions, thawed**
- 4 **medium carrots, cut into 2-inch pieces**

COBBLER TOPPING

- 2 **cups biscuit/baking mix**
- ⅔ **cup 2% milk**
  Fresh thyme leaves

TOP TIP

Biscuits that are baked on top of casseroles, stews and potpies can easily become doughy on the bottom. For better heat circulation, use a shallow baking dish (unless the recipe states otherwise) and arrange the biscuits so they're not touching too closely. If using refrigerated biscuit dough, bake your dish at the same temperature or higher than the directions call for on the package. Be sure to add the biscuits near the end of the casserole's baking time, when the mixture is hot and bubbly.

Hamburger Noodle Bake

Cream cheese and cottage cheese balance the saucy ground beef and noodles in this hearty casserole. It's been a favorite in our house for years.

—**CHARISSA DUNN** BARTLESVILLE, OK

PREP: 35 MIN. • **BAKE:** 20 MIN.
MAKES: 2 SERVINGS

- 2 **cups uncooked egg noodles**
- ½ **pound lean ground beef (90% lean)**
- 2 **tablespoons finely chopped onion**
- 1 **can (8 ounces) tomato sauce**
- ¼ **teaspoon sugar**
- ⅛ **teaspoon salt**
- ⅛ **teaspoon garlic salt**
  Dash pepper
- ¼ **cup cream-style cottage cheese**
- 2 **ounces cream cheese, softened**
- 1 **tablespoon thinly sliced green onion**
- 1 **tablespoon chopped green pepper**
- 1 **tablespoon sour cream**
- 2 **tablespoons grated Parmesan cheese**

1. Preheat oven to 350°. Cook noodles according to package directions.
2. Meanwhile, in a large skillet, cook beef and onion until the meat is no longer pink; drain. Remove from heat; stir in tomato sauce, sugar, salt, garlic salt and pepper.
3. In a small bowl, combine cottage cheese, cream cheese, green onion, green pepper and sour cream.
4. Drain noodles; place half of noodles in a greased 1-qt. baking dish. Spoon half of the beef mixture over the top. Layer with the cottage cheese mixture and remaining noodles. Top with the remaining beef mixture; sprinkle with Parmesan cheese.
5. Cover and bake 20-25 minutes or until heated through.

Beef 'n' Biscuit Casserole

This piping hot dish is perfect for a weeknight meal. It boasts terrific flavor and is quick and easy. With its beef and corn combo, it's comfort food at its best.

—**ERIN SCHNEIDER** ST. PETERS, MO

START TO FINISH: 30 MIN.
MAKES: 6-8 SERVINGS

- 1 **pound ground beef**
- 1 **can (16 ounces) kidney beans, rinsed and drained**
- 1 **can (15¼ ounces) whole kernel corn, drained**
- 1 **can (10¾ ounces) condensed tomato soup, undiluted**
- ¼ **cup milk**
- 2 **tablespoons finely chopped onion**
- ½ **teaspoon chili powder**
- ¼ **teaspoon salt**
- 1 **cup cubed process cheese (Velveeta)**
- 1 **tube (12 ounces) refrigerated biscuits**
- 2 **to 3 tablespoons butter, melted**
- ⅓ **cup yellow cornmeal**

1. Preheat oven to 375°. In a saucepan over medium heat, cook beef until no longer pink; drain. Add beans, corn, soup, milk, onion, chili powder and salt; bring to a boil. Remove from heat; stir in cheese until melted. Spoon into a greased 2½-qt. baking dish. Bake, uncovered, 10 minutes.
2. Meanwhile, brush all sides of biscuits with butter; roll in cornmeal. Place on top of bubbling meat mixture. Return to oven 10-12 minutes or until the biscuits are lightly browned and cooked through.

BEEF 'N' BISCUIT CASSEROLE

BAKED SPAGHETTI

Baked Spaghetti

My family asks for this classic pasta dish when they crave comfort food. You could use spiral or tube pasta in place of the spaghetti. Add a salad and breadsticks to round out a memorable menu.

—**BETTY RABE** MAHTOMEDI, MN

PREP: 20 MIN. • **BAKE:** 30 MIN. + STANDING
MAKES: 6-8 SERVINGS

- 8 **ounces uncooked spaghetti, broken into thirds**
- 1 **egg**
- ½ **cup milk**
- ½ **teaspoon salt**
- ½ **pound ground beef**
- ½ **pound bulk Italian sausage**
- 1 **small onion, chopped**
- ¼ **cup chopped green pepper**
- 1 **jar (14 ounces) meatless spaghetti sauce**
- 1 **can (8 ounces) tomato sauce**
- 1 **to 2 cups (4 to 8 ounces) shredded part-skim mozzarella cheese**

1. Preheat oven to 350°. Cook the spaghetti according to package directions.
2. Meanwhile, in a large bowl, beat egg, milk and salt. Drain spaghetti; add to egg mixture and toss to coat. Transfer to a greased 13x9-in. baking dish.
3. In a large skillet, cook the beef, sausage, onion and green pepper over medium heat until the meat is no longer pink; drain. Stir in the spaghetti sauce and tomato sauce. Spoon over spaghetti mixture.
4. Bake, uncovered, for 20 minutes. Sprinkle with the cheese. Bake for 10 minutes longer or until cheese is melted. Let casserole stand 10 minutes before cutting.

Scalloped Potatoes 'n' Ham Casserole

I'm a home health nurse, and a client recently shared this recipe with me. It had been one of her standbys for years, and now it's one of my family's favorites, too. The casserole will never curdle, thanks to the secret ingredient of powdered nondairy creamer.

—**KATHY JOHNSON** LAKE CITY, SD

PREP: 25 MIN. • **BAKE:** 1 HOUR
MAKES: 6 SERVINGS

- ¾ **cup powdered nondairy creamer**
- 1¾ **cups water**
- 3 **tablespoons butter**
- 3 **tablespoons all-purpose flour**
- 2 **tablespoons dried minced onion**
- 1 **teaspoon salt**
- ¾ **teaspoon paprika**
- 6 **large potatoes, peeled and thinly sliced**
- 2 **cups diced fully cooked ham**
- 1 **cup (4 ounces) shredded cheddar cheese**

1. Preheat oven to 350°. In a small bowl, mix creamer and water until smooth. In a small saucepan, heat butter over medium heat. Stir in flour, onion, salt and paprika until smooth; gradually add creamer mixture. Bring to a boil; cook and stir 1-2 minutes or until thickened.
2. In a greased 13x9-in. baking dish, layer potatoes and ham; pour sauce over top. Bake, covered, 15 minutes. Uncover; bake 40-50 minutes longer or until potatoes are tender. Sprinkle with cheese; bake 5-10 minutes or until edges are bubbly and cheese is melted.

FREEZE IT Potluck Hot Dish

This beef and pork dish is my favorite item to take to bring-a-dish dinners. It's easy to whip together, and the down-home ingredients make it a guaranteed crowd-pleaser. The recipe is often requested, and I'm always happy to share it.

—**DOROTHY FRIEZ** MCLAUGHLIN, SD

PREP: 15 MIN. • **BAKE:** 1 HOUR
MAKES: 12 SERVINGS

- 1 **pound ground pork**
- 1 **pound ground beef**
- 1 **large onion, chopped**
- 1 **medium green pepper, chopped**
- 1 **package (7 ounces) elbow or ring macaroni, cooked and drained**
- 2 **cans (14¾ ounces each) cream-style corn**
- 2 **cans (10½ ounces each) condensed chicken with rice soup, undiluted**
- 1 **can (10¾ ounces) condensed cream of mushroom soup, undiluted**
- 1 **teaspoon salt**
- ½ **teaspoon pepper**
  Seasoned salt to taste
- ½ **cup dry bread crumbs**
- 2 **tablespoons butter, melted**

1. Preheat oven to 350°. In a 6-qt. stockpot, cook pork, beef, onion and green pepper over medium heat 10-12 minutes or until meat is no longer pink, breaking into crumbles; drain. Stir in macaroni, corn, soups and seasonings.

2. Transfer to a greased 13x9-in. baking dish. In a small bowl, mix bread crumbs and butter; sprinkle over top. Bake, covered, 45 minutes. Bake, uncovered, 15 minutes longer or until heated through.

FREEZE OPTION *Transfer meat mixture to a greased 13x9-in. baking dish, reserving buttered bread crumbs for topping when baking. Cool unbaked casserole; cover and freeze. To use, partially thaw in the refrigerator overnight. Remove from refrigerator 30 minutes before baking. Preheat oven to 350°. Prepare bread crumbs as directed; sprinkle over top. Bake casserole as directed, increasing time as necessary to heat through and for a thermometer inserted into center to read 165°.*

Corn Dog Casserole

Reminiscent of traditional corn dogs, this fun main dish really hits the spot. It tastes especially good right from the oven.

—**MARCY SUZANNE OLIPANE** BELLEVILLE, IL

PREP: 25 MIN. • **BAKE:** 30 MIN.
MAKES: 12 SERVINGS

- 2 **cups thinly sliced celery**
- 2 **tablespoons butter**
- 1½ **cups sliced green onions**
- 1½ **pounds hot dogs**
- 2 **eggs**
- 1½ **cups 2% milk**
- 2 **teaspoons rubbed sage**
- ¼ **teaspoon pepper**
- 2 **packages (8½ ounces each) corn bread/muffin mix**
- 2 **cups (8 ounces) shredded sharp cheddar cheese, divided**

1. In a small skillet, saute celery in butter 5 minutes. Add onions; saute 5 minutes longer or until vegetables are tender. Place in a large bowl; set aside.

2. Preheat oven to 400°. Cut hot dogs lengthwise into quarters, then cut into thirds. In the same skillet, saute hot dogs 5 minutes or until lightly browned; add to vegetables. Set aside 1 cup.

3. In a large bowl, whisk eggs, milk, sage and pepper. Add remaining hot dog mixture. Stir in corn bread mixes. Add 1½ cups cheese. Spread into a shallow 3-qt. baking dish. Top with reserved hot dog mixture and remaining cheese.

4. Bake, uncovered, 30 minutes or until golden brown.

CORN DOG CASSEROLE

Creamy Pork Chop Casserole

Tender pork chops are treated to a sweet-tangy marinade and topped with gooey melted Mexican cheese in this delightful meal.

—**DEBBIE HANKINS** IRONTON, OH

PREP: 15 MIN. + MARINATING
BAKE: 50 MIN.
MAKES: 2 SERVINGS

- ¼ cup reduced-sodium teriyaki sauce
- 2 bone-in pork loin chops (8 ounces each and ½-inch thick)
- 1 can (10¾ ounces) condensed cream of mushroom soup, undiluted
- 1 cup frozen peas and carrots
- ¾ cup water
- ½ small sweet red pepper, chopped
- ⅓ cup uncooked long grain rice
- 1 teaspoon dried minced onion
- ⅛ teaspoon pepper
- ¼ cup shredded Mexican cheese blend

1. Place teriyaki sauce in a large resealable plastic bag; add pork chops. Seal bag and turn to coat; refrigerate for at least 1 hour.

2. Preheat oven to 350°. In a large bowl, combine soup, peas and carrots, water, red pepper, rice, onion and pepper. Transfer to an 11x7-in. baking dish coated with cooking spray.

3. Drain and discard marinade. Place pork chops over rice mixture. Cover and bake 40 minutes. Uncover; sprinkle with cheese. Bake 10-20 minutes longer or until a thermometer reads 145° and cheese is melted. Let stand 5 minutes before serving.

HAM & CHEESE PENNE

Ham & Cheese Penne

This versatile dish is a crowd-pleaser. You can easily take the recipe and make it your own by changing up the cheeses or veggie. My family loves it!

—**DONNA BAILEY** ORELAND, PA

PREP: 25 MIN. • **BAKE:** 20 MIN.
MAKES: 6 SERVINGS

- 1 package (16 ounces) ziti
- ¼ cup butter, cubed
- ¼ cup all-purpose flour
- 2 cups 2% milk
- 2 cups (8 ounces) shredded white cheddar cheese
- ¼ cup grated Parmesan cheese
- 1 teaspoon garlic powder
- ½ teaspoon pepper
- 3 cups cubed fully cooked ham
- 1 package (10 ounces) frozen chopped spinach, thawed and squeezed dry

1. Prepare ziti according to package directions. Meanwhile, in a Dutch oven, melt butter. Stir in flour until smooth; gradually add milk. Bring to a boil; cook and stir for 2 minutes or until thickened. Reduce heat; add the cheeses, garlic powder and pepper. Cook and stir until cheese is melted.

2. Drain ziti; add to sauce mixture. Stir in ham and spinach. Transfer to a greased 13x9-in. baking dish. Bake, uncovered, at 375° for 20-25 minutes or until heated through.

CREAMY PORK CHOP CASSEROLE

Corny Pork Chops

My grandmother first made this hearty recipe in the 1950s, and it remains a family favorite today. As simple as it seems, the corn dressing complements the pork beautifully.

—RALPH PETTERSON SALT LAKE CITY, UT

PREP: 15 MIN. • **BAKE:** 40 MIN.
MAKES: 4 SERVINGS

- 4 **bone-in pork loin chops (¾- to 1-inch thick and 7 ounces each)**
- 1 **teaspoon salt, divided**
- ¼ **teaspoon pepper, divided**
- 1 **tablespoon canola oil**
- 1 **can (15¼ ounces) whole kernel corn, drained**
- 2 **celery ribs, diced**
- 1 **cup soft bread crumbs**
- ⅓ **cup ketchup**
- 1 **tablespoon chopped green onion**

1. Preheat oven to 325°. Season pork chops with ½ teaspoon salt and ⅛ teaspoon pepper. In a large skillet, cook chops in oil over medium heat 2-3 minutes on each side or until chops are lightly browned; drain.

2. Combine corn, celery, bread crumbs, ketchup, onion and remaining salt and pepper; place in a greased 11x7-in. baking dish. Top with chops.

3. Cover and bake 40-45 minutes or until meat is tender.

Southwestern Potpie with Cornmeal Biscuits

My Southwestern-inspired potpie is full of sweet and spicy pork, corn, beans and chilies. It's a sure-fire winner for any gathering. The cornmeal gives the biscuits a delightful crunch.

—ANDREA BOLDEN UNIONVILLE, TN

PREP: 35 MIN. + SIMMERING
BAKE: 15 MIN. + STANDING
MAKES: 12 SERVINGS

SOUTHWESTERN POTPIE WITH CORNMEAL BISCUITS

- ¼ **cup all-purpose flour**
- 1½ **pounds boneless pork loin roast, cut into ½-inch cubes**
- 2 **tablespoons butter**
- 1 **jalapeno pepper, seeded and chopped**
- 2 **garlic cloves, minced**
- 2 **cups beef broth**
- 1 **can (14½ ounces) diced tomatoes, undrained**
- 1 **teaspoon ground cumin**
- ½ **teaspoon chili powder**
- ¼ **to ½ teaspoon ground cinnamon**
- 1 **can (15¼ ounces) whole kernel corn, drained**
- 1 **can (15 ounces) pinto beans, rinsed and drained**
- 1 **can (4 ounces) chopped green chilies**

BISCUITS

- 3 **cups biscuit/baking mix**
- ¾ **cup cornmeal**
- ½ **cup shredded cheddar cheese**
- 4½ **teaspoons sugar**
- 1 **cup 2% milk**

1. Place flour in a large resealable plastic bag. Add pork, a few pieces at a time, and shake to coat. In a Dutch oven, brown pork in butter in batches. Remove and set aside.

2. In same pan, saute jalapeno and garlic in drippings 1 minute. Stir in broth, tomatoes, cumin, chili powder, cinnamon and pork. Bring to a boil. Reduce heat; cover and simmer 1 hour or until pork is tender.

3. Preheat oven to 400°. Add corn, beans and chilies; heat through. Transfer to a greased 13x9-in. baking dish.

4. In a large bowl, combine biscuit mix, cornmeal, cheese and sugar; stir in milk just until moistened. Turn onto a lightly floured surface; knead 8-10 times.

5. Pat or roll out to ½-in. thickness; cut with a floured 2½-in. biscuit cutter. Arrange over meat mixture. Bake 15-18 minutes or until golden brown. Let stand 10 minutes before serving.

NOTE *Wear disposable gloves when cutting hot peppers; the oils can burn skin. Avoid touching your face.*

FREEZE IT Italian Sausage Rigatoni Bake

Here's a dish that combines all of our favorite Italian flavors. It's great served alongside a green salad and crusty French bread.

—BLAIR LONERGAN ROCHELLE, VA

PREP: 30 MIN. • **BAKE:** 25 MIN.
MAKES: 2 CASSEROLES (4 SERVINGS EACH)

- 1 **package (16 ounces) rigatoni**
- 1 **pound bulk Italian sausage**
- 8 **ounces sliced fresh mushrooms**
- 1 **medium sweet red pepper, chopped**
- 5 **cups marinara sauce**
- ¼ **cup grated Parmesan cheese**
- 2 **tablespoons half-and-half cream**
- 16 **ounces sliced part-skim mozzarella cheese**

1. Preheat oven to 375°. Cook rigatoni according to package directions; drain.

2. In a large skillet, cook sausage, mushrooms and pepper over medium-high heat 8-10 minutes or until sausage is no longer pink and vegetables are tender, breaking up sausage into crumbles; drain. Stir in marinara sauce, Parmesan cheese and cream. Add rigatoni and toss to coat.

3. In each of two greased 8-in.-square baking dishes, layer one-fourth of the rigatoni mixture and one-fourth of the mozzarella cheese. Repeat layers. Bake, uncovered, 25-35 minutes or until heated through and cheese is melted. (Cover loosely with foil if top browns too quickly.)

FREEZE OPTION *Cool unbaked casseroles; cover and freeze. To use, partially thaw in the refrigerator overnight. Remove from refrigerator 30 minutes before baking. Preheat oven to 375°. Bake casseroles as directed, increasing time as necessary to heat through and for a thermometer inserted into center to read 165°.*

SMOKED PORK CHOPS WITH SWEET POTATOES

⑤ INGREDIENTS Smoked Pork Chops with Sweet Potatoes

Apple and sweet potato make a great complement to pork. My family enjoys simple dinners like this one.

—HELEN SANDERS FORT MYERS, FL

PREP: 15 MIN. • **COOK:** 40 MIN.
MAKES: 6 SERVINGS

- 6 **smoked boneless pork chops (7 ounces each)**
- 1 **tablespoon canola oil**
- 4 **large sweet potatoes, cooked, peeled and cut lengthwise into thirds**
- ½ **cup packed brown sugar**
- ⅛ **teaspoon pepper**
- 2 **large tart apples, peeled and thinly sliced**
- ¼ **cup apple juice or water**

1. Preheat oven to 325°. In a large skillet, cook chops in oil over medium heat 2-3 minutes on each side or until lightly browned; drain.

2. Transfer to a greased 13x9-in. baking dish. Top with sweet potatoes. Combine brown sugar and pepper; sprinkle over sweet potatoes. Top with apples; drizzle with apple juice.

3. Cover and bake 30 minutes. Uncover; bake 10-15 minutes longer or until meat is tender.

ITALIAN SAUSAGE RIGATONI BAKE

HAM-NOODLE BAKE

Ham-Noodle Bake

After a long day of doing chores on the farm, my husband and I have quite the appetite. My hot, creamy ham and noodle dish really hits the spot.

—**MARY RICHARDS** ELLENDALE, MN

PREP: 10 MIN. • **BAKE:** 30 MIN.
MAKES: 4-6 SERVINGS

- ¼ **cup butter, cubed**
- ¼ **cup all-purpose flour**
- ½ **teaspoon salt**
- ⅛ **teaspoon pepper**
- 2½ **cups milk**
- 3 **to 4 teaspoons prepared horseradish**
- 1 **tablespoon prepared mustard**
- 6 **cups cooked wide egg noodles**
- 2 **cups cubed fully cooked ham**
- 1 **cup cubed cheddar cheese**
- ½ **cup soft bread crumbs, toasted**

1. Preheat oven to 350°. In a large saucepan over medium heat, melt butter. Stir in flour, salt and pepper until smooth. Gradually add milk. Bring to a boil. Cook and stir 2 minutes or until thickened and bubbly. Add horseradish and mustard; mix well. Stir in noodles, ham and cheese.
2. Pour into a greased 2½-qt. baking dish. Cover and bake 20 minutes. Uncover; sprinkle with bread crumbs. Bake 10-15 minutes longer or until bubbly and heated through.

TOP TIP

The next time you cook a ham, cut up the leftovers into cubes and freeze them in separate freezer bags. Add the meat whenever you cook scrambled eggs, potato soup, jambalaya, macaroni and cheese and other casseroles.

Broccoli-Ham Hot Dish

One of my best friends shared this recipe with me. My family loves it because it includes one of our favorite vegetables: broccoli. It's a delicious and colorful way to use up leftover ham.

—MARGARET ALLEN ABINGDON, VA

PREP: 20 MIN. • **BAKE:** 30 MIN.
MAKES: 8 SERVINGS

- 2 packages (10 ounces each) frozen cut broccoli
- 2 cups cooked rice
- 6 tablespoons butter, cubed
- 2 cups fresh bread crumbs (about 2½ slices)
- 1 medium onion, chopped
- 3 tablespoons all-purpose flour
- 1 teaspoon salt
- ¼ teaspoon pepper
- 3 cups milk
- 1½ pounds fully cooked ham, cubed
  Shredded cheddar or Swiss cheese

1. Preheat oven to 350°. Cook broccoli according to package directions; drain. Spoon rice into a 13x9-in. baking pan. Place broccoli over rice.
2. Melt butter in a large skillet. Sprinkle 2 tablespoons of melted butter over the bread crumbs and set aside. Saute onion in remaining butter until soft. Add flour, salt and pepper, stirring constantly until blended; stir in milk. Bring to a boil; cook and stir 2 minutes or until thickened. Add ham.
3. Pour over rice and broccoli. Sprinkle with crumbs. Bake 30 minutes or until heated through. Sprinkle with cheese; let stand 5 minutes before serving.

PORK NOODLE CASSEROLE

FREEZE IT **5 INGREDIENTS**

Pork Noodle Casserole

Less expensive cuts of pork become tender and tasty in this creamy, meal-in-one casserole.

—BERNICE MORRIS MARSHFIELD, MO

PREP: 25 MIN. • **BAKE:** 45 MIN.
MAKES: 8 SERVINGS

- 2 cups uncooked egg noodles
- 2 pounds boneless pork, cut into ¾-inch cubes
- 2 medium onions, chopped
- 2 cans (15¼ ounces each) whole kernel corn, drained
- 2 cans (10¾ ounces each) condensed cream of mushroom soup, undiluted
- ½ teaspoon salt
- ½ teaspoon pepper

1. Preheat oven to 350°. Cook noodles according to package directions.
2. Meanwhile, in a large skillet, cook pork and onions over medium heat until meat is no longer pink. Drain noodles. Stir noodles, corn, soup, salt and pepper into the pork mixture.
3. Transfer to a greased 3-qt. baking dish. Cover and bake 30 minutes. Uncover; bake 15 minutes longer.
FREEZE OPTION *Cool unbaked casserole; cover and freeze. To use, partially thaw in the refrigerator overnight. Remove from refrigerator 30 minutes before baking. Preheat oven to 350°. Bake casserole as directed, increasing time as necessary to heat through and for a thermometer inserted into center to read 165°.*

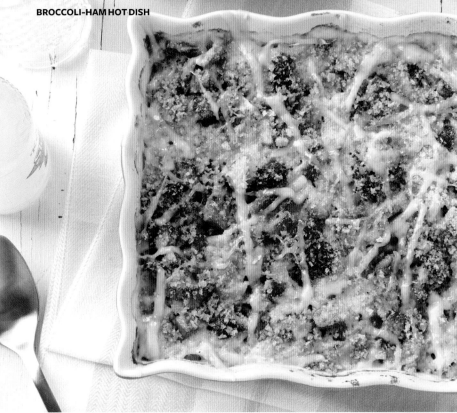

BROCCOLI-HAM HOT DISH

Penne and Smoked Sausage

My sausage-pasta dish is a must-try. It tastes so good when it's hot and bubbly from the oven. The cheddar French-fried onions lend a cheesy, crunchy touch.

—**MARGARET WILSON** SUN CITY, CA

PREP: 15 MIN. • **BAKE:** 30 MIN.
MAKES: 6 SERVINGS

- **2 cups uncooked penne pasta**
- **1 pound smoked sausage, cut into ¼-inch slices**
- **1½ cups 2% milk**
- **1 can (10¾ ounces) condensed cream of celery soup, undiluted**
- **1½ cups cheddar French-fried onions, divided**
- **1 cup (4 ounces) shredded part-skim mozzarella cheese, divided**
- **1 cup frozen peas**

1. Preheat oven to 375°. Cook pasta according to package directions.
2. Meanwhile, in a large skillet, brown sausage over medium heat 5 minutes; drain. In a large bowl, combine milk and soup. Stir in ½ cup onions, ½ cup cheese, peas and sausage. Drain pasta; stir into sausage mixture.
3. Transfer to a greased 13x9-in. baking dish. Cover and bake 25-30 minutes or until bubbly. Sprinkle with remaining onions and cheese. Bake, uncovered, 3-5 minutes longer or until cheese is melted.

Potluck Casserole

Whenever I take this dish to potlucks, people compare it to the hominess of tuna casserole. It reminds them of the comfort foods we all enjoyed growing up.

—**JANET WIELHOUWER** GRAND RAPIDS, MI

PREP: 10 MIN. • **COOK:** 45 MIN.
MAKES: 4 SERVINGS

- **½ pound boneless pork, cut into ¾-inch cubes**
- **1 cup sliced celery**
- **¼ cup chopped onion**
- **2 tablespoons water**
- **2 cups cooked noodles**
- **1 can (10¾ ounces) condensed cream of mushroom soup, undiluted**
- **1 cup frozen peas**
- **¼ teaspoon salt, optional**
- **⅛ teaspoon pepper**
- **3 tablespoons seasoned or plain dry bread crumbs**

1. In a large skillet coated with cooking spray, brown pork over medium-high heat on all sides for 2-3 minutes or until lightly browned. Add celery, onion and water; cover and simmer 20-25 minutes or until vegetables are tender.
2. Meanwhile, preheat oven to 350°. Remove skillet from heat; add noodles, soup, peas, salt if desired and pepper.
3. Transfer to an ungreased 11x7-in. baking dish; sprinkle with bread crumbs. Bake, uncovered, for 20-25 minutes or until meat is tender.

POTLUCK CASSEROLE

Perfect Pork Chop Bake

This recipe is especially useful on busy days when we're short on time. I love that it cooks hands-free while I'm doing other things.

—JAN LUTZ STEVENS POINT, WI

PREP: 15 MIN. • **BAKE:** 40 MIN.
MAKES: 6 SERVINGS

- 6 **boneless pork loin chops (5 ounces each)**
- ½ **teaspoon salt, divided, optional**
- 1 **medium onion, thinly sliced and separated into rings**
- 3 **medium potatoes, peeled and thinly sliced**
- 6 **medium carrots, thinly sliced**
- 1 **teaspoon dried marjoram**
- 3 **tablespoons all-purpose flour**
- ¾ **cup milk**
- 1 **can (10¾ ounces) condensed cream of mushroom soup, undiluted**

1. Preheat oven to 350°. Coat a large skillet with cooking spray; cook chops over medium heat 2-3 minutes on each side or until lightly browned. Place in an ungreased 13x9-in. baking dish; sprinkle with ¼ teaspoon salt if desired. Layer with onion, potatoes and carrots. Sprinkle with marjoram and remaining salt if desired.

2. In a small bowl, whisk flour and milk until smooth; add soup. Pour over vegetables.

3. Cover and bake 30-35 minutes. Uncover; bake 10-15 minutes longer or until meat is tender.

PERFECT PORK CHOP BAKE

Ham 'n' Tater Casserole

This casserole reminds me of a loaded baked potato. I usually make it several times a month—I've even served it to company. I'm always asked for the recipe, which I got from my sister.

—PEGGY GRIEME PINEHURST, NC

PREP: 10 MIN. • **BAKE:** 40 MIN.
MAKES: 6-8 SERVINGS

- 1 package (28 ounces) frozen steak fries
- 3 cups frozen chopped broccoli, thawed and drained
- 1½ cups diced fully cooked ham
- 1 can (10¾ ounces) condensed cream of broccoli soup, undiluted
- ¾ cup milk
- ½ cup mayonnaise
- 1 cup (4 ounces) shredded cheddar cheese

1. Preheat oven to 350°. Arrange fries in a greased 3-qt. baking dish; layer with broccoli and then ham. Combine soup, milk and mayonnaise until smooth; pour over ham.
2. Cover and bake 20 minutes. Sprinkle with cheese; bake, uncovered, 20-25 minutes longer or until bubbly.

HAM 'N' TATER CASSEROLE

BACON-CHEESE STUFFED SHELLS

Bacon-Cheese Stuffed Shells

I make these rich shells for parties and potlucks. Pasta, bacon and cheese is a combination that's hard to pass up. Everyone will be asking for seconds.

—REBECCA ANDERSON DRIFTWOOD, TX

PREP: 45 MIN. • **BAKE:** 40 MIN.
MAKES: 12 SERVINGS

- 24 uncooked jumbo pasta shells
- 1 cup chopped fresh mushrooms
- 1 cup finely chopped onion
- 1 tablespoon plus ¼ cup butter, divided
- 1½ cups ricotta cheese
- 1 package (8 ounces) cream cheese, softened, divided
- 1½ cups shredded Asiago cheese, divided
- 1 cup shredded Parmesan cheese
- 1 cup crumbled cooked bacon
- 2 tablespoons minced fresh parsley, divided
- ½ teaspoon garlic salt
- ½ teaspoon ground nutmeg
- ¼ teaspoon pepper
- 2 tablespoons all-purpose flour
- 2 cups heavy whipping cream
- ½ cup chicken broth
- ½ cup 2% milk
- 2 cups shredded Romano cheese
- 1½ cups shredded part-skim mozzarella cheese

1. Cook pasta according to package directions.
2. Meanwhile, in a large skillet, saute mushrooms and onion in 1 tablespoon butter until tender.
3. In a large bowl, beat ricotta and 4 ounces cream cheese until blended. Stir in ½ cup Asiago cheese, Parmesan cheese, bacon, 1 tablespoon parsley, garlic salt, nutmeg, pepper and mushroom mixture. Spoon into shells; place in a greased 13x9-in. baking dish.
4. Preheat oven to 350°. In a large saucepan, melt remaining butter. Stir in flour until smooth; gradually add cream, broth and milk. Bring to a boil; cook and stir 1-2 minutes or until thickened. Stir in Romano cheese and the remaining cream cheese, Asiago and parsley.
5. Pour over shells. Sprinkle with mozzarella cheese. Cover and bake 30 minutes. Uncover; bake 10-15 minutes longer or until bubbly.

PORK CHOP-CRANBERRY DISH

Farm-Style Sausage Bake

This dish is a hearty meal all by itself. My family thinks it's fantastic. Maybe yours will, too.

—**CATHERINE O'HARA** BRIDGETON, NJ

PREP: 30 MIN. • **BAKE:** 30 MIN.
MAKES: 6 SERVINGS

- 6 medium potatoes (about 2 pounds), peeled and cubed
- ¾ cup milk
- 2 tablespoons butter
- 3 to 4 green onions, sliced
- 2 garlic cloves, minced
- 2 egg yolks
  Dash each pepper and ground nutmeg
- 1 pound smoked sausage, sliced
- ½ cup cubed part-skim mozzarella cheese
- 2 tablespoons grated Parmesan cheese
- 2 tablespoons dried parsley flakes
- 1 teaspoon dried thyme or rubbed sage

1. Place potatoes in a large saucepan and cover with water. Bring to a boil. Reduce heat; cover and simmer for 15-20 minutes or until tender.
2. Preheat oven to 400°. Drain potatoes and transfer to a large bowl; mash potatoes. Beat in milk, butter, green onions, garlic, egg yolks, pepper and nutmeg until light and fluffy.
3. Stir in sausage, cheeses and parsley. Spoon into a greased 2-qt. baking dish. Sprinkle with thyme. Bake, uncovered, 30 minutes or until a thermometer reads 160°.

Pork Chop-Cranberry Dish

The original recipe was for pork chops and apples and it was good. I added cranberries and onion, and the result was even more sensational. I like to serve this with mashed potatoes or buttered noodles.

—**SHELVY RITTER** PORTAGE, WI

PREP: 20 MIN. • **BAKE:** 45 MIN.
MAKES: 2 SERVINGS

- 2 boneless pork loin chops (5 ounces each)
- 2 teaspoons butter
- 2 medium apples, peeled and sliced
- ¾ cup whole-berry cranberry sauce
- 1 small sweet onion, halved and thinly sliced
- 2 tablespoons brown sugar
- ¼ teaspoon ground cinnamon

1. Preheat oven to 325°. In a small nonstick skillet, brown pork chops in butter.
2. Meanwhile, in a small bowl, combine apples, cranberry sauce and onion. Transfer to an 8-in.-square baking dish coated with cooking spray. Combine brown sugar and cinnamon; sprinkle over apple mixture. Top with pork chops.
3. Cover and bake 45-50 minutes or until pork reaches 145° and apples are tender.

FARM-STYLE SAUSAGE BAKE

PORK CHOP AND CHILIES CASSEROLE

Pork Chop and Chilies Casserole

A real estate agent who wanted to list my house dropped off this recipe at my door. I didn't sell the house, but the recipe has saved my life many times! It is easy to make and guests always like the flavor of this unique spin on pork chops.

—**MICKEY O'NEAL** CHULA VISTA, CA

PREP: 15 MIN. • **BAKE:** 30 MIN.
MAKES: 4 SERVINGS

- 4 pork rib chops (¾- to 1-inch thick)
- 1 tablespoon canola oil
- 1 medium onion, chopped
- 1 can (4 ounces) chopped green chilies
- ½ cup chopped celery
- 1½ cups uncooked instant rice
- 1 can (10¾ ounces) condensed cream of mushroom soup, undiluted
- 1⅓ cups water
- 3 tablespoons reduced-sodium soy sauce

1. Preheat oven to 350°. In a large skillet, cook chops in oil over medium heat for 2-3 minutes on each side or until chops are lightly browned; drain. Remove and set aside.

2. In the same skillet, saute onion, chilies and celery until onion is tender. Stir in rice; saute until lightly browned. Add remaining ingredients.

3. Place in a greased 2-qt. baking dish. Top with pork chops. Bake at 30-40 minutes or until meat is tender.

FREEZE IT Sausage Lasagna Rolls

Who said lasagna noodles have to lie flat? This artful interpretation of layered comfort food—with a twist—is what we like to call "casser-roll."

—**KALI WRASPIR** OLYMPIA, WA

PREP: 45 MIN. • **BAKE:** 45 MIN.
MAKES: 2 CASSEROLES (6 SERVINGS EACH)

- 12 lasagna noodles
- 1 pound bulk Italian sausage
- 2 jars (26 ounces each) spaghetti sauce
- 1 carton (15 ounces) ricotta cheese
- 2 cups (8 ounces) shredded part-skim mozzarella cheese, divided
- ¾ cup shredded Parmesan cheese, divided
- 1 egg
- 2 tablespoons minced fresh parsley or 2 teaspoons dried parsley flakes
- 2½ teaspoons minced fresh rosemary or ¾ teaspoon dried rosemary, crushed
- 2 teaspoons lemon juice
- 1½ teaspoons minced fresh thyme or ½ teaspoon dried thyme
- 1 teaspoon grated lemon peel
- 1 teaspoon coarsely ground pepper
- ½ teaspoon salt

1. Preheat oven to 350°. Cook noodles according to package directions.

2. Meanwhile, in a large skillet, cook sausage over medium heat until no longer pink; drain. Stir in spaghetti sauce.

3. In a large bowl, combine ricotta, 1 cup mozzarella, ¼ cup Parmesan, egg, parsley, rosemary, lemon juice, thyme, lemon peel, pepper and salt. Drain noodles. Spread 2 tablespoons cheese mixture on each noodle; carefully roll up.

4. Spread ⅔ cup meat sauce into each of two greased 11x7-in. baking dishes. Place roll-ups seam side down over sauce. Top with remaining meat sauce. Sprinkle with remaining mozzarella and Parmesan cheeses.

5. Cover and bake 45-50 minutes or until bubbly.

FREEZE OPTION *Cover and freeze unbaked casseroles up to 3 months. To use, thaw in the refrigerator overnight. Remove from refrigerator 30 minutes before baking. Preheat oven to 350°. Cover and bake 50-60 minutes or until bubbly.*

SAUSAGE LASAGNA ROLLS

Ham and Broccoli Biscuit Bake

Whenever I cook this creamy dish, I'm on alert to make sure my husband doesn't nibble on it before I bring it to the table!
—**AMY WHEELER** BALTIMORE, MD

PREP: 20 MIN. • **BAKE:** 25 MIN.
MAKES: 6 SERVINGS

- 2½ cups frozen chopped broccoli
- 1 can (10¾ ounces) condensed cream of potato soup, undiluted
- 1¼ cups 2% milk, divided
- 1 teaspoon garlic pepper blend
- ½ teaspoon crushed red pepper flakes
- ¼ teaspoon pepper
- 2 cups cubed fully cooked ham
- 1 cup (4 ounces) shredded cheddar-Monterey Jack cheese
- 1½ cups biscuit/baking mix
- 1 egg

1. Preheat oven to 350°. Combine broccoli, soup, ¾ cup milk and seasonings in a large saucepan; bring to a boil. Reduce heat; stir in ham and cheese. Cook and stir until cheese is melted. Pour into a greased 11x7-in. baking dish.
2. Combine biscuit mix, egg and remaining milk in a small bowl just until moistened. Drop by tablespoonfuls over ham mixture; spread gently.
3. Bake, uncovered, 25-30 minutes or until golden brown.

DID YOU KNOW?

Pastitsio is a traditional Greek baked pasta dish that includes a cinnamon-flavored meat filling of lean ground lamb or beef and a creamy white Béchamel sauce on top. Feel free to add a pinch of nutmeg to the sauce for extra flavor.

PASTITSIO

Pastitsio

Guests always seem to gobble up this authentic Greek lamb and pasta casserole. The creamy white sauce is delicious.
—**AMANDA BRIGGS** GREENFIELD, WI

PREP: 35 MIN. • **BAKE:** 30 MIN. + STANDING
MAKES: 12 SERVINGS

- 1 package (7 ounces) uncooked elbow macaroni
- 1 pound ground lamb or beef
- 1 medium onion, chopped
- 1 garlic clove, minced
- 1 can (8 ounces) tomato sauce
- 1 teaspoon salt, divided
- ¼ teaspoon dried oregano
- ⅛ teaspoon pepper
- ¼ teaspoon ground cinnamon, optional
- ½ cup grated Parmesan cheese, divided
- 3 tablespoons butter
- 3 tablespoons all-purpose flour
- 1½ cups 2% milk
- 1 egg, lightly beaten

1. Cook macaroni according to package directions. Meanwhile, in a large skillet, cook lamb and onion over medium heat until meat is no longer pink. Add garlic; cook 1 minute longer. Drain. Stir in the tomato sauce, ½ teaspoon salt, oregano, pepper and, if desired, cinnamon; heat through.
2. Drain macaroni; place half of macaroni in a greased 9-in.-square baking pan. Sprinkle with ¼ cup cheese. Layer with meat mixture and remaining macaroni. Set aside.
3. Preheat oven to 350°. In a small saucepan, melt butter; stir in flour and remaining salt until smooth. Gradually add milk. Bring to a boil; cook and stir 2 minutes or until thickened.
4. Remove from the heat. Stir a small amount of the hot mixture into egg; return all to the pan, stirring constantly. Bring to a gentle boil; cook and stir 2 minutes. Remove from heat; stir in remaining cheese. Pour sauce over macaroni.
5. Bake, uncovered, 30-35 minutes or until golden brown. Let stand 10 minutes before serving.

FREEZE IT Polish Casserole

When I first made this dish, my 2-year-old liked it so much that he wanted it for every meal! You can use any pasta that will hold the sauce.

—**CRYSTAL BRUNS** ILIFF, CO

PREP: 25 MIN. • **BAKE:** 45 MIN.
MAKES: 2 CASSEROLES (6 SERVINGS EACH)

- 4 cups uncooked penne pasta
- 1½ pounds smoked Polish sausage or kielbasa, cut into ½-inch slices
- 2 cans (10¾ ounces each) condensed cream of mushroom soup, undiluted
- 1 jar (16 ounces) sauerkraut, rinsed and well drained
- 3 cups (12 ounces) shredded Swiss cheese, divided
- 1⅓ cups 2% milk
- 4 green onions, chopped
- 2 tablespoons Dijon mustard
- 4 garlic cloves, minced

1. Preheat oven to 350°. Cook pasta according to package directions; drain and transfer to a large bowl. Stir in sausage, soup, sauerkraut, 2 cups cheese, milk, onions, mustard and garlic.

2. Spoon into two greased 8-in.-square baking dishes; sprinkle with remaining cheese. Bake, uncovered, 45-50 minutes or until casserole is golden brown and bubbly.

FREEZE OPTION *Cover and freeze unbaked casserole up to 3 months. Thaw in the refrigerator overnight. Remove from refrigerator 30 minutes before baking. Preheat oven to 350°. Bake, uncovered, 50-55 minutes or until golden brown and bubbly.*

POLISH CASSEROLE

Autumn Sausage Casserole

Apple, raisins and spices give this tasty sausage-rice entree a taste of autumn. We enjoy it with a green salad on a cool fall day. It would be a nice potluck dish, too—just double the recipe if needed.

—**DIANE BRUNELL** WASHINGTON, MA

PREP: 20 MIN. • **BAKE:** 25 MIN.
MAKES: 4-6 SERVINGS

- 1 pound bulk pork sausage
- 1 medium apple, peeled and chopped
- 1 medium onion, chopped
- ½ cup chopped celery
- 3 cups cooked long grain rice
- ½ cup raisins
- ⅓ cup minced fresh parsley
- 1 tablespoon brown sugar
- ½ teaspoon salt
- ¼ teaspoon ground allspice
- ¼ teaspoon ground cinnamon
- ⅛ teaspoon pepper

1. Preheat oven to 350°. In a large skillet, cook sausage, apple, onion and celery over medium heat until meat is no longer pink; drain. Stir in the remaining ingredients.
2. Transfer to a greased 2-qt. baking dish. Cover and bake 25-30 minutes or until heated through.

⑤ INGREDIENTS Pork Chops with Orange Rice

My husband is delighted every time we have this pork and rice bake for dinner. I've also made it for new moms who need meals brought over.

—**KAREN HOSSINK** LANSING, MI

PREP: 15 MIN. • **BAKE:** 25 MIN.
MAKES: 4 SERVINGS

- 4 bone-in pork loin chops
  (½-inch thick and 8 ounces each)
- 1 tablespoon canola oil
- 1⅓ cups uncooked instant rice

- 1 cup orange juice
  Salt and pepper to taste
- 1 can (10½ ounces) condensed chicken with rice soup, undiluted

1. Preheat oven to 350°. In a large skillet, brown pork chops in oil on both sides. Sprinkle rice into a greased 9-in.-square baking dish. Add juice; arrange chops over rice. Sprinkle with salt and pepper. Pour soup over chops.
2. Cover and bake 25-30 minutes or until a thermometer reads 145° and rice is tender. Let meat stand 5 minutes before serving.

Pepperoni Pizza Pasta

Pizza taste without the takeout? Believe it! With great pepperoni flavor, this recipe will give the whole family an easy alternative on pizza night.

—**MARY SHIVERS** ADA, OK

PREP: 20 MIN. • **BAKE:** 20 MIN. + STANDING
MAKES: 6 SERVINGS

- 1½ cups uncooked elbow macaroni
- 2 eggs, lightly beaten
- ⅓ cup grated Parmesan cheese
- ¼ cup sour cream
- ½ teaspoon Italian seasoning
- 1½ cups pizza sauce
- 2 cups (8 ounces) shredded part-skim mozzarella cheese
- 30 slices pepperoni
- 1 can (2¼ ounces) sliced ripe olives, drained

1. Preheat oven to 375°. Cook macaroni according to package directions; drain. Stir in the eggs, Parmesan cheese, sour cream and Italian seasoning. Transfer to a greased 11x7-in. baking dish. Bake 10 minutes.
2. Spread macaroni mixture with pizza sauce. Sprinkle with mozzarella cheese; top with pepperoni and olives. Bake 10-15 minutes longer or until cheese is melted. Let stand 10 minutes before serving.

PEPPERONI PIZZA PASTA

Firefighter's Chicken Spaghetti

I love to spend time in the kitchen making a variety of dishes for family, neighbors and our local fire department, where my husband works as a firefighter. This casserole is a favorite with his team.

—**KRISTA DAVIS-KEITH** NEW CASTLE, IN

PREP: 20 MIN. • **BAKE:** 45 MIN.
MAKES: 12-14 SERVINGS

- 12 **ounces uncooked spaghetti, broken in half**
- 1 **can (10¾ ounces) condensed cream of chicken soup, undiluted**
- 1 **can (10¾ ounces) condensed cream of mushroom soup, undiluted**
- 1 **cup (8 ounces) sour cream**
- ½ **cup milk**
- ¼ **cup butter, melted, divided**
- 2 **tablespoons dried parsley flakes**
- ½ **teaspoon garlic powder**
- ½ **teaspoon salt**
- ¼ **teaspoon pepper**
- 2 **cups (8 ounces) shredded part-skim mozzarella cheese**
- 1 **cup grated Parmesan cheese**
- 2 **to 3 celery ribs, chopped**
- 1 **medium onion, chopped**
- 1 **can (4 ounces) mushroom stems and pieces, drained**
- 5 **cups cubed cooked chicken**
- 1½ **cups crushed cornflakes**

1. Preheat oven to 350°. Cook spaghetti according to package directions; drain.
2. In a large bowl, combine soups, sour cream, milk, 2 tablespoons butter and seasonings. Add the cheeses, celery, onion and mushrooms. Stir in the chicken and spaghetti.
3. Transfer to a greased 3-qt. baking dish (dish will be full). Combine the cornflakes and remaining butter; sprinkle over the top.
4. Bake, uncovered, 45-50 minutes or until bubbly.

FIREFIGHTER'S CHICKEN SPAGHETTI

Barbecue Chicken Casserole

I am a minister's wife and have cooked for countless fellowships, potlucks and other church activities. This is one of my go-to recipes that I use for those occasions where I need a crowd-pleaser.

—**GAIL RECTOR** BELLE, MO

PREP: 25 MIN. • **BAKE:** 50 MIN.
MAKES: 4-6 SERVINGS

- 1 cup all-purpose flour
- 1 broiler/fryer chicken (3 to 4 pounds), cut up
- 2 tablespoons canola oil
- 1 cup chopped onion
- 1 cup chopped green pepper
- 1 cup thinly sliced celery
- 1 cup ketchup
- ½ cup water
- 3 tablespoons brown sugar
- 3 tablespoons Worcestershire sauce
- ½ teaspoon salt
- ¼ teaspoon pepper
- 1 package (16 ounces) frozen corn, thawed

1. Preheat oven to 350°. Place flour in a large resealable plastic bag. Add chicken, a few pieces at a time, and shake to coat. In a large skillet, brown chicken in oil; transfer to an ungreased 13x9-in. baking dish.

2. Drain the skillet, reserving 2 tablespoons drippings. In drippings, saute onion, green pepper and celery until tender. In a small bowl, combine the ketchup, water, brown sugar, Worcestershire sauce, salt and pepper; add to vegetables. Bring to a boil. Pour over chicken.

3. Cover; bake 30 minutes. Sprinkle with corn. Bake 18-20 minutes longer or until chicken juices run clear and corn is tender.

FREEZE IT Simple Creamy Chicken Enchiladas

This is one of the first recipes I created and cooked for my husband right after we got married. He was so impressed! We fix these creamy enchiladas for friends regularly.

—**MELISSA ROGERS** TUSCALOOSA, AL

PREP: 30 MIN. • **BAKE:** 30 MIN.
MAKES: 2 CASSEROLES (5 SERVINGS EACH)

- 1 rotisserie chicken
- 2 cans (14½ ounces each) diced tomatoes with mild green chilies, undrained
- 2 cans (10¾ ounces each) condensed cream of chicken soup, undiluted
- 1 can (10¾ ounces) condensed cheddar cheese soup, undiluted
- ¼ cup 2% milk
- 1 tablespoon ground cumin
- 1 tablespoon chili powder
- 2 teaspoons garlic powder
- 2 teaspoons dried oregano
- 1 package (8 ounces) cream cheese, cubed
- 20 flour tortillas (8 inches), warmed
- 4 cups shredded Mexican cheese blend

1. Preheat oven to 350°. Remove meat from bones; discard bones. Shred chicken with two forks and set aside. In a large bowl, combine the tomatoes, soups, milk and seasonings. Transfer 3½ cups to another bowl; add chicken and cream cheese.

2. Spread ¼ cup soup mixture into each of two greased 13x9-in. baking dishes. Place ⅓ cup chicken mixture down the center of each tortilla. Roll up and place seam side down in baking dishes. Pour remaining soup mixture over tops; sprinkle with cheese.

3. Bake, uncovered, 30-35 minutes or until heated through and cheese is melted.

FREEZE OPTION *Cover and freeze unbaked casseroles up to 3 months. To use, partially thaw in refrigerator overnight. Remove from refrigerator 30 minutes before baking. Preheat oven to 350°. Cover casserole with foil; bake as directed, increasing covered time to 45 minutes or until heated through and a thermometer inserted in center reads 165°. Uncover; bake 5-10 minutes longer or until cheese is melted.*

SIMPLE CREAMY CHICKEN ENCHILADAS

PORTOBELLO PASTA

Portobello Pasta

I always plan to use this recipe right after Thanksgiving Day. Leftover turkey never tasted so good.

—**PRECI D'SILVA** DUBAI, UAE

PREP: 20 MIN. • **BAKE:** 20 MIN.
MAKES: 4 SERVINGS

- 2½ cups uncooked multigrain spiral pasta
- 3 large portobello mushrooms
- 1 tablespoon olive oil
- 1 tablespoon butter
- 3 garlic cloves, minced
- 3 tablespoons all-purpose flour
- 1½ cups 2% milk
- ⅓ cup heavy whipping cream
- 2 cups cubed cooked turkey
- ¾ teaspoon salt
- ¼ teaspoon pepper
- 1 cup (4 ounces) shredded part-skim mozzarella cheese, divided
- 2 tablespoons grated Parmesan cheese

1. Preheat oven to 350°. Cook pasta according to package directions. With a spoon, scrape and remove gills of mushrooms; slice caps.
2. In a large skillet, heat oil and butter over medium-high heat. Add sliced mushrooms; cook and stir until tender. Add garlic; cook 1 minute longer. Stir in flour until blended; gradually add milk and cream. Bring to a boil; cook and stir 2 minutes or until thickened. Stir in turkey, salt and pepper; heat through.
3. Drain pasta; add to the turkey mixture and toss to coat. Stir in ¾ cup mozzarella cheese.
4. Transfer to a greased 8-in.-square baking dish. Sprinkle with Parmesan cheese and remaining mozzarella cheese. Bake, uncovered, 20-25 minutes or until cheese is melted.

Chicken Artichoke Bake

The first time I tasted this creamy casserole at a friend's get-together, I noted how much everyone loved it. All of the party guests went for seconds...and thirds.

—**TODD RICHARDS** WEST ALLIS, WI

PREP: 15 MIN. • **BAKE:** 55 MIN.
MAKES: 6 SERVINGS

- 2 cans (10¾ ounces each) condensed cream of celery soup, undiluted
- 1 cup mayonnaise
- 3 cups cubed cooked chicken
- 1 can (14 ounces) water-packed artichoke hearts, rinsed, drained and chopped
- 1 can (8 ounces) sliced water chestnuts, drained
- 1 package (6 ounces) long grain and wild rice mix
- 1 cup sliced fresh mushrooms
- 1 medium onion, finely chopped
- 1 jar (2 ounces) diced pimientos, drained
- ¼ teaspoon pepper
- 1 cup seasoned stuffing cubes

1. Preheat oven to 350°. In a large bowl, combine soup and mayonnaise. Stir in chicken, artichokes, water chestnuts, rice mix with contents of seasoning packet, mushrooms, onion, pimientos and pepper.
2. Spoon the mixture into a greased 2½-qt. baking dish. Sprinkle with stuffing cubes. Bake, uncovered, 55-65 minutes or until edges are bubbly and rice is tender.

Savory Chicken Potpie

Roasting chunky chicken and veggies in a creamy sauce and topped with a puff pastry crust, these mini potpies are sure to satisfy! They take some time to prep, but the oohs and aahs you'll hear coming from happy tasters is well worth the effort.

—TASTE OF HOME COOKING SCHOOL

PREP: 1½ HOURS + COOLING • **BAKE:** 40 MIN.
MAKES: 4 SERVINGS

- 1 **broiler/fryer chicken, cut up (3 to 4 pounds)**
- 3 **tablespoons olive oil, divided**
  Salt and pepper to taste
- 1 **pound potatoes (about 2 medium), peeled and cut into 1-inch cubes**
- 3 **medium carrots, cut into 1-inch pieces**
- 8 **fresh mushrooms, quartered**
- 2 **celery ribs, cut into 1-inch pieces**
- 1 **leek, cut into ½-inch slices**
- 24 **frozen pearl onions**
- 2 **garlic cloves, minced**
- 2 **tablespoons minced fresh parsley**
- 1 **teaspoon dried rosemary**
- 1 **teaspoon dried thyme**
- ½ **teaspoon dried sage**
- 1 **cup frozen peas**
- 1 **jar (2 ounces) diced pimientos, drained**
- ¼ **cup butter, cubed**
- 6 **tablespoons all-purpose flour**
- 4 **cups chicken broth**
- 1 **package (17.3 ounces) frozen puff pastry, thawed**
- 1 **egg yolk**
- ½ **cup heavy whipping cream**

1. Preheat oven to 375°. Rub chicken with 1 tablespoon olive oil and season with salt and pepper to taste; transfer to a shallow roasting pan. In a large bowl, toss the potatoes, carrots, mushrooms, celery, leek, onions and garlic with herbs and remaining oil; place around chicken.

2. Bake, uncovered, 1 hour or until chicken juices run clear and vegetables are tender. Remove chicken from pan to cool. Remove vegetables with a slotted spoon to a large bowl; add peas and pimientos. Pour drippings and loosened browned bits from roasting pan into a measuring cup. Skim fat, reserving 2 tablespoons fat.

3. Increase oven setting to 400°. In a large saucepan, melt butter with reserved fat over medium heat. Stir in flour until blended. Gradually whisk in broth and cooking juices. Bring to a boil, stirring constantly; cook and stir 1-2 minutes or until thickened. Stir into vegetables.

4. Remove chicken from bones; discard skin and bones. Cut chicken into ¾-in. pieces; stir into gravy mixture. Divide among four 12-oz. ovenproof bowls or a 2-qt. baking dish.

5. Unfold puff pastry. Roll to ⅛-in. thickness; cut out four circles to fit ramekins. Place dough over chicken mixture, pressing to seal edges. In a small bowl, whisk egg yolk with cream; brush over pastry. Place potpies on a baking sheet. Bake 20-25 minutes or until lightly browned.

SAVORY CHICKEN POTPIE

CHEDDAR
TURKEY PASTA

FREEZE IT Cheddar Turkey Pasta

This recipe boasts lots of mass appeal, thanks to its cheesy sauce. Simply toss together pasta, veggies and leftover turkey, and bake for a filling dinner.

—**STEVE FOY** KIRKWOOD, MO

PREP: 20 MIN. • **BAKE:** 35 MIN.
MAKES: 6 SERVINGS

- 4 **cups uncooked spiral pasta**
- 1 **garlic clove, minced**
- 3 **tablespoons butter**
- 3 **tablespoons all-purpose flour**
- 1 **teaspoon salt**
- ¼ **teaspoon prepared mustard**
- ¼ **teaspoon dried thyme**
- ¼ **teaspoon pepper**
- 2 **cups 2% milk**
- 1½ **cups (6 ounces) shredded cheddar cheese**
- 2 **cups cubed cooked turkey**
- 2 **cups frozen mixed vegetables, thawed**
- ½ **cup slivered almonds**

1. Preheat oven to 350°. Cook pasta according to package directions.
2. Meanwhile, in a large saucepan, saute garlic in butter until tender. Stir in the flour, salt, mustard, thyme and pepper. Gradually stir in milk. Bring to a boil; cook and stir 2 minutes or until thickened. Remove from heat; stir in cheese until melted. Drain pasta; place in a large bowl. Toss with the turkey, vegetables and cheese sauce.
3. Transfer to a greased 13x9-in.

baking dish. Sprinkle with almonds. Bake, uncovered, 35-40 minutes or until heated through.
FREEZER OPTION *Cover and freeze unbaked casserole up to 3 months. To use, thaw in the refrigerator overnight. Remove from refrigerator 30 minutes before baking. Preheat oven to 350°. Bake according to directions.*

FREEZE IT Thanksgiving Leftovers Casserole

Sometimes leftovers are just as good as the original meal. Watch your family dig in to this Thanksgiving-inspired shepherd's pie that makes Turkey Day twice as nice.

—*TASTE OF HOME* TEST KITCHEN

PREP: 30 MIN. • **BAKE:** 25 MIN.
MAKES: 4 SERVINGS

- 3 **medium potatoes, peeled and cut into chunks**
- 3 **cups leftover cooked stuffing**
- 2 **cups cubed cooked turkey**
- 1 **can (10¾ ounces) condensed cream of chicken soup, undiluted**
- ½ **teaspoon garlic powder**
- 2 **tablespoons plus ¼ cup sour cream, divided**
- 2 **ounces cream cheese, softened**
- ¼ **teaspoon pepper**
- ⅛ **teaspoon salt**
- ¾ **cup shredded cheddar cheese**

1. Place potatoes in a Dutch oven and cover with water. Bring to a boil. Reduce heat; cover and cook for 15-20 minutes or until tender.
2. Meanwhile, preheat oven to 350°. Spread stuffing into a greased 8-in.-square baking dish. In a large bowl, combine turkey, soup, garlic powder and 2 tablespoons sour cream; spoon over stuffing.
3. Drain potatoes; mash in a small bowl. Beat in cream cheese, pepper, salt and the remaining sour cream; spread over turkey mixture. Sprinkle with cheese.
4. Bake, uncovered, 25-30 minutes or until heated through.
FREEZE OPTION *Cover and freeze unbaked casseroles up to 3 months. To use, thaw in the refrigerator overnight. Remove from refrigerator 30 minutes before baking. Preheat oven to 350°. Bake according to directions.*

THANKSGIVING LEFTOVERS CASSEROLE

Biscuit-Topped Lemon Chicken

Here's a homey dish that combines two of my favorite things—hot, crusty biscuits and chicken smothered in a flavorful lemon-pepper sauce. I often serve it with sides of potatoes and carrots.

—PATTIE ISHEE STRINGER, MS

PREP: 40 MIN. • **BAKE:** 35 MIN.
MAKES: 15 SERVINGS (30 BISCUITS)

- 2 large onions, finely chopped
- 4 celery ribs, finely chopped
- 1 cup butter, cubed
- 2 garlic cloves, minced
- 8 green onions, thinly sliced
- ⅔ cup all-purpose flour
- 8 cups 2% milk
- 12 cups cubed cooked chicken
- 2 cans (10¾ ounces each) condensed cream of chicken soup, undiluted
- ½ cup lemon juice
- 2 tablespoons grated lemon peel
- 2 teaspoons pepper
- 1 teaspoon salt

CHEDDAR BISCUITS
- 5 cups self-rising flour
- 2 cups 2% milk
- 2 cups (8 ounces) shredded cheddar cheese
- ¼ cup butter, melted

1. In a Dutch oven, saute onions and celery in butter. Add garlic; cook 1 minute longer. Add green onions. Stir in flour until blended; gradually add milk. Bring to a boil; cook and stir 2 minutes or until thickened.

2. Stir in chicken, soup, lemon juice and peel, pepper and salt; heat through. Pour into two greased 13x9-in. baking dishes; set aside.

3. Preheat oven to 350°. In a large bowl, combine biscuit ingredients just until moistened. Turn onto a lightly floured surface; knead 8-10 times. Pat or roll out to ¾-in. thickness. With a floured 2½-in. biscuit cutter, cut out 30 biscuits.

4. Place over chicken mixture. Bake, uncovered, 35-40 minutes or until golden brown.

NOTE *As a substitute for each cup of self-rising flour, place 1½ teaspoons baking powder and ½ teaspoon salt in a measuring cup. Add all-purpose flour to measure 1 cup.*

CHICKEN MOLE CASSEROLE

Chicken Mole Casserole

The secret to a good mole dish is its rich, brown sauce with a hint of chocolate. The cocoa in this Mexican-inspired recipe lends richness without sweetness.

—*TASTE OF HOME* TEST KITCHEN

PREP: 25 MIN. • **BAKE:** 20 MIN.
MAKES: 6 SERVINGS

- 1 pound boneless skinless chicken breasts, cut into ½-inch cubes
- 1 medium green pepper, cut into strips
- 1 small onion, chopped
- 1 tablespoon butter
- 2 tablespoons baking cocoa
- 2 teaspoons brown sugar
- 1 teaspoon chili powder
- ½ teaspoon ground cumin
- ¼ teaspoon salt
- ¼ teaspoon ground coriander
- ¼ teaspoon cayenne pepper
- 2½ cups frozen corn, thawed
- 1 jar (16 ounces) chunky salsa
- 1 tube (10.2 ounces) large refrigerated flaky biscuits
- 2 teaspoons butter, melted
- ¾ teaspoon cornmeal

1. Preheat oven to 375°. In a large skillet, saute chicken, green pepper and onion in butter until chicken juices run clear and vegetables are tender.

2. Add cocoa, brown sugar and seasonings; cook and stir over medium heat for 1 minute. Stir in corn and salsa; heat through. Transfer to a greased 11x7-in. baking dish.

3. Cut each biscuit in half. Arrange biscuit pieces over chicken mixture with cut sides facing outer edge of dish, overlapping slightly. Brush with melted butter; sprinkle with cornmeal.

4. Bake, uncovered, 20-25 minutes or until biscuits are golden brown.

HEARTY CHICKEN CASSEROLE

FREEZE IT Hearty Chicken Casserole

Bring the zesty flavors of the Southwest to the table with this delectable high-fiber dish. The best part is you can enjoy this crowd-pleaser without any guilt. No-salt and reduced-fat ingredients keep it on the lighter side without taking away any of the rich, creamy goodness.

—**JENNY EBERT** EAU CLAIRE, WI

PREP: 15 MIN. • **BAKE:** 25 MIN.
MAKES: 6 SERVINGS

- 2 **celery ribs, chopped**
- 1 **small onion, chopped**
- 1½ **teaspoons olive oil**
- 3 **cups cubed cooked chicken breast**
- 1 **can (16 ounces) kidney beans, rinsed and drained**
- 1 **can (15 ounces) black beans, rinsed and drained**
- 1 **tablespoon chili powder**
- 2 **teaspoons ground cumin**
- 1 **can (14½ ounces) no-salt-added diced tomatoes, undrained**
- 1 **can (10¾ ounces) reduced-fat reduced-sodium condensed cream of mushroom soup, undiluted**
- 1 **cup (4 ounces) shredded reduced-fat cheddar cheese**

1. Preheat oven to 350°. In a large nonstick skillet coated with cooking spray, saute celery and onion in oil until tender. Stir in chicken, beans, chili powder and cumin; heat through.
2. Transfer to a shallow 2½-qt. baking dish coated with cooking spray. Combine tomatoes and soup; pour over chicken mixture.
3. Bake, uncovered, 20 minutes. Sprinkle with the cheese. Bake 5-10 minutes longer or until heated through and cheese is melted.
FREEZE OPTION *Cover and freeze unbaked casserole up to 3 months. To use, thaw in the refrigerator overnight. Remove from refrigerator 30 minutes before baking. Preheat oven to 350°. Bake according to directions.*

Makeover Poppy Seed Chicken

Poppy seed chicken is a traditional Southern dish and an amazingly delicious comfort food. But how do you turn an ooey-gooey casserole filled with sour cream, cheese and butter into a light entree? This makeover dish proves it can be done.

—**CAROLYN KEESE** SENECA, SC

PREP: 10 MIN. • **BAKE:** 30 MIN.
MAKES: 6 SERVINGS

- 3 **cups cubed cooked chicken breast**
- 2 **cans (10¾ ounces each) reduced-fat reduced-sodium condensed cream of chicken soup, undiluted**
- 1 **cup (8 ounces) reduced-fat sour cream**
- 2 **teaspoons poppy seeds**
- 1 **cup crushed reduced-fat butter-flavored crackers (about 25 crackers)**
- 3 **tablespoons reduced-fat butter, melted**
- ⅓ **cup grated Parmesan cheese**

1. Preheat oven to 350°. In a large bowl, combine chicken, soup, sour cream and poppy seeds. In a small bowl, combine cracker crumbs and butter; set aside ½ cup for topping. Stir remaining crumbs into the chicken mixture.
2. Transfer to an 11x7-in. baking dish coated with cooking spray. Top with reserved crumbs; sprinkle with cheese. Bake, uncovered, 30-35 minutes or until bubbly.

MAKEOVER POPPY SEED CHICKEN

CORDON BLEU BAKE

FREEZE IT Cordon Bleu Bake

A friend gave me the recipe for this treasured dish, and it's become my go-to make-ahead freezer meal. I share it with neighbors or pull it out of the freezer for a night when I'll be crunched for time.

—**REA NEWELL** DECATUR, IL

PREP: 20 MIN. • **BAKE:** 40 MIN.
MAKES: 2 CASSEROLES (6 SERVINGS EACH)

- 2 **packages (6 ounces each) reduced-sodium stuffing mix**
- 1 **can (10¾ ounces) condensed cream of chicken soup, undiluted**
- 1 **cup milk**
- 8 **cups cubed cooked chicken**
- ½ **teaspoon pepper**
- ¾ **pound sliced deli ham, cut into 1-inch strips**
- 1 **cup (4 ounces) shredded Swiss cheese**
- 3 **cups (12 ounces) shredded cheddar cheese**

1. Preheat oven to 350°. Prepare stuffing mixes according to package directions.
2. Meanwhile, in a large bowl, combine soup and milk; set aside.
3. Divide the chicken between two greased 13x9-in. baking dishes. Sprinkle with pepper. Layer with ham, Swiss cheese, 1 cup cheddar cheese, soup mixture and stuffing. Sprinkle with remaining cheddar cheese.
4. Cover and bake 30 minutes. Uncover; bake 10-15 minutes longer or until cheese is melted.
FREEZE OPTION *Cover and freeze unbaked casseroles up to 3 months. To use, thaw in the refrigerator overnight. Remove from refrigerator 30 minutes before baking. Preheat oven to 350°. Cover and bake 45 minutes. Uncover; bake 10-15 minutes longer or until heated through and cheese is melted.*

HOT CHICKEN CASSEROLE

FREEZE IT Hot Chicken Casserole

A comforting hot dish with a crispy topping, this hearty casserole will warm you from the inside out.

—**CAROL WILSON** DEKALB, IL

PREP: 15 MIN. • **BAKE:** 40 MIN.
MAKES: 8 SERVINGS

- 3 **cups cubed cooked chicken breast**
- 2 **cups mayonnaise**
- 1 **can (10¾ ounces) condensed cream of chicken soup, undiluted**
- 2 **celery ribs, finely chopped**
- 2 **cups cooked rice**
- 1 **can (8 ounces) sliced water chestnuts, drained**
- 1 **teaspoon grated onion**
- 1 **teaspoon lemon juice**

TOPPING

- 2 **cups crushed cornflakes**
- ½ **cup slivered almonds**
- ½ **cup butter, melted**

1. Preheat oven to 350°. In a large bowl, combine first eight ingredients. Transfer to a greased 13x9-in. baking dish.
2. Combine topping ingredients; sprinkle over top. Bake, uncovered, 40-45 minutes or until bubbly.

FREEZE OPTION *Cover and freeze unbaked casserole up to 3 months. To use, remove from the freezer 30 minutes before baking (do not thaw). Preheat oven to 350°. Cover with foil and bake 1½ hours. Uncover; bake 10-15 minutes longer or until bubbly and heated through.*

TOP TIP

An easy way to crush cornflakes with little mess is to put them in a large, wide-mouthed cup or mug. Use a tall narrow tumbler that fits inside the cup or mug to crush the cornflakes.

MOM'S TURKEY TETRAZZINI

Mom's Turkey Tetrazzini

 My mother-in-law gave me her famous recipe for this classic turkey casserole in 1954. It's comfort food at its best!

—**JUDY BATSON** TAMPA, FL

PREP: 25 MIN. • **BAKE:** 25 MIN. + STANDING
MAKES: 6 SERVINGS

- 1 **package (12 ounces) fettuccine**
- ½ **pound sliced fresh mushrooms**
- 1 **medium onion, chopped**
- ¼ **cup butter, cubed**
- 3 **tablespoons all-purpose flour**
- 3 **cups 2% milk**
- 1 **cup white wine or chicken broth**
- 3 **cups cubed cooked turkey**
- ¾ **teaspoon salt**
- ½ **teaspoon pepper**
- ½ **teaspoon hot pepper sauce**
- ½ **cup shredded Parmesan cheese**
  Paprika, optional

1. Preheat oven to 375°. Cook fettuccine according to package directions.
2. Meanwhile, in a large skillet, saute mushrooms and onion in butter until tender. Stir in flour until blended; gradually add milk and wine. Bring to a boil; cook and stir 2 minutes or until thickened. Stir in turkey, salt, pepper and pepper sauce.
3. Drain fettuccine. Layer half of the fettuccine, turkey mixture and cheese in a greased 13x9-in. baking dish. Repeat layers. Sprinkle with paprika if desired.
4. Cover and bake 25-30 minutes or until heated through. Let stand 10 minutes before serving.

Crescent-Topped Turkey Amandine

Quick to prepare, this tasty main dish is loaded with turkey flavor and has a nice crunch from celery and water chestnuts. Topped with a golden crescent roll crust and a sprinkling of almonds and cheese, it's bound to become a favorite.

—BECKY LARSON MALLARD, IA

PREP: 20 MIN. • **BAKE:** 30 MIN.
MAKES: 4 SERVINGS

- 3 **cups cubed cooked turkey**
- 1 **can (10¾ ounces) condensed cream of mushroom soup, undiluted**
- 1 **can (8 ounces) sliced water chestnuts, drained**
- ⅔ **cup mayonnaise**
- ½ **cup chopped celery**
- ½ **cup chopped onion**
- 1 **tube (4 ounces) refrigerated crescent rolls**
- ⅔ **cup shredded Swiss cheese**
- ½ **cup sliced almonds**
- ¼ **cup butter, melted**

1. Preheat oven to 375°. In a large saucepan, combine the first six ingredients; heat through. Transfer to a greased 2-qt. baking dish. Unroll the crescent dough and place over the turkey mixture.
2. In a small bowl, combine cheese, almonds and butter. Spoon over dough. Bake, uncovered, 30-35 minutes or until crust is golden brown and filling is bubbly.

Lemony Chicken & Rice

I couldn't say who loves this recipe best, because every time I serve it, it gets raves! Occasionally I even get a phone call or email from a friend requesting the recipe, and it's certainly a favorite for my grown children and 15 grandchildren.

—MARYALICE ANN WOOD LANGLEY, BC

PREP: 15 MIN. + MARINATING • **BAKE:** 55 MIN.
MAKES: 2 CASSEROLES (4 SERVINGS EACH)

- 2 **cups water**
- ½ **cup reduced-sodium soy sauce**
- ¼ **cup lemon juice**

LEMONY CHICKEN & RICE

- ¼ **cup olive oil**
- 2 **garlic cloves, minced**
- 2 **teaspoons ground ginger**
- 2 **teaspoons pepper**
- 16 **bone-in chicken thighs, skin removed (about 6 pounds)**
- 2 **cups uncooked long grain rice**
- 4 **tablespoons grated lemon peel, divided**
- 2 **medium lemons, sliced**

1. In a large resealable plastic bag, combine the first seven ingredients. Add chicken; seal bag and turn to coat. Refrigerate 4 hours or overnight.
2. Preheat oven to 325°. Spread 1 cup rice into each of two greased 13x9-in. baking dishes. Top each with 1 tablespoon grated lemon peel, 8 chicken thighs and half of the marinade. Top with sliced lemons.
3. Bake, covered, 40 minutes. Bake, uncovered, 15-20 minutes longer or until a thermometer inserted in chicken reads 180°. Sprinkle with remaining lemon peel.

CRESCENT-TOPPED TURKEY AMANDINE

Chicken and Dumpling Casserole

Basil adds just the right touch of flavor and fills the house with a wonderful aroma while this dish cooks. My husband loves the fluffy dumplings with plenty of gravy poured over them.

—SUE MACKEY JACKSON, WI

PREP: 30 MIN. • **BAKE:** 40 MIN.
MAKES: 6-8 SERVINGS

- ½ cup chopped onion
- ½ cup chopped celery
- ¼ cup butter, cubed
- 2 garlic cloves, minced
- ½ cup all-purpose flour
- 2 teaspoons sugar
- 1 teaspoon salt
- 1 teaspoon dried basil
- ½ teaspoon pepper
- 4 cups chicken broth
- 1 package (10 ounces) frozen green peas
- 4 cups cubed cooked chicken

DUMPLINGS
- 2 cups biscuit/baking mix
- 2 teaspoons dried basil
- ⅔ cup 2% milk

1. Preheat oven to 350°. In a large saucepan, saute onion and celery in butter until tender. Add garlic; cook 1 minute longer. Stir in flour, sugar, salt, basil and pepper until blended. Gradually add broth; bring to a boil. Cook and stir 1 minute or until thickened; reduce heat. Add peas and cook 5 minutes, stirring constantly. Stir in chicken. Pour into a greased 13x9-in. baking dish.
2. For dumplings, in a small bowl, combine baking mix and basil. Stir in milk with a fork until moistened. Drop by tablespoonfuls into 12 mounds over chicken mixture.
3. Bake, uncovered, 30 minutes. Cover and bake 10 minutes longer or until a toothpick inserted in a dumpling comes out clean.

Broccoli Chicken Lasagna

I'm a working mom with four kids, so I rely on casseroles to feed my clan. This lasagna features a yummy white sauce instead of the traditional tomato-based sauce.

—DAWN OWENS PALATKA, FL

PREP: 20 MIN. • **BAKE:** 50 MIN. + STANDING
MAKES: 12 SERVINGS

- ½ pound sliced fresh mushrooms
- 1 large onion, chopped
- ¼ cup butter, cubed
- ½ cup all-purpose flour
- ½ teaspoon salt
- ¼ teaspoon pepper
- ⅛ teaspoon ground nutmeg
- 1 can (14½ ounces) chicken broth
- 1¾ cups milk
- ⅔ cup grated Parmesan cheese
- 1 package (16 ounces) frozen broccoli cuts, thawed
- 9 lasagna noodles, cooked and drained
- 1⅓ cups julienned fully cooked ham, divided
- 2 cups (8 ounces) shredded Monterey Jack cheese, divided
- 2 cups cubed cooked chicken

1. Preheat oven to 350°. In a large skillet, saute mushrooms and onion in butter until tender. Stir in flour, salt, pepper and nutmeg until blended. Gradually stir in broth and milk. Bring to a boil; cook and stir 2 minutes or until thickened. Stir in Parmesan cheese and broccoli; heat through.
2. Spread ½ cup broccoli mixture in a greased 13x9-in. baking dish. Layer with three noodles, a third of the remaining broccoli mixture, 1 cup ham and 1 cup Monterey Jack cheese. Top with three noodles, half the remaining broccoli mixture, all the chicken and ½ cup Monterey Jack cheese. Top with remaining noodles, broccoli mixture and ham.
3. Cover and bake 45-50 minutes or until bubbly. Sprinkle with remaining Monterey Jack cheese. Bake 5 minutes longer or until cheese is melted. Let stand 15 minutes before cutting.

BROCCOLI CHICKEN LASAGNA

CHICKEN FLORENTINE CASSEROLE

Chicken Florentine Casserole

This hot and steamy bake is sure to be a hit at dinnertime. The herbs and seasonings give it a fantastic flavor, while the buttered bread crumb topping delivers the perfect bit of crunch.

—**DORI JACKSON** GULF BREEZE, FL

PREP: 20 MIN. • **BAKE:** 40 MIN.
MAKES: 6 SERVINGS

- 2 **cups uncooked elbow macaroni**
- 3 **cups shredded cooked chicken**
- 1 **can (10¾ ounces) condensed cream of mushroom soup, undiluted**
- 2 **cups (8 ounces) shredded Swiss cheese**
- 1 **package (10 ounces) frozen creamed spinach, thawed**
- ½ **cup mayonnaise**
- ¼ **cup loosely packed minced fresh basil**
- 1 **teaspoon garlic powder**
- ½ **teaspoon dried thyme**
- ½ **teaspoon pepper**
- ½ **cup seasoned bread crumbs**
- 2 **tablespoons butter, melted**

1. Preheat oven to 350°. Cook macaroni according to package directions.
2. Meanwhile, in a large bowl, combine chicken, soup, cheese, spinach, mayonnaise, basil, garlic powder, thyme and pepper.
3. Drain macaroni; gently stir into chicken mixture. Transfer to an ungreased 2½-qt. baking dish. Toss bread crumbs and butter; sprinkle over casserole.
4. Bake, uncovered, 40-45 minutes or until bubbly.

Turkey Enchilada Lasagna

I get recipe requests every time I serve this zippy entree. It's layered with tortillas instead of traditional lasagna noodles.

—**DEBRA MARTIN** BELLEVILLE, MI

PREP: 30 MIN. • **BAKE:** 25 MIN.
MAKES: 10 SERVINGS

- 1 **pound lean ground turkey**
- 1 **medium green pepper, chopped**
- 1 **medium onion, chopped**
- 3 **garlic cloves, minced**
- 2 **cans (15 ounces each) black beans, rinsed and drained**
- 1 **jar (16 ounces) salsa**
- 1 **can (15 ounces) tomato sauce**
- 1 **can (14½ ounces) Mexican stewed tomatoes**
- 1 **teaspoon each onion powder, garlic powder and ground cumin**
- 12 **corn tortillas (6 inches)**
- 2 **cups (8 ounces) shredded reduced-fat cheddar cheese, divided**

1. In a large nonstick saucepan coated with cooking spray, cook turkey, green pepper and onion over medium heat until meat is no longer pink. Add garlic; cook 1 minute longer. Drain. Stir in beans, salsa, tomato sauce, tomatoes, onion powder, garlic powder and cumin. Bring to a boil. Reduce heat; simmer, uncovered, 10 minutes.
2. Preheat oven to 350°. Spread 1 cup meat sauce into a 13x9-in. baking dish coated with cooking spray. Top with six tortillas. Spread with half the remaining meat sauce; sprinkle with 1 cup cheese. Layer with remaining tortillas and meat sauce.
3. Cover and bake 20 minutes. Uncover; sprinkle with remaining cheese. Bake 5-10 minutes longer or until bubbly and cheese is melted.

TURKEY ENCHILADA LASAGNA

Turkey & Spinach Stuffing Casserole

START TO FINISH: 25 MIN.
MAKES: 4 SERVINGS

- 1 can (14½ ounces) reduced-sodium chicken broth
- 3 tablespoons butter
- 3 cups stuffing mix
- 3 cups cubed cooked turkey
- 2 cups fresh baby spinach
- ½ cup dried cranberries
- ¾ cup shredded cheddar cheese

1. Preheat oven to 350°. In a large saucepan, bring broth and butter to a boil. Remove from heat. Add stuffing mix; stir until moistened. Stir in turkey, spinach and cranberries.

2. Transfer to a greased 11x7-in. baking dish. Sprinkle with cheese. Bake, uncovered, 10-15 minutes or until cheese is melted.

TURKEY & SPINACH STUFFING CASSEROLE

CHICKEN & EGG NOODLE CASSEROLE

CHICKEN 'N' CORN BREAD BAKE

Chicken & Egg Noodle Casserole

My heart broke for my friend Michelle and her family after a fire at their home. I took them this homemade chicken casserole to let them know they were in my thoughts. Loaded with oodles of noodles and sprinkled with crumbs, it's the perfect way to spread a little love.

—LIN KRANKEL OXFORD, MI

PREP: 20 MIN. • **BAKE:** 30 MIN.
MAKES: 8 SERVINGS

- 6 **cups uncooked egg noodles (about 12 ounces)**
- 2 **cans (10¾ ounces each) condensed cream of chicken soup, undiluted**
- 1 **cup (8 ounces) sour cream**
- ¾ **cup 2% milk**
- ¼ **teaspoon salt**
- ¼ **teaspoon pepper**
- 3 **cups cubed cooked chicken breasts**
- 1 **cup crushed butter-flavored crackers (about 20 crackers)**
- ¼ **cup butter, melted**

1. Preheat oven to 350°. Cook noodles according to package directions for al dente; drain.

2. In a large bowl, whisk soup, sour cream, milk, salt and pepper until blended. Stir in chicken and noodles. Transfer to a greased 13x9-in. baking dish. In a small bowl, mix crushed crackers and butter; sprinkle over top. Bake 30-35 minutes or until bubbly.

Chicken 'n' Corn Bread Bake

Here's Southern comfort food at its best! It's fantastic prepared with chicken or turkey and often on the menu when I cook for my large family—my husband, our four kids, their spouses and our 10 grandkids.

—ANN HILLMEYER SANDIA PARK, NM

PREP: 25 MIN. • **BAKE:** 25 MIN.
MAKES: 8 SERVINGS

- 2½ **cups reduced-sodium chicken broth**
- 1 **small onion, chopped**
- 1 **celery rib, chopped**
- ⅛ **teaspoon pepper**
- 4½ **cups corn bread stuffing mix, divided**
- 4 **cups cubed cooked chicken**
- 1½ **cups (12 ounces) sour cream**
- 1 **can (10¾ ounces) condensed cream of chicken soup, undiluted**
- 3 **green onions, thinly sliced**
- ¼ **cup butter, cubed**

1. Preheat oven to 325°. In a large saucepan, combine broth, onion, celery and pepper. Bring to a boil. Reduce heat; cover and simmer 5-6 minutes or until vegetables are tender. Stir in 4 cups stuffing mix.

2. Transfer to a greased 13x9-in. baking dish. Top with chicken. In a small bowl, combine sour cream, soup and green onions. Spread over chicken. Sprinkle with remaining stuffing mix; dot with butter.

3. Bake, uncovered, 25-30 minutes or until heated through.

SOUTHWESTERN TURKEY BAKE

CREAMY CHICKEN-RICE CASSEROLE

Southwestern Turkey Bake

It's hard to resist a big scoop of this tasty dish with its crispy tortilla chip topping. It's an easy way to sneak veggies into a meal.
—**CRYSTAL KOLADY** HENRIETTA, NY

PREP: 20 MIN. • **BAKE:** 25 MIN.
MAKES: 12 SERVINGS

- 2 **large onions, chopped**
- 2 **jalapeno peppers, seeded and chopped**
- 2 **tablespoons butter**
- 6 **cups cubed cooked turkey**
- 2 **cans (10¾ ounces each) condensed cream of chicken soup, undiluted**
- 2 **cups (16 ounces) sour cream**
- 1 **package (10 ounces) frozen chopped spinach, thawed and squeezed dry**
- 2 **cups (8 ounces) shredded Monterey Jack cheese**
- 1 **package (12½ ounces) nacho tortilla chips, crushed**
- 4 **green onions, sliced**

1. Preheat oven to 350°. In a Dutch oven, saute onions and jalapenos in butter until tender. Stir in turkey, soup, sour cream and spinach. In a greased 13x9-in. baking dish, layer half of the turkey mixture, cheese and tortilla chips. Repeat layers.
2. Bake, uncovered, 25-30 minutes or until bubbly. Let stand 5 minutes before serving. Sprinkle with the sliced green onions.
NOTE *Wear disposable gloves when cutting hot peppers; the oils can burn skin. Avoid touching your face.*

Creamy Chicken-Rice Casserole

Gravy, chicken soup and sour cream make this rich casserole one you'll want to add to your "keepers" file. Be prepared to make it often, as it fills 'em up fast and tastes delish!
—**NANCY FOUST** STONEBORO, PA

PREP: 20 MIN. • **BAKE:** 50 MIN.
MAKES: 9 SERVINGS

- 3 **cups cubed cooked chicken**
- 2⅔ **cups chicken gravy**
- 2 **cups uncooked instant rice**
- 1 **can (10¾ ounces) condensed cream of chicken soup, undiluted**
- 1 **cup (8 ounces) sour cream**
- 1 **can (8 ounces) mushroom stems and pieces, drained**
- 1 **medium onion, chopped**
- ⅔ **cup chopped celery**
- ⅔ **cup water**
- ¼ **cup chopped pitted green olives**
- ¼ **cup chopped ripe olives**
- 2 **teaspoons dried parsley flakes**
- ⅛ **teaspoon pepper**

1. Preheat oven to 375°. In a large bowl, combine all ingredients. Transfer to a greased 13x9-in. baking dish.
2. Cover and bake 30 minutes. Uncover and stir; bake 20-25 minutes longer or until bubbly and the rice and vegetables are tender.

MACARONI TUNA CASSEROLE

Baked Sole and Spinach

This crunched-for-time casserole can be fixed from start to finish in less than an hour. A cheesy pasta layer is topped with fish, spinach and almonds to make a complete meal that's a nice change of pace from the ordinary.

—**ANNA FUERY** TAFTVILLE, CT

PREP: 25 MIN. • **BAKE:** 30 MIN.
MAKES: 6 SERVINGS

- 1 **package (8 ounces) egg noodles**
- 3 **tablespoons butter**
- 3 **tablespoons all-purpose flour**
- 3 **cups 2% milk**
- 1½ **cups (6 ounces) shredded cheddar cheese, divided**
- 1 **tablespoon lemon juice**
- 1 **teaspoon salt**
- 1 **teaspoon ground mustard**
- 1 **teaspoon Worcestershire sauce**
- ⅛ **teaspoon ground nutmeg**
- ⅛ **teaspoon pepper**
- 2 **packages (10 ounces each) frozen chopped spinach, thawed and squeezed dry**
- 1½ **pounds sole fillets**
- ¼ **cup slivered almonds, toasted**

1. Cook noodles according to package directions.

2. Meanwhile, in a large saucepan, melt butter. Stir in flour until smooth; gradually add milk. Bring to a boil; cook and stir 2 minutes or until thickened.

3. Stir in 1 cup cheese, lemon juice, salt, mustard, Worcestershire sauce, nutmeg and pepper, stirring until the cheese is melted. Set aside half of the cheese sauce.

4. Preheat oven to 375°. Drain noodles; add to the remaining sauce. Transfer to a greased 13x9-in. baking dish. Layer with spinach, sole, reserved cheese sauce and remaining cheese; sprinkle with almonds.

5. Bake, uncovered, 30-35 minutes or until fish flakes easily with a fork.

Macaroni Tuna Casserole

So easy to fix, this dish has a homemade flavor that beats any boxed tuna casserole I've tried. It was a staple when I was in college since a box of macaroni and cheese and a can of tuna cost so little.

—**SUZANNE ZICK** OSCEOLA, AR

PREP: 15 MIN. • **BAKE:** 20 MIN.
MAKES: 4 SERVINGS

- 1 **package (7¼ ounces) macaroni and cheese**
- 1 **can (10¾ ounces) condensed cream of celery soup, undiluted**
- 1 **can (5 ounces) tuna, drained and flaked**
- ½ **cup milk**
- 1 **cup (4 ounces) shredded cheddar cheese**
  Minced fresh parsley, optional

Preheat oven to 350°. Prepare macaroni and cheese according to package directions. Stir in soup, tuna and milk. Pour into a greased 2-qt. baking dish. Sprinkle with cheese and, if desired, parsley. Bake, uncovered, 20-25 minutes or until cheese is melted.

⑤INGREDIENTS Crumb-Topped Haddock

My delightful fish with a creamy sauce and crispy topping is a breeze to make. Pollock is also good in this recipe. Keep an eye on the fish as it's baking to avoid overcooking it.

—DEBBIE SOLT LEWISTOWN, PA

PREP: 5 MIN. • **BAKE:** 35 MIN.
MAKES: 6 SERVINGS

- 2 pounds haddock or cod fillets
- 1 can (10¾ ounces) condensed cream of shrimp soup, undiluted
- 1 teaspoon grated onion
- 1 teaspoon Worcestershire sauce
- 1 cup crushed butter-flavored crackers (about 25 crackers)

1. Preheat oven to 375°. Arrange fillets in a greased 13x9-in. baking dish. Combine soup, onion and Worcestershire sauce; pour over fish.
2. Bake, uncovered, 20 minutes. Sprinkle with cracker crumbs. Bake 15 minutes longer or until fish flakes easily with a fork.

Blend of the Bayou

My sister-in-law shared this recipe when I first moved to Louisiana. It's been handed down in my husband's family for generations, and I've passed it on to my children, too.

—RUBY WILLIAMS BOGALUSA, LA

PREP: 20 MIN. • **BAKE:** 25 MIN.
MAKES: 6-8 SERVINGS

- 1 package (8 ounces) cream cheese, cubed
- 4 tablespoons butter, divided
- 1 large onion, chopped
- 2 celery ribs, chopped
- 1 large green pepper, chopped
- 1 pound cooked medium shrimp, peeled and deveined
- 2 cans (6 ounces each) crabmeat, drained, flaked and cartilage removed
- 1 can (10¾ ounces) condensed cream of mushroom soup, undiluted
- ¾ cup cooked rice
- 1 jar (4½ ounces) sliced mushrooms, drained
- 1 teaspoon garlic salt
- ¾ teaspoon hot pepper sauce
- ½ teaspoon cayenne pepper
- ¾ cup shredded cheddar cheese
- ½ cup crushed butter-flavored crackers (about 12 crackers)

1. Preheat oven to 350°. In a small saucepan, cook and stir cream cheese and 2 tablespoons butter over low heat until melted and smooth.
2. In a large skillet, saute onion, celery and green pepper in remaining butter until tender. Stir in the shrimp, crab, soup, rice, mushrooms, garlic salt, pepper sauce, cayenne and cream cheese mixture.
3. Transfer to a greased 2-qt. baking dish. Combine cheddar cheese and cracker crumbs; sprinkle over top. Bake, uncovered, 25-30 minutes or until bubbly.

BLEND OF THE BAYOU

BAKED ORANGE ROUGHY AND RICE

Baked Orange Roughy and Rice

It might sound too good to be true, but we're crossing our hearts when we tell you this delectable fish dinner will dirty just one dish. Your family will be lining up to dig in once they see the beautiful results.

—*TASTE OF HOME* TEST KITCHEN

PREP: 10 MIN. • **BAKE:** 30 MIN.
MAKES: 4 SERVINGS

- 2 cups uncooked instant rice
- 1 package (16 ounces) frozen broccoli-cauliflower blend, thawed
- 4 orange roughy fillets (6 ounces each)
- 1 can (14½ ounces) chicken broth
- 1 can (14½ ounces) fire-roasted diced tomatoes, undrained
- 1 teaspoon garlic powder
- 1 teaspoon lemon-pepper seasoning
- ¼ to ½ teaspoon cayenne pepper
- ½ cup shredded cheddar cheese

1. Preheat oven to 375°. Place rice in a greased 13x9-in. baking dish. Layer with vegetables and fish. Pour broth and tomatoes over the top; sprinkle with seasonings.

2. Cover and bake 25-30 minutes or until fish flakes easily with a fork and rice is tender. Sprinkle with cheese; bake 5 minutes longer or until cheese is melted.

Crab 'n' Penne Casserole

Purchased Alfredo sauce lends creaminess to this crab casserole while red pepper flakes kick up the flavor. Summer squash and zucchini give it garden-fresh goodness.

—**BERNADETTE BENNETT** WACO, TX

PREP: 20 MIN. • **BAKE:** 40 MIN.
MAKES: 6 SERVINGS

- 1½ cups uncooked penne pasta
- 1 jar (15 ounces) Alfredo sauce
- 1½ cups imitation crabmeat, chopped
- 1 medium yellow summer squash, sliced
- 1 medium zucchini, sliced
- 1 tablespoon dried parsley flakes
- ⅛ to ¼ teaspoon crushed red pepper flakes
- 1½ cups (6 ounces) shredded part-skim mozzarella cheese
- 2 tablespoons dry bread crumbs
- 2 teaspoons butter, melted

1. Preheat oven to 325°. Cook pasta according to package directions.

2. Meanwhile, in a large bowl, combine Alfredo sauce, crab, yellow squash, zucchini, parsley and pepper flakes. Drain pasta; add to the sauce mixture and toss to coat. Transfer to a greased 13x9-in. baking dish. Sprinkle with cheese.

3. Cover and bake 35 minutes or until heated through. Toss bread crumbs and butter; sprinkle over casserole. Bake, uncovered, 5-6 minutes longer or until browned.

CRAB 'N' PENNE CASSEROLE

Lightened-Up Shrimp Rice Casserole

I love this lighter version of my shrimp casserole. It has only half the calories and sodium and less fat than my original recipe, but tastes every bit as good.
—**MARIE ROBERTS** LAKE CHARLES, LA

PREP: 40 MIN. • **BAKE:** 30 MIN.
MAKES: 6 SERVINGS

- 1 **pound uncooked medium shrimp, peeled and deveined**
- 2 **tablespoons butter, divided**
- 12 **ounces fresh mushrooms, sliced**
- 1 **large green pepper, chopped**
- 1 **medium onion, chopped**
- 3 **tablespoons all-purpose flour**
- ¾ **teaspoon salt**
- ⅛ **teaspoon cayenne pepper**
- 1⅓ **cups fat-free milk**
- 3 **cups cooked brown rice**
- 1 **cup (4 ounces) shredded reduced-fat cheddar cheese, divided**

1. In a large nonstick skillet, saute shrimp in 1 tablespoon butter for 2-3 minutes or until shrimp turn pink. Remove and set aside. In the same skillet, saute the mushrooms, green pepper and onion in remaining butter until tender.

2. Stir in the flour, salt and cayenne. Gradually add milk until blended. Bring to a boil; cook and stir for 2 minutes or until thickened. Add the rice, ½ cup cheese and shrimp; stir until combined.

3. Pour into a 1½-qt. baking dish coated with cooking spray. Cover and bake at 325° for 30-35 minutes or until heated through. Sprinkle with remaining cheese; cover and let stand for 5 minutes or until cheese is melted.

CORN BREAD-TOPPED SALMON

Corn Bread-Topped Salmon

There's no need to serve bread when you've already baked it into this main dish. The economical casserole also works well with tuna or chicken.
—**BILLIE WILSON** MASONIC HOME, KY

PREP: 15 MIN. • **BAKE:** 30 MIN.
MAKES: 6-8 SERVINGS

- 2 **cans (10¾ ounces each) condensed cream of mushroom soup, undiluted**
- ¼ **cup milk**
- 1 **can (14¾ ounces) salmon, drained, bones and skin removed**
- 1½ **cups frozen peas, thawed**
- 1 **package (8½ ounces) corn bread/muffin mix**
- 1 **jar (4 ounces) diced pimientos, drained**
- ¼ **cup finely chopped green pepper**
- 1 **teaspoon finely chopped onion**
- ½ **teaspoon celery seed**
- ¼ **teaspoon dried thyme**

1. Preheat oven to 400°. In a large saucepan, bring soup and milk to a boil; add salmon and peas. Pour into a greased shallow 2½-qt. baking dish. Prepare corn bread batter according to package directions; stir in the remaining ingredients. Spoon over the salmon mixture.

2. Bake, uncovered, 30-35 minutes or until a toothpick inserted in the corn bread comes out clean.

TOP TIP

You can remove the bones from canned salmon if you prefer, but they are edible and can add calcium to your diet. If you don't like the texture, mash the drained salmon in a bowl with the back of a spoon. The bones will become undetectable in seconds.

SEAFOOD 'N' SHELLS CASSEROLE

Seafood 'n' Shells Casserole

Poaching the cod before baking this casserole is the easiest method for cooking the fish and also prevents it from watering down the dish. This recipe is sure to warm you up on a chilly night.

—TASTE OF HOME TEST KITCHEN

PREP: 25 MIN. • **BAKE:** 25 MIN.
MAKES: 6 SERVINGS

- 6 **cups water**
- 1 **teaspoon lemon-pepper seasoning**
- 1 **bay leaf**
- 2 **pounds cod fillets, cut into 1-inch pieces**
- 1 **cup uncooked small pasta shells**
- 1 **medium sweet red pepper, chopped**
- 1 **medium green pepper, chopped**
- 1 **medium onion, chopped**
- 1 **tablespoon butter**
- 3 **tablespoons all-purpose flour**
- 2½ **cups fat-free evaporated milk**
- ¾ **teaspoon salt**
- ½ **teaspoon dried thyme**
- ¼ **teaspoon pepper**
- 1 **cup (4 ounces) shredded Mexican cheese blend**

1. In a large skillet, bring the water, lemon pepper and bay leaf to a boil. Reduce heat; carefully add cod. Cover and simmer 5-8 minutes or until fish flakes easily with a fork; drain and set aside. Discard bay leaf.

2. Cook pasta according to package directions.

3. Meanwhile, preheat oven to 350°. In a large saucepan, saute peppers and onion in butter over medium heat until tender. Stir in flour until blended. Gradually stir in the milk. Bring to a boil; cook and stir 2 minutes or until thickened. Stir in salt, thyme and pepper. Remove from the heat; stir in cheese until melted.

4. Drain pasta. Stir fish and pasta into sauce. Transfer to a 2-qt. baking dish coated with cooking spray. Cover and bake 25-30 minutes or until heated through.

Captain Russell's Jambalaya

A tour guide in New Orleans gave me this recipe. I love that it's so simple to prepare. The deliciously authentic Cajun flavors make it one of my favorite recipes.

—DONNA LAMANO OLATHE, KS

PREP: 15 MIN. • **BAKE:** 40 MIN.
MAKES: 6 SERVINGS

- 1 **can (10½ ounces) condensed French onion soup**
- 1¼ **cups reduced-sodium beef broth**
- 1 **can (8 ounces) tomato sauce**
- ½ **cup butter, cubed**
- 1 **small green pepper, chopped**
- 1 **small onion, chopped**
- 1½ **teaspoons Creole seasoning**
- 1 **teaspoon hot pepper sauce**
- 1 **pound uncooked medium shrimp, peeled and deveined**
- ½ **pound fully cooked andouille sausage links, halved lengthwise and cut into ½-inch slices**
- 2 **cups uncooked long grain rice**

1. Preheat oven to 375°. In a large saucepan, combine the first eight ingredients. Bring to a boil. Remove from heat; stir in shrimp, sausage and rice. Transfer to a greased 13x9-in. baking dish.

2. Cover and bake 30 minutes. Remove cover and stir; cover and bake 10-15 minutes longer or until rice is tender.

NOTE *The following spices may be substituted for 1 teaspoon Creole seasoning: ¼ teaspoon each salt, garlic powder and paprika; and a pinch each of dried thyme, ground cumin and cayenne pepper.*

CAPTAIN RUSSELL'S JAMBALAYA

Special Seafood Casserole

I first sampled this fantastic creation at a baby shower. When I kept going back for more, I knew the recipe was a keeper!

—ANGELA SCHWARTZ MARIETTA, GA

PREP: 25 MIN. • **BAKE:** 25 MIN. + STANDING
MAKES: 6 SERVINGS

- ½ pound sea scallops
- 1 small onion, finely chopped
- 1 celery rib, finely chopped
- 6 tablespoons butter, cubed
- 7 tablespoons all-purpose flour
- 1½ cups half-and-half cream
- 1 cup (4 ounces) shredded sharp cheddar cheese
- 6 tablespoons sherry or apple juice
- ¾ teaspoon salt
- ¼ teaspoon cayenne pepper
- 1 pound cooked medium shrimp, peeled and deveined
- 1 can (6 ounces) crab
- 1 can (14 ounces) water-packed artichoke hearts, drained, rinsed, chopped and patted dry
- 1 can (8 ounces) sliced water chestnuts, drained
- ½ cup sliced almonds
- ¼ cup grated Parmesan cheese

1. Preheat oven to 350°. In a Dutch oven, saute scallops, onion and celery in butter until scallops are firm and opaque. Stir in flour until blended. Add cream. Bring to a boil; cook and stir 2 minutes or until thickened. Reduce heat; add cheddar cheese, sherry, salt and cayenne, stirring until cheese is melted. Remove from heat; set aside.
2. In a greased 11x7-in. baking dish, layer the shrimp, crab, artichokes and water chestnuts. Top with sauce. Sprinkle with almonds and Parmesan.
3. Bake, uncovered, 25-30 minutes or until heated through. Let stand 10 minutes before serving.

Salmon Puff

Take advantage of this recipe on nights when you're looking for an economical way to serve seafood. The salmon makes the fluffy dish so tasty. I also take it to parties when I need a dish to pass.

—MARILYN KUTZLI CLINTON, IA

PREP: 15 MIN. • **BAKE:** 50 MIN.
MAKES: 6-8 SERVINGS

- 4 eggs, lightly beaten
- ½ cup milk
- 1 can (10¾ ounces) condensed cream of mushroom soup, undiluted
- 1 can (14¾ ounces) salmon, drained, bones and skin removed
- 2 cups soft bread cubes (about 2½ slices)
- 1 tablespoon minced parsley
- 1 small onion, minced
- 2 tablespoons butter, melted
- ½ teaspoon lemon juice

1. Preheat oven to 350°. In a large bowl, combine eggs, milk and soup; stir in remaining ingredients.
2. Pour into a greased 11x7-in. baking dish. Bake 50 minutes or until set. Let stand 5 minutes before serving.

SPECIAL SEAFOOD CASSEROLE

Tuna Bake
with Cheese Swirls

My family thinks this dish is a delicious alternative to regular tuna casserole. The proof is that there are never any leftovers.

—VIRGINIA MAGEE REENE, NH

PREP: 30 MIN. • **BAKE:** 20 MIN.
MAKES: 6-8 SERVINGS

- 3 tablespoons chopped onion
- 3 tablespoons chopped green pepper
- ⅓ cup butter
- ⅓ cup all-purpose flour
- 3 cups milk
- 1 can (10¾ ounces) condensed cream of mushroom soup, undiluted
- 1 can (12 ounces) tuna, drained and flaked
- 1 tablespoon lemon juice
- 1 teaspoon salt

DOUGH

- 2 cups biscuit/baking mix
- ½ cup milk
- ½ cup shredded cheddar cheese
- ½ cup diced pimientos
- ¼ cup minced fresh parsley
- 1 egg
- 2 teaspoons water

1. In a saucepan, saute onion and green pepper in butter. Blend in flour until smooth. Gradually stir in milk; bring to a boil over medium heat. Cook and stir 2 minutes. Remove from heat; stir in soup, tuna, lemon juice and salt. Pour into an ungreased 13x9-in. baking dish.
2. Preheat oven to 400°. For dough, combine biscuit mix and milk until blended. On a lightly floured surface, roll the dough into a 12x9-in. rectangle. Sprinkle with the cheese, pimientos and parsley. Roll up, jelly-roll style, starting with a long side. Cut into 1-in. slices; place over tuna mixture. Beat egg and water; brush over swirls.
3. Bake, uncovered, 20-25 minutes or until top is lightly browned.

SEAFOOD AU GRATIN

Seafood Au Gratin

I'm from the Maritimes and my father was a fisherman, so we ate fish almost every day while I was growing up. Over the years I've tried many seafood dishes, but this one is my favorite. It's great to serve at parties, and guests always rave about the flavor.

—HAZEL MCMULLIN AMHERST, NS

PREP: 30 MIN. • **BAKE:** 15 MIN.
MAKES: 6 SERVINGS

- 4 tablespoons butter, divided
- 2 tablespoons all-purpose flour
- ⅛ teaspoon pepper
- 1 cup chicken broth
- ½ cup 2% milk
- ½ cup grated Parmesan cheese, divided
- ½ pound sea scallops
- 1 pound haddock or cod fillets, cut into six pieces
- 1½ cups sliced fresh mushrooms
- ½ cup shredded part-skim mozzarella cheese
- ½ cup shredded cheddar cheese

1. In a large saucepan, melt 2 tablespoons butter. Stir in flour and pepper until smooth; gradually add broth and milk. Bring to a boil; cook and stir 2 minutes or until thickened. Stir in ¼ cup Parmesan cheese; set aside.
2. Preheat oven to 350°. Place scallops in another saucepan; cover with water. Simmer, uncovered, 4-5 minutes or until firm and opaque.
3. Meanwhile, place fillets in a shallow 2-qt. microwave-safe dish. Cover and microwave on high 2-4 minutes or until fish flakes easily with a fork. Drain scallops. Arrange fish and scallops in a greased 11x7-in. baking dish.
4. In a small skillet, saute mushrooms in remaining butter until tender; stir into cheese sauce. Spoon over seafood. Sprinkle with mozzarella, cheddar and remaining Parmesan cheese.
5. Cover and bake 15-20 minutes or until bubbly and cheese is melted. **NOTE** *This recipe was tested in a 1,100-watt microwave.*

> The recipe serves eight, but plan to double it if you're having folks over. Fresh mushrooms and lump crabmeat make it hard to turn down seconds of this dish.
>
> —BARBARA CARLUCCI ORANGE PARK, FL

Crab Imperial Casserole

PREP: 20 MIN. • **BAKE:** 25 MIN.
MAKES: 8 SERVINGS

- 3 cups uncooked spiral pasta
- 1¾ cups sliced fresh mushrooms
- 5 tablespoons butter, cubed
- 2 tablespoons all-purpose flour
- ¾ teaspoon pepper
- ½ teaspoon salt
- 1½ cups 2% milk
- 4 cans (6 ounces each) lump crabmeat, drained
- 1 can (10¾ ounces) condensed cream of mushroom soup, undiluted
- ¼ cup crushed butter-flavored crackers

1. Preheat oven to 350°. Cook pasta according to package directions.
2. Meanwhile, in a large skillet, saute mushrooms in butter until tender. Stir in flour, pepper and salt until blended; gradually add milk. Bring to a boil. Cook and stir 2 minutes or until thickened. Stir in crab and soup until blended.
3. Drain pasta. Add crab mixture; toss to coat. Transfer to a greased 13x9-in. baking dish; sprinkle with cracker crumbs.
4. Bake, uncovered, 25-30 minutes or until bubbly.

CRAB IMPERIAL CASSEROLE

Mini Scallop Casseroles

Tiny and tender bay scallops take center stage in these miniature dishes. They're reminiscent of potpies, creamy and packed with flavorful veggies in every bite.

—VIVIAN MANARY NEPEAN, ON

PREP: 30 MIN. • **BAKE:** 20 MIN.
MAKES: 4 SERVINGS

- 3 **celery ribs, chopped**
- 1 **cup sliced fresh mushrooms**
- 1 **medium green pepper, chopped**
- 1 **small onion, chopped**
- 2 **tablespoons butter**
- ⅓ **cup all-purpose flour**
- ¼ **teaspoon salt**
- ¼ **teaspoon pepper**
- 2 **cups fat-free milk**
- 1 **pound bay scallops**

TOPPING

- 1 **cup soft bread crumbs**
- 1 **tablespoon butter, melted**
- ¼ **cup shredded cheddar cheese**

1. In a large skillet, saute celery, mushrooms, green pepper and onion in butter until tender. Stir in flour, salt and pepper until blended; gradually add milk. Bring to a boil; cook and stir 2 minutes or until thickened.

2. Reduce heat; add scallops. Cook, stirring occasionally, 3-4 minutes or until scallops are firm and opaque.

3. Preheat oven to 350°. Divide mixture among four 10-oz. ramekins or custard cups. In a small bowl, combine crumbs and butter; sprinkle over scallop mixture.

4. Bake, uncovered, 15-20 minutes or until bubbly. Sprinkle with cheese; bake 5 minutes longer or until cheese is melted.

Seafood-Stuffed Shells

Even non-fish lovers will enjoy this dish. Serve with garlic bread and a salad for a complete meal.

—EZRA WEAVER WOLCOTT, NY

PREP: 35 MIN. • **BAKE:** 30 MIN.
MAKES: 10 SERVINGS

- 30 **uncooked jumbo pasta shells**
- ½ **pound bay scallops**
- 2 **teaspoons butter**
- 2 **eggs**
- 2 **cups (16 ounces) cream-style cottage cheese**
- 1 **carton (15 ounces) ricotta cheese**
- ½ **teaspoon ground nutmeg**
- ¼ **teaspoon pepper**
- 1 **can (6 ounces) lump crabmeat, drained**
- ¾ **pound cooked small shrimp, peeled and deveined**
- 1 **jar (15 ounces) Alfredo sauce**

1. Cook pasta shells according to package directions.

2. Meanwhile, in a small skillet over medium heat, cook scallops in butter 1-2 minutes or until opaque. Transfer to a large bowl.

3. Preheat oven to 350°. Place one egg and half the cottage cheese, ricotta, nutmeg and pepper in a blender; cover and process until smooth. Add to scallops. Repeat with remaining egg, cottage cheese, ricotta, nutmeg and pepper. Add to scallops. Stir in crab and shrimp.

4. Drain shells and rinse in cold water. Stuff with seafood mixture. Place in a greased 13x9-in. baking dish. Top with Alfredo sauce.

5. Cover and bake 30-35 minutes or until bubbly.

SEAFOOD-STUFFED SHELLS

ZUCCHINI ENCHILADAS

Upside-Down Meatless Pizza

I experimented with a recipe for upside-down pizza and made it into a meatless dish. This is guaranteed to satisfy your deepest pizza cravings!

—**MARIE FIGUEROA** WAUWATOSA, WI

PREP: 25 MIN. • **BAKE:** 20 MIN.
MAKES: 8 SERVINGS

- 1 **small onion, chopped**
- ¼ **cup chopped green pepper**
- 3 **tablespoons canola oil, divided**
- 2 **tablespoons plus 1 cup all-purpose flour, divided**
- ½ **teaspoon dried basil**
- ½ **teaspoon fennel seed**
- 1 **package (10 ounces) frozen chopped spinach, thawed and squeezed dry**
- 1 **cup sliced fresh mushrooms**
- 1 **can (15 ounces) tomato sauce**
- 2 **cups (8 ounces) shredded cheddar cheese**
- 2 **eggs**
- ¾ **cup 2% milk**
- ½ **teaspoon salt**
- 2 **tablespoons grated Parmesan cheese**

1. Preheat oven to 425°. In a large skillet, saute onion and green pepper in 2 tablespoons oil until tender. Stir in 2 tablespoons flour, basil and fennel until blended. Add the spinach, mushrooms and tomato sauce. Bring to a boil; cook and stir 2 minutes or until thickened.

2. Pour into a greased 11x7-in. baking dish. Sprinkle with cheddar cheese. Place the remaining flour in a large bowl. Add eggs, milk, salt and the remaining oil; beat until smooth. Stir in Parmesan cheese. Pour over the vegetable mixture.

3. Bake, uncovered, 20-25 minutes or until a thermometer reads 160°.

Zucchini Enchiladas

This is my go-to recipe when I have a bounty of garden-fresh zucchini to use up.

—**ANGELA LEINENBACH** MECHANICSVILLE, VA

PREP: 1½ HOURS • **BAKE:** 30 MIN.
MAKES: 12 SERVINGS

- 1 **medium sweet yellow pepper, chopped**
- 1 **medium green pepper, chopped**
- 1 **large sweet onion, chopped**
- 2 **tablespoons olive oil**
- 2 **garlic cloves, minced**
- 2 **cans (15 ounces each) tomato sauce**
- 2 **cans (14½ ounces each) no-salt-added diced tomatoes, undrained**
- 2 **tablespoons chili powder**
- 2 **teaspoons sugar**
- 2 **teaspoons dried marjoram**
- 1 **teaspoon dried basil**
- 1 **teaspoon ground cumin**
- ¼ **teaspoon salt**
- ¼ **teaspoon cayenne pepper**
- 1 **bay leaf**
- 3 **pounds zucchini, shredded (about 8 cups)**
- 24 **corn tortillas (6 inches), warmed**
- 4 **cups (16 ounces) shredded reduced-fat cheddar cheese**
- 2 **cans (2¼ ounces each) sliced ripe olives, drained**
- ½ **cup minced fresh cilantro
  Reduced-fat sour cream, optional**

1. In a large saucepan, saute peppers and onion in oil until tender. Add garlic; cook 1 minute longer. Stir in tomato sauce, tomatoes, chili powder, sugar, marjoram, basil, cumin, salt, cayenne and bay leaf. Bring to a boil. Reduce heat; simmer, uncovered, 30-35 minutes or until slightly thickened. Discard bay leaf.

2. Preheat oven to 350°. Place ⅓ cup zucchini down the center of each tortilla; top with 2 tablespoons cheese and 2 teaspoons olives. Roll up and place seam side down in two 13x9-in. baking dishes coated with cooking spray. Pour sauce over the top; sprinkle with remaining cheese.

3. Bake, uncovered, 30-35 minutes or until heated through. Sprinkle with cilantro. Serve with sour cream if desired.

Very Veggie Lasagna

People sometimes tell me you can't call something "lasagna" if it doesn't have the traditional meat-based sauce. Then they try this dish and ask for the recipe.

—**KIM BENDER** AURORA, CO

PREP: 20 MIN. • **BAKE:** 1 HOUR + STANDING
MAKES: 12 SERVINGS

- 2 **cups (16 ounces) 1% cottage cheese**
- 1 **carton (15 ounces) reduced-fat ricotta cheese**
- 2 **tablespoons minced fresh parsley**
- 1 **jar (26 ounces) meatless spaghetti sauce**
- 9 **uncooked lasagna noodles**
- 2 **medium carrots, shredded**
- 1½ **cups broccoli florets**
- 4 **ounces fresh mushrooms, sliced**
- 1 **small zucchini, thinly sliced**
- 1 **small yellow summer squash, thinly sliced**
- 2 **cups fresh spinach**
- 2 **cups (8 ounces) shredded part-skim mozzarella cheese**

1. Preheat oven to 350°. In a bowl, combine the cottage cheese, ricotta and parsley. Spread ½ cup spaghetti sauce in a 13x9-in. baking dish coated with cooking spray. Top with three noodles and a third of the cheese mixture. Sprinkle with half the carrots, broccoli, mushrooms, zucchini and squash. Top with a third of the remaining sauce.
2. Arrange half the spinach over the spaghetti sauce; sprinkle with a third of the mozzarella cheese. Repeat layers of noodles, cheese mixture, vegetables, sauce, spinach and mozzarella. Top with the remaining noodles, cheese mixture, sauce and mozzarella.
3. Cover tightly and bake 45 minutes. Uncover; bake 15 minutes longer or until noodles are tender. Let stand 15 minutes before cutting.

Black Bean Nacho Bake

Pasta, black beans and nacho cheese soup combine in this speedy six-ingredient supper. Top servings with cheddar cheese and crunchy tortilla chips.

—**MELODIE GAY** SALT LAKE CITY, UT

PREP: 15 MIN. • **BAKE:** 30 MIN.
MAKES: 4 SERVINGS

- 1 **package (7 ounces) small pasta shells, cooked and drained**
- 1 **can (15 ounces) black beans, rinsed and drained**
- 1 **can (11 ounces) condensed nacho cheese soup, undiluted**
- ⅓ **cup 2% milk**
- ½ **cup crushed tortilla chips**
- ½ **cup shredded cheddar cheese**

1. Preheat oven to 350°. In a large bowl, combine macaroni and beans. In a small bowl, combine soup and milk; stir into macaroni mixture.
2. Transfer to a greased 8-in.-square baking dish. Cover dish and bake 25 minutes. Uncover; sprinkle with tortilla chips and the cheese. Bake 5-10 minutes longer or until pasta is tender and cheese is melted.

BLACK BEAN NACHO BAKE

Italian Cheese-Stuffed Shells

I found this recipe in a church cookbook and thought it was an excellent twist on traditional lasagna. I omitted the meat, and it's just as yummy. Italian stewed tomatoes add robust flavor.

—PATTY TAPPENDORF GALESVILLE, WI

PREP: 1 HOUR • **BAKE:** 50 MIN.
MAKES: 7 SERVINGS

- 1 medium onion, chopped
- ½ cup chopped green pepper
- ½ cup chopped sweet red pepper
- ½ pound sliced fresh mushrooms
- 2 garlic cloves, minced
- 1½ cups water
- 1 can (14½ ounces) Italian stewed tomatoes
- 1 can (6 ounces) tomato paste
- 1½ teaspoons Italian seasoning
- 2 eggs, lightly beaten
- 1 carton (15 ounces) reduced-fat ricotta cheese
- 2 cups (8 ounces) shredded part-skim mozzarella cheese, divided
- ½ cup grated Parmesan cheese
- 21 jumbo pasta shells, cooked and drained

1. In a large nonstick skillet coated with cooking spray, cook onion and peppers over medium heat 2 minutes. Add mushrooms; cook 4-5 minutes until tender. Add garlic; cook 1 minute longer Stir in water, tomatoes, tomato paste and Italian seasoning. Bring to a boil. Reduce heat; cover and simmer 30 minutes.

2. Meanwhile, preheat oven to 350°. In a small bowl, combine eggs, the ricotta, ½ cup mozzarella and the Parmesan. Stuff into shells. Spread 1 cup vegetable sauce in a 13x9-in. baking dish coated with cooking spray. Arrange shells over sauce; top with remaining sauce.

3. Cover and bake 45 minutes. Uncover; sprinkle with remaining mozzarella. Bake 5-10 minutes longer or until bubbly and cheese is melted. Let stand 5 minutes before serving.

PROVOLONE ZITI BAKE

Provolone Ziti Bake

As easy as it is filling and delicious, this Italian meal appeals to everyone—and no one will even miss the meat. Serve it with salad and hot French bread, and watch it disappear.

—VICKY PALMER ALBUQUERQUE, NM

PREP: 20 MIN. • **BAKE:** 65 MIN.
MAKES: 8 SERVINGS

- 1 tablespoon olive oil
- 1 medium onion, chopped
- 3 garlic cloves, minced
- 2 cans (28 ounces each) Italian crushed tomatoes
- 1½ cups water
- ½ cup dry red wine or reduced-sodium chicken broth
- 1 tablespoon sugar
- 1 teaspoon dried basil
- 1 package (16 ounces) ziti or small tube pasta
- 8 slices provolone cheese

1. Preheat oven to 350°. In a 6-qt. stockpot, heat oil over medium-high heat. Add the onion; cook and stir 3-4 minutes or until tender. Add garlic; cook 1 minute longer. Stir in tomatoes, water, wine, sugar and basil. Bring to a boil; remove from heat. Stir in ziti.

2. Transfer to a 13x9-in. baking dish coated with cooking spray. Bake, covered, 1 hour. Top with cheese. Bake, uncovered, 4-6 minutes longer or until ziti is tender and cheese is melted.

ITALIAN CHEESE-STUFFED SHELLS

Zesty Rice 'n' Bean Casserole

A savory mix of seasonings adds zip to this satisfying dish that's loaded with beans, rice, vegetables and cheese. We enjoy it as a light entree with garlic bread and a fresh spinach salad. It also makes a super side dish at potluck gatherings.

—**DAPHNE BLANDFORD** GANDER, NL

PREP: 35 MIN. • **BAKE:** 15 MIN.
MAKES: 8 SERVINGS

- 2 **medium green peppers, chopped**
- 1½ **cups sliced fresh mushrooms**
- 1 **medium onion, chopped**
- ½ **cup water**
- 1 **teaspoon canola oil**
- 2 **garlic cloves, minced**
- 1 **can (28 ounces) diced tomatoes, undrained**
- 1 **can (16 ounces) kidney beans, rinsed and drained**
- ¾ **cup uncooked long grain rice**
- 2 **teaspoons ground cumin**
- 1 **teaspoon chili powder**
- ¼ **teaspoon cayenne pepper**
- 1 **cup (4 ounces) shredded part-skim mozzarella cheese, divided**

1. Preheat oven to 350°. In a large nonstick skillet, saute green peppers, mushrooms and onion in water and oil until onion is tender. Add garlic; cook 1 minute longer. Add tomatoes, beans, rice and seasonings. Bring to a boil.
2. Reduce heat; cover and simmer 25 minutes or until rice is tender and most of the liquid is absorbed. Remove from heat; stir in ½ cup cheese.
3. Transfer to a 2½-qt. baking dish coated with cooking spray. Sprinkle with the remaining cheese. Bake, uncovered, 15-20 minutes or until cheese is melted.

Vegetarian Tex-Mex Peppers

Folks who enjoy stuffed peppers will love this Tex-Mex twist. The filling holds together well and has a good amount of heat to match the sweetness of the peppers.

—**CELE KNIGHT** NACOGDOCHES, TX

PREP: 20 MIN. • **BAKE:** 45 MIN.
MAKES: 4 SERVINGS

- 4 **large green peppers**
- 2 **eggs, beaten**
- 2 **cups cooked brown rice**
- 1 **cup frozen vegetarian meat crumbles**
- 1 **cup canned black beans, rinsed and drained**
- ½ **teaspoon pepper**
- ¼ **teaspoon hot pepper sauce**
- ¼ **teaspoon ground cardamom, optional**
- 1 **can (14½ ounces) diced tomatoes, drained**
- 1 **can (10 ounces) diced tomatoes and green chilies**
- 1 **can (8 ounces) no-salt-added tomato sauce**
- ½ **cup shredded Colby cheese**

1. Preheat oven to 350°. Cut peppers in half lengthwise and remove seeds. Discard stems. In a Dutch oven, cook peppers in boiling water 3-5 minutes. Drain and rinse in cold water; set aside.
2. In a large bowl, combine eggs, rice, meat crumbles, beans, pepper, pepper sauce and, if desired, cardamom. Spoon into peppers. Place in a 13x9-in. baking dish coated with cooking spray.
3. In a small bowl, combine diced tomatoes, tomatoes and green chilies, and tomato sauce. Spoon over peppers. Cover and bake 40-45 minutes or until a thermometer reads 160°. Sprinkle with cheese; bake 5 minutes longer or until cheese is melted.

NOTE *Vegetarian meat crumbles are a nutritious protein source made from soy. Look for them in the natural foods freezer section.*

VEGETARIAN TEX-MEX PEPPERS

VEGGIE CHEESE SQUARES

Veggie Cheese Squares

I developed this recipe in my kitchen one busy afternoon when I looked in the fridge and not much was there. With no time to shop, I used what I had. Now this nice and easy dish is a suppertime standby.

—**DIXIE TERRY** GOREVILLE, IL

PREP: 20 MIN. • **BAKE:** 30 MIN.
MAKES: 4-6 SERVINGS

- 1½ cups fresh broccoli florets
- 1 medium sweet red pepper, julienned
- 2 tablespoons olive oil
- 2 garlic cloves, minced
- 4 eggs
- 1 cup milk
- 1 cup (4 ounces) shredded cheddar cheese, divided
- ½ teaspoon dried thyme
- ¼ teaspoon salt

1. Preheat oven to 350°. In a large skillet, saute broccoli and red pepper in oil. Add garlic; cook 1 minute longer. Spoon into a greased 9-in.-square baking dish. In another large bowl, combine eggs, milk, ¾ cup cheese, thyme and salt.

2. Pour the egg mixture over the broccoli mixture. Bake, uncovered, 25-30 minutes. Sprinkle with the remaining cheese. Bake 5 minutes longer or until cheese is melted. Let stand 5 minutes before cutting.

Vegetarian Potato au Gratin

Fill up on veggies and load up on flavor with this creamy baked entree. You'll appreciate the homey bread-crumb topping and hands-free bake time at the end of a long day.

—*TASTE OF HOME* **TEST KITCHEN**

PREP: 15 MIN. • **BAKE:** 50 MIN. + STANDING
MAKES: 6 SERVINGS

- 3 medium carrots, thinly sliced
- 1 medium green pepper, chopped
- 4 tablespoons butter, divided
- 3 tablespoons all-purpose flour
- 1 teaspoon dried oregano
- ½ teaspoon salt
- 2½ cups 2% milk
- 1 can (15 ounces) black beans, rinsed and drained
- 3 cups (12 ounces) shredded Swiss cheese, divided
- 4 medium Yukon Gold potatoes, thinly sliced
- ½ cup seasoned bread crumbs

1. Preheat oven to 400°. In a large saucepan, saute carrots and pepper in 3 tablespoons butter until tender. Stir in flour, oregano and salt until blended; gradually add milk. Bring to a boil; cook and stir 2 minutes or until thickened. Stir in beans and 2 cups cheese until cheese is melted.

2. Layer half of the potatoes and sauce in a greased 13x9-in. baking dish; repeat layers. Sprinkle with remaining cheese. In a microwave, melt the remaining butter. Stir in bread crumbs. Sprinkle over top.

3. Cover and bake 50-55 minutes. Let stand 10 minutes before serving.

VEGETARIAN POTATO AU GRATIN

These authentic eggplant roll-ups may take some time to prepare, but the end result is restaurant-quality. Your family will request it time and again.

—NANCY SOUSLEY LAFAYETTE, IN

Eggplant Rollatini

PREP: 1 HOUR • **BAKE:** 30 MIN.
MAKES: 5 SERVINGS

- 1 **large eggplant**
- 1 **tablespoon salt**

SAUCE

- 1 **small onion, chopped**
- ¼ **cup olive oil**
- 2 **garlic cloves, minced**
- 1 **can (15 ounces) tomato sauce**
- 1 **can (14½ ounces) diced tomatoes**
- ½ **cup chicken broth**
- ¼ **cup tomato paste**
- 2 **tablespoons minced fresh parsley**
- 2 **teaspoons sugar**
- ½ **teaspoon salt**
- ½ **teaspoon dried basil**
- ¼ **teaspoon pepper**
- ⅛ **teaspoon crushed red pepper flakes**

FILLING

- 1 **carton (15 ounces) ricotta cheese**
- 1 **cup (4 ounces) shredded part-skim mozzarella cheese**
- ½ **cup grated Parmesan cheese**
- ¼ **cup minced fresh parsley**
- 1 **egg, lightly beaten**
- ⅛ **teaspoon pepper**

COATING

- 3 **eggs, lightly beaten**
- 1 **cup seasoned bread crumbs**
- 1 **cup grated Parmesan cheese, divided**
- 2 **garlic cloves, minced**
- 2 **tablespoons minced fresh parsley Dash each salt and pepper**

1. Peel and slice eggplant lengthwise into fifteen ⅛-in.-thick slices. Place in a colander over a plate; sprinkle with salt and toss. Let stand 30 minutes.
2. Meanwhile, for sauce, in a large saucepan, saute onion in oil. Add the garlic; cook 1 minute longer. Stir in remaining ingredients. Bring to a boil. Reduce heat; simmer, uncovered, 20-25 minutes or until flavors are blended, stirring occasionally. Rinse and drain eggplant.
3. In a large bowl, combine filling ingredients; set aside.
4. Place eggs in a shallow bowl. In another shallow bowl, combine the bread crumbs, ½ cup Parmesan cheese, garlic, parsley, salt and pepper. Dip eggplant in eggs, then the bread crumb mixture.

5. In an electric skillet, heat ½ in. of oil to 375°. Fry eggplant in batches 2-3 minutes on each side or until golden brown. Drain on paper towels.
6. Preheat oven to 375°. Spoon 1 cup sauce into an ungreased 13x9-in. baking dish. Spread 2 rounded tablespoons filling over each eggplant slice. Carefully roll up and place seam side down in baking dish. Spoon remaining sauce over the roll-ups. Sprinkle with remaining Parmesan cheese. Cover and bake 30-35 minutes or until bubbly.

EGGPLANT ROLLATINI

DID YOU KNOW?

Salting an eggplant draws out some of the moisture, giving the flesh a denser texture. This means it will give off less moisture and absorb less fat during cooking. Salting may cut some of the bitterness from an eggplant.

TORTELLINI SPINACH CASSEROLE

tortellini; place in a large bowl. Stir in mushroom mixture and spinach. Add cheese sauce and toss to coat.

4. Transfer to a greased 13x9-in. baking dish; sprinkle with mozzarella cheese. Cover and bake 15 minutes. Uncover; bake 5-10 minutes longer or until heated through and cheese is melted.

5 INGREDIENTS Polenta Chili Casserole

We love this delicious vegetarian bean and polenta bake that combines spicy chili, mixed veggies and homemade polenta.
—**DAN KELMENSON** WEST BLOOMFIELD, MI

PREP: 20 MIN. • **BAKE:** 35 MIN. + STANDING
MAKES: 8 SERVINGS

- 1¼ cups yellow cornmeal
- ½ teaspoon salt
- 4 cups boiling water
- 2 cups (8 ounces) shredded cheddar cheese, divided
- 3 cans (15 ounces each) vegetarian chili with beans
- 1 package (16 ounces) frozen mixed vegetables, thawed and well drained

1. Preheat oven to 350°. In a large saucepan, combine cornmeal and salt. Gradually whisk in boiling water. Cook and stir over medium heat 5 minutes or until thickened. Remove from heat. Stir in ¼ cup cheddar cheese until melted.

2. Spread into a 13x9-in. baking dish coated with cooking spray. Bake, uncovered, at 20 minutes. Meanwhile, heat chili according to package directions.

3. Spread vegetables over polenta; top with chili. Sprinkle with remaining cheese. Bake 12-15 minutes longer or until cheese is melted. Let stand 10 minutes before serving.

Tortellini Spinach Casserole

Here's a casserole with a fresh taste that will delight even those who say they don't like spinach. In fact, people are often surprised at just how good it is! Whenever I take it to a gathering, it doesn't sit around for long.
—**BARBARA KELLEN** ANTIOCH, IL

PREP: 20 MIN. • **BAKE:** 20 MIN.
MAKES: 12 SERVINGS

- 1 package (19 ounces) frozen cheese tortellini
- 1 pound sliced fresh mushrooms
- 1 teaspoon garlic powder
- ¼ teaspoon onion powder
- ¼ teaspoon pepper
- ½ cup butter, divided
- 1 can (12 ounces) evaporated milk
- ½ pound brick cheese, cubed
- 3 packages (10 ounces each) frozen chopped spinach, thawed and squeezed dry
- 2 cups (8 ounces) shredded part-skim mozzarella cheese

1. Preheat oven to 350°. Cook tortellini according to the package directions.

2. Meanwhile, in a large skillet, saute mushrooms, garlic powder, onion powder and pepper in ¼ cup butter until mushrooms are tender. Remove and keep warm.

3. In same skillet, combine milk and remaining butter. Bring to a gentle boil; stir in brick cheese until smooth. Drain

POLENTA CHILI CASSEROLE

Creamy Broccoli Lasagna

Nothing warms you up faster on a cold day than a piping hot lasagna. Folks can't resist the combination of a rich homemade white sauce, broccoli, mushrooms and Swiss cheese.

—**LAUNA SHOEMAKER** LANDRUM, SC

PREP: 15 MIN. • **BAKE:** 35 MIN. + STANDING
MAKES: 12 SERVINGS

- 9 uncooked lasagna noodles
- ¼ cup chopped onion
- ¼ cup butter
- ¼ cup all-purpose flour
- 2 teaspoons chicken bouillon granules
- ¾ teaspoon garlic salt
- ¼ teaspoon pepper
- ¼ teaspoon dried thyme
- 2½ cups milk
- 6 cups broccoli florets
- 1½ cups (12 ounces) 4% cottage cheese
- 2 jars (4½ ounces each) sliced mushrooms, drained
- 2 packages (6 ounces each) slices Swiss cheese

1. Preheat oven to 350°. Cook noodles according to package directions.

2. Meanwhile, in a large saucepan, saute onion in butter until tender. Add flour, bouillon, garlic salt, pepper and thyme; stir until smooth. Gradually add milk. Bring to a boil; cook and stir 2 minutes or until thickened. Add broccoli; cook 3-5 minutes. Stir in cottage cheese and mushrooms. Drain noodles.

3. In a greased 13x9-in. baking dish, layer three noodles, a third of the sauce and a third of the Swiss cheese. Repeat layers twice.

4. Bake, uncovered, 35-40 minutes or until bubbly and broccoli is tender. Let stand 10 minutes before cutting.

Zippy Macaroni and Cheese

When I was asked to teach an advanced 4-H foods class, I included this recipe. The kids loved it and have been making it for their families ever since.

—**GLENDA SCHWARZ** MORDEN, MB

PREP: 20 MIN. • **BAKE:** 25 MIN.
MAKES: 4 SERVINGS

ZIPPY MACARONI AND CHEESE

- 1⅓ cups uncooked elbow macaroni
- 1 cup (8 ounces) 4% cottage cheese
- 1 cup (4 ounces) shredded part-skim mozzarella cheese
- ½ cup shredded cheddar cheese
- 1 teaspoon cornstarch
- 1 cup milk
- 1 small onion, grated
- ¼ cup finely chopped green pepper
- 1 teaspoon Dijon mustard
- ½ teaspoon salt
- ¼ to ½ teaspoon crushed red pepper flakes
- ½ cup crushed cornflakes
- 1 tablespoon butter, melted

1. Preheat oven to 350°. Cook macaroni according to package directions; drain. Add cottage, mozzarella and cheddar cheeses; set aside.

2. In a large saucepan, combine cornstarch and milk until smooth. Stir in onion, green pepper, mustard, salt and pepper flakes. Bring to a boil; cook and stir 2 minutes or until thickened. Pour over macaroni mixture; gently stir to coat.

3. Transfer to a greased 2-qt. baking dish. Combine cornflakes and butter; sprinkle over top. Bake, uncovered, 25-30 minutes or until bubbly and the top is golden brown.

CREAMY BROCCOLI LASAGNA

Meatless Stuffed Cabbage

These stuffed cabbage bundles make a delicious and healthy alternative to the meat-filled ones.

—**LINDA EVANCOE-COBLE** LEOLA, PA

PREP: 45 MIN. • **BAKE:** 40 MIN.
MAKES: 6 SERVINGS

- ½ cup uncooked brown rice
- 1 cup water
- 1 medium head cabbage
- 1 package (12 ounces) frozen vegetarian meat crumbles, thawed
- 1 large onion, chopped
- ½ teaspoon pepper
- 1 can (10¾ ounces) reduced-sodium condensed tomato soup, undiluted, divided
- 1 can (8 ounces) Italian tomato sauce, divided
- 1 can (14½ ounces) Italian diced tomatoes, undrained

1. In a small saucepan, bring rice and water to a boil. Reduce heat; cover and simmer 25-30 minutes or until tender.

2. Meanwhile, cook cabbage in boiling water just until outer leaves pull away easily from head. Set aside 12 large leaves for rolls (refrigerate remaining cabbage for another use).

3. Preheat oven to 350°. In a large bowl, combine meat crumbles, onion, pepper, cooked rice and half of the soup. Cut out the thick vein from bottom of each reserved leaf, making a V-shaped cut. Place ⅓ cup rice mixture on each cabbage leaf; overlap cut ends. Fold in sides, beginning from cut end. Roll up completely to enclose filling.

4. Spread half the tomato sauce into a 13x9-in. baking dish coated with cooking spray. Place rolls seam side down in dish.

5. In a small bowl, combine tomatoes with the remaining soup and tomato sauce. Pour over rolls. Cover and bake 40-45 minutes or until bubbly and cabbage is tender.

NOTE *Vegetarian meat crumbles are a nutritious protein source made from soy. Look for them in the natural foods freezer section.*

Vegetarian Tortilla Stack

Nearly all the meals I make are meatless. This tasty layered creation is one of my husband's favorites. If you don't like as much heat, limit the amount of jalapenos.

—**WENDY FENSTERMACHER** ALLENTOWN, PA

PREP: 25 MIN. • **BAKE:** 35 MIN.
MAKES: 6 SERVINGS

- 1 medium green pepper, chopped
- 1 medium sweet red pepper, chopped
- 1 small onion, chopped
- 2 teaspoons olive oil
- 1 package (12 ounces) frozen vegetarian meat crumbles, thawed
- 2 tablespoons minced fresh cilantro
- 1 teaspoon ground cumin
- 1½ cups salsa
- 5 flour tortillas (8 inches)
- 1¼ cups shredded reduced-fat Mexican cheese blend, divided
- ⅓ cup pickled jalapeno slices
- 5 tablespoons sliced ripe olives

1. Preheat oven to 350°. In a large nonstick skillet coated with cooking spray, saute peppers and onion in oil until tender. Stir in meat crumbles, cilantro and cumin; heat through.

2. Spread ¼ cup salsa into a 9-in. deep-dish pie plate coated with cooking spray. Layer with one tortilla, a fourth of the meat crumble mixture, ¼ cup salsa, ¼ cup cheese, 2 or 3 jalapeno slices and 1 tablespoon olives. Repeat layers three times. Top with remaining tortilla, salsa, olives and jalapeno slices.

3. Cover and bake 30 minutes. Uncover; sprinkle with remaining cheese. Bake 5-10 minutes longer or until heated through and the cheese is melted.

NOTE *Vegetarian meat crumbles are a nutritious protein source made from soy. Look for them in the natural foods freezer section.*

VEGETARIAN TORTILLA STACK

Hearty Tomato-Olive Penne

Who needs meat when you have a pasta dish loaded with tomatoes, olives and Havarti cheese? I often assemble it in advance, refrigerate it overnight and bake it the next day, adding a few minutes to the cooking time.

—JACQUELINE FRANK GREEN BAY, WI

PREP: 50 MIN. • **BAKE:** 25 MIN.
MAKES: 8 SERVINGS

- 2 **large onions, chopped**
- 6 **tablespoons olive oil**
- 3 **garlic cloves, minced**
- 3 **pounds plum tomatoes, seeded and chopped (about 10 tomatoes)**
- 1 **cup vegetable or chicken broth**
- 1 **tablespoon dried basil**
- 1 **teaspoon crushed red pepper flakes**
- ½ **teaspoon salt**
- ¼ **teaspoon pepper**
- 1 **package (16 ounces) uncooked penne pasta**
- 1 **block (24 ounces) Havarti cheese, cut into ½-in. cubes**
- 1 **cup pitted Greek olives**
- ⅓ **cup grated Parmesan cheese**

1. In a Dutch oven, saute onions in oil until tender. Add garlic; cook 1 minute longer. Stir in tomatoes, broth, basil, pepper flakes, salt and pepper. Bring to a boil. Reduce heat; cover and simmer 25-30 minutes or until sauce is slightly thickened.

2. Meanwhile, cook penne according to package directions; drain.

3. Preheat oven to 375°. Stir Havarti cheese, olives and cooked penne into the sauce. Transfer to a greased 13x9-in. baking dish; sprinkle with Parmesan cheese.

4. Cover and bake 20 minutes. Uncover; bake 5 minutes longer or until cheese is melted.

HEARTY TOMATO-OLIVE PENNE

Stacked Vegetables and Ravioli

Fresh squash, zucchini and basil meet ricotta cheese and ravioli in this crowd-pleasing entree with delicious summer flavors. One bite and you'll agree—this is what fresh tastes like.
—**TASTE OF HOME** TEST KITCHEN

PREP: 20 MIN. • **BAKE:** 30 MIN. + STANDING
MAKES: 6 SERVINGS

- 2 **yellow summer squash**
- 2 **medium zucchini**
- 1 **package (9 ounces) refrigerated cheese ravioli**
- 1 **cup ricotta cheese**
- 1 **egg**
- ½ **teaspoon garlic salt**
- 1 **jar (24 ounces) marinara or spaghetti sauce**
- 10 **fresh basil leaves, divided**
- ¾ **cup shredded Parmesan cheese**

1. Preheat oven to 350°. Using a vegetable peeler, cut squash and zucchini into very thin lengthwise strips. In a Dutch oven, cook ravioli according to package directions, adding vegetable strips during last 3 minutes of cooking.

2. Meanwhile, in a small bowl, combine ricotta cheese, egg and garlic salt; set aside. Drain ravioli and vegetables.

3. Spread ½ cup marinara sauce into a greased 11x7-in. baking dish. Layer with half the ravioli and vegetables, half the ricotta mixture, seven basil leaves and 1 cup marinara sauce. Layer with the remaining ravioli, vegetables and marinara sauce. Dollop remaining ricotta mixture over top; sprinkle with Parmesan cheese.

4. Cover and bake 25 minutes. Uncover; bake 5-10 minutes longer or until cheese is melted. Let stand 10 minutes before cutting. Thinly slice remaining basil; sprinkle over top.

BLACK BEAN CORNMEAL PIE

Black Bean Cornmeal Pie

My hearty, meatless Southwestern pie is tasty and nutritious. Feel free to vary the beans to suit your tastes. I like to serve this with salsa and reduced-fat sour cream.
—**TARI AMBLER** SHOREWOOD, IL

PREP: 30 MIN. • **BAKE:** 20 MIN.
MAKES: 6 SERVINGS

- 1 **large onion, chopped**
- 1 **large green pepper, chopped**
- 1 **teaspoon canola oil**
- 1½ **teaspoons chili powder**
- 1 **garlic clove, minced**
- ¾ **teaspoon ground cumin**
- ¼ **teaspoon pepper**
- 1 **can (14½ ounces) diced tomatoes, undrained**
- 2 **cans (15 ounces each) black beans, rinsed and drained**
- 1 **cup frozen corn**

TOPPING
- ¾ **cup whole wheat pastry flour**
- ¾ **cup yellow cornmeal**
- 2 **teaspoons sugar**
- 2 **teaspoons baking powder**
- 2 **teaspoons chopped seeded jalapeno pepper**
- ¼ **teaspoon salt**
- 1 **egg**
- ¾ **cup fat-free milk**
- 1 **tablespoon canola oil**
  Salsa and reduced-fat sour cream, optional

1. In a large skillet, saute onion and green pepper in oil until tender. Add chili powder, garlic, cumin and pepper; saute 1 minute longer. Add tomatoes and bring to a boil. Reduce heat; cover and simmer 5 minutes.

2. Stir in beans and corn; heat through. Transfer to an 11x7-in. baking dish coated with cooking spray.

3. Preheat oven to 375°. For topping, in a small bowl, combine the flour, cornmeal, sugar, baking powder, jalapeno and salt. Whisk egg, milk and oil; stir into dry ingredients just until moistened. Spoon over filling; gently spread to cover the top.

4. Bake 20-25 minutes or until filling is bubbly and a toothpick inserted into topping comes out clean. Serve with salsa and sour cream if desired.

NOTE *Wear disposable gloves when cutting hot peppers; the oils can burn skin. Avoid touching your face.*

Southwestern Veggie Bake

Refrigerated corn bread twists become an appealing lattice top on this zippy main dish. The original recipe called for cooked chicken instead of kidney beans and celery, but my family prefers my meatless version. It's a time-saver so I make it often.

—JULIE ZEAGER KENT, OH

PREP: 20 MIN. • **BAKE:** 20 MIN.
MAKES: 8 SERVINGS

- 3 medium carrots, sliced
- 2 celery ribs, chopped
- 1 small onion, chopped
- 2 to 3 teaspoons chili powder
- 1 teaspoon ground cumin
- ¼ teaspoon cayenne pepper
- 2 tablespoons butter
- 3 tablespoons all-purpose flour
- ½ cup milk
- 1 can (16 ounces) kidney beans, rinsed and drained
- 1 can (15 ounces) black beans, rinsed and drained
- 1 can (15¼ ounces) whole kernel corn, drained
- 1 can (14½ ounces) diced tomatoes, undrained
- 1 can (4 ounces) chopped green chilies
- 1 tube (11½ ounces) refrigerated corn bread twists

1. Preheat oven to 350°. In a large skillet, saute carrots, celery, onion and seasonings in butter until vegetables are crisp-tender. Stir in flour until blended. Gradually add milk. Bring to a boil; cook and stir 2 minutes or until thickened and bubbly.

2. Remove from the heat; add beans, corn, tomatoes and chilies. Spoon into an ungreased 13x9-in. baking dish. Separate corn bread twists; weave a lattice crust over filling.

3. Bake, uncovered, 20-25 minutes or until corn bread is golden brown.

Sweet Potato Chili Bake

I don't consume meat but wanted to create some dishes that are a little heartier than traditional vegetarian fare. Here's one that hits the spot whenever I'm craving comfort food.

—JILLIAN TOURNOUX MASSILLON, OH

PREP: 30 MIN. • **BAKE:** 20 MIN.
MAKES: 7 SERVINGS

- 2 cups cubed peeled sweet potato
- 1 medium sweet red pepper, chopped
- 1 tablespoon olive oil
- 1 garlic clove, minced
- 1 can (28 ounces) diced tomatoes, undrained
- 2 cups vegetable broth
- 1 can (15 ounces) black beans, rinsed and drained
- 4½ teaspoons brown sugar
- 3 teaspoons chili powder
- 1 teaspoon salt
- ½ teaspoon pepper
- 1 package (6½ ounces) corn bread/ muffin mix
- ½ cup shredded cheddar cheese
  Optional toppings: sour cream, shredded cheddar cheese and chopped seeded jalapeno pepper

1. In an ovenproof Dutch oven, saute sweet potato and red pepper in oil until crisp-tender. Add garlic; cook 1 minute longer. Add tomatoes, broth, beans, brown sugar, chili powder, salt and pepper. Bring to a boil. Reduce heat; simmer, uncovered, 15-20 minutes or until potatoes are tender.

2. Meanwhile, preheat oven to 400°. Prepare corn bread batter according to package directions; stir in cheese. Drop by tablespoonfuls over chili.

3. Cover and bake 18-20 minutes or until a toothpick inserted in center comes out clean. Serve with toppings of your choice.

NOTE *Wear disposable gloves when cutting hot peppers; the oils can burn skin. Avoid touching your face.*

SWEET POTATO CHILI BAKE

Four-Vegetable Bake

Several members of my family enjoy meatless dishes and I'm partial to casseroles, so this tasty dish pleases everyone. It lets the goodness of the veggies come through.

—RUBY WILLIAMS BOGALUSA, LA

PREP: 20 MIN. • **BAKE:** 20 MIN.
MAKES: 8 SERVINGS

- 3 medium zucchini, cut into ¼-inch slices
- 1 pound sliced fresh mushrooms
- 1 medium onion, chopped
- ½ cup chopped green onions
- 8 tablespoons butter, divided
- ¼ cup all-purpose flour
- 1 cup 2% milk
- 1 can (14 ounces) water-packed artichoke hearts, rinsed, drained and quartered
- ¾ cup shredded Swiss cheese
- ½ teaspoon salt
- ¼ teaspoon pepper
- ¾ cup seasoned bread crumbs

1. Preheat oven to 350°. In a large skillet, saute zucchini, mushrooms and onions in 3 tablespoons butter until zucchini is crisp-tender; remove and set aside.

2. In same skillet, melt 3 tablespoons butter. Stir in flour until smooth. Gradually stir in milk until blended. Bring to a boil; cook and stir 2 minutes or until thickened. Stir in zucchini mixture, artichokes, cheese, salt and pepper.

3. Transfer to a greased 11x7-in. baking dish. Melt remaining butter; toss with bread crumbs. Sprinkle over top. Bake, uncovered, 20-25 minutes or until bubbly and topping is lightly browned.

EGGPLANT PARMESAN

Eggplant Parmesan

My recipe says to bake the eggplant instead of frying it, so it's much healthier. The prep time is little longer than other comparable recipes, but the classic Italian flavors and rustic elegance make it worth the extra effort.

—LACI HOOTEN MCKINNEY, TX

PREP: 40 MIN. • **COOK:** 25 MIN.
MAKES: 8 SERVINGS

- 3 eggs, beaten
- 2½ cups panko (Japanese) bread crumbs
- 3 medium eggplants, cut into ¼-inch slices
- 2 jars (4½ ounces each) sliced mushrooms, drained
- ½ teaspoon dried basil
- ⅛ teaspoon dried oregano
- 2 cups (8 ounces) shredded part-skim mozzarella cheese
- ½ cup grated Parmesan cheese
- 1 jar (28 ounces) spaghetti sauce

1. Preheat oven to 350°. Place eggs and bread crumbs in separate shallow bowls. Dip eggplant in eggs, then coat in crumbs. Place on baking sheets coated with cooking spray. Bake 15-20 minutes or until tender and golden brown, turning once.

2. In a small bowl, combine the mushrooms, basil and oregano. In another small bowl, combine the mozzarella and Parmesan cheeses.

3. Spread ½ cup sauce into a 13x9-in. baking dish coated with cooking spray. Layer with a third of the mushroom mixture, a third of the eggplant, ¾ cup sauce and a third of the cheese mixture. Repeat layers twice.

4. Bake, uncovered, for 25-30 minutes or until heated through and cheese is melted.

New Orleans-Style Scalloped Corn

I serve a zippy version of scalloped corn during the holidays, at summer picnics and for other family gatherings. It's a New Orleans tradition that I've incorporated into my menus. My sons love it, and now it's part of their treasured recipe collections.

—PRISCILLA GILBERT
INDIAN HARBOUR BEACH, FL

PREP: 20 MIN. • **BAKE:** 35 MIN.
MAKES: 8 SERVINGS

- 4 teaspoons butter
- 1 large onion, finely chopped
- 1 large sweet red pepper, finely chopped
- 4 cups frozen corn
- 2 eggs
- 1 cup fat-free milk
- 1 tablespoon sugar
- 1 to 2 teaspoons hot pepper sauce
- ½ teaspoon dried thyme
- ¼ teaspoon salt
- ¼ teaspoon pepper
- 1¼ cups crushed reduced-fat butter-flavored crackers (about 30 crackers)
- 5 green onions, sliced

1. Preheat oven to 350°. In a large skillet, heat butter over medium-high heat. Add onion and pepper; cook and stir until tender. Add corn; heat through, stirring occasionally. Remove from heat.
2. In a small bowl, whisk eggs, milk, sugar, pepper sauce, thyme, salt and pepper; add to corn mixture. Stir in crushed crackers and green onions.
3. Transfer to a 2-qt. baking dish coated with cooking spray. Bake, uncovered, 35-40 minutes or until a knife inserted near the center comes out clean.

CHILI-CHEESE RICE BAKE

Chili-Cheese Rice Bake

This three-cheese baked rice side dish is so comforting you could make a meal out of it. On occasion, I top it with French-fried onions or crumbled potato chips before baking; they add a little extra crunch.

—CATHLENE WILLIS RIGBY, ID

START TO FINISH: 30 MIN.
MAKES: 2 SERVINGS

- ½ cup uncooked instant rice
- ½ cup chopped onion
- 1 tablespoon butter
- ½ cup sour cream
- ¼ cup canned chopped green chilies
- 2 tablespoons cream-style cottage cheese
- 2 tablespoons ricotta cheese
- ⅛ teaspoon salt
  Dash pepper
- ½ cup shredded sharp cheddar cheese
- 1 teaspoon minced fresh parsley

1. Preheat oven to 375°. Cook rice according to package directions.
2. Meanwhile, in a large skillet, saute onion in butter until tender. Remove from heat; stir in sour cream, chilies, cottage cheese, ricotta cheese, salt, pepper and rice.
3. Transfer rice mixture to a 2-cup baking dish coated with cooking spray. Sprinkle with cheddar cheese. Bake 15-20 minutes or until cheese is melted. Sprinkle with parsley.

NEW ORLEANS-
STYLE SCALLOPED CORN

Creamy Vegetable Casserole

I add extra white pepper to this veggie bake for a little extra kick. I've used an Italian cheese blend instead of Swiss, and the results were equally good.

—**CHRISTIE NELSON** TAYLORVILLE, IL

PREP: 25 MIN. • **BAKE:** 20 MIN.
MAKES: 8 SERVINGS

- 2 cups fresh baby carrots
- 2 cups fresh broccoli florets
- 2 cups fresh cauliflowerets
- 1¾ cups sliced fresh mushrooms
- 2 tablespoons butter
- 2 tablespoons all-purpose flour
- 2 cups half-and-half cream
- 1 teaspoon chicken bouillon granules
- ½ teaspoon onion powder
- ¼ teaspoon white pepper
- 1 cup (4 ounces) shredded Swiss cheese
- ½ cup crushed butter-flavored crackers (about 15 crackers)

1. Preheat oven to 350°. Place carrots in a steamer basket; place in a large saucepan over 1 in. of water. Bring to a boil; cover and steam 3 minutes.

2. Add broccoli and cauliflower; steam 5 minutes longer or until vegetables are tender. Transfer to a greased 2½-qt. baking dish.

3. In a large skillet, saute mushrooms in butter until tender. Stir in flour until blended. Gradually stir in cream, bouillon, onion powder and pepper. Bring to a boil; cook and stir for 2 minutes or until thickened. Stir in cheese.

4. Pour over vegetables and stir to coat. Sprinkle with cracker crumbs. Bake, uncovered, 20-25 minutes or until bubbly.

Parmesan-Baked Mashed Potatoes

Here's a family favorite side dish I serve for Christmas, although it's so good you may want it all year long. My clan looks forward to a big scoop of these Parmesan mashed potatoes next to their ham or turkey.

—**ROSEMARY JANZ** CONCORD, NC

PREP: 20 MIN. • **BAKE:** 25 MIN.
MAKES: 4 SERVINGS

- 1¾ pounds red potatoes (about 6 medium), peeled and cubed
- ⅔ cup sour cream
- 2 egg whites, lightly beaten
- ¼ cup butter
- ¼ cup minced fresh parsley
- 2 green onions, thinly sliced
- ¾ teaspoon salt
- ¼ teaspoon pepper
    Dash ground nutmeg
- 3 tablespoons grated Parmesan cheese

1. Preheat oven to 400°. Place potatoes in a large saucepan; add water to cover. Bring to a boil. Reduce heat; cook, uncovered, 10-15 minutes or until tender.

2. Drain; return to pan. Mash potatoes, gradually adding sour cream, egg whites and butter. Stir in parsley, green onions, salt, pepper and nutmeg.

3. Transfer to a greased 1½-qt. baking dish; sprinkle with cheese. Bake for 25-30 minutes or until golden brown.

PARMESAN-BAKED MASHED POTATOES

BASIL CORN & TOMATO BAKE

Basil Corn & Tomato Bake

I turn to this recipe when sweet Jersey corn is in season. The flavor combination offers broad appeal, so you can serve it for brunch, lunch or dinner.

—ERIN CHILCOAT CENTRAL ISLIP, NY

PREP: 30 MIN. • **BAKE:** 45 MIN. + STANDING
MAKES: 10 SERVINGS

- 2 teaspoons olive oil
- 1 medium onion, chopped
- 2 eggs
- 1 can (10¾ ounces) reduced-fat reduced-sodium condensed cream of celery soup, undiluted
- 4 cups fresh or frozen corn
- 1 small zucchini, chopped
- 1 medium tomato, seeded and chopped
- ¾ cup soft whole wheat bread crumbs
- ⅓ cup minced fresh basil
- ½ teaspoon salt
- ½ cup shredded part-skim mozzarella cheese
  Additional minced fresh basil, optional

1. Preheat oven to 350°. In a small skillet, heat oil over medium heat. Add onion; cook and stir until tender. In a large bowl, whisk eggs and condensed soup until blended. Stir in vegetables, bread crumbs, basil, salt and onion. Transfer mixture to an 11x7-in. baking dish coated with cooking spray.
2. Bake, uncovered, 40-45 minutes or until bubbly. Sprinkle with cheese. Bake 5-10 minutes longer or until cheese is melted. Let stand 10 minutes before serving. If desired, sprinkle with additional basil.

NOTE *To make soft bread crumbs, tear bread into pieces and place in a food processor or blender. Cover and pulse until crumbs form. One slice of bread yields ½ to ¾ cup crumbs.*

Buttery Sweet Potato Casserole

Whenever we get together as a family for major holidays, my kids, nieces and nephews ask me to make this dish. It goes together in minutes with canned sweet potatoes, making it ideal for the busy holiday season.

—SUE MILLER MARS, PA

PREP: 15 MIN. • **BAKE:** 20 MIN.
MAKES: 6-8 SERVINGS

- 2 cans (15¾ ounces each) sweet potatoes, drained and mashed
- ½ cup sugar
- 1 egg
- ¼ cup butter, melted
- ½ teaspoon ground cinnamon
  Dash salt

TOPPING

- 1 cup coarsely crushed butter-flavored crackers (about 25 crackers)
- ½ cup packed brown sugar
- ¼ cup butter, melted

1. Preheat oven to 350°. In a large bowl, combine first six ingredients. Transfer to a greased 8-in.-square baking dish. Combine topping ingredients; sprinkle over sweet potato mixture.
2. Bake, uncovered, 20-25 minutes or until a thermometer reads 160°.

BUTTERY SWEET POTATO CASSEROLE

TWO-CHEESE
MAC 'N CHEESE

Two-Cheese Mac 'n Cheese

A lot of stories say that mac and cheese was created by Thomas Jefferson, Marco Polo or the cooks of China. My favorite theory? An Italian housewife invented it to introduce non-Italian Americans to macaroni noodles.

—STEPHANIE SORBIE GLENDALE, AZ

PREP: 35 MIN. • **BAKE:** 35 MIN.
MAKES: 15 SERVINGS

- 1 package (16 ounces) spiral pasta
- 3 tablespoons butter
- 3 garlic cloves, minced, optional
- 3 tablespoons all-purpose flour
- ⅛ teaspoon pepper
    Dash salt
- 4 cups 2% milk
- 5 cups (20 ounces) shredded sharp cheddar cheese, divided
- 1 cup shredded Asiago cheese

1. In a Dutch oven, cook pasta according to package directions.
2. Meanwhile, in a large saucepan, melt butter over medium heat. Add garlic if desired; cook and stir for 1 minute. Stir in flour, pepper and salt until blended; cook and stir until golden brown, about 5 minutes. Gradually whisk in milk, stirring until smooth. Bring to a boil; cook 2 minutes longer or until thickened.
3. Remove from heat. Stir in 4 cups cheddar cheese and Asiago cheese until melted. Mixture will thicken.
4. Preheat oven to 350°. Drain pasta; stir in cheese sauce. Transfer to a greased 13x9-in. baking dish. Sprinkle with remaining cheddar cheese.
5. Bake, uncovered, 35-40 minutes or until golden brown. Let stand 5 minutes before serving.

Creamy Spinach Casserole

Rich and satisfying, this savory spinach casserole will be a welcome addition to the table. You will love the short prep time and decadent taste.

—ANNETTE MARIE YOUNG
WEST LAFAYETTE, IN

PREP: 10 MIN. • **BAKE:** 35 MIN.
MAKES: 10 SERVINGS

- 2 cans (10¾ ounces each) reduced-fat reduced-sodium condensed cream of chicken soup, undiluted
- 1 package (8 ounces) reduced-fat cream cheese, cubed
- ½ cup fat-free milk
- ½ cup grated Parmesan cheese
- 4 cups herb seasoned stuffing cubes
- 2 packages (10 ounces each) frozen chopped spinach, thawed and squeezed dry

1. Preheat oven to 350°. In a large bowl, beat soup, cream cheese, milk and Parmesan cheese until blended. Stir in stuffing cubes and spinach.
2. Spoon into a 2-qt. baking dish coated with cooking spray. Bake, uncovered, 35-40 minutes or until heated through.

CREAMY SPINACH CASSEROLE

Two-Cheese & Bacon Grits Bake

To a Southerner, grits are a true staple. When combined with bacon and cheese, even Northerners will be asking for a second helping.

—MELISSA ROGERS TUSCALOOSA, AL

PREP: 25 MIN. • **BAKE:** 40 MIN. + STANDING
MAKES: 12 SERVINGS

- 6 **thick-sliced bacon strips, chopped**
- 3 **cups water**
- 3 **cups chicken stock**
- 1 **teaspoon garlic powder**
- ½ **teaspoon pepper**
- 2 **cups quick-cooking grits**
- 12 **ounces process cheese (Velveeta), cubed (about 2⅓ cups)**
- ½ **cup butter, cubed**
- ½ **cup 2% milk**
- 4 **eggs, lightly beaten**
- 2 **cups (8 ounces) shredded white cheddar cheese**

1. Preheat oven to 350°. In a large saucepan, cook bacon over medium heat until crisp, stirring occasionally. Remove pan from heat. Remove the bacon with a slotted spoon; drain on paper towels.

2. Add water, stock, garlic powder and pepper to bacon drippings; bring to a boil. Slowly stir in grits. Reduce heat to medium-low; cook, covered, for 5-7 minutes or until thickened, stirring occasionally. Remove from heat.

3. Add process cheese and butter; stir until melted. Stir in milk. Slowly stir in eggs until blended. Transfer to a greased 13x9-in. baking dish. Sprinkle with bacon and shredded cheese. Bake, uncovered, 40-45 minutes or until edges are golden brown and cheese is melted. Let stand 10 minutes before serving.

TWO-CHEESE & BACON GRITS BAKE

Wild Rice Casserole

My daughter is a vegetarian, so I'm always looking for meatless dishes she'd enjoy. This creamy rice dish gets a flavor boost with sauted veggies. When cooking for a vegetarian, use vegetable broth instead of chicken broth.

—**VICKI SCHRUPP** LITTLE FALLS, MN

PREP: 55 MIN. • **BAKE:** 25 MIN.
MAKES: 3 SERVINGS

- ½ cup uncooked wild rice
- 1 cup chicken broth
- ½ cup water
- 1 celery rib, sliced
- 1 small onion, chopped
- ½ cup sliced fresh mushrooms
- 2 teaspoons butter
- ⅔ cup condensed cream of mushroom soup, undiluted
- ⅛ teaspoon salt

1. In a small saucepan, bring rice, broth and water to a boil. Reduce heat; cover and simmer 45-50 minutes or until rice is tender and liquid is absorbed.
2. Preheat oven to 350°. In a large nonstick skillet, saute celery, onion and mushrooms in butter until tender. Stir in soup, salt and rice; transfer to a 3-cup baking dish coated with cooking spray. Cover and bake 25-30 minutes or until heated through.

Vidalia Onion Bake

The mild taste of Vidalias makes this bake appealing to onion lovers and nonfans alike. It's an excellent accompaniment to beef, pork or chicken.

—**KATRINA STITT** ZEPHYRHILLS, FL

PREP: 25 MIN. • **BAKE:** 20 MIN.
MAKES: 8 SERVINGS

- 6 large sweet onions, sliced (about 12 cups)
- ½ cup butter, cubed

- 2 cups crushed butter-flavored crackers
- 1 cup shredded Parmesan cheese
- ½ cup shredded cheddar cheese
- ¼ cup shredded Romano cheese

1. Preheat oven to 325°. In a large skillet, saute onions in butter until tender and liquid has evaporated. Place half the onions in a greased 2-qt. baking dish; sprinkle with half the cracker crumbs and cheeses. Repeat layers.
2. Bake, uncovered, 20-25 minutes or until golden brown.

Go for the Grains Casserole

A friend of mine gave me the recipe for this satisfying casserole when I was looking for healthy dishes that would keep me full. This colorful medley has "good for you" written all over it.

—**MELANIE BLAIR** WARSAW, IN

PREP: 25 MIN. • **BAKE:** 55 MIN.
MAKES: 10 SERVINGS

- 5 medium carrots, thinly sliced
- 2 cups frozen corn, thawed
- 1 medium onion, diced
- 1 cup quick-cooking barley
- ½ cup bulgur
- ⅓ cup minced fresh parsley
- 1 teaspoon salt
- ½ teaspoon pepper
- 3 cups vegetable broth
- 1 can (15 ounces) black beans, rinsed and drained
- 1½ cups (6 ounces) shredded reduced-fat cheddar cheese

1. Preheat oven to 350°. In a large bowl, combine carrots, corn, onion, barley, bulgur, parsley, salt and pepper. Stir in broth and beans. Transfer to a 13x9-in. baking dish coated with cooking spray.
2. Cover and bake 50-55 minutes or until grains are tender, stirring once. Sprinkle with cheese. Bake, uncovered, 3-5 minutes longer or until the cheese is melted.

GO FOR THE GRAINS CASSEROLE

SPICY SPANISH RICE

Spicy Spanish Rice

Try this rice dish the next time you're looking for something to perk up a ho-hum dinner. We especially like it with chicken enchiladas. It's also great for potlucks and family get-togethers. You can make the rice less spicy by choosing a milder variety of the canned tomatoes with green chilies.

—**MARILYN WARNER** SHIRLEY, AR

PREP: 10 MIN. • **BAKE:** 55 MIN.
MAKES: 6-8 SERVINGS

- 1 **cup uncooked long grain rice**
- 1 **small onion, chopped**
- 1 **can (2¼ ounces) sliced ripe olives, drained**
- 1 **teaspoon ground cumin**
- 2 **cans (10 ounces each) diced tomatoes and green chilies, undrained**
- 1 **cup water**
- 2 **tablespoons canola oil**
- 1 **cup (4 ounces) shredded Monterey Jack cheese**
- 2 **tablespoons minced fresh cilantro, optional**

1. Preheat oven to 350°. In a greased 2-qt. baking dish, combine rice, onion, olives, cumin, tomatoes, water and oil. Cover and bake 45 minutes.

2. Stir in cheese. Bake, uncovered, 10-15 minutes longer or until rice is tender and liquid is absorbed. Stir in cilantro if desired.

German Noodle Bake

I serve this noodle bake each year for my holiday open house. It is always a hit. Store-bought noodles can be substituted, but I prefer homemade noodles—and so does everyone else.

—**KATHLEEN MEINEKE** COLOGNE, NJ

PREP: 45 MIN. + STANDING • **BAKE:** 30 MIN.
MAKES: 8 SERVINGS

- 1 **cup all-purpose flour**
- ½ **teaspoon salt**
- 2 **eggs, lightly beaten**
- 2 **quarts water**

CHEESE SAUCE
- 3 **tablespoons butter**
- 3 **tablespoons all-purpose flour**
- ½ **teaspoon salt**
- ½ **teaspoon paprika**
- 1½ **cups milk**
- 8 **ounces Swiss cheese, diced**
- 2 **eggs, well beaten**

1. In a small bowl, combine flour and salt. Make a well in center; add eggs. Stir together, forming a dough.

2. Turn dough onto a floured surface; knead 5-6 minutes. Divide dough in half. Roll each portion into a 12x9-in. rectangle. Dust both sides of dough with flour; roll up, jelly-roll style. Cut into ¼-in. slices. Unroll noodles on paper towels; let dry for up to 2 hours.

3. Preheat oven to 350°. In a Dutch oven, bring water to a rapid boil. Add noodles; cook 7-9 minutes or until tender.

4. Meanwhile, in a small saucepan, melt butter. Stir in flour, salt and paprika until smooth; gradually add milk. Bring to a boil; cook and stir 2 minutes or until thickened. Remove from heat; stir in cheese until melted. Stir in eggs.

5. Drain noodles; transfer to a greased 11x7-in. baking dish. Top with cheese sauce. Cover and bake 20 minutes. Uncover; bake 10-15 minutes longer or until bubbly.

GERMAN NOODLE BAKE

Fancy Bean Casserole

My daughter gave me this wonderful recipe, and I've since shared it with many of my friends. This lightened-up version retains all its crunchy, creamy goodness.

—**VENOLA SHARPE** CAMPBELLSVILLE, KY

PREP: 15 MIN. • **BAKE:** 35 MIN.
MAKES: 6 SERVINGS

- 3 **cups frozen French-style green beans, thawed**
- 1 **can (10¾ ounces) reduced-fat reduced-sodium condensed cream of chicken soup, undiluted**
- 1½ **cups frozen corn, thawed**
- 1 **can (8 ounces) sliced water chestnuts, drained**
- 1 **medium onion, chopped**
- ½ **cup reduced-fat sour cream**
- ¼ **cup cubed reduced-fat process cheese (Velveeta)**
- 5 **teaspoons reduced-fat butter**
- ⅓ **cup crushed butter-flavored crackers**
- 2 **tablespoons slivered almonds**

1. Preheat oven to 350°. In a large bowl, combine first seven ingredients. Transfer to an 11x7-in. baking dish coated with cooking spray.
2. In a small skillet, melt butter. Add cracker crumbs and almonds; cook and stir until lightly browned. Sprinkle over top.
3. Bake, uncovered, 35-40 minutes or until heated through and topping is golden brown.
NOTE *This recipe was tested with Land O'Lakes light stick butter.*

DID YOU KNOW?

French-style green beans are green beans that are cut lengthwise into very thin strips.

SWEET POTATO PRALINE SWIRL

Sweet Potato Praline Swirl

Tired of the same old marshmallows on your sweet potatoes? Set this rich, tasty side dish beside the turkey this year and introduce your family to a new favorite.

—**AMANDA DALVINE** ORANGE PARK, FL

PREP: 25 MIN. • **BAKE:** 30 MIN.
MAKES: 6 SERVINGS

- 2 **medium sweet potatoes, peeled and cubed**
- ½ **cup heavy whipping cream**
- 2 **eggs**
- ¼ **cup packed brown sugar**
- 3 **teaspoons vanilla extract**
- 1 **teaspoon ground cinnamon**
- ½ **teaspoon ground ginger**
- ½ **cup chopped pecans**

PRALINE SAUCE
- ⅓ **cup packed brown sugar**
- ¼ **cup sweetened condensed milk**
- 2 **teaspoons butter, melted**
- ½ **teaspoon vanilla extract**

1. Place sweet potatoes in a large saucepan and cover with water. Bring to a boil. Reduce heat; cover and cook 10-15 minutes or until tender. Drain potatoes and place in a large bowl; mash until smooth.
2. Preheat oven to 325°. Beat cream, eggs, brown sugar, vanilla, cinnamon and ginger with sweet potatoes; fold in pecans.
3. Transfer to a greased 8-in.-square baking dish. Combine the sauce ingredients; spoon over potato mixture. Cut through with a knife to swirl the sauce.
4. Bake, uncovered, 30-40 minutes or until a thermometer reads 160°.

ZUCCHINI & SWEET CORN SOUFFLE

Zucchini & Sweet Corn Souffle

As novice gardeners, my husband and I sowed zucchini seeds—15 hills' worth! That's a lot to use up, so I'm happy my family loves this dish. It's a keeper!

—CAROL ELLERBROEK GLADSTONE, IL

PREP: 40 MIN. + STANDING • **BAKE:** 45 MIN.
MAKES: 10 SERVINGS

- 2 **medium zucchini (about 1½ pounds), shredded**
- 2½ **teaspoons salt, divided**
- 6 **eggs**
- 2 **medium ears sweet corn, husks removed**
- 6 **tablespoons butter**
- 2 **green onions, chopped**
- 6 **tablespoons all-purpose flour**
- ¼ **teaspoon pepper**
- 1¼ **cups 2% milk**
- ½ **cup shredded Swiss cheese**

1. Place zucchini in a colander over a plate; sprinkle with 1 teaspoon salt and toss. Let stand 30 minutes. Rinse and drain well; blot dry with paper towels. Meanwhile, separate eggs; let stand at room temperature 30 minutes. Grease a 2½-qt. souffle dish; dust lightly with flour.

2. Preheat oven to 350°. Place corn in a large saucepan; add water to cover. Bring to a boil. Reduce heat; cook, covered, 3-5 minutes or until crisp-tender; drain. Cool slightly. Cut corn from cobs and place in a large bowl.

3. In a large skillet, heat butter over medium-high heat. Add green onions and zucchini; cook and stir until tender. Stir in flour, pepper and remaining salt until blended; gradually stir in milk. Bring to a boil, stirring constantly; cook and stir 1-2 minutes or until sauce is thickened. Add to corn; stir in cheese.

4. Stir a small amount of hot zucchini mixture into egg yolks; return all to bowl, stirring constantly. Cool slightly.

5. In a large bowl, beat egg whites on high speed until stiff but not dry. With a rubber spatula, gently stir a fourth of the egg whites into zucchini mixture. Fold in remaining egg whites. Transfer to prepared dish.

6. Bake 45-50 minutes or until top is puffed and center appears set. Serve immediately.

Sweet Corn & Potato Gratin

This old-fashioned side pairs two popular vegetables, making it a real crowd-pleaser. The garlic and onion flavors appeal to adults, and the crispy topping has kids asking for seconds.

—JENNIFER OLSON PLEASANTON, CA

PREP: 30 MIN. • **BAKE:** 45 MIN. + STANDING
MAKES: 8 SERVINGS

- 1 **medium onion, thinly sliced**
- 2 **tablespoons butter**
- 2 **tablespoons all-purpose flour**
- 2 **garlic cloves, minced**
- 1 **teaspoon salt**
- ½ **teaspoon pepper**
- 1 **cup whole milk**
- 2 **pounds medium Yukon Gold potatoes, peeled and cut into ⅛-inch slices**
- 2 **cups fresh or frozen corn**
- 1 **can (8¼ ounces) cream-style corn**
- ¾ **cup panko (Japanese) bread crumbs**
- 1 **tablespoon butter, melted**

1. Preheat oven to 350°. In a large saucepan, saute onion in butter until tender. Stir in flour, garlic, salt and pepper until blended; gradually add milk. Stir in potatoes. Bring to a boil. Reduce heat; cook and stir 8-10 minutes or until potatoes are crisp-tender.

2. Stir in corn and cream-style corn. Transfer to an 8-in.-square baking dish coated with cooking spray.

3. In a small bowl, combine bread crumbs and butter; sprinkle over potatoes. Bake 45-50 minutes or until golden brown and potatoes are tender. Let stand 10 minutes before serving.

SWEET CORN & POTATO GRATIN

MAKEOVER HASH BROWN CASSEROLE

8 bacon strips, cooked and crumbled
2 green onions, thinly sliced
¼ cup grated Parmesan cheese
¼ cup chopped sun-dried tomatoes (not packed in oil)
¼ cup chicken broth
1 garlic clove, minced
½ teaspoon pepper

1. Preheat oven to 350°. In a large bowl, combine all ingredients. Transfer to a greased 8-in.-square baking dish.
2. Bake, uncovered, 20-25 minutes or until bubbly.
TO MAKE AHEAD *Cook rice and bacon ahead of time and refrigerate for up to 3 days.*

(5)INGREDIENTS Baked Shredded Carrots

Everyone who samples this crisp and tender carrot dish loves it. I make it often when we have fresh produce from our garden. Its bright orange color looks so pretty on our Thanksgiving table.
—**CAROLE HARTWIG** HORICON, WI

PREP: 10 MIN. • **BAKE:** 45 MIN.
MAKES: 6 SERVINGS

6 cups shredded carrots (about 2 pounds)
¾ cup chopped green onions
2 tablespoons sugar
½ teaspoon salt
½ teaspoon celery salt
¼ cup butter, cubed

1. Preheat oven to 325°. In a large bowl, combine carrots, onions, sugar, salt and celery salt. Transfer to an ungreased 1½-qt. baking dish. Dot with butter.
2. Cover and bake 45-50 minutes or until carrots are crisp-tender.

Makeover Hash Brown Casserole

This revised and lightened-up recipe is just as tasty as the original full-fat version!
—**KELLY KIRBY** VICTORIA, BC

PREP: 15 MIN. • **BAKE:** 40 MIN.
MAKES: 12 SERVINGS

1 package (30 ounces) frozen shredded hash brown potatoes, thawed
1 can (10¾ ounces) reduced-fat reduced-sodium condensed cream of chicken soup, undiluted
1 cup (4 ounces) shredded reduced-fat sharp cheddar cheese
⅔ cup reduced-fat sour cream
1 small onion, chopped
½ teaspoon salt
½ teaspoon pepper
¼ cup crushed cornflakes
1 tablespoon butter, melted

1. Preheat oven to 350°. In a large bowl, mix the first seven ingredients. Transfer to a 13x9-in. or 3-qt. baking dish coated with cooking spray.
2. In a small bowl, toss cornflakes with melted butter; sprinkle over top. Bake 40-45 minutes or until golden brown.

Alfredo Rice Casserole

Rice lovers won't be able to get enough of this creamy, savory side. Substitute a mushroom Alfredo or three-cheese sauce for equally scrumptious results.
—**AYSHA SCHURMAN** AMMON, ID

START TO FINISH: 30 MIN.
MAKES: 5 SERVINGS

1⅓ cups refrigerated Alfredo sauce
1 cup cooked brown rice
1 cup cooked wild rice
1 cup marinated quartered artichoke hearts, chopped

**BRUSSELS SPROUTS
AU GRATIN**

Brussels Sprouts au Gratin

Brussels sprouts have always been a mainstay in our house. When I topped them with a creamy sauce, Swiss cheese and bread crumbs, they became a new holiday dinner tradition.

—**GWEN GREGORY** RIO OSO, CA

PREP: 30 MIN. • **BAKE:** 20 MIN.
MAKES: 6 SERVINGS

- 2 pounds fresh Brussels sprouts, quartered
- 1 tablespoon olive oil
- ½ teaspoon salt, divided
- ¼ teaspoon pepper, divided
- ¾ cup cubed sourdough or French bread
- 1 tablespoon butter
- 1 tablespoon minced fresh parsley
- 2 garlic cloves, coarsely chopped
- 1 cup heavy whipping cream
- ⅛ teaspoon crushed red pepper flakes
- ⅛ teaspoon ground nutmeg
- ½ cup shredded white sharp cheddar or Swiss cheese

1. Preheat oven to 450°. Place Brussels sprouts in a large bowl. Add oil, ¼ teaspoon salt and ⅛ teaspoon pepper; toss to coat. Transfer to two ungreased 15x10x1-in. baking pans. Roast 8-10 minutes or until lightly browned and crisp-tender. Reduce oven setting to 400°.

2. Meanwhile, place bread, butter, parsley and garlic in a food processor; pulse until fine crumbs form.

3. Place roasted sprouts in a greased 8-in.-square baking dish. In a small bowl, mix cream, pepper flakes, nutmeg, and remaining salt and pepper. Pour over Brussels sprouts; sprinkle with cheese. Top with the crumb mixture. Bake, uncovered, 15-20 minutes or until bubbly and topping is lightly browned.

Butternut Squash Casserole

This recipe has stood the test of time in my kitchen. Tart apples balance the sweetness of the squash, and it pairs perfectly with pork or chicken.

—**CATHERINE DWYER** FREEDOM, NH

START TO FINISH: 30 MIN.
MAKES: 3 SERVINGS

- 2 **cups sliced tart apples**
- 1 **tablespoon sugar**
- 2 **tablespoons butter, divided**
- 1 **cup mashed cooked butternut squash**
- 1 **teaspoon brown sugar**
- ⅛ **teaspoon salt**
  Dash white pepper

TOPPING
- ½ **cup frosted cornflakes, coarsely crushed**
- 2 **tablespoons chopped pecans**
- 2 **tablespoons brown sugar**
- 2 **teaspoons butter, melted**

1. Preheat oven to 350°. In a large skillet, saute the apples and sugar in 1 tablespoon butter 4-5 minutes or until crisp-tender. Place in a 1-qt. baking dish coated with cooking spray; set aside.
2. In a bowl, combine squash, brown sugar, salt, pepper and remaining butter; spoon over apples. Combine the topping ingredients; sprinkle over casserole.
3. Bake, uncovered, 15-20 minutes or until heated through and topping is browned.

Hearty Maple Beans

These beans work well for any gathering because they can be made in advance and kept warm in a slow cooker for hours without losing any flavor.

—**MARGARET GLASSIC** EASTON, PA

PREP: 15 MIN. • **BAKE:** 25 MIN.
MAKES: 8 SERVINGS

HEARTY MAPLE BEANS

- 6 **bacon strips, diced**
- ½ **pound smoked kielbasa or Polish sausage, sliced**
- 1 **small onion, chopped**
- 1 **can (15¾ ounces) pork and beans**
- 1 **can (16 ounces) kidney beans, rinsed and drained**
- 1 **can (16 ounces) butter beans, rinsed and drained**
- ½ **cup maple syrup**
- 3 **tablespoons white vinegar**
- 3 **tablespoons ketchup**
- 3 **tablespoons prepared mustard**

1. Preheat oven to 350°. In a large skillet, cook bacon over medium heat until crisp. Using a slotted spoon, remove to paper towels. Drain, reserving 1 tablespoon drippings. In drippings, cook sausage and onion over medium-high heat until sausage is lightly browned. Stir in bacon and remaining ingredients.
2. Transfer to an ungreased 2-qt. baking dish. Bake, uncovered, 25-30 minutes or until bubbly.

BUTTERNUT SQUASH CASSEROLE

Special Cauliflower

Dijon mustard adds a little zip to cauliflower. Yogurt, mayonnaise and cheddar cheese lend a creamy texture.

—RITA REINKE WAUWATOSA, WI

START TO FINISH: 30 MIN.
MAKES: 6 SERVINGS

- 4 cups fresh cauliflowerets
- 2 tablespoons plain yogurt
- 2 tablespoons mayonnaise
- 1 teaspoon Dijon mustard
- ¼ teaspoon dill weed
- ¼ teaspoon salt
- ¼ teaspoon garlic powder
- ½ cup shredded cheddar cheese

1. Preheat oven to 350°. Place cauliflower in a steamer basket; place in a large saucepan over 1 in. of water. Bring to a boil; cover and steam 6-8 minutes or until crisp-tender.
2. Meanwhile, in a bowl, combine yogurt, mayonnaise, mustard, dill, salt and garlic powder.
3. Transfer cauliflower to an ungreased 3-cup baking dish; top with yogurt mixture and cheese. Bake, uncovered, 8-10 minutes or until heated through and cheese is melted.

Broccoli and Carrot Cheese Bake

A creamy cheese sauce makes vegetables so much more appealing to my crowd. So this holiday side dish is guaranteed to please even the pickiest veggie-phobics. It calls for vegetables that are available year round, so it works for Easter as well as winter holiday menus.

—TRISHA KRUSE EAGLE, ID

PREP: 25 MIN. • **BAKE:** 30 MIN. + STANDING
MAKES: 9 SERVINGS

- 2 cups thinly sliced fresh carrots
- 2 cups fresh broccoli florets
- 3 eggs
- 2 cups 2% milk
- ¼ cup butter, melted
- ½ teaspoon salt
- ¼ teaspoon ground nutmeg
- ¼ teaspoon pepper
- 1½ cups (6 ounces) grated Gruyere or Swiss cheese, divided
- 6 cups cubed egg bread

1. Place carrots and broccoli in a steamer basket; place in a large saucepan over 1 in. of water. Bring to a boil; cover and steam 3-4 minutes or until vegetables are crisp-tender.
2. Preheat oven to 325°. In a large bowl, whisk eggs, milk, butter, salt, nutmeg and pepper. Stir in vegetables and 1 cup cheese. Gently stir in bread.
3. Transfer to a greased 11x7-in. baking dish; sprinkle with remaining cheese. Bake, uncovered, 30-35 minutes or until a knife inserted near the center comes out clean. Let stand 10 minutes before serving.

TO MAKE AHEAD *This recipe can be made a day ahead; cover and refrigerate. Remove from the refrigerator 30 minutes before baking. Bake as directed.*

BROCCOLI AND CARROT CHEESE BAKE

TEX-MEX SUMMER SQUASH CASSEROLE

Crunchy Broccoli Bake

Lima beans combine nicely with broccoli in this veggie casserole. Water chestnuts and a cereal topping add a fun crunch.

—**RON SLIVON** SURPRISE, AZ

PREP: 15 MIN. • **BAKE:** 30 MIN.
MAKES: 9 SERVINGS

- 6 **cups frozen chopped broccoli, thawed**
- 1½ **cups frozen lima beans, thawed**
- 1 **can (10¾ ounces) condensed cream of mushroom soup, undiluted**
- 1 **cup (8 ounces) sour cream**
- 1 **envelope onion soup mix**
- 1 **can (8 ounces) water chestnuts, drained and chopped**
- ¼ **teaspoon garlic powder**
- 3 **cups crisp rice cereal, crushed**
- ½ **cup butter, melted**

1. Preheat oven to 325°. Place broccoli and beans in a greased 2-qt. baking dish. Combine soup, sour cream, soup mix, water chestnuts and garlic powder. Spread over vegetables.
2. Combine cereal and butter; sprinkle over top. Bake, uncovered, for 30-35 minutes or until edges begin to brown.

DID YOU KNOW?

Summer squash have edible thin skins and soft seeds. Zucchini, pattypan and yellow are the most common varieties. Choose firm summer squash with brightly colored skin that's free from spots and bruises. Generally, the smaller the squash, the more tender it will be. Refrigerate summer squash in a plastic bag for up to 5 days. Before using, wash squash and trim both ends. One pound summer squash equals about 3 medium or 2½ cups chopped.

Tex-Mex Summer Squash Casserole

Mild-flavored yellow squash gets a big boost from flavor-packed chilies, jalapenos and red onion. You can also make this dish with zucchini.

—**TOMMY LOMBARDO** EUCLID, OH

PREP: 15 MIN. • **BAKE:** 40 MIN. + STANDING
MAKES: 10 SERVINGS

- 7 **medium yellow summer squash, sliced (about 10 cups)**
- 2¼ **cups (9 ounces) shredded cheddar cheese, divided**
- 1 **medium onion, chopped**
- 1 **can (4 ounces) chopped green chilies**
- 1 **can (4 ounces) diced jalapeno peppers, drained**
- ¼ **cup all-purpose flour**
- ½ **teaspoon salt**
- ¾ **cup salsa**
- 4 **green onions, sliced**
- ¼ **cup chopped red onion**

1. Preheat oven to 400°. In a large bowl, combine squash, ¾ cup cheese, onion, chilies and jalapenos. Sprinkle with flour and salt; toss to combine.
2. Transfer to a greased 13x9-in. baking dish. Bake, covered, 30-40 minutes or until squash is tender.
3. Spoon salsa over top; sprinkle with remaining 1½ cups cheese. Bake, uncovered, 10-15 minutes longer or until golden brown. Let stand 10 minutes. Top with green and red onions before serving.

Slow Cooker

WITH A LITTLE HELP FROM YOUR SLOW COOKER, YOU CAN SERVE UP HOT AND HEARTY COMFORTS...EVEN ON YOUR BUSIEST NIGHT!

SWEET & SPICY CHICKEN WINGS
PAGE 115

GRANDMA SCHWARTZ'S ROULADEN *PAGE 153*

MOLTEN MOCHA CAKE
PAGE 221

JALAPENO SPINACH DIP

In a 1½-qt. slow cooker, combine the first 10 ingredients. Cover and cook on low for 2-3 hours or until heated through. Serve with chips.

NOTE *Wear disposable gloves when cutting hot peppers; the oils can burn skin. Avoid touching your face.*

Cranberry Hot Wings

Chicken wings get special treatment from cranberry sauce and a hint of citrus in this yummy appetizer.

—**ROBIN HAAS** CRANSTON, RI

PREP: 50 MIN. • **COOK:** 2 HOURS
MAKES: ABOUT 2½ DOZEN

- 1 can (14 ounces) jellied cranberry sauce, cubed
- 2 tablespoons ground mustard
- 2 tablespoons hot pepper sauce
- 2 tablespoons reduced-sodium soy sauce
- 2 tablespoons honey
- 1 tablespoon cider vinegar
- 2 teaspoons garlic powder
- 1 teaspoon grated orange peel
- 3 pounds chicken wings
  Blue cheese salad dressing and celery ribs

1. In a 5-qt. slow cooker, combine the first eight ingredients. Cover and cook on low for 45 minutes or until cranberry sauce is melted.

2. Meanwhile, cut wings into three sections; discard wing tip sections. Place wings on a greased broiler pan. Broil 4-6 in. from the heat for 15-20 minutes or until lightly browned, turning occasionally.

3. Transfer wings to slow cooker; toss to coat. Cover and cook on high for 2-3 hours or until tender. Serve wings with salad dressing and celery ribs.

NOTE *Uncooked chicken wing sections (wingettes) may be substituted for whole chicken wings.*

Jalapeno Spinach Dip

Everyone loves spinach dip, and this version gets a little kick from jalapeno. Just mix the ingredients together in the slow cooker for a savory and creamy dip.

—**MICHAELA DEBELIUS** WADDELL, AZ

PREP: 10 MIN. • **COOK:** 2 HOURS
MAKES: 16 SERVINGS (¼ CUP EACH)

- 2 packages (10 ounces each) frozen chopped spinach, thawed and squeezed dry
- 2 packages (8 ounces each) cream cheese, softened
- 1 cup grated Parmesan cheese
- 1 cup half-and-half cream
- ½ cup finely chopped onion
- ¼ cup chopped seeded jalapeno peppers
- 2 teaspoons Worcestershire sauce
- 2 teaspoons hot pepper sauce
- 1 teaspoon garlic powder
- 1 teaspoon dill weed
  Tortilla chips

Sweet & Spicy Peanuts

With a caramel-like coating, these crunchy peanuts have a touch of heat from the hot sauce. They make a tasty snack, or bag them up to sell at charity bake sales.

—*TASTE OF HOME* TEST KITCHEN

PREP: 10 MIN. • **COOK:** 1½ HOURS + COOLING
MAKES: 4 CUPS

- 3 **cups salted peanuts**
- ½ **cup sugar**
- ⅓ **cup packed brown sugar**
- 2 **tablespoons hot water**
- 2 **tablespoons butter, melted**
- 1 **tablespoon Sriracha Asian hot chili sauce or hot pepper sauce**
- 1 **teaspoon chili powder**

1. Place peanuts in a greased 1½-qt. slow cooker. In a small bowl, combine the sugars, water, butter, hot sauce and chili powder. Pour over peanuts. Cover and cook on high for 1½ hours, stirring once.

2. Spread on waxed paper to cool. Store in an airtight container.

CARAMEL APPLE CIDER

SWEET & SPICY PEANUTS

Caramel Apple Cider

Spiced with cinnamon sticks, allspice and caramel, this warm-you-up sipper is sure to chase away winter's chill. Serve brimming mugs of the hot beverage alongside a platter of sugar cookies at your next get-together.

—*TASTE OF HOME* TEST KITCHEN

PREP: 5 MIN. • **COOK:** 2 HOURS
MAKES: 12 SERVINGS (¾ CUP EACH)

- 8 **cups apple cider or juice**
- 1 **cup caramel flavoring syrup**
- ¼ **cup lemon juice**
- 1 **vanilla bean**
- 2 **cinnamon sticks (3 inches)**
- 1 **tablespoon whole allspice**
  Whipped cream, hot caramel ice cream topping and cinnamon sticks (3 inches), optional

1. In a 3-qt. slow cooker, combine the apple cider, caramel syrup and lemon juice. Split the vanilla bean and scrape seeds; add seeds to cider mixture. Place the bean, cinnamon sticks and allspice on a double thickness of cheesecloth; bring up corners of the cloth and tie with string to form a bag. Add to the cider mixture.

2. Cover and cook on low for 2-3 hours or until heated through. Discard spice bag. Pour cider into mugs; garnish with whipped cream, caramel topping and additional cinnamon sticks if desired.

NOTE *This recipe was tested with Torani brand flavoring syrup. Look for it in the coffee section.*

Barbecued Party Starters

These sweet and tangy bites are sure to tide everyone over until dinner. At the buffet, set out some fun toothpicks to make for easy nibbling.

—ANASTASIA WEISS PUNXSUTAWNEY, PA

PREP: 30 MIN. • **COOK:** 2¼ HOURS
MAKES: 16 SERVINGS (⅓ CUP EACH)

- 1 **pound ground beef**
- ¼ **cup finely chopped onion**
- 1 **package (16 ounces) miniature hot dogs, drained**
- 1 **jar (12 ounces) apricot preserves**
- 1 **cup barbecue sauce**
- 1 **can (20 ounces) pineapple chunks, drained**

1. In a large bowl, combine beef and onion, mixing lightly but thoroughly. Shape into 1-in. balls. In a large skillet over medium heat, cook meatballs in two batches until cooked through, turning occasionally.

2. Using a slotted spoon, transfer meatballs to a 3-qt. slow cooker. Add the hot dogs; stir in the preserves and barbecue sauce. Cook, covered, on high 2-3 hours or until heated through.

3. Stir in the pineapple; cook, covered, 15-20 minutes longer or until mixture is heated through.

Mini Teriyaki Turkey Sandwiches

Pulled turkey in a delicious teriyaki sauce makes for incredible snack-sized sandwiches. Serve the turkey on lightly toasted sweet dinner rolls to add a little crunch.

—AMANDA HOOP SEAMAN, OH

PREP: 20 MIN. • **COOK:** 5½ HOURS
MAKES: 20 SERVINGS

- 2 **boneless skinless turkey breast halves (2 pounds each)**
- ⅔ **cup packed brown sugar**
- ⅔ **cup reduced-sodium soy sauce**
- ¼ **cup cider vinegar**

MINI TERIYAKI TURKEY SANDWICHES

- 3 **garlic cloves, minced**
- 1 **tablespoon minced fresh gingerroot**
- ½ **teaspoon pepper**
- 2 **tablespoons cornstarch**
- 2 **tablespoons cold water**
- 20 **Hawaiian sweet rolls**
- 2 **tablespoons butter, melted**

1. Place turkey in a 5- or 6-qt. slow cooker. In a small bowl, combine the brown sugar, soy sauce, vinegar, garlic, ginger and pepper; pour over turkey. Cook, covered, on low 5-6 hours or until meat is tender.

2. Remove turkey from slow cooker. In a small bowl, mix cornstarch and cold water until smooth; gradually stir into cooking liquid. When cool enough to handle, shred meat with two forks and return meat to slow cooker. Cook, covered, on high 30-35 minutes or until sauce is thickened.

3. Preheat oven to 325°. Split rolls and brush cut sides with butter; place on an ungreased baking sheet, cut side up. Bake 8-10 minutes or until toasted and golden brown. Spoon ⅓ cup turkey mixture on roll bottoms. Replace tops.

BARBECUED PARTY STARTERS

I've been making this recipe for years. Everyone flips over the wonderful flavors. When cooled, this cheesy appetizer is also fantastic as a spread for crackers or cut veggies.

—**CLEO GONSKE** REDDING, CA

Garlic Swiss Fondue

PREP: 10 MIN. • **COOK:** 2 HOURS
MAKES: 3 CUPS

- 4 **cups (16 ounces) shredded Swiss cheese**
- 1 **can (10¾ ounces) condensed cheddar cheese soup, undiluted**
- 2 **tablespoons sherry or chicken broth**
- 1 **tablespoon Dijon mustard**
- 2 **garlic cloves, minced**
- 2 **teaspoons hot pepper sauce**
  Cubed French bread baguette, sliced apples and seedless red grapes

In a 1½-qt. slow cooker, mix the first six ingredients. Cook, covered, on low 2 to 2½ hours or until the cheese is melted, stirring every 30 minutes. Serve warm with bread cubes and fruit.

GARLIC SWISS FONDUE

Buffalo Wing Dip

If you love spicy wings, you'll adore this dip! The creamy texture and Buffalo sauce make for an addictive combination.
—*TASTE OF HOME* TEST KITCHEN

PREP: 20 MIN. • **COOK:** 2 HOURS
MAKES: 6 CUPS

- 2 packages (8 ounces each) cream cheese, softened
- ½ cup ranch salad dressing
- ½ cup sour cream
- 5 tablespoons crumbled blue cheese
- 2 cups shredded cooked chicken
- ½ cup Buffalo wing sauce
- 2 cups (8 ounces) shredded cheddar cheese, divided
- 1 green onion, sliced
  Tortilla chips

1. In a small bowl, combine the cream cheese, dressing, sour cream and blue cheese. Transfer to a 3-qt. slow cooker. Layer with chicken, wing sauce and 1 cup cheese. Cover and cook on low for 2-3 hours or until heated through.
2. Sprinkle with remaining cheese and onion. Serve with tortilla chips.

Southwestern Pulled Pork Crostini

Look to the Southwest for a hearty, unique take on crostini. Perfect for casual parties any time of year, these bites are always popular. Apricot preserves lend the perfect hint of sweetness.
—**RANDY CARTWRIGHT** LINDEN, WI

PREP: 45 MIN. • **COOK:** 6 HOURS
MAKES: 32 APPETIZERS

- 1 boneless pork shoulder butt roast (about 2 pounds)
- ½ cup lime juice
- 2 envelopes mesquite marinade mix
- ¼ cup sugar
- ¼ cup olive oil

SALSA
- 1 cup frozen corn, thawed
- 1 cup canned black beans, rinsed and drained
- 1 small tomato, finely chopped
- 2 tablespoons finely chopped seeded jalapeno pepper
- 2 tablespoons lime juice
- 2 tablespoons olive oil
- 1½ teaspoons ground cumin
- 1 teaspoon chili powder
- ½ teaspoon salt
- ¼ teaspoon crushed red pepper flakes

SAUCE
- 1 can (4 ounces) chopped green chilies
- ⅓ cup apricot preserves
- ⅛ teaspoon salt

CROSTINI
- 32 slices French bread baguette (¼ inch thick)
- ¼ cup olive oil
- ⅔ cup crumbled queso fresco or feta cheese
  Lime wedges, optional

1. Place roast in a 3-qt. slow cooker. In a small bowl, whisk lime juice, marinade mix, sugar and oil until blended; pour over roast. Cook, covered, on low 6-8 hours or until meat is tender.
2. For salsa, in a small bowl, combine corn, beans, tomato and jalapeno. Stir in lime juice, oil and seasonings. In a small saucepan, combine sauce ingredients; cook and stir over low heat until blended.
3. For crostini, preheat broiler. Brush bread slices on both sides with oil; place on ungreased baking sheets. Broil 3-4 in. from heat 1-2 minutes on each side or until golden brown.
4. Remove roast from slow cooker; cool slightly. Shred pork with two forks. To serve, layer toasts with salsa, pork and cheese. Top with sauce. If desired, serve with lime wedges.

BUFFALO WING DIP

SOUTHWESTERN PULLED PORK CROSTINI

(5) INGREDIENTS Creamy Cranberry Meatballs

Here's a rich and juicy take on an all-time party staple. After your event is over, turn these slow-cooked meatballs into a satisfying entree. Simply serve the leftovers on a bed of fluffy rice or buttered noodles.

—AMY WARREN MAINEVILLE, OH

PREP: 10 MIN. • **COOK:** 3 HOURS
MAKES: ABOUT 5 DOZEN

- 2 **envelopes brown gravy mix**
- 1 **package (32 ounces) frozen fully cooked Swedish meatballs**
- ⅔ **cup jellied cranberry sauce**
- 2 **teaspoons Dijon mustard**
- ¼ **cup heavy whipping cream**

Prepare gravy mix according to package directions. In a 4-qt. slow cooker, combine the meatballs, cranberry sauce, mustard and gravy. Cover and cook on low for 3-4 hours or until heated through, adding cream during the last 30 minutes of cooking.

TOP TIP

Taking a slow-cooked appetizer to a party? Slow cookers are ideal for keeping warm foods warm, but remember to help out the hostess by bringing an extension cord as well. If you're going to a covered-dish event like a charity potluck, consider bringing a few along to help out everyone with a slow cooker in tow.

CREAMY CRANBERRY MEATBALLS

Sweet & Spicy Chicken Wings

The meat literally falls from the bones of these wings. Spice lovers will get a kick out of the big sprinkle of red pepper flakes.

—**SUE BAYLESS** PRIOR LAKE, MN

PREP: 25 MIN. • **COOK:** 5 HOURS
MAKES: ABOUT 2½ DOZEN

- 3 **pounds chicken wings**
- 1½ **cups ketchup**
- 1 **cup packed brown sugar**
- 1 **small onion, finely chopped**
- ¼ **cup finely chopped sweet red pepper**
- 2 **tablespoons chili powder**
- 2 **tablespoons Worcestershire sauce**
- 1½ **teaspoons crushed red pepper flakes**
- 1 **teaspoon ground mustard**
- 1 **teaspoon dried basil**
- 1 **teaspoon dried thyme**
- 1 **teaspoon pepper**

Cut wings into three sections; discard wing tip sections. Place chicken in a 4-qt. slow cooker. In a small bowl, combine the remaining ingredients. Pour over chicken; stir until coated. Cover and cook on low for 5-6 hours or until chicken juices run clear.
NOTE *Uncooked chicken wing sections (wingettes) may be substituted for whole chicken wings.*

SWEET KAHLUA COFFEE

Sweet Kahlua Coffee

Want to perk up your java? With Kahlua, creme de cacao and a dollop of whipped cream, this chocolaty coffee makes the perfect after-dinner treat.

—**RUTH GRUCHOW** YORBA LINDA, CA

PREP: 10 MIN. • **COOK:** 3 HOURS
MAKES: 8 SERVINGS (2¼ QUARTS)

- 2 **quarts hot water**
- ½ **cup Kahlua (coffee liqueur)**
- ¼ **cup creme de cacao**
- 3 **tablespoons instant coffee granules**
- 2 **cups heavy whipping cream**
- ¼ **cup sugar**
- 1 **teaspoon vanilla extract**
- 2 **tablespoons grated semisweet chocolate**

1. In a 4-qt. slow cooker, mix water, Kahlua, creme de cacao and coffee granules. Cook, covered, on low for 3-4 hours or until heated through.
2. In a large bowl, beat cream until it begins to thicken. Add sugar and vanilla; beat until soft peaks form. Serve warm coffee with whipped cream and chocolate.

SWEET & SPICY CHICKEN WINGS

REUBEN SPREAD

Reuben Spread

I'm a big fan of Reuben sandwiches and I adore anything with that flavor combo. The sandwich becomes sharable fun when you blend corned beef with Swiss, sauerkraut and Thousand Island dressing to make a spread for rye bread or crackers.
—**JUNE HERKE** WATERTOWN, SD

PREP: 10 MIN. • **COOK:** 4 HOURS
MAKES: 30 SERVINGS
(2 TABLESPOONS EACH)

- 2 **packages (8 ounces each) cream cheese, cubed**
- 4 **cups (16 ounces) shredded Swiss cheese**
- 1 **can (14 ounces) sauerkraut, rinsed and well drained**
- 4 **packages (2 ounces each) thinly sliced deli corned beef, chopped**
- ½ **cup Thousand Island salad dressing**
  Snack rye bread or rye crackers

1. Place the first five ingredients in a 1½-qt. slow cooker; stir to combine. Cook, covered, on low 4 to 4½ hours or until heated through.
2. Stir to blend. Serve spread with bread.

Creamy Artichoke Dip

My sister, Teresa, got a creamy dip recipe from a friend and she passed it along to me. It has since become a family favorite. It's loaded with cheese, artichokes and just the right amount of spice for a crowd-pleasing party starter!
—**MARY SPENCER** GREENDALE, WI

PREP: 20 MIN. • **COOK:** 1 HOUR
MAKES: 5 CUPS

- 2 **cans (14 ounces each) water-packed artichoke hearts, rinsed, drained and coarsely chopped**
- 2 **cups (8 ounces) shredded part-skim mozzarella cheese**
- 1 **package (8 ounces) cream cheese, cubed**
- 1 **cup shredded Parmesan cheese**
- ½ **cup mayonnaise**
- ½ **cup shredded Swiss cheese**
- 2 **tablespoons lemon juice**
- 2 **tablespoons plain yogurt**
- 1 **tablespoon seasoned salt**
- 1 **tablespoon chopped seeded jalapeno pepper**
- 1 **teaspoon garlic powder**
  Tortilla chips

In a 3-qt. slow cooker, combine the first 11 ingredients. Cover and cook on low for 1 hour or until heated through. Serve with tortilla chips.
NOTE *Wear disposable gloves when cutting hot peppers; the oils can burn skin. Avoid touching your face.*

CREAMY ARTICHOKE DIP

Loaded Veggie Dip

Packed with veggies and bursting with flavor, this chunky dip is sure to be a hit at your next get-together. Serve it with thick crackers that can be used as scoops.

—**PATRICE SLAUGHTER** PALM BAY, FL

PREP: 1 HOUR • **COOK:** 1 HOUR
MAKES: 5 CUPS

- ¾ **cup finely chopped fresh broccoli**
- ½ **cup finely chopped cauliflower**
- ½ **cup finely chopped fresh carrot**
- ½ **cup finely chopped red onion**
- ½ **cup finely chopped celery**
- 2 **garlic cloves, minced**
- 4 **tablespoons olive oil, divided**
- 1 **can (14 ounces) water-packed artichoke hearts, rinsed, drained and chopped**
- 1 **package (6½ ounces) spreadable garlic and herb cream cheese**
- 1 **package (1.4 ounces) vegetable recipe mix (Knorr)**
- 1 **teaspoon garlic powder**
- ½ **teaspoon white pepper**
- ⅛ **to ¼ teaspoon cayenne pepper**
- ¼ **cup vegetable broth**
- ¼ **cup half-and-half cream**
- 3 **cups (12 ounces) shredded Italian cheese blend**
- ½ **cup minced fresh basil**
- 1 **package (9 ounces) fresh spinach, finely chopped**
  Assorted crackers or baked pita chips

1. In a large skillet, saute the broccoli, cauliflower, carrot, onion, celery and garlic in 2 tablespoons oil until tender. Stir in the artichokes, cream cheese, vegetable recipe mix, garlic powder, white pepper and cayenne; set aside.
2. In a 3-qt. slow cooker, combine broth, cream and remaining oil. Stir in broccoli mixture, Italian cheese blend and basil. Fold in spinach. Cover and cook on low for 1-2 hours or until cheese is melted and spinach is tender. Serve with crackers.

Chai Tea

A wonderfully heartwarming aroma always wafts from the slow cooker as this pleasantly flavored chai tea simmers.

—**CRYSTAL BRUNS** ILIFF, CO

PREP: 20 MIN. • **COOK:** 8 HOURS
MAKES: 12 SERVINGS (3 QUARTS)

- 3½ **ounces fresh gingerroot, peeled and thinly sliced**
- 25 **whole cloves**
- 15 **cardamom pods, crushed**
- 3 **cinnamon sticks (3 inches)**
- 3 **whole peppercorns**
- 3½ **quarts water**
- 8 **individual black tea bags**
- 1 **can (14 ounces) sweetened condensed milk**

1. Place the ginger, cloves, cardamom, cinnamon sticks and peppercorns on a double thickness of cheesecloth; bring up corners of cloth and tie with string to form a bag. Add spice bag and water to a 5- or 6-qt. slow cooker. Cover and cook on low for 8 hours.
2. Add tea bags; cover and steep for 3-5 minutes. Discard tea bags and spice bag. Stir in milk; heat through. Serve warm.

CHAI TEA

Spiced Ambrosia Punch

The flavor of chai inspired this twist on a basic spiced cider punch. Apricot and peach nectars are a wonderful surprise when you take the first sip.

—AYSHA SCHURMAN AMMON, ID

PREP: 15 MIN. • **COOK:** 3 HOURS
MAKES: 10 SERVINGS (¾ CUP EACH)

- 3½ cups apple cider or juice
- 3 cups apricot nectar
- 1 cup peach nectar or additional apricot nectar
- ¼ cup water
- 3 tablespoons lemon juice
- ½ teaspoon ground cardamom
- ½ teaspoon ground nutmeg
- 2 cinnamon sticks (3 inches)
- 1 teaspoon finely chopped fresh gingerroot
- 1 teaspoon grated orange peel
- 8 whole cloves
  Lemon or orange slices, optional

1. In a 3- or 4-qt. slow cooker, combine the first seven ingredients. Place the cinnamon sticks, ginger, orange peel and cloves on a double thickness of cheesecloth. Gather corners of cloth to enclose seasonings; tie securely with string. Place bag in slow cooker.
2. Cook, covered, on low 3-4 hours or until heated through. Remove and discard spice bag. Serve warm, with lemon slices, if desired.

TOP TIP

Fresh gingerroot should have smooth skin. If wrinkled and cracked, the root is dry. When stored in a heavy-duty resealable plastic bag, unpeeled gingerroot can be frozen for up to 1 year. When needed, peel and grate.

SPICED AMBROSIA PUNCH

Crispy Snack Mix

Here's a recipe that proves you can make just about anything in a slow cooker, even a delightfully crispy snack mix!

—**JANE PAIR SIMS** DE LEON, TX

PREP: 10 MIN. • **COOK:** 2½ HOURS
MAKES: ABOUT 2½ QUARTS

- 4½ cups crispy chow mein noodles
- 4 cups Rice Chex
- 1 can (9¾ ounces) salted cashews
- 1 cup flaked coconut, toasted
- ½ cup butter, melted
- 2 tablespoons reduced-sodium soy sauce
- 2¼ teaspoons curry powder
- ¾ teaspoon ground ginger

1. In a 5-qt. slow cooker, combine the noodles, cereal, cashews and coconut. In a small bowl, whisk the butter, soy sauce, curry powder and ginger; drizzle over cereal mixture and mix well.
2. Cover and cook on low for 2½ hours, stirring every 30 minutes. Serve warm or at room temperature.

CRISPY SNACK MIX

WARM CRAB DIP

Warm Crab Dip

Slow-cooked dips are ideal for entertaining since they free up the oven. As a bonus, leftovers are great served over a baked potato the next day.

—**SUSAN D'AMORE** WEST CHESTER, PA

PREP: 20 MIN. • **COOK:** 1½ HOURS
MAKES: 2⅓ CUPS

- 1 package (8 ounces) cream cheese, softened
- 2 green onions, chopped
- ¼ cup chopped sweet red pepper
- 2 tablespoons minced fresh parsley
- 2 tablespoons mayonnaise
- 1 tablespoon Dijon mustard
- 1 teaspoon Worcestershire sauce
- ¼ teaspoon salt
- ¼ teaspoon pepper
- 2 cans (6 ounces each) lump crabmeat, drained
- 2 tablespoons capers, drained
  Dash hot pepper sauce
  Assorted crackers

1. In a 1½-qt. slow cooker, combine the first nine ingredients; stir in crab.
2. Cover and cook on low for 1-2 hours. Stir in capers and pepper sauce; cook 30 minutes longer to allow flavors to blend. Serve with crackers.

GINGER CHICKEN NOODLE SOUP

Ginger Chicken Noodle Soup

This is one of my favorite soup recipes to serve in the winter because it's easy to make and fills the whole house with a wonderful aroma. My whole family loves it!

—**BRANDY STANSBURY** EDNA, TX

PREP: 15 MIN. • **COOK:** 3½ HOURS
MAKES: 8 SERVINGS (2½ QUARTS)

- 1 **pound boneless skinless chicken breasts, cubed**
- 2 **medium carrots, shredded**
- 3 **tablespoons sherry or reduced-sodium chicken broth**
- 2 **tablespoons rice vinegar**
- 1 **tablespoon reduced-sodium soy sauce**
- 2 **to 3 teaspoons minced fresh gingerroot**
- ¼ **teaspoon pepper**
- 6 **cups reduced-sodium chicken broth**
- 1 **cup water**
- 2 **cups fresh snow peas, halved**
- 2 **ounces uncooked angel hair pasta, broken into thirds**

1. In a 5-qt. slow cooker, combine the first seven ingredients; stir in broth and water. Cook, covered, on low 3-4 hours or until chicken is tender.
2. Stir in snow peas and pasta. Cook, covered, on low 30 minutes longer or until snow peas and pasta are tender.

Cuban-Style Pork Sandwiches

My lighter version of a favorite restaurant-style sandwich is loaded with tangy flavor. If you don't have a panini maker, tuck the sandwiches under the broiler until the bread browns and the cheese melts.

—**ROBIN HAAS** CRANSTON, RI

PREP: 20 MIN. • **COOK:** 6 HOURS + STANDING
MAKES: 10 SERVINGS

- 1 **large onion, cut into wedges**
- ¾ **cup reduced-sodium chicken broth**
- 1 **cup minced fresh parsley**
- 7 **garlic cloves, minced and divided**
- 2 **tablespoons cider vinegar**
- 1 **tablespoon plus 1½ teaspoons lemon juice, divided**
- 2 **teaspoons ground cumin**
- 1 **teaspoon ground mustard**
- 1 **teaspoon dried oregano**
- ½ **teaspoon salt**
- ½ **teaspoon pepper**
- 1 **boneless pork shoulder butt roast (3 to 4 pounds)**
- 1¼ **cups fat-free mayonnaise**
- 2 **tablespoons Dijon mustard**
- 10 **whole wheat hamburger buns, split**
- 1¼ **cups (5 ounces) shredded reduced-fat Swiss cheese**
- 1 **medium onion, thinly sliced and separated into rings**
- 2 **whole dill pickles, sliced**

1. Place onion wedges and broth in a 5-qt. slow cooker. In a small bowl, combine the parsley, 5 garlic cloves, vinegar, 1 tablespoon lemon juice, cumin, mustard, oregano, salt and pepper; rub over pork. Add to slow cooker. Cover and cook on low for 6-8 hours or until meat is tender.
2. Remove meat; let stand for 10 minutes before slicing. In another small bowl, combine the mayonnaise, mustard and remaining garlic and lemon juice; spread over buns. Layer bun bottoms with pork, cheese, sliced onion and pickles; replace tops.
3. Cook on a panini maker or indoor grill for 2-3 minutes or until buns brown and cheese melts.

CUBAN-STYLE PORK SANDWICHES

Pork & Rice Noodle Soup

My husband and I are crazy about the Korean noodle bowls at our favorite restaurant. I came up with this quick soup to enjoy those wonderful flavors at home. Look for rice noodles and coconut milk in the Asian section of the grocery store.

PREP: 15 MIN. • **COOK:** 6½ HOURS
MAKES: 8 SERVINGS (3 QUARTS)

- 1½ pounds boneless country-style pork ribs, cut into 1-inch cubes
- 6 garlic cloves, minced
- 2 tablespoons minced fresh gingerroot
- 2 cans (14½ ounces each) reduced-sodium chicken broth
- 2 cans (13.66 ounces each) coconut milk
- ¼ cup reduced-sodium soy sauce
- 4 ounces uncooked thin rice noodles
- 2 cups frozen pepper strips, thawed
- 1 can (8 ounces) sliced water chestnuts, drained
- ¼ cup minced fresh cilantro
- 2 tablespoons lime juice

1. In a 5-qt. slow cooker, combine the first six ingredients. Cook, covered, on low 6-8 hours or until meat is tender.
2. Add rice noodles, pepper strips and water chestnuts; cook 30-35 minutes longer or until noodles are tender. If desired, skim soup. Just before serving, stir in cilantro and lime juice.

Butternut Squash Soup

The deep golden color and creamy texture of this soup are comforting on a chilly fall day. The cinnamon, ginger and garlic are warm and soothing .
—**JACKIE CAMPBELL** STANHOPE, NJ

PREP: 30 MIN. • **COOK:** 6¼ HOURS
MAKES: 14 SERVINGS (2½ QUARTS)

- 1 medium onion, chopped
- 2 tablespoons butter
- 1 medium butternut squash (about 4 pounds), peeled and cubed
- 3 cans (14½ ounces each) vegetable broth
- 1 tablespoon brown sugar
- 1 tablespoon minced fresh gingerroot
- 1 garlic clove, minced
- 1 cinnamon stick (3 inches)
- 1 package (8 ounces) cream cheese, softened and cubed

1. In a small skillet, saute onion in butter until tender. Transfer to a 5-or 6-quart slow cooker; add squash. Combine the broth, brown sugar, ginger, garlic and cinnamon; pour over squash. Cover and cook on low for 6-8 hours or until squash is tender.
2. Cool slightly. Discard cinnamon stick. In a blender, process soup in batches until smooth. Return all to slow cooker. Whisk in cream cheese; cover and cook 15 minutes longer or until cheese is melted.

TOP TIP

Add a few roasted carrots or potatoes to make this butternut squash soup heartier. You can intensify the flavor with another garlic clove, or if you prefer a sweeter taste, add a touch more of brown sugar or some nutmeg.

BUTTERNUT SQUASH SOUP

Mexican Shredded Beef Wraps

The first time I served these wraps was at my son's baptism celebration. I made a double batch and fed a crowd of 20. The tender beef can also be served on buns.

—**AMY LENTS** GRAND FORKS, ND

PREP: 20 MIN. • **COOK:** 6 HOURS
MAKES: 6 SERVINGS

- 1 **small onion, finely chopped**
- 1 **jalapeno pepper, seeded and minced**
- 3 **garlic cloves, minced**
- 1 **boneless beef chuck roast (2 to 3 pounds)**
- ½ **teaspoon salt**
- ½ **teaspoon pepper**
- 1 **can (8 ounces) tomato sauce**
- ¼ **cup lime juice**
- 1 **tablespoon chili powder**
- 1 **teaspoon ground cumin**
- ¼ **teaspoon cayenne pepper**
- 6 **flour or whole wheat tortillas (8 inches)**
  Optional toppings: torn romaine, chopped tomatoes and sliced avocado

1. Place onion, jalapeno and garlic in a 4-qt. slow cooker. Sprinkle roast with salt and pepper; place over vegetables. In a small bowl, mix tomato sauce, lime juice, chili powder, cumin and cayenne; pour over roast.

2. Cook, covered, on low 6-8 hours or until meat is tender. Remove roast; cool slightly. Shred meat with two forks; return to slow cooker. Serve beef on tortillas with toppings of your choice.

NOTE *Wear disposable gloves when cutting hot peppers; the oils can burn skin. Avoid touching your face.*

SAUSAGE PEPPER SANDWICHES

(5) INGREDIENTS Sausage Pepper Sandwiches

Peppers and onions add a fresh taste to a classic sausage filling for sandwiches. My mother gave me this recipe. It's fun to eat and serve, perfect for a casual night.

—**SUZETTE GESSEL** ALBUQUERQUE, NM

PREP: 15 MIN. • **COOK:** 6 HOURS
MAKES: 6 SERVINGS

- 6 **Italian sausage links (4 ounces each)**
- 1 **medium green pepper, cut into 1-inch pieces**
- 1 **large onion, cut into 1-inch pieces**
- 1 **can (8 ounces) tomato sauce**
- ⅛ **teaspoon pepper**
- 6 **hoagie or submarine sandwich buns, split**

1. In a large skillet, brown sausage links over medium heat. Cut into ½-in. slices; place in a 3-qt. slow cooker. Stir in the green pepper, onion, tomato sauce and pepper.

2. Cover and cook on low for 6-8 hours or until sausage is no longer pink and vegetables are tender. Use a slotted spoon to serve on buns.

MEXICAN SHREDDED BEEF WRAPS

Seafood Cioppino

Looking for a great slow cooker recipe that uses of the catch of the day? This classic stew originated in San Francisco and is filled with clams, crab, fish and shrimp. Serve it as part of a formal meal or any time you have a hankering for seafood.

—LISA MORIARTY WILTON, NH

PREP: 20 MIN. • **COOK:** 4½ HOURS
MAKES: 8 SERVINGS (2½ QUARTS)

- 1 **can (28 ounces) diced tomatoes, undrained**
- 2 **medium onions, chopped**
- 3 **celery ribs, chopped**
- 1 **bottle (8 ounces) clam juice**
- 1 **can (6 ounces) tomato paste**
- ½ **cup white wine or vegetable broth**
- 5 **garlic cloves, minced**
- 1 **tablespoon red wine vinegar**
- 1 **tablespoon olive oil**
- 1 **to 2 teaspoons Italian seasoning**
- ½ **teaspoon sugar**
- 1 **bay leaf**
- 1 **pound haddock fillets, cut into 1-inch pieces**
- 1 **pound uncooked small shrimp, peeled and deveined**
- 1 **can (6 ounces) lump crabmeat, drained**
- 1 **can (6 ounces) chopped clams**
- 2 **tablespoons minced fresh parsley or 2 teaspoons dried parsley flakes**

In a 4- or 5-qt. slow cooker, combine the first 12 ingredients. Cover and cook on low for 4-5 hours. Stir in the haddock, shrimp, crabmeat and clams. Cover and cook 30 minutes longer or until fish flakes easily with a fork and shrimp turn pink. Stir in parsley. Discard bay leaf.

SEAFOOD CIOPPINO

Veggie Beef Barley Soup

Seasoned beef and a host of fresh veggies make this soup taste just like something my mother would make. Add a green salad and crusty rolls, and you'll have a great meal on the table in minutes.

—TARA MCDONALD KANSAS CITY, MO

PREP: 45 MIN. • **COOK:** 7 HOURS
MAKES: 8 SERVINGS (2¾ QUARTS)

- 1 teaspoon seasoned salt
- 1 teaspoon onion powder
- 1 teaspoon garlic powder
- 1½ pounds beef stew meat, cut into 1-inch cubes
- 2 tablespoons canola oil
- 3 cups water
- 3 medium potatoes, peeled and diced
- 1 cup sliced fresh carrots
- 1 cup chopped celery
- ½ cup chopped onion
- 1 teaspoon beef bouillon granules
- 1 can (15¼ ounces) whole kernel corn, drained
- 1 can (14½ ounces) diced tomatoes, undrained
- 1 can (8½ ounces) peas, drained
- 1 cup tomato juice
- ¾ cup medium pearl barley
- ½ teaspoon salt
- ¼ teaspoon pepper

1. In a large resealable plastic bag, combine the seasoned salt, onion powder and garlic powder. Add beef and toss to coat. In a large skillet, brown beef in oil until meat is no longer pink; drain.

2. Transfer to a 5- or 6-qt. slow cooker. Add the water, potatoes, carrots, celery, onion and bouillon. Cover and cook on low for 5-6 hours or until meat and vegetables are almost tender.

3. Add the corn, tomatoes, peas, tomato juice, barley, salt and pepper; cover and cook 2 hours longer or until barley is tender.

⑤ INGREDIENTS

Carolina-Style Vinegar BBQ Chicken

I live in Georgia but I appreciate the tangy, sweet and slightly spicy taste of Carolina Vinegar Chicken. I make my version in the slow cooker and when you walk in the door after being gone all day, the aroma will knock you off your feet!

—RAMONA PARRIS ACWORTH, GA

PREP: 10 MIN. • **COOK:** 4 HOURS
MAKES: 6 SERVINGS

- 2 cups water
- 1 cup white vinegar
- ¼ cup sugar
- 1 tablespoon reduced-sodium chicken base
- 1 teaspoon crushed red pepper flakes
- ¾ teaspoon salt
- 1½ pounds boneless skinless chicken breasts
- 6 whole wheat hamburger buns, split, optional

1. In a small bowl, mix the first six ingredients. Place chicken in a 3-qt. slow cooker; add vinegar mixture. Cook, covered, on low 4-5 hours or until chicken is tender.

2. Remove chicken; cool slightly. Reserve 1 cup cooking juices; discard remaining juices. Shred chicken with two forks. Return meat and reserved cooking juices to slow cooker; heat through. If desired, serve chicken mixture on buns.

NOTE *Look for chicken base near the broth and bouillon.*

CAROLINA-STYLE VINEGAR BBQ CHICKEN

Over-the-Rainbow Minestrone

A rainbow of vegetables go into this vegetarian soup. You can use any multi-colored pasta in place of the rotini.

—**CRYSTAL SCHLUETER** NORTHGLENN, CO

PREP: 20 MIN. • **COOK:** 6 HOURS 20 MIN.
MAKES: 10 SERVINGS (3¾ QUARTS)

- 4 **stalks Swiss chard (about ½ pound)**
- 2 **tablespoons olive oil**
- 1 **medium red onion, finely chopped**
- 6 **cups vegetable broth**
- 2 **cans (14½ ounces each) fire-roasted diced tomatoes, undrained**
- 1 **can (16 ounces) kidney beans, rinsed and drained**
- 1 **can (15 ounces) garbanzo beans or chickpeas, rinsed and drained**
- 1 **medium yellow summer squash or zucchini, halved and cut into ¼-inch slices**
- 1 **medium sweet red or yellow pepper, finely chopped**
- 1 **medium carrot, finely chopped**
- 2 **garlic cloves, minced**
- 1½ **cups uncooked spiral pasta**
- ¼ **cup prepared pesto**

1. Cut stems from chard; chop stems and leaves separately. Reserve leaves for adding later. In a large skillet, heat oil over medium heat. Add onion and chard stems; cook and stir 3-5 minutes or until tender. Transfer to a 6-qt. slow cooker.

2. Stir in broth, tomatoes, beans, squash, pepper and carrot. Cook, covered, on low 6-8 hours or until vegetables are tender.

3. Stir in pasta and reserved chard leaves. Cook, covered, on low 20-25 minutes longer or until pasta is tender. Top servings with pesto.

LEMON CHICKEN & RICE SOUP

Lemon Chicken & Rice Soup

You'll love the bright, fresh flavor of this nutrient-rich soup. Have the butcher cut the chicken into cubes for you and save yourself some prep time.

—**KRISTIN CHERRY** BOTHELL, WA

PREP: 35 MIN. • **COOK:** 4¼ HOURS
MAKES: 12 SERVINGS (4 QUARTS)

- 2 **tablespoons olive oil**
- 2 **pounds boneless skinless chicken breasts, cut into ½-inch pieces**
- 5 **cans (14½ ounces each) reduced-sodium chicken broth**
- 8 **cups coarsely chopped Swiss chard, kale or spinach**
- 2 **large carrots, finely chopped**
- 1 **small onion, chopped**
- 1 **medium lemon, halved and thinly sliced**
- ¼ **cup lemon juice**
- 4 **teaspoons grated lemon peel**
- ½ **teaspoon pepper**
- 4 **cups cooked brown rice**

1. In a large skillet, heat 1 tablespoon oil over medium-high heat. Add half of the chicken; cook and stir until browned. Transfer to a 6-qt. slow cooker. Repeat with remaining oil and chicken.

2. Stir broth, vegetables, lemon slices, lemon juice, peel and pepper into chicken. Cook, covered, on low 4-5 hours or until chicken is tender. Stir in rice; heat through.

Beef & Veggie Sloppy Joes

I'm always looking for new ways to serve my family food that's tasty and good for us, so I started experimenting with my favorite vegetables and ground beef. I came up with these sandwiches that my kids now request regularly. This is a vegetable-rich version of the childhood favorite.

—**MEGAN NIEBUHR** YAKIMA, WA

PREP: 35 MIN. • **COOK:** 5 HOURS
MAKES: 12 SERVINGS

- 4 **medium carrots, shredded (about 3½ cups)**
- 1 **medium yellow summer squash, shredded (about 2 cups)**
- 1 **medium zucchini, shredded (about 2 cups)**
- 1 **medium sweet red pepper, finely chopped**
- 2 **medium tomatoes, seeded and chopped**
- 1 **small red onion, finely chopped**
- ½ **cup ketchup**
- 3 **tablespoons minced fresh basil or 3 teaspoons dried basil**
- 3 **tablespoons molasses**
- 2 **tablespoons cider vinegar**
- 2 **garlic cloves, minced**
- ½ **teaspoon salt**
- ½ **teaspoon pepper**
- 2 **pounds lean ground beef (90% lean)**
- 12 **whole wheat hamburger buns, split**

1. In a 5- or 6-qt. slow cooker, combine the first 13 ingredients. In a large skillet, cook beef over medium heat 8-10 minutes or until no longer pink, breaking into crumbles. Drain; transfer beef to slow cooker. Stir to combine.

2. Cook, covered, on low 5-6 hours or until heated through and vegetables are tender. Using a slotted spoon, serve beef mixture on buns.

BEEF & VEGGIE SLOPPY JOES

SLOW COOKER PASTA E FAGIOLI

Slow Cooker Pasta e Fagioli

Welcome your family home with steaming bowls of this hearty Italian soup. Loaded with veggies, pasta, ground beef and beans, it's almost a meal on its own.

—PENNY NOVY BUFFALO GROVE, IL

PREP: 30 MIN. • **COOK:** 7½ HOURS
MAKES: 8 SERVINGS (2½ QUARTS)

- 1 **pound ground beef**
- 1 **medium onion, chopped**
- 1 **carton (32 ounces) chicken broth**
- 2 **cans (14½ ounces each) diced tomatoes, undrained**
- 1 **can (15 ounces) white kidney or cannellini beans, rinsed and drained**
- 2 **medium carrots, chopped**
- 1½ **cups finely chopped cabbage**
- 1 **celery rib, chopped**
- 2 **tablespoons minced fresh basil or 2 teaspoons dried basil**
- 2 **garlic cloves, minced**
- ½ **teaspoon salt**
- ½ **teaspoon pepper**
- 1 **cup ditalini or other small pasta Grated Parmesan cheese, optional**

1. In a large skillet, cook beef and onion over medium heat until beef is no longer pink and onion is tender; drain.
2. Transfer to a 4- or 5-qt. slow cooker. Stir in the broth, tomatoes, beans, carrots, cabbage, celery, basil, garlic, salt and pepper. Cover and cook on low for 7-8 hours or until vegetables are tender.
3. Stir in pasta. Cover and cook on high 30 minutes longer or until pasta is tender. Sprinkle with cheese if desired.

Anything Goes Sausage Soup

I call this recipe "anything goes" because you can add or take out ingredients, and the soup still turns out delicious. It's impossible to have just one bowl, unless of course your first bowl is huge and filled to the brim!

—SHEENA WELLARD NAMPA, ID

PREP: 40 MIN. • **COOK:** 9½ HOURS
MAKES: 15 SERVINGS (ABOUT 4 QUARTS)

- 1 **pound bulk pork sausage**
- 4 **cups water**
- 1 **can (10¾ ounces) condensed cream of mushroom soup, undiluted**
- 1 **can (10¾ ounces) condensed cheddar cheese soup, undiluted**
- 5 **medium red potatoes, cubed**
- 4 **cups chopped cabbage**
- 3 **large carrots, thinly sliced**
- 4 **celery ribs, chopped**
- 1 **medium zucchini, chopped**
- 1 **large onion, chopped**
- 5 **chicken bouillon cubes**
- 1 **tablespoon dried parsley flakes**
- ¾ **teaspoon pepper**
- 1 **can (12 ounces) evaporated milk**

1. In a large skillet, cook sausage over medium heat until no longer pink; drain. Transfer to a 6-qt. slow cooker. Stir in the water and soups until blended. Add the vegetables, bouillon, parsley and pepper.
2. Cover and cook on low for 9-10 hours or until vegetables are tender. Stir in milk; cover and cook 30 minutes longer.

ANYTHING GOES SAUSAGE SOUP

SPICY CHICKEN AND HOMINY SOUP

Spicy Chicken and Hominy Soup

Posole is another name for this soup. It's a traditional good luck New Year's meal in my native New Mexico. Each cook's version is unique. Mine solves the age-old chili dilemma, "red or green?"—because it uses both.

—JANET CHRISTINE MCDANIEL
ARLINGTON, TX

PREP: 15 MIN. • **COOK:** 4 HOURS
MAKES: 4 SERVINGS

- 1 **pound boneless skinless chicken breasts, cubed**
- 2 **tablespoons olive oil**
- 1 **medium onion, chopped**
- 3 **garlic cloves, minced**
- 2 **chipotle peppers in adobo sauce**
- 2 **cans (14½ ounces each) chicken broth, divided**
- 1 **can (15 ounces) hominy, rinsed and drained**
- 1 **can (4 ounces) chopped green chilies**
- 1 **teaspoon dried oregano**
- 1 **teaspoon ground cumin**
- ¼ **teaspoon pepper**

1. In a large skillet, brown chicken in oil. With a slotted spoon, transfer chicken to a 3- or 4-qt. slow cooker. In the same skillet, saute onion and garlic in drippings until tender; add to the chicken.

2. Place chipotle peppers and ¼ cup broth in a blender or food processor; cover and process until blended. Add to chicken mixture. Stir in the hominy, chilies, seasonings and remaining broth. Cover and cook on low for 4-5 hours or until chicken is tender.

Very Best Barbecue Beef Sandwiches

Chuck roast makes delicious sweet and tangy shredded beef sandwiches after simmering in a rich sauce all day.

—TASTE OF HOME TEST KITCHEN

PREP: 20 MIN. • **COOK:** 8 HOURS
MAKES: 12 SERVINGS

- 1 **boneless beef chuck roast (3 to 4 pounds)**
- 1½ **cups ketchup**
- 1 **small onion, finely chopped**
- ¼ **cup packed brown sugar**
- ¼ **cup red wine vinegar**
- 1 **tablespoon Dijon mustard**
- 1 **tablespoon Worcestershire sauce**
- 2 **garlic cloves, minced**
- ½ **teaspoon salt**
- ¼ **teaspoon celery seed**
- ¼ **teaspoon paprika**
- ¼ **teaspoon pepper**
- 2 **tablespoons cornstarch**
- 2 **tablespoons cold water**
- 12 **kaiser rolls, split**
  Dill pickle slices, optional

1. Cut roast in half. Place in a 5-qt. slow cooker. In a small bowl, combine the ketchup, onion, brown sugar, vinegar, mustard, Worcestershire sauce, garlic, salt, celery seed, paprika and pepper; pour over roast. Cover and cook on low for 8-10 hours or until meat is tender.

2. Remove meat. Skim fat from cooking juices; transfer to a large saucepan. Bring to a boil. Combine cornstarch and water until smooth; gradually stir into juices. Return to a boil; cook and stir for 2 minutes or until thickened.

3. When meat is cool enough to handle, shred with two forks. Return to slow cooker and stir in sauce mixture; heat through. Serve on rolls with pickle slices if desired.

VERY BEST BARBECUE BEEF SANDWICHES

Chicken Cassoulet Soup

After my sister spent a year in France as an au pair, I created this lighter, easier version of traditional French cassoulet for her. It uses chicken instead of the usual duck.

—**BRIDGET KLUSMAN** OTSEGO, MI

PREP: 35 MIN. • **COOK:** 6 HOURS
MAKES: 7 SERVINGS (2¾ QUARTS)

- ½ **pound bulk pork sausage**
- 5 **cups water**
- ½ **pound cubed cooked chicken**
- 1 **can (16 ounces) kidney beans, rinsed and drained**
- 1 **can (15 ounces) black beans, rinsed and drained**
- 1 **can (15 ounces) garbanzo beans or chickpeas, rinsed and drained**
- 2 **medium carrots, shredded**
- 1 **medium onion, chopped**
- ¼ **cup dry vermouth or chicken broth**
- 5 **teaspoons chicken bouillon granules**
- 4 **garlic cloves, minced**
- 1 **teaspoon dried lavender flowers, optional**
- ½ **teaspoon dried thyme**
- ¼ **teaspoon fennel seed, crushed**
- ½ **pound bacon strips, cooked and crumbled**

1. In a large skillet, cook sausage over medium heat until no longer pink; drain.

2. Transfer to a 4- or 5-qt. slow cooker. Add the water, chicken, beans, carrots, onion, vermouth, bouillon, garlic, lavender if desired, thyme and fennel. Cover and cook on low for 6-8 hours or until heated through.

3. Divide among bowls; sprinkle with bacon.

NOTE *Look for dried lavender flowers in spice shops. If using lavender from the garden, make sure it hasn't been treated with chemicals.*

HAWAIIAN SAUSAGE SUBS

(5)INGREDIENTS Hawaiian Sausage Subs

Try these subs if you're looking for a different way to use kielbasa. The sweet and mildly spicy flavor is a nice change of pace.

—**JUDY DAMES** BRIDGEVILLE, PA

PREP: 15 MIN. • **COOK:** 3 HOURS
MAKES: 12 SERVINGS

- 3 **pounds smoked kielbasa or Polish sausage, cut into 3-inch pieces**
- 2 **bottles (12 ounces each) chili sauce**
- 1 **can (20 ounces) pineapple tidbits, undrained**
- ¼ **cup packed brown sugar**
- 12 **hoagie buns, split**

Place kielbasa in a 3-qt. slow cooker. Combine the chili sauce, pineapple and brown sugar; pour over kielbasa. Cover and cook on low for 3-4 hours or until heated through. Serve on buns.

SWEET & SPICY PULLED PORK SANDWICHES

Sweet & Spicy Pulled Pork Sandwiches

One day I mixed together some sauces and seasonings I had on hand and poured it over a pork roast. I put it in the slow cooker and the result was a fantastic pulled pork. It has become a staple sandwich filling for large get-togethers. Serve the pork on rolls, on toasted crostini or in empanadas.
—**LORI TERRY** CHICAGO, IL

PREP: 30 MIN. • **COOK:** 8 HOURS
MAKES: 10 SERVINGS

- 2 medium onions, sliced (about 2 cups)
- 2 tablespoons brown sugar
- 1 tablespoon smoked paprika
- 1½ teaspoons salt
- ½ teaspoon pepper
- 1 boneless pork shoulder roast (4 to 5 pounds)
- ½ cup chicken or vegetable broth
- ¼ cup cider vinegar
- 3 tablespoons reduced-sodium soy sauce
- 3 tablespoons Worcestershire sauce
- 2 tablespoons Sriracha Asian hot chili sauce
- 1 tablespoon molasses
- 2 garlic cloves, minced
- 2 teaspoons Dijon mustard
- 3 cups coleslaw mix
- 3 tablespoons lime juice
- 10 kaiser or onion rolls, split

1. Place onions in a 4- or 5-qt. slow cooker. Mix brown sugar, paprika, salt and pepper; rub over roast. Place over onions.

2. In a small bowl, mix broth, vinegar, soy sauce, Worcestershire sauce, chili sauce, molasses, garlic and mustard; pour over roast. Cook, covered, on low 8-10 hours or until meat is tender.

3. Remove roast; cool slightly. Skim fat from cooking juices. In a small bowl, toss coleslaw mix with lime juice. Shred pork with two forks. Return pork to slow cooker; heat through. Serve on rolls with coleslaw.

FREEZE IT Spinach Bean Soup

As a college nursing professor, I know the importance of a healthy diet. So I do my best to eat right. I was looking for a soup recipe that was easy to make and full of nutrients. This one hit the spot!
—**BRENDA JEFFERS** OTTUMWA, IA

PREP: 20 MIN. • **COOK:** 6¼ HOURS
MAKES: 8 SERVINGS (2 QUARTS)

- 3 cans (14½ ounces each) vegetable broth
- 1 can (15½ ounces) great northern beans, rinsed and drained
- 1 can (15 ounces) tomato puree
- ½ cup finely chopped onion
- ½ cup uncooked converted long grain rice
- 2 garlic cloves, minced
- 1 teaspoon dried basil
- ½ teaspoon salt
- ¼ teaspoon pepper
- 1 package (6 ounces) fresh baby spinach, coarsely chopped
- ¼ cup shredded Parmesan cheese

In a 4-qt. slow cooker, combine the first nine ingredients. Cover and cook on low for 6-7 hours or until heated through. Stir in spinach. Cover and cook for 15 minutes or until spinach is wilted. Sprinkle with cheese.

FREEZE OPTION *Before adding cheese, cool soup. Freeze soup in freezer containers. To use, partially thaw in refrigerator overnight. Heat through in a saucepan, stirring occasionally and adding a little broth or water if necessary. Sprinkle each serving with cheese.*

SPINACH BEAN SOUP

FRENCH ONION SOUP WITH MEATBALLS

Polynesian Ham Sandwiches

The sweetness of the brown sugar and pineapple combined with the tanginess of the Dijon mustard make a perfect match in this tasty sandwich filling.

—**JACKIE SMULSKI** LYONS, IL

PREP: 20 MIN. • **COOK:** 3 HOURS
MAKES: 12 SERVINGS

- 2 **pounds fully cooked ham, finely chopped**
- 1 **can (20 ounces) crushed pineapple, undrained**
- ¾ **cup packed brown sugar**
- ⅓ **cup chopped green pepper**
- ¼ **cup Dijon mustard**
- 1 **green onion, chopped**
- 1 **tablespoon dried minced onion**
- 12 **hamburger buns or kaiser rolls, split**

In a 3-qt. slow cooker, combine the first seven ingredients. Cover and cook on low for 3-4 hours or until heated through. Using a slotted spoon, place ½ cup on each bun.

POLYNESIAN HAM SANDWICHES

French Onion Soup with Meatballs

I got the idea for how to make this soup after I went to a brewhouse restaurant that put ale in their gravy. I make this every time the weather starts to cool down in the fall—it's comfort food for the soul.

—**CRYSTAL HOLSINGER** SURPRISE, AZ

PREP: 15 MIN. • **COOK:** 8 HOURS
MAKES: 6 SERVINGS

- 1 **package (12 ounces) frozen fully cooked Italian meatballs**
- 2 **large sweet onions, sliced**
- 2 **garlic cloves, minced**
- 1 **teaspoon beef bouillon granules**
- ½ **teaspoon dried thyme**
- ¼ **teaspoon salt**
- ¼ **teaspoon pepper**
- 5 **cups beef broth**
- 1 **bottle (12 ounces) pale ale or additional beef broth**
- 18 **slices French bread baguette (¼ inch thick)**
- 12 **slices Muenster or cheddar cheese**

1. In a 4-qt. slow cooker, combine the first nine ingredients. Cook, covered, on low 8-10 hours or until the onions are tender.

2. Ladle soup into six broiler-safe 16-oz. ramekins. Top each with three slices of bread and two slices of cheese. Broil 4-6 in. from heat 2-3 minutes or until the cheese is melted. Serve soup immediately.

Mango & Coconut Chicken Soup

I consider preparing dinner in a slow cooker "carefree cooking." This chicken dish uses ingredients that I enjoy, such as coconut milk, edamame and fresh ginger. The Asian-style entree is perfect for a potluck party.

—ROXANNE CHAN ALBANY, CA

PREP: 25 MIN. • **COOK:** 6 HOURS
MAKES: 6 SERVINGS

- 1 broiler/fryer chicken (3 to 4 pounds), skin removed and cut up
- 2 tablespoons canola oil
- 1 can (15 ounces) whole baby corn, drained
- 1 package (10 ounces) frozen chopped spinach, thawed
- 1 cup frozen shelled edamame, thawed
- 1 small sweet red pepper, chopped
- 1 can (13.66 ounces) light coconut milk
- ½ cup mango salsa
- 1 teaspoon minced fresh gingerroot
- 1 medium mango, peeled and chopped
- 2 tablespoons lime juice
- 2 green onions, chopped

1. In a large skillet, brown chicken in oil in batches. Transfer chicken and drippings to a 5-qt. slow cooker. Add the corn, spinach, edamame and pepper. In a small bowl, combine the coconut milk, salsa and ginger; pour over vegetables.

2. Cover and cook on low for 6-8 hours or until chicken is tender. Remove chicken; cool slightly. When cool enough to handle, remove meat from bones; cut or shred meat into bite-size pieces. Return meat to slow cooker.

3. Just before serving, stir in mango and lime juice. Sprinkle servings with green onions.

TURKEY PEPPER CHILI

Turkey Pepper Chili

I love this chili recipe because it's a delicious, easy meal I can prepare in the morning and when I return home in the evening, there's a wholesome dinner ready to go.

—TERRI CRANDALL GARDNERVILLE, NV

PREP: 30 MIN. • **COOK:** 7¼ HOURS
MAKES: 8 SERVINGS (2¾ QUARTS)

- 2 tablespoons olive oil
- 1½ pounds ground turkey
- 1 medium onion, chopped
- 2 tablespoons ground ancho chili pepper
- 1 tablespoon chili powder
- 1½ teaspoons salt
- 1½ teaspoons ground cumin
- 1½ teaspoons paprika
- 2 cans (14½ ounces each) fire-roasted diced tomatoes, undrained
- 1 medium sweet yellow pepper, chopped
- 1 medium sweet red pepper, chopped
- 1 can (4 ounces) chopped green chilies
- 1 garlic clove, minced
- 1 cup brewed coffee
- ¾ cup dry red wine or chicken broth
- 1 can (16 ounces) kidney beans, rinsed and drained
- 1 can (15 ounces) white kidney or cannellini beans, rinsed and drained
  Sliced avocado and chopped green onions

1. In a large skillet, heat oil over medium heat. Add turkey and onion; cook 8-10 minutes or until meat is no longer pink, breaking up turkey into crumbles.

2. Transfer to a 5-qt. slow cooker; stir in seasonings. Add tomatoes, sweet peppers, chilies and garlic; stir in coffee and wine.

3. Cook, covered, on low 7-9 hours. Stir in beans; cook 15-20 minutes longer or until heated through. Top servings with avocado and green onions.

SLOW COOKER POTATO & HAM SOUP

EASY PHILLY CHEESESTEAKS

Slow Cooker Potato & Ham Soup

In our house, this soup is a win-win. It uses everyday convenience items so it's easy for me to whip up. The rich texture and great taste make it easy for my family to devour. Serve with crusty bread for dipping.

—LINDA HAGLUND BUFFALO, MN

PREP: 10 MIN. • **COOK:** 6¼ HOURS
MAKES: 8 SERVINGS (2½ QUARTS)

- 1 carton (32 ounces) chicken broth
- 1 package (30 ounces) frozen shredded hash brown potatoes, thawed
- 1 small onion, finely chopped
- ¼ teaspoon pepper
- 4 ounces cream cheese, softened and cubed
- 1 cup cubed deli ham
- 1 can (5 ounces) evaporated milk
  Sour cream and chopped green onions, optional

1. In a 4- or 5-qt. slow cooker, combine broth, potatoes, onion and pepper. Cook, covered, on low 6-8 hours or until vegetables are tender.
2. Mash potatoes to desired consistency. Whisk in cream cheese until melted. Stir in ham and milk. Cook, covered, 15-20 minutes longer or until heated through. Serve with sour cream and green onions if desired.

Easy Philly Cheesesteaks

Since we live in a rural area far from any restaurants or pubs that serve this classic sandwich, I thought it would be fun to make it at home. For extra flavor, add a splash of steak sauce.

—LENETTE A. BENNETT COMO, CO

PREP: 20 MIN. • **COOK:** 6 HOURS
MAKES: 6 SERVINGS

- 2 medium onions, halved and sliced
- 2 medium sweet red or green peppers, halved and sliced
- 1 beef top sirloin steak (1½ pounds), cut into thin strips
- 1 envelope onion soup mix
- 1 can (14½ ounces) reduced-sodium beef broth
- 6 hoagie buns, split
- 12 slices provolone cheese, halved
  Pickled hot cherry peppers, optional

1. Place onions and red peppers in a 4- or 5-qt. slow cooker. Add the beef, soup mix and broth. Cook, covered, on low 6-8 hours or until the meat is tender.
2. Arrange buns on a baking sheet, cut side up. Using tongs, place meat mixture on bun bottoms; top with cheese.
3. Broil 2-3 in. from heat 30-60 seconds or until cheese is melted and bun tops are toasted. If desired, serve with cherry peppers.

ITALIAN BEEF SANDWICHES

PEPPERONI PIZZA SOUP

(5)INGREDIENTS Italian Beef Sandwiches

Since I can let this beef chuck roast simmer for 8 to 10 hours, I prep the meat mixture before I leave for work in the morning. When I arrive home, we are ready to dig-in. These sandwiches are also great for picnics and get-togethers.

—**CAROL ALLEN** MCLEANSBORO, IL

PREP: 15 MIN. • **COOK:** 8 HOURS
MAKES: 10-12 SERVINGS

- 1 boneless beef chuck roast (3 to 4 pounds)
- 3 tablespoons dried basil
- 3 tablespoons dried oregano
- 1 cup water
- 1 envelope onion soup mix
- 10 to 12 Italian rolls or sandwich buns

1. Cut roast in half; place in a 5-qt. slow cooker. Combine the basil, oregano and water; pour over roast. Sprinkle with soup mix.

2. Cover and cook on low for 8-10 hours or until meat is tender. Remove meat; shred with two forks and keep warm. Strain broth and skim fat. Serve meat on rolls; use broth for dipping if desired.

Pepperoni Pizza Soup

Once upon a time, my husband and I owned a pizzeria, and this soup was always a top favorite with our patrons. We sold the restaurant, but I still make this recipe for potlucks and other gatherings.

—**ESTELLA PETERSON** MADRAS, OR

PREP: 20 MIN. • **COOK:** 8¼ HOURS
MAKES: 6 SERVINGS (2¼ QUARTS)

- 2 cans (14½ ounces each) Italian stewed tomatoes, undrained
- 2 cans (14½ ounces each) reduced-sodium beef broth
- 1 small onion, chopped
- 1 small green pepper, chopped
- ½ cup sliced fresh mushrooms
- ½ cup sliced pepperoni, halved
- 1½ teaspoons dried oregano
- ⅛ teaspoon pepper
- 1 package (9 ounces) refrigerated cheese ravioli
  Shredded part-skim mozzarella cheese and sliced ripe olives

1. In a 4-qt. slow cooker, combine the first eight ingredients. Cook, covered, on low 8-9 hours.

2. Stir in ravioli; cook, covered, on low 15-30 minutes or until pasta is tender. Top servings with cheese and olives.

TOP TIP

Pasta, if added to a slow cooker when dry, tends to become very sticky. It's better to cook it according to the package directions, if the recipe directs to do so, and stir it into the slow cooker just before serving.

TOMATO-BASIL STEAK

Tomato-Basil Steak

I use basil and bell peppers from my garden to make this dish. It's so easy to prepare and so rich and delicious.

—**SHERRY LITTLE** SHERWOOD, AR

PREP: 15 MIN. • **COOK:** 6 HOURS
MAKES: 4 SERVINGS

- 1¼ **pounds boneless beef shoulder top blade or flat iron steaks**
- ½ **pound whole fresh mushrooms, quartered**
- 1 **medium sweet yellow pepper, julienned**
- 1 **can (14½ ounces) stewed tomatoes, undrained**
- 1 **can (8 ounces) tomato sauce**
- 1 **envelope onion soup mix**
- 2 **tablespoons minced fresh basil**
  Hot cooked rice

1. Place steaks in a 4-qt. slow cooker. Add mushrooms and pepper. In a bowl, mix tomatoes, tomato sauce, soup mix and basil; pour over top.
2. Cook, covered, on low 6-8 hours or until beef and vegetables are tender. Serve with rice.

Chili & Cheese Crustless Quiche

Start your day off right with a filling Tex-Mex egg casserole. Add a salad, and it's a perfect dinner option.

—**GAIL WATKINS** NORWALK, CA

PREP: 15 MIN. • **COOK:** 3 HOURS + STANDING
MAKES: 6 SERVINGS

- 3 **corn tortillas (6 inches)**
- 2 **cans (4 ounces each) whole green chilies**
- 1 **can (15 ounces) chili con carne**
- 1½ **cups (6 ounces) shredded cheddar cheese, divided**
- 4 **eggs**
- 1½ **cups 2% milk**
- 1 **cup biscuit/baking mix**
- ¼ **teaspoon salt**
- ¼ **teaspoon pepper**
- 1 **teaspoon hot pepper sauce, optional**
- 1 **can (4 ounces) chopped green chilies**
- 2 **medium tomatoes, sliced**
  Sour cream, optional

1. In a greased 4- or 5-qt. slow cooker, layer tortillas, whole green chilies, chili con carne and 1 cup cheese.
2. In a small bowl, whisk eggs, milk, biscuit mix, salt, pepper and, if desired, pepper sauce until blended; pour into slow cooker. Top with chopped green chilies and tomatoes.
3. Cook, covered, on low 3-4 hours or until a thermometer reads 160°, sprinkling with remaining cheese during the last 30 minutes of cooking. Turn off slow cooker; remove insert. Let stand 15 minutes before serving. If desired, top with sour cream.

CHILI & CHEESE CRUSTLESS QUICHE

Slow-Cooked Shepherd's Pie

Shepherd's pie is to the British as meat loaf is to Americans. When I was a young child living in the UK, shepherd's pie was a weekly staple. This is my go-to recipe when I'm longing for the sights and smells of my mother's kitchen.

—MARI SITKIEWICZ DOWNERS GROVE, IL

PREP: 35 MIN. • **COOK:** 5¼ HOURS
MAKES: 5 SERVINGS

- 2 **pounds medium Yukon Gold potatoes, peeled and quartered**
- 2 **tablespoons butter**
- ¼ **to ⅓ cup 2% milk**
- ¾ **teaspoon salt, divided**
- ½ **teaspoon pepper, divided**
- 1 **pound ground beef**
- 1 **large onion, chopped**
- 2 **garlic cloves, minced**
- 3 **tablespoons tomato paste**
- 1¾ **cups sliced fresh mushrooms**
- 2 **medium carrots, chopped**
- 1 **cup beef broth**
- ¼ **cup dry white wine**
- 2 **teaspoons Worcestershire sauce**
- ½ **teaspoon dried thyme**
- ⅓ **cup frozen peas**
- ½ **cup shredded Monterey Jack cheese**
- 1 **tablespoon minced fresh parsley**

SLOW-COOKED SHEPHERD'S PIE

1. Place potatoes in a large saucepan and cover with water. Bring to a boil. Reduce heat; cover and cook for 10-15 minutes or until tender. Drain, then shake potatoes over low heat for 1 minute to dry. Mash potatoes, gradually adding butter and enough milk to reach desired consistency. Stir in ½ teaspoon salt and ¼ teaspoon pepper.

2. Meanwhile, in a large skillet, cook the beef, onion and garlic over medium heat until meat is no longer pink; drain.

3. Add the tomato paste; cook for 2 minutes. Add the mushrooms, carrots, broth, wine, Worcestershire sauce and thyme. Bring to a boil. Reduce heat; simmer, uncovered, until most of the liquid is evaporated. Stir in peas. Season with remaining salt and pepper.

4. Transfer beef mixture to a greased 4-qt. slow cooker. Spread mashed potatoes over top. Cover and cook on low for 5-6 hours or until bubbly. Sprinkle with cheese. Cover and cook 10 minutes longer or until cheese is melted. Just before serving, sprinkle with parsley.

TOP TIP

Shepherd's pie is a one-dish staple in homes from coast to coast. If you don't have time to prepare it in the slow cooker, as this recipe suggests, simply set the cooked filling in a baking dish or deep dish pie pan. Top with cooked mashed potatoes as directed, and bake at 350° for roughly 30 minutes or until heated through.

Coffee-Braised Short Ribs

When the leaves start falling, I crave comfort foods like hearty stews and braised meats. I love this recipe because the short ribs smell and taste impressive, but they are a cinch to make.

—MELISSA TURKINGTON
CAMANO ISLAND, WA

PREP: 25 MIN. • **COOK:** 6 HOURS
MAKES: 8 SERVINGS

- 4 **pounds bone-in beef short ribs**
- 1½ **teaspoons salt, divided**
- 1 **teaspoon ground coriander**
- ½ **teaspoon pepper**
- 2 **tablespoons olive oil**
- 1½ **pounds small red potatoes, cut in half**
- 1 **medium onion, chopped**
- 1 **cup reduced-sodium beef broth**
- 1 **whole garlic bulb, cloves separated, peeled and slightly crushed**
- 4 **cups strong brewed coffee**
- 2 **teaspoons red wine vinegar**
- 3 **tablespoons butter**

1. Sprinkle ribs with 1 teaspoon salt, coriander and pepper. In a large skillet, brown ribs in oil in batches. Using tongs, transfer ribs to a 6-qt. slow cooker. Add potatoes and onion.
2. Add broth to the skillet, stirring to loosen browned bits. Bring to a boil; cook until liquid is reduced by half. Stir in garlic and remaining salt; add to slow cooker. Pour coffee over top. Cover and cook on low for 6-8 hours or until meat is tender.
3. Remove ribs and potatoes to a serving platter; keep warm. Strain cooking juices into a small saucepan; skim fat. Bring to a boil; cook until liquid is reduced by half. Stir in vinegar. Remove from the heat; whisk in butter. Serve with ribs and potatoes.

TEX-MEX SHREDDED BEEF SANDWICHES

(5) INGREDIENTS

Tex-Mex Shredded Beef Sandwiches

It takes just a few ingredients to make my delicious shredded beef. As the meat cooks to tender perfection, I have all day to attend to other things.

—KATHERINE WHITE CLEMMONS, NC

PREP: 5 MIN. • **COOK:** 8 HOURS
MAKES: 8 SERVINGS

- 1 **boneless beef chuck roast (3 pounds)**
- 1 **envelope chili seasoning**
- ½ **cup barbecue sauce**
- 8 **onion rolls, split**
- 8 **slices cheddar cheese**

1. Cut roast in half; place in a 3-qt. slow cooker. Sprinkle with chili seasoning. Pour barbecue sauce over top. Cover and cook on low for 8-10 hours or until meat is tender.
2. Remove roast; cool slightly. Shred meat with two forks. Skim fat from cooking juices. Return meat to slow cooker; heat through. Using a slotted spoon, place ½ cup meat mixture on each roll bottom; top with cheese. Replace tops.

COFFEE-BRAISED SHORT RIBS

Sweet-and-Sour Beef Stew

This all-in-one dinner makes terrific use of nutrient-packed vegetables. It has a splendid sweet and tangy flavor.

—**FRANCES CONKLIN** GRANGEVILLE, ID

PREP: 25 MIN. • **COOK:** 8 HOURS
MAKES: 8 SERVINGS

- 2 **pounds beef top round steak, cut into 1-inch cubes**
- 2 **tablespoons olive oil**
- 1 **can (15 ounces) tomato sauce**
- 2 **large onions, chopped**
- 4 **medium carrots, thinly sliced**
- 1 **large green pepper, cut into 1-inch pieces**
- 1 **cup canned pineapple chunks, drained**
- ½ **cup cider vinegar**
- ¼ **cup packed brown sugar**
- ¼ **cup light corn syrup**
- 2 **teaspoons chili powder**
- 2 **teaspoons paprika**
- ½ **teaspoon salt**
  Hot cooked rice, optional

1. In a large skillet, brown beef in oil in batches; drain. Transfer to a 4- or 5-qt. slow cooker.

2. In a large bowl, combine the tomato sauce, onions, carrots, green pepper, pineapple, vinegar, brown sugar, corn syrup, chili powder, paprika and salt; pour over beef.

3. Cover and cook on low for 8-10 hours or until beef is tender. Serve with rice if desired.

FREEZE OPTION *Freeze cooled stew in freezer containers. To use, partially thaw in the refrigerator overnight. Heat through in a saucepan, stirring occasionally and adding a little broth or water if necessary.*

Beef-Stuffed Cabbage Rolls

My family is quick to come to the table when I serve these cabbage rolls. They are satisfying, quick to put together and make great use of my slow cooker.

—**LYNN BOWEN** GERALDINE, AL

PREP: 20 MIN. • **COOK:** 6 HOURS
MAKES: 6 SERVINGS

- 12 **cabbage leaves**
- 1 **cup cooked brown rice**
- ¼ **cup finely chopped onion**
- 1 **egg, lightly beaten**
- ¼ **cup fat-free milk**
- ½ **teaspoon salt**
- ¼ **teaspoon pepper**
- 1 **pound lean ground beef (90% lean)**

SAUCE

- 1 **can (8 ounces) tomato sauce**
- 1 **tablespoon brown sugar**
- 1 **tablespoon lemon juice**
- 1 **teaspoon Worcestershire sauce**

1. In batches, cook cabbage in boiling water 3-5 minutes or until it is crisp-tender. Drain; cool slightly. Trim the thick vein from the bottom of each cabbage leaf, making a V-shaped cut.

2. In a large bowl, combine rice, onion, egg, milk, salt and pepper. Add beef; mix lightly but thoroughly. Place about ¼ cup beef mixture on each cabbage leaf. Pull together cut edges of leaf to overlap; fold over filling. Fold in sides and roll up.

3. Place six rolls in a 4- or 5-qt. slow cooker, seam side down. In a bowl, mix sauce ingredients; pour half of the sauce over cabbage rolls. Top with remaining rolls and sauce. Cook, covered, on low 6-8 hours or until a thermometer inserted in beef reads 160° and cabbage is tender.

BEEF-STUFFED CABBAGE ROLLS

**BEER-BRAISED ROAST
WITH ROOT VEGETABLES**

Beer-Braised Roast with Root Vegetables

My nephew is an avid hunter and makes an effort to share his bounty with his family members. My wife and I like the combination of vegetables, lean meat and seasonings in this recipe. They all complement one another so well! I serve the roast with a garden salad and crusty multigrain bread.

—**MALCOLM CIESZKO** WASHINGTON, NC

PREP: 35 MIN. • **COOK:** 8 HOURS
MAKES: 6 SERVINGS

- 2 **tablespoons olive oil**
- 1 **boneless beef chuck or venison roast (3 to 3½ pounds), trimmed**
- 2 **large onions, sliced**
- 3 **celery ribs, cut into 1-inch pieces**
- 3 **medium carrots, cut into 1-inch pieces**
- 1 **medium sweet potato, peeled and cut into 1-inch cubes**
- ½ **pound fresh whole mushrooms, quartered**
- 1 **bottle (12 ounces) dark beer or 1½ cups beef broth**
- 4 **tablespoons minced fresh parsley, divided**
- 3 **tablespoons Worcestershire sauce**
- 3 **tablespoons seedless blackberry spreadable fruit**
- 1 **teaspoon salt**
- 1 **teaspoon pepper**
- 2 **tablespoons cornstarch**
- ½ **cup cold water**

1. In a large skillet, heat oil over medium heat. Brown roast on all sides. Place vegetables in a 6-qt. slow cooker. Place roast over vegetables. In a bowl, combine beer, 2 tablespoons parsley, Worcestershire sauce, spreadable fruit, salt and pepper; pour over meat. Cook, covered, on low 8-10 hours or until meat and vegetables are tender.

2. Using a slotted spoon, remove roast and vegetables to a serving platter; keep warm. Pour cooking juices into a small saucepan; skim fat and bring to a boil. Mix cornstarch and cold water until smooth; stir into cooking juices. Return to a boil; cook and stir 1-2 minutes or until thickened. Serve with roast and vegetables; sprinkle with remaining parsley.

Slow Cooker Beef Vegetable Stew

Come home to warm, comforting food! This is based on my mom's wonderful recipe, though I tweaked it a bit. Add a sprinkle of Parmesan to each bowl for a tasty finishing touch.

—**MARCELLA WEST** WASHBURN, IL

PREP: 20 MIN. • **COOK:** 6½ HOURS
MAKES: 8 SERVINGS (3 QUARTS)

- 1½ **pounds boneless beef chuck roast, cut into 1-inch cubes**
- 3 **medium potatoes, peeled and cubed**
- 3 **cups hot water**
- 1½ **cups fresh baby carrots**
- 1 **can (10¾ ounces) condensed tomato soup, undiluted**
- 1 **medium onion, chopped**
- 1 **celery rib, chopped**
- 2 **tablespoons Worcestershire sauce**
- 1 **tablespoon browning sauce, optional**
- 2 **teaspoons beef bouillon granules**
- 1 **garlic clove, minced**
- 1 **teaspoon sugar**
- ¾ **teaspoon salt**
- ¼ **teaspoon pepper**
- ¼ **cup cornstarch**
- ¾ **cup cold water**
- 2 **cups frozen peas, thawed**

1. Place the beef, potatoes, hot water, carrots, soup, onion, celery, Worcestershire sauce, browning sauce if desired, bouillon granules, garlic, sugar, salt and pepper in a 5- or 6-qt. slow cooker. Cover and cook on low for 6-8 hours or until meat is tender.

2. Combine cornstarch and cold water in a small bowl until smooth; gradually stir into stew. Stir in peas. Cover and cook on high 30 minutes or until thickened.

Best Short Ribs Vindaloo

PREP: 30 MIN. + MARINATING
COOK: 8¼ HOURS
MAKES: 4 SERVINGS

- 1 **tablespoon cumin seeds**
- 2 **teaspoons coriander seeds**
- 1 **tablespoon butter**
- 1 **medium onion, finely chopped**
- 8 **garlic cloves, minced**
- 1 **tablespoon minced fresh gingerroot**
- 2 **teaspoons mustard seed**
- ½ **teaspoon ground cloves**
- ¼ **teaspoon kosher salt**
- ¼ **teaspoon ground cinnamon**
- ¼ **teaspoon cayenne pepper**
- ½ **cup red wine vinegar**
- 4 **bay leaves**
- 2 **pounds bone-in beef short ribs**
- 1 **cup fresh sugar snap peas, halved**
  Hot cooked rice and plain yogurt

1. In a dry small skillet over medium heat, toast cumin and coriander seeds until aromatic, stirring frequently. Cool. Coarsely crush seeds in a spice grinder or with a mortar and pestle.
2. In a large saucepan, heat butter over medium heat. Add onion, garlic and ginger; cook and stir for 1 minute. Add the mustard seed, cloves, salt, cinnamon, cayenne pepper and crushed seeds; cook and stir 1 minute longer. Cool completely.
3. In a large resealable plastic bag, combine the vinegar, bay leaves and onion mixture. Add ribs; seal bag and turn to coat. Refrigerate overnight.
4. Transfer rib mixture to a 4-qt. slow cooker. Cover and cook on low for 8-10 hours or until meat is tender. Stir in peas; cook 8-10 minutes longer or until peas are crisp-tender. Skim fat; discard bay leaves. Serve rib mixture with rice and yogurt.

BEST SHORT RIBS VINDALOO

MEXICAN BEEF-STUFFED PEPPERS

Mexican Beef-Stuffed Peppers

I grew up eating stuffed peppers and thought my husband would immediately love them as well. He didn't at first, but then I created this unique version. He enjoys fajitas and tacos, so I made these peppers with all of his favorite flavors tucked inside.

—**NICOLE SULLIVAN** ARVADA, CO

PREP: 15 MIN. • **COOK:** 5 HOURS
MAKES: 4 SERVINGS

- 4 medium green or sweet red peppers
- 1 pound ground beef
- 1 package (8.8 ounces) ready-to-serve Spanish rice
- 2 cups (8 ounces) shredded Colby-Monterey Jack cheese, divided
- 1½ cups salsa
- 1 tablespoon hot pepper sauce
- 1 cup water
- 2 tablespoons minced fresh cilantro

1. Cut tops off peppers and remove seeds; set aside. In a large skillet, cook beef over medium heat until no longer pink; drain.
2. Stir in the rice, 1½ cups cheese, salsa and pepper sauce. Spoon into peppers. Transfer to a 5-qt. slow cooker. Pour water around peppers.
3. Cover and cook on low for 5-6 hours or until peppers are tender and filling is heated through. Top with remaining cheese; sprinkle with cilantro.

Garlic-Sesame Beef

My mom received this marinade recipe from a neighbor while she lived in Seoul, Korea, from where I was adopted. Mom created a fun "heritage night" for my brother and me. She'd make Korean foods alongside sticky rice, and we'd eat with chopsticks. This dish helps me keep the tradition alive for my four kids.

—**JACKIE BROWN** FAIRVIEW, NC

PREP: 15 MIN. + MARINATING
COOK: 5 HOURS
MAKES: 6 SERVINGS

- 6 green onions, sliced
- ½ cup sugar
- ½ cup water
- ½ cup reduced-sodium soy sauce
- ¼ cup sesame oil
- 3 tablespoons sesame seeds, toasted
- 2 tablespoons all-purpose flour
- 4 garlic cloves, minced
- 1 beef sirloin tip roast (3 pounds), thinly sliced
  Additional sliced green onions and toasted sesame seeds
  Hot cooked rice

1. In a large resealable plastic bag, mix the first eight ingredients. Add beef; seal bag and turn to coat. Refrigerate 8 hours or overnight.
2. Pour beef and marinade into a 3-qt. slow cooker. Cook, covered, on low 5-7 hours or until meat is tender.
3. Using a slotted spoon, remove beef to a serving platter; sprinkle with additional green onions and sesame seeds. Serve with rice.

GARLIC-SESAME BEEF

Short Ribs in Red Wine

These ribs are an easy alternative to traditionally braised short ribs—you don't need to pay any attention to them once you get them started.

—**REBEKAH BEYER** SABETHA, KS

PREP: 30 MIN. • **COOK:** 6¼ HOURS
MAKES: 6 SERVINGS

- 3 **pounds bone-in beef short ribs**
- ½ **teaspoon salt**
- ½ **teaspoon pepper**
- 1 **tablespoon canola oil**
- 4 **medium carrots, cut into 1-inch pieces**
- 1 **cup beef broth**
- 4 **fresh thyme sprigs**
- 1 **bay leaf**
- 2 **large onions, cut into ½-inch wedges**
- 6 **garlic cloves, minced**
- 1 **tablespoon tomato paste**
- 2 **cups dry red wine or beef broth**
- 4 **teaspoons cornstarch**
- 3 **tablespoons cold water**
  Salt and pepper to taste

1. Sprinkle ribs with ½ teaspoon each salt and pepper. In a large skillet, heat oil over medium heat. In batches, brown ribs on all sides; transfer to a 4- or 5-qt. slow cooker. Add carrots, broth, thyme and bay leaf to ribs.
2. Add onions to the same skillet; cook and stir over medium heat 8-9 minutes or until tender. Add garlic and tomato paste; cook and stir 1 minute longer. Stir in the wine. Bring to a boil; cook 8-10 minutes or until liquid is reduced by half. Add to the slow cooker. Cook, covered, on low 6-8 hours or until meat is tender.
3. Remove ribs and vegetables; keep warm. Transfer cooking juices to a small saucepan; skim fat. Discard thyme and bay leaf. Bring juices to a boil. In a small bowl, mix cornstarch and water until smooth; stir into cooking juices. Return to a boil; cook and stir 1-2 minutes or until thickened. Season with salt and pepper to taste. Serve with ribs and vegetables.

LOUISIANA ROUND STEAK

Louisiana Round Steak

The men in our family really enjoy this slow-cooked entree. After simmering for hours, the steak takes on a robust taste, and everyone gets a substantial portion.

—**MEGAN ROHLCK** VERMILLION, SD

PREP: 20 MIN. • **COOK:** 7 HOURS
MAKES: 6 SERVINGS

- 2 **pounds sweet potatoes, peeled and cut into 1-inch pieces**
- 1 **large onion, chopped**
- 1 **medium green pepper, sliced**
- 2 **beef top round steaks (¾ inch thick and 1 pound each)**
- 1 **teaspoon salt, divided**
- 2 **tablespoons olive oil**
- 1 **garlic clove, minced**
- 3 **tablespoons all-purpose flour**
- 1 **can (28 ounces) diced tomatoes, undrained**
- ½ **cup beef broth**
- 1 **teaspoon sugar**
- ½ **teaspoon dried thyme**
- ½ **teaspoon pepper**
- ¼ **teaspoon hot pepper sauce**

1. Place the sweet potatoes, onion and green pepper in a 6-qt. slow cooker. Cut each steak into three serving-size pieces; sprinkle with ½ teaspoon salt. In a large skillet over medium heat, brown steaks in oil in batches on both sides. Place steaks over vegetables, reserving drippings in pan.
2. Add garlic to drippings; cook and stir for 1 minute. Stir in flour until blended. Stir in the remaining ingredients and remaining salt. Bring to a boil, stirring constantly. Cook and stir for 4-5 minutes or until thickened. Pour over meat. Cover and cook on low for 7-9 hours or until beef is tender.

Portobello Beef Burgundy

Rely on the convenience of your slow cooker for a meal that boasts stick-to-your-ribs goodness. These tender cubes of beef—loaded with a fantastic mushroom flavor and draped in a rich, Burgundy sauce—are sure to have your guests asking for seconds and dreaming of thirds.

—MELISSA GALINAT LAKELAND, FL

PREP: 30 MIN. • **COOK:** 7½ HOURS
MAKES: 6 SERVINGS

- ¼ cup all-purpose flour
- ½ teaspoon salt
- ½ teaspoon seasoned salt
- 1½ teaspoons minced fresh thyme or ½ teaspoon dried thyme
- ¾ teaspoon minced fresh marjoram or ¼ teaspoon dried thyme
- ½ teaspoon pepper
- 2 pounds beef sirloin tip steak, cubed
- 2 bacon strips, diced
- 3 tablespoons canola oil
- 1 garlic clove, minced
- 1 cup Burgundy wine or beef broth
- 1 teaspoon beef bouillon granules
- 1 pound sliced baby portobello mushrooms
    Hot cooked noodles, optional

1. In a large resealable plastic bag, combine the first six ingredients. Add beef, a few pieces at a time, and shake to coat.

2. In a large skillet, cook bacon over medium heat until crisp. Remove to paper towels with a slotted spoon; drain. In same skillet, brown beef in oil in batches, adding garlic to the last batch; cook 1-2 minutes longer. Drain.

3. Transfer to a 4-qt. slow cooker. Add wine to skillet, stirring to loosen browned bits from pan. Add bouillon; bring to a boil. Stir into slow cooker. Stir in bacon. Cover and cook on low for 7-9 hours or until meat is tender.

4. Stir in mushrooms. Cover and cook on high 30-45 minutes longer or until mushrooms are tender and sauce is slightly thickened. Serve with noodles if desired.

BEEFY CABBAGE BEAN STEW

Beefy Cabbage Bean Stew

While on a quilting retreat, one of my friends made this wonderful stew for dinner. We all loved it and have since passed it around for others to enjoy. Now I'm passing it on to you.

—MELISSA GLANCY LA GRANGE, KY

PREP: 20 MIN. • **COOK:** 6 HOURS
MAKES: 6 SERVINGS

- ½ pound lean ground beef (90% lean)
- 3 cups shredded cabbage or angel hair coleslaw mix
- 1 can (16 ounces) red beans, rinsed and drained
- 1 can (14½ ounces) diced tomatoes, undrained
- 1 can (8 ounces) tomato sauce
- ¾ cup salsa or picante sauce
- 1 medium green pepper, chopped
- 1 small onion, chopped
- 3 garlic cloves, minced
- 1 teaspoon ground cumin
- ½ teaspoon pepper

1. In a large skillet, cook beef over medium heat 4-6 minutes or until no longer pink, breaking into crumbles; drain.

2. Transfer meat to a 4-qt. slow cooker. Stir in remaining ingredients. Cook, covered, on low 6-8 hours or until cabbage is tender.

PORTOBELLO BEEF BURGUNDY

Mediterranean Pot Roast Dinner

I first made this recipe one cold winter day. My family (adults, kids and dogs) had a blast sledding and playing in the snow all day, and when we came inside supper was ready. This pot roast is perfect served with mashed potatoes, rice or crusty dinner rolls.

—**HOLLY BATTISTE** BARRINGTON, NJ

PREP: 30 MIN. • **COOK:** 8 HOURS
MAKES: 8 SERVINGS

- 2 **pounds potatoes (about 6 medium), peeled and cut into 2-inch pieces**
- 5 **medium carrots (about ¾ pound), cut into 1-inch pieces**
- 2 **tablespoons all-purpose flour**
- 1 **boneless beef chuck roast (3 to 4 pounds)**
- 1 **tablespoon olive oil**
- 8 **large fresh mushrooms, quartered**
- 2 **celery ribs, chopped**
- 1 **medium onion, thinly sliced**
- ¼ **cup sliced Greek olives**
- ½ **cup minced fresh parsley, divided**
- 1 **can (14½ ounces) fire-roasted diced tomatoes, undrained**
- 1 **tablespoon minced fresh oregano or 1 teaspoon dried oregano**
- 1 **tablespoon lemon juice**
- 2 **teaspoons minced fresh rosemary or ½ teaspoon dried rosemary, crushed**
- 2 **garlic cloves, minced**
- ¾ **teaspoon salt**
- ¼ **teaspoon pepper**
- ¼ **teaspoon crushed red pepper flakes, optional**

1. Place potatoes and carrots in a 6-qt. slow cooker. Sprinkle flour over all surfaces of roast. In a large skillet, heat oil over medium-high heat. Brown roast on all sides. Place over vegetables.
2. Add mushrooms, celery, onion, olives and ¼ cup parsley to slow cooker. In a small bowl, mix remaining ingredients; pour over top.
3. Cook, covered, on low 8-10 hours or until the meat and vegetables are tender. Remove beef. Stir remaining parsley into vegetables. Serve beef with vegetables.

Beef Roast with Cranberry Gravy

Cranberries, cranberry juice and balsamic vinegar give beef roast a slight tartness. Serve the gravy over noodles or mashed potatoes. It's so good!

—**DIANE NEMITZ** LUDINGTON, MI

PREP: 40 MIN. • **COOK:** 7 HOURS
MAKES: 6 SERVINGS

- 1 **boneless beef chuck roast (3 to 4 pounds)**
- 2 **teaspoons salt**
- 1 **teaspoon pepper**
- 2 **tablespoons canola oil**
- 2 **medium carrots, finely chopped**
- 1 **medium onion, chopped**
- 2 **garlic cloves, minced**
- 1 **cup cranberry juice**
- ¾ **cup water**
- ½ **cup fresh or frozen cranberries**
- ½ **cup balsamic vinegar**
- 2 **fresh thyme sprigs**
- 1 **bay leaf**
- 3 **tablespoons cornstarch**
- 3 **tablespoons cold water**

1. Sprinkle beef with salt and pepper. In a large skillet, heat oil over medium heat. Brown roast on all sides. Transfer to a 5-qt. slow cooker.
2. Add carrots and onion to drippings; cook and stir over medium heat 4-5 minutes or until tender. Add garlic; cook 1 minute longer. Spoon vegetables around roast; add cranberry juice, ¾ cup water, cranberries, vinegar, thyme and bay leaf. Cook, covered, on low 7-9 hours or until meat is tender.
3. Using a slotted spoon, remove roast and vegetables to a serving platter; keep warm. Pour cooking juices into a small saucepan; skim fat. Discard thyme and bay leaf. Bring cooking juices to a boil. Mix cornstarch and water until smooth; gradually stir into pan. Return to a boil, stirring constantly; cook and stir 1-2 minutes or until thickened. Serve with roast.

BEEF ROAST WITH CRANBERRY GRAVY

HEARTY BEEF ENCHILADA

three tortillas, beef mixture, broth, tomato sauce and enchilada sauce; sprinkle with ½ cup cheese. Add three tortillas, beans, Mexicorn, green chilies, half of the olives and ½ cup cheese. Top with remaining tortillas, cheese and olives.

3. Cover and cook on low for 6-7 hours. Serve with sour cream and avocado if desired.

Flank Steak with Green Chilies

This flavorful, tender beef dish has been a go-to recipe for many years; it's a true lifesaver on days when I know I'm going to arrive home late.

—ANNE MERRILL CROGHAN, NY

PREP: 20 MIN. • **COOK:** 6 HOURS
MAKES: 4 SERVINGS

- 1 **tablespoon canola oil**
- 1 **beef flank steak (1½ pounds)**
- 1 **large onion, sliced**
- ⅓ **cup water**
- 1 **can (4 ounces) chopped green chilies**
- 2 **tablespoons cider vinegar**
- 2 **to 3 teaspoons chili powder**
- 1 **teaspoon garlic powder**
- 1 **teaspoon sugar**
- ½ **teaspoon salt**
- ⅛ **teaspoon pepper**

1. In a large skillet, heat oil over medium-high heat; brown steak on both sides. Transfer to a 3-qt. slow cooker.

2. Add onion to same skillet; cook and stir 1-2 minutes or until crisp-tender. Add water to pan; cook 30 seconds, stirring to loosen browned bits from pan. Stir in remaining ingredients; return to a boil. Pour over steak.

3. Cook, covered, on low 6-8 hours or until meat is tender. Slice steak across the grain; serve with onion mixture.

Hearty Beef Enchilada

Deliciously spicy, meaty and cheesy, this enchilada will please everyone in your family. Serve it with sour cream, avocado and additional enchilada sauce. It is perfect for potlucks and other fun get-togethers!

—MARINA CASTLE CANYON COUNTRY, CA

PREP: 10 MIN. • **COOK:** 6 HOURS
MAKES: 10 SERVINGS

- 1½ **pounds lean ground beef (90% lean)**
- 1 **small onion, chopped**
- 1 **garlic clove, minced**
- 1 **envelope taco seasoning**
- ½ **teaspoon salt**
- ½ **teaspoon pepper**
- 9 **corn tortillas (6 inches)**
- ½ **cup chicken broth**
- ½ **cup tomato sauce**
- 1 **can (10 ounces) enchilada sauce**
- 1½ **cups (6 ounces) shredded cheddar cheese**
- 2 **cans (15 ounces each) pinto beans, rinsed and drained**
- 1 **can (11 ounces) Mexicorn, drained**
- 1 **can (4 ounces) chopped green chilies, drained**
- 1 **can (2¼ ounces) chopped ripe olives, drained**
  Optional ingredients: sour cream and avocado slices

1. In a large skillet, cook the beef, onion and garlic over medium heat until meat is no longer pink; drain. Stir in the taco seasoning, salt and pepper.

2. In a greased 5-qt. slow cooker, layer

FLANK STEAK WITH GREEN CHILIES

Mushroom Pot Roast

Packed with wholesome veggies and tender beef, this is one entree that all ages will like. Serve with mashed potatoes to soak up every last drop of the beefy gravy. It's great for company.

—ANGIE STEWART TOPEKA, KS

PREP: 25 MIN. • **COOK:** 6 HOURS
MAKES: 10 SERVINGS

- 1 boneless beef chuck roast (3 to 4 pounds)
- ½ teaspoon salt
- ¼ teaspoon pepper
- 1 tablespoon canola oil
- 1½ pounds sliced fresh shiitake mushrooms
- 2½ cups thinly sliced onions
- 1½ cups reduced-sodium beef broth
- 1½ cups dry red wine or additional reduced-sodium beef broth
- 1 can (8 ounces) tomato sauce
- ¾ cup chopped peeled parsnips
- ¾ cup chopped celery
- ¾ cup chopped carrots
- 8 garlic cloves, minced
- 2 bay leaves
- 1½ teaspoons dried thyme
- 1 teaspoon chili powder
- ¼ cup cornstarch
- ¼ cup water
  Mashed potatoes

1. Sprinkle roast with salt and pepper. In a Dutch oven, brown roast in oil on all sides. Transfer to a 6-qt. slow cooker. Add the mushrooms, onions, broth, wine, tomato sauce, parsnips, celery, carrots, garlic, bay leaves, thyme and chili powder. Cover and cook on low for 6-8 hours or until meat is tender.

2. Remove meat and vegetables to a serving platter; keep warm. Discard bay leaves. Skim fat from cooking juices; transfer to a small saucepan. Bring liquid to a boil. Combine cornstarch and water until smooth; gradually stir into the pan. Bring to a boil; cook and stir for 2 minutes or until thickened. Serve with mashed potatoes, meat and vegetables.

MUSHROOM POT ROAST

Guinness Corned Beef and Cabbage

A dear friend of my mother's shared this recipe years ago. My husband and kids request it for special occasions such as birthdays and, of course, St. Patrick's Day.

—KARIN BRODBECK RED HOOK, NY

PREP: 20 MIN. • **COOK:** 8 HOURS
MAKES: 9 SERVINGS

- 2 pounds red potatoes, quartered
- 1 pound carrots, cut into 3-inch pieces
- 2 celery ribs, cut into 3-inch pieces
- 1 small onion, quartered
- 1 corned beef brisket with spice packet (3 to 3½ pounds)
- 8 whole cloves
- 6 whole peppercorns
- 1 bay leaf
- 1 bottle (12 ounces) Guinness stout or reduced-sodium beef broth
- ½ small head cabbage, thinly sliced
  Prepared horseradish

1. In a 6-qt. slow cooker, combine potatoes, carrots, celery and onion. Add corned beef (discard spice packet or save for another use).

2. Place cloves, peppercorns and bay leaf on a double thickness of cheesecloth. Gather corners of cloth to enclose seasonings; tie securely with string. Place in slow cooker. Pour stout over top.

3. Cook, covered, on low 8-10 hours or until the meat and vegetables are tender, adding cabbage during the last hour of cooking. Discard spice bag.

4. Cut beef diagonally across the grain into thin slices. Serve beef with vegetables and horseradish.

Sweet Pepper Steak

Pepper steak is one of my favorite dishes, but I was always disappointed with beef that was too tough. This recipe solves that problem. I've stored leftovers in one big resealable bag and also in individual portions for quick lunches.

—JULIE RHINE ZELIENOPLE, PA

PREP: 30 MIN. • **COOK:** 6¼ HOURS
MAKES: 12 SERVINGS

- 1 **beef top round roast (3 pounds)**
- 1 **large onion, halved and sliced**
- 1 **large green pepper, cut into ½-inch strips**
- 1 **large sweet red pepper, cut into ½-inch strips**
- 1 **cup water**
- 4 **garlic cloves, minced**
- ⅓ **cup cornstarch**
- ½ **cup reduced-sodium soy sauce**
- 2 **teaspoons sugar**
- 2 **teaspoons ground ginger**
- 8 **cups hot cooked brown rice**

1. Place roast, onion and peppers in a 5-qt. slow cooker. Add water and garlic. Cook, covered, on low 6-8 hours or until meat is tender.

2. Remove beef to a cutting board. Transfer vegetables and cooking juices to a large saucepan. Bring to a boil. In a small bowl, mix cornstarch, soy sauce, sugar and ginger until smooth; stir into vegetable mixture. Return to a boil, stirring constantly; cook and stir 1-2 minutes or until thickened.

3. Cut beef into slices. Stir gently into sauce; heat through. Serve with rice.

FREEZE OPTION *Freeze cooled beef mixture in freezer containers. To use, partially thaw in the refrigerator overnight. Heat through in a saucepan, stirring occasionally and adding a little water if necessary.*

SPINACH & FETA STUFFED FLANK STEAK

Spinach & Feta Stuffed Flank Steak

Spinach, feta and sun-dried tomatoes lend Mediterranean flair to simple flank steak. Elegant enough for company, the colorful rolls look pretty on a plate.

—STEVEN SCHEND GRAND RAPIDS, MI

PREP: 30 MIN. • **COOK:** 6 HOURS
MAKES: 6 SERVINGS

- 1 **beef flank steak (1½ pounds)**
- 2 **cups (8 ounces) crumbled feta cheese**
- 3 **cups fresh baby spinach**
- ½ **cup oil-packed sun-dried tomatoes, drained and chopped**
- ½ **cup finely chopped onion**
- 5 **tablespoons all-purpose flour, divided**
- ½ **teaspoon salt**
- ½ **teaspoon pepper**
- 2 **tablespoons canola oil**
- 1 **cup beef broth**
- 1 **tablespoon Worcestershire sauce**
- 2 **teaspoons tomato paste**
- ⅓ **cup dry red wine or additional beef broth**
  Hot cooked egg noodles, optional

1. Starting at one long side, cut steak horizontally in half to within ½ in. of opposite side. Open steak flat; cover with plastic wrap. Pound with a meat mallet to ½-in. thickness. Remove plastic.

2. Sprinkle 1 cup cheese over steak to within 1 in. of edges. Layer with spinach, tomatoes, onion and remaining cheese. Roll up jelly-roll style, starting with a long side; tie at 1½-in. intervals with kitchen string. Sprinkle beef with 2 tablespoons flour, salt and pepper.

3. In a large skillet, heat oil over medium heat. Brown beef on all sides; drain. Transfer to a 6-qt. oval slow cooker. In a small bowl, mix the broth, Worcestershire sauce and tomato paste; pour over top. Cook, covered, on low 6-8 hours or until meat is tender.

4. Remove beef to a platter; keep warm. Transfer cooking juices to a small saucepan; skim fat. Bring juices to a boil. Mix remaining flour and the wine until smooth; gradually stir into pan. Return to a boil; cook and stir 1-2 minutes or until thickened. Serve beef with gravy and, if desired, noodles.

Beef Stew Provencal

When I was young, beef stew was my favorite food to order in a restaurant. My mother and I decided to create our own and experimented with different ingredients until we came up with this recipe. Everyone liked this version so much that now it's a tradition every time the whole family is together.

—**CHELSEY LARSEN** SPARKS, NV

PREP: 25 MIN. • **COOK:** 6 HOURS
MAKES: 6 SERVINGS

- 4 **medium carrots, chopped**
- 4 **celery ribs, chopped**
- 1 **cup beef broth**
- 1 **jar (7 ounces) julienned oil-packed sun-dried tomatoes, drained**
- 1 **can (6 ounces) tomato paste**
- 1 **small onion, chopped**
- ⅓ **cup honey**
- ¼ **cup balsamic vinegar**
- 1 **garlic clove, minced**
- 1 **teaspoon dried thyme**
- ½ **teaspoon onion powder**
- ¼ **teaspoon white pepper**
- 1 **boneless beef chuck roast (2½ pounds), cut into 2-inch cubes**
- ½ **cup all-purpose flour**
- ½ **teaspoon salt**
- ½ **teaspoon pepper**
- 2 **tablespoons olive oil**
  Hot cooked mashed potatoes or egg noodles

1. In a 4-qt. slow cooker, combine the first 12 ingredients. In a large bowl, combine the beef, flour, salt and pepper; toss to coat. In a large skillet, brown beef in oil in batches. Transfer to slow cooker.

2. Cover and cook on low for 6-8 hours or until beef is tender. Serve with mashed potatoes.

BEEF STEW PROVENCAL

DOUBLE-ONION BEEF BRISKET

Double-Onion Beef Brisket

Gentle simmering makes this brisket tender. It gets a wonderful sweet-hot flavor from chili sauce, cider vinegar and brown sugar.

—**ELAINE SWEET** DALLAS, TX

PREP: 35 MIN. • **COOK:** 6 HOURS
MAKES: 10 SERVINGS

- 1 fresh beef brisket (4 pounds)
- 1½ teaspoons kosher salt
- 1½ teaspoons coarsely ground pepper
- 2 tablespoons olive oil
- 3 medium onions, halved and sliced
- 3 celery ribs, chopped
- 1 cup chili sauce
- ¼ cup packed brown sugar
- ¼ cup cider vinegar
- 1 envelope onion soup mix

1. Cut brisket in half; sprinkle all sides with salt and pepper. In a large skillet, brown brisket in oil; remove and set aside. In the same skillet, cook and stir onions over low heat for 15-20 minutes or until caramelized.

2. Place half of the onions in a 5-qt. slow cooker; top with celery and brisket. Combine the chili sauce, brown sugar, vinegar and soup mix. Pour over brisket; top with remaining onions.

3. Cover and cook on low for 6-7 hours or until meat is tender. Let stand for 5 minutes before slicing. Skim fat from cooking juices; serve juices with meat.
NOTE *This is a fresh beef brisket, not corned beef.*

Mexican Beef & Bean Stew

Comfort food is even better when it comes together quickly. The beans, veggies and spices blend nicely, and it really warms me up on blustery days.

—**TACY FLEURY** CLINTON, SC

PREP: 20 MIN. • **COOK:** 8 HOURS
MAKES: 10 SERVINGS (2½ QUARTS)

- 1 cup all-purpose flour
- ¼ teaspoon salt
- ⅛ teaspoon pepper
- 1 pound beef stew meat, cut into 1-inch cubes
- 2 tablespoons canola oil
- 1 can (16 ounces) kidney beans, rinsed and drained
- 1 can (15¼ ounces) whole kernel corn, drained
- 2 medium potatoes, cubed
- 2 small carrots, sliced
- 2 celery ribs, sliced
- 1 small onion, chopped
- 2 cans (15 ounces each) tomato sauce
- 1 cup water
- 1 envelope taco seasoning
- ½ teaspoon ground cumin
  Tortilla chips and shredded cheddar cheese

1. Combine the flour, salt and pepper in a large resealable plastic bag. Add beef, a few pieces at a time, and shake to coat.

2. Brown meat in batches in oil in a large skillet; drain. Transfer to a 5-qt. slow cooker. Add the beans, corn, potatoes, carrots, celery and onion.

3. Whisk the tomato sauce, water, taco seasoning and cumin; pour over top. Cover and cook on low for 8-10 hours or until meat is tender. Serve with tortilla chips and cheese.

MEXICAN BEEF & BEAN STEW

BEEF BRACIOLE

Beef Braciole

My great aunt used to make the most amazing braciole, tossed with olive oil and Romano cheese and served sliced over orzo. It was *delicioso,* but also a laborious and time-consuming effort. I took her basic recipe and transformed it into a slow-cooker version, making it easier for today's busy families. The result is impressive yet simple.

—**LISA RENSHAW** KANSAS CITY, MO

PREP: 30 MIN. • **COOK:** 6 HOURS
MAKES: 6 SERVINGS

- 2 jars (24 ounces each) tomato basil pasta sauce
- 1 teaspoon crushed red pepper flakes
- 1 beef flank steak (1½ pounds)
- ½ teaspoon salt
- ½ teaspoon pepper
- 2 eggs, beaten
- ½ cup seasoned bread crumbs
- 8 thin slices prosciutto or deli ham
- 1 cup (4 ounces) shredded Italian cheese blend
- 2 tablespoons olive oil

1. In a 5- or 6-qt. oval slow cooker, combine pasta sauce and pepper flakes. Pound steak with a meat mallet to ½-in. thickness; sprinkle with salt and pepper.

2. In a small bowl, combine eggs and bread crumbs. Spoon over beef to within 1 in. of edges; press onto meat. Layer with prosciutto and cheese. Roll up jelly-roll style, starting with a long side; tie at 2-in. intervals with kitchen string.

3. In a Dutch oven, brown meat in oil on all sides. Transfer to slow cooker; spoon sauce over meat. Cover and cook on low for 6-8 hours or until beef is tender.

4. Remove meat from sauce and discard string. Cut into slices; serve with sauce.

Cheddar-Topped Barbecue Meat Loaf

The bold barbecue flavor of this tender meat loaf is always a hit with my family. Since it's a snap to make, it's a hit with me.

—**DAVID SNODGRASS** COLUMBIA, MO

PREP: 20 MIN. • **COOK:** 3¼ HOURS
MAKES: 8 SERVINGS

- 3 eggs, lightly beaten
- ¾ cup old-fashioned oats
- 1 large sweet red or green pepper, chopped (about 1½ cups)
- 1 small onion, finely chopped
- 1 envelope onion soup mix
- 3 garlic cloves, minced
- ½ teaspoon salt
- ¼ teaspoon pepper
- 2 pounds lean ground beef (90% lean)
- 1 cup ketchup
- 2 tablespoons brown sugar
- 1 tablespoon barbecue seasoning
- 1 teaspoon ground mustard
- 1 cup (4 ounces) shredded cheddar cheese

1. Cut three 18x3-in. strips of heavy-duty foil; crisscross so they resemble spokes of a wheel. Place strips on bottom and up sides of a 3-qt. slow cooker. Coat strips with cooking spray.

2. In a large bowl, combine eggs, oats, chopped pepper, onion, soup mix, garlic, salt and pepper. Add beef; mix lightly but thoroughly. Shape into a 7-in. round loaf. Place loaf in center of strips in slow cooker. Cook, covered, on low 3-4 hours or until a thermometer reads at least 160°.

3. In a small bowl, mix ketchup, brown sugar, barbecue seasoning and mustard; pour over meat loaf and sprinkle with cheese. Cook, covered, on low 15 minutes longer or until cheese is melted. Let stand 5 minutes. Using foil strips as handles, remove meat loaf to a platter.

Sausage-Stuffed Flank Steak

I won a slow cooker in a recipe contest. I hadn't used one in years so I didn't have any slow-cooker recipes on hand. This tasty beef was my first creation, and it got rave reviews.

—JULIE MERRIMAN SEATTLE, WA

PREP: 35 MIN. • **COOK:** 6 HOURS
MAKES: 4 SERVINGS

- ¼ cup dried cherries
- ¾ cup dry red wine or beef broth, divided
- 1 beef flank steak (1½ pounds)
- ¾ teaspoon salt, divided
- ½ teaspoon pepper, divided
- 1 medium onion, finely chopped
- 3 tablespoons olive oil, divided
- 4 garlic cloves, minced
- ½ cup seasoned bread crumbs
- ¼ cup pitted Greek olives, halved
- ¼ cup grated Parmesan cheese
- ¼ cup minced fresh basil
- ½ pound bulk hot Italian sausage
- 1 jar (24 ounces) marinara sauce
  Hot cooked pasta

1. In a small bowl, combine cherries and ¼ cup wine; let stand 10 minutes. Meanwhile, cut steak into four serving-size pieces; flatten to ¼-in. thickness. Sprinkle both sides with ½ teaspoon salt and ¼ teaspoon pepper.
2. In a large skillet, saute onion in 1 tablespoon oil until tender. Add garlic; cook 1 minute longer. Transfer to a bowl; stir in bread crumbs, olives, cheese, basil, cherry mixture and remaining salt and pepper. Crumble sausage over mixture and mix well.
3. Spread ½ cup sausage mixture over each steak piece. Roll up jelly-roll style, starting with a long side; tie with kitchen string.
4. In the same skillet, brown meat in remaining oil on all sides. Transfer to

GRANDMA SCHWARTZ'S ROULADEN

a greased 3-qt. slow cooker. Top with marinara sauce and remaining wine. Cook and cook on low for 6-8 hours or until beef is tender. Serve with pasta.

Grandma Schwartz's Rouladen

My Grandma Schwartz made rouladen for her family. Grandpa Schwartz was a German butcher, and this was one of his (and our) favorite meals. It's an extra-special beef entree when served with mashed potatoes made with butter and sour cream.

—LYNDA SHARAI SUMMER LAKE, OR

PREP: 35 MIN. • **COOK:** 6 HOURS
MAKES: 6 SERVINGS

- 3 bacon strips, chopped
- 1½ pounds beef top round steak
- 2 tablespoons Dijon mustard
- 3 medium carrots, quartered lengthwise
- 6 dill pickle spears
- ¼ cup finely chopped onion
- 1 cup sliced fresh mushrooms
- 1 small parsnip, peeled and chopped
- 1 celery rib, chopped
- 1 can (10¾ ounces) condensed golden cream of mushroom soup, undiluted
- ⅓ cup dry red wine
- 2 tablespoons Worcestershire sauce
- 2 tablespoons minced fresh parsley

1. In a large skillet, cook bacon over medium heat until crisp. Remove to paper towels with a slotted spoon; drain, reserving drippings.
2. Meanwhile, cut steak into six serving-size pieces; pound with a meat mallet to ¼-in. thickness. Spread tops with mustard. Top each with two carrot pieces and one pickle spear; sprinkle with onion. Roll up from a short side and secure with toothpicks.
3. In a large skillet, brown roll-ups in bacon drippings over medium-high heat. Place roll-ups in a 4-qt. slow cooker. Top with mushrooms, parsnip, celery and cooked bacon.
4. In a small bowl, whisk the soup, wine and Worcestershire sauce. Pour over top. Cover and cook on low for 6-8 hours or until beef is tender. Sprinkle with parsley.

SAVORY MUSTARD PORK ROAST

Savory Mustard Pork Roast

The mustard sauce for this tender pork roast has a kiss of honey and molasses. Even though the recipe makes a large batch, I rarely have leftovers when I serve this family favorite.

—EZRA ELKON CHARLES TOWN, WV

PREP: 20 MIN. • **COOK:** 6 HOURS + STANDING
MAKES: 8 SERVINGS

- 1 **boneless pork shoulder butt roast (3 to 4 pounds)**
- ¾ **teaspoon salt**
- ¼ **teaspoon pepper**
- 1 **tablespoon canola oil**
- 1 **can (14½ ounces) diced tomatoes, drained**
- 1 **medium onion, chopped**
- 1 **can (14½ ounces) beef broth**
- ½ **cup dry red wine**
- ¾ **cup stone-ground mustard**
- 6 **garlic cloves, minced**
- 2 **tablespoons honey**
- 2 **tablespoons molasses**
- 1 **teaspoon dried thyme**
- 2 **tablespoons cornstarch**
- 2 **tablespoons cold water**

1. Sprinkle roast with salt and pepper; brown in oil in a large skillet on all sides. Transfer to a 5-qt. slow cooker. Add tomatoes and onion; pour broth and wine around meat. Combine the mustard, garlic, honey, molasses and thyme; pour over pork. Cover and cook on low for 6-7 hours or until meat is tender.

2. Remove roast; cover and let stand for 15 minutes before slicing. Meanwhile, skim fat from cooking juices; transfer juices to a small saucepan. Bring to a boil. Combine cornstarch and water until smooth; gradually stir into the pan. Bring to a boil; cook and stir for 2 minutes or until thickened. Slice pork and serve with sauce.

(5) INGREDIENTS Five-Ingredient Chili Verde

I love chili verde and order it at restaurants whenever I have the chance. I figured out how to make an easy homemade version. Guests have the option to eat it with a fork or stuffed in tortillas with a variety of toppings such as cheese, cilantro, minced onions or lime wedges. I get rave reviews every time I serve it.

—JULIE ROWLAND SALT LAKE CITY, UT

PREP: 10 MIN. • **COOK:** 5 HOURS
MAKES: 12 SERVINGS (3 QUARTS)

- 1 **boneless pork shoulder roast (4 to 5 pounds), cut into 1-inch pieces**
- 3 **cans (10 ounces each) green enchilada sauce**
- 1 **cup salsa verde**
- 1 **can (4 ounces) chopped green chilies**
- ½ **teaspoon salt**
   Hot cooked rice
   Sour cream, optional

In a 5-qt. slow cooker, combine pork, enchilada sauce, salsa verde, green chilies and salt. Cook, covered, on low 5-6 hours or until pork is tender. Serve with rice. If desired, top with sour cream.

FIVE-INGREDIENT CHILI VERDE

Simple Sparerib & Sauerkraut Supper

This sparerib recipe is old-fashioned goodness at its best. It has a little bit of everything for a delicious meal-in-one.
—**DONNA HARP** CINCINNATI, OH

PREP: 30 MIN. • **COOK:** 6 HOURS
MAKES: 4 SERVINGS

- 1 **pound fingerling potatoes**
- 1 **medium onion, chopped**
- 1 **medium Granny Smith apple, peeled and chopped**
- 3 **slices thick-sliced bacon strips, cooked and crumbled**
- 1 **jar (16 ounces) sauerkraut, undrained**
- 2 **pounds pork spareribs**
- ½ **teaspoon salt**
- ¼ **teaspoon pepper**
- 1 **tablespoon vegetable oil**
- 3 **tablespoons brown sugar**
- ¼ **teaspoon caraway seeds**
- ½ **pound smoked Polish sausage, cut into 1-inch slices**
- 1 **cup beer**

1. In a 6-qt. slow cooker, place the potatoes, onion, apple and bacon. Drain sauerkraut, reserving ⅓ cup of the liquid; add sauerkraut and reserved liquid to slow cooker.
2. Cut spareribs into serving-size portions; sprinkle with salt and pepper. In a large skillet, heat oil over medium-high heat; brown ribs in batches. Transfer to slow cooker; sprinkle with brown sugar and caraway seeds.
3. Add sausage; pour in beer. Cover and cook on low for 6-7 hours or until ribs are tender.

SLOW-COOKED PORK VERDE

Slow-Cooked Pork Verde

Comforting and hearty, our midweek entree is perfect winter fare. Serve with French bread and a green salad for a well-rounded meal.
—*TASTE OF HOME* TEST KITCHEN

PREP: 15 MIN. • **COOK:** 4½ HOURS
MAKES: 8 SERVINGS

- 3 **medium carrots, sliced**
- 1 **boneless pork shoulder butt roast (3 to 4 pounds)**
- 1 **can (15 ounces) black beans, rinsed and drained**
- 1 **can (10 ounces) green enchilada sauce**
- ¼ **cup minced fresh cilantro**
- 1 **tablespoon cornstarch**
- ¼ **cup cold water**
   Hot cooked rice

1. Place carrots in a 5-qt. slow cooker. Cut roast in half; place in slow cooker. Add the beans, enchilada sauce and cilantro. Cover and cook on low for 4½ to 5 hours or until a meat thermometer reads 160°. Remove roast to a serving platter; keep warm.
2. Skim fat from cooking juices. Transfer the cooking liquid, carrots and beans to a small saucepan. Bring to a boil. Combine cornstarch and water until smooth. Gradually stir into the pan. Bring to a boil; cook and stir for 2 minutes or until thickened. Serve with meat and rice.

Pork with Peach Sauce

I get excited when fresh peaches are in season because it means it's time to enjoy these pork ribs with family and friends. With just six ingredients, you'll be amazed at how tasty they turn out.

—CONNIE JENISTA VALRICO, FL

PREP: 20 MIN. + CHILLING • **COOK:** 5½ HOURS
MAKES: 4 SERVINGS

- **2 pounds boneless country-style pork ribs**
- **2 tablespoons taco seasoning**
- **½ cup mild salsa**
- **¼ cup peach preserves**
- **¼ cup barbecue sauce**
- **2 cups chopped fresh peeled peaches or frozen unsweetened sliced peaches, thawed and chopped**

1. In a large bowl, toss pork ribs with taco seasoning. Cover and refrigerate overnight.

2. Place pork in a 3-qt. slow cooker. In a small bowl, combine the salsa, preserves and barbecue sauce. Pour over ribs. Cover and cook on low for 5-6 hours or until meat is tender.

3. Add peaches; cover and cook 30 minutes longer or until peaches are tender.

Lamb with Orzo

Looking to switch up your slow-cooker staples? Consider this lamb and orzo entree. A terrific meal-in-one, it certainly adds flair to dinnertime doldrums. A splash of lemon juice and zesty lemon peel complement the flavors of fresh spinach and feta cheese.

—DAN KELMENSON WEST BLOOMFIELD, MI

PREP: 30 MIN. • **COOK:** 8 -10 HOURS
MAKES: 9 SERVINGS

- **1 boneless lamb shoulder roast (3 pounds)**

LAMB WITH ORZO

- **3 tablespoons lemon juice**
- **3 garlic cloves, minced**
- **2 teaspoons dried oregano**
- **2 teaspoons grated lemon peel**
- **¼ teaspoon salt**
- **1 package (16 ounces) orzo pasta**
- **2 packages (9 ounces each) fresh spinach, torn, divided**
- **1 cup (4 ounces) crumbled feta cheese, divided**

1. Cut roast in half. Place in a 5-qt. slow cooker. Drizzle with lemon juice. Sprinkle with the garlic, oregano, lemon peel and salt. Cover and cook on low for 8-10 hours or until meat is tender.

2. Cook orzo according to package directions. Remove lamb from slow cooker. Shred meat with two forks; set aside and keep warm.

3. Skim fat from cooking juices if necessary; return 1 cup cooking juices to slow cooker. Add one package of spinach. Cook on high for 5-10 minutes or until spinach is wilted. Drain orzo; add to spinach mixture. Stir in reserved meat and ½ cup feta cheese.

4. To serve, arrange remaining fresh spinach on nine individual plates. Top with lamb mixture. Sprinkle each with remaining feta cheese.

PORK WITH PEACH SAUCE

Glazed Lamb Shanks

These lamb shanks become so tender and savory after simmering with the potatoes and herbs. The Guinness and honey nicely balance with the meat, while garlic lends zing.

—ELIZABETH MITCHELL COCHRANVILLE, PA

PREP: 30 MIN. + MARINATING • **COOK:** 6 HOURS
MAKES: 4 SERVINGS

- 4 **lamb shanks (about 20 ounces each)**
- 4 **garlic cloves, thinly sliced**
- 1 **cup lemon juice**
- 4 **tablespoons olive oil, divided**
- 1 **tablespoon each minced fresh thyme, rosemary and parsley**
- 1 **teaspoon salt**
- ½ **teaspoon pepper**

SAUCE

- 1 **cup Guinness (dark beer)**
- ¼ **cup honey**
- 3 **fresh thyme sprigs**
- 2 **bay leaves**
- 1 **tablespoon Dijon mustard**
- 2 **garlic cloves, minced**
- ½ **teaspoon salt**
- ¼ **teaspoon pepper**
- ⅛ **teaspoon crushed red pepper flakes**
- 2 **pounds Yukon Gold potatoes, peeled and cut into chunks**

1. Cut slits into each lamb shank; insert garlic slices. In a large resealable plastic bag, combine the lemon juice, 2 tablespoons oil, thyme, rosemary, parsley, salt and pepper. Add the lamb; seal bag and turn to coat. Refrigerate overnight.

2. Drain and discard marinade. In large skillet, brown shanks in remaining oil on all sides in batches. Place shanks in a 5- or 6-qt. slow cooker.

3. In the same skillet, combine the beer, honey, thyme, bay leaves, Dijon, garlic, salt, pepper and pepper flakes. Bring to a boil, stirring constantly. Pour over meat. Cover and cook on low for 6-8 hours or until meat and potatoes are tender, adding the potatoes during the last 2 hours of cooking.

4. Remove lamb and potatoes from slow cooker. Strain sauce and discard bay leaves. If desired, thicken sauce. Serve with lamb and potatoes.

⑤INGREDIENTS Cherry Balsamic Pork Loin

After sampling a wonderful cherry topping for Brie at a local market, I had to come up with one for pork. If you love cherries, feel free to add more.

—SUSAN STETZEL GAINESVILLE, NY

PREP: 20 MIN. • **COOK:** 3 HOURS + STANDING
MAKES: 8 SERVINGS (1⅓ CUPS SAUCE)

- 1 **boneless pork loin roast (3 to 4 pounds)**
- 1 **teaspoon salt**
- ½ **teaspoon pepper**
- 1 **tablespoon canola oil**
- ¾ **cup cherry preserves**
- ½ **cup dried cherries**
- ⅓ **cup balsamic vinegar**
- ¼ **cup packed brown sugar**

1. Sprinkle roast with salt and pepper. In a large skillet, heat oil over medium-high heat. Brown roast on all sides.

2. Transfer to a 6-qt. slow cooker. In a small bowl, mix preserves, cherries, vinegar and brown sugar until blended; pour over roast. Cook, covered, on low 3-4 hours or until tender (a thermometer inserted in pork should read at least 145°).

3. Remove roast from slow cooker; tent with foil. Let stand 15 minutes before slicing. Skim fat from cooking juices. Serve pork with sauce.

CHERRY BALSAMIC PORK LOIN

Slow Cooker Breakfast Casserole

Here's a down-home breakfast casserole that's easy on the time-crunched cook. Do all the prep work the night before you plan to serve it, and it will be ready at sunrise. It's the perfect recipe when you're hosting weekend guests.

—ELLA STUTHEIT LAS VEGAS, NV

PREP: 25 MIN. • **COOK:** 7 HOURS
MAKES: 12 SERVINGS

- 1 package (30 ounces) frozen shredded hash brown potatoes
- 1 pound bulk pork sausage, cooked and drained
- 1 medium onion, chopped
- 1 can (4 ounces) chopped green chilies
- 1½ cups (6 ounces) shredded cheddar cheese
- 12 eggs
- 1 cup 2% milk
- ½ teaspoon salt
- ½ teaspoon pepper

In a greased 5- or 6-qt. slow cooker, layer half of the potatoes, sausage, onion, chilies and cheese. Repeat layers. In a large bowl, whisk the eggs, milk, salt and pepper; pour over top. Cover and cook on low for 7-9 hours or until eggs are set.

Slow Cooker Two-Meat Manicotti

I wanted to create my ideal version of a stuffed manicotti, with a fantastic filling and a meat sauce that's to die for. This recipe is the result, and I don't mind saying it's a success!

—SHALIMAR WIECH GLASSPORT, PA

PREP: 45 MIN. • **COOK:** 4 HOURS
MAKES: 7 SERVINGS

- ½ pound medium fresh mushrooms, chopped

SLOW COOKER
TWO-MEAT MANICOTTI

- 2 small green peppers, chopped
- 1 medium onion, chopped
- 1½ teaspoons canola oil
- 4 garlic cloves, minced
- ¾ pound ground sirloin
- ¾ pound bulk Italian sausage
- 2 jars (23½ ounces each) Italian sausage and garlic spaghetti sauce
- 1 carton (15 ounces) ricotta cheese
- 1 cup minced fresh parsley
- ½ cup shredded part-skim mozzarella cheese, divided
- ½ cup grated Parmesan cheese, divided
- 2 eggs, lightly beaten
- ½ teaspoon salt
- ¼ teaspoon pepper
- ⅛ teaspoon ground nutmeg
- 1 package (8 ounces) manicotti shells

1. In a large skillet, saute the mushrooms, peppers and onion in oil until tender. Add garlic; cook 1 minute longer. Remove from pan.

2. In the same skillet, cook beef and sausage over medium heat until no longer pink; drain. Stir in mushroom mixture and spaghetti sauce; set aside.

3. In a small bowl, combine the ricotta cheese, parsley, ¼ cup mozzarella cheese, ¼ cup Parmesan cheese, eggs and seasonings. Stuff into uncooked manicotti shells.

4. Spread 2¼ cups sauce onto the bottom of a 6-qt. slow cooker. Arrange five stuffed manicotti shells over sauce; repeat two times, using four shells on the top layer. Top with remaining sauce. Sprinkle with remaining cheeses. Cover and cook on low for 4-5 hours or until pasta is tender.

Bacon-Pineapple Tater Tot Bake

My favorite style of pizza is Hawaiian with bacon and pineapple. I used that combo to come up with this slow cooker creation. The Tater Tots make it family-friendly.

—**LISA RENSHAW** KANSAS CITY, MO

PREP: 15 MIN. • **COOK:** 4 HOURS + STANDING
MAKES: 8 SERVINGS

- 1 **package (32 ounces) frozen Tater Tots, thawed**
- 8 **ounces Canadian bacon, chopped**
- 1 **cup frozen pepper strips, thawed and chopped**
- 1 **medium onion, finely chopped**
- 1 **can (8 ounces) pineapple tidbits, drained**
- 2 **eggs**
- 3 **cans (5 ounces each) evaporated milk**
- 1 **can (15 ounces) pizza sauce**
- 1 **cup (4 ounces) shredded provolone cheese**
- ½ **cup grated Parmesan cheese, optional**

1. Place half of the Tater Tots in a greased 5-qt. slow cooker. Layer with Canadian bacon, peppers, onion and pineapple. Top with remaining Tater Tots. In a large bowl, whisk eggs, milk and pizza sauce; pour over top. Sprinkle with provolone cheese.
2. Cook, covered, on low 4-5 hours or until heated through. If desired, sprinkle with Parmesan cheese; let stand, covered, 20 minutes.

DID YOU KNOW?

Closer to ham than bacon, Canadian bacon is typically derived from a loin cut and is leaner and meatier than conventional bacon. This cut is cured, smoked and fully cooked and needs only to be warmed.

ASIAN RIBS

Asian Ribs

My husband loves these ribs, and I love the aroma that wafts through our house when I make it. The tangy, salty-sweet sauce with fresh ginger and garlic is delicious with rice or noodles.

—**JULIE KO** ROGERS, AR

PREP: 15 MIN. • **COOK:** 6 HOURS
MAKES: 6 SERVINGS (ABOUT 4 CUPS SAUCE)

- 6 **pounds pork baby back ribs, cut into serving-size pieces**
- 1⅓ **cups packed brown sugar**
- 1 **cup reduced-sodium soy sauce**
- ¼ **cup rice vinegar**
- ¼ **cup sesame oil**
- ¼ **cup minced fresh gingerroot**
- 6 **garlic cloves, minced**
- 1 **teaspoon crushed red pepper flakes**
- ¼ **cup cornstarch**
- ¼ **cup cold water**
  Thinly sliced green onions and sesame seeds, optional

1. Place ribs in a 6-qt. slow cooker. In a small bowl, combine the brown sugar, soy sauce, vinegar, oil, ginger, garlic and pepper flakes; pour over ribs. Cover and cook on low for 6-7 hours or until meat is tender.
2. Remove meat to a serving platter; keep warm. Skim fat from cooking juices; transfer to a small saucepan. Bring to a boil.
3. Combine cornstarch and water until smooth. Gradually stir into the pan. Bring to a boil; cook and stir for 2 minutes or until thickened. Serve with ribs. Garnish with onions and sesame seeds if desired.

Root Beer BBQ Ribs

You won't be disappointed with my rib recipe. The root beer soaks into the ribs while slow cooking and gives them a fantastic flavor.

—**MAIRYN S.** SANDY, UT

PREP: 25 MIN. • **COOK:** 6 HOURS
MAKES: 5 SERVINGS

- 1 **cup root beer**
- 1 **cup ketchup**
- ¼ **cup orange juice**
- 3 **tablespoons Worcestershire sauce**
- 2 **tablespoons molasses**
- 1 **teaspoon onion powder**
- 1 **teaspoon garlic powder**
- ½ **teaspoon ground ginger**
- ½ **teaspoon paprika**
- ¼ **teaspoon crushed red pepper flakes**
- 4½ **pounds pork baby back ribs**
- 1 **teaspoon salt**
- ½ **teaspoon pepper**

1. In a small saucepan, combine the first 10 ingredients. Bring to a boil over medium heat. Reduce heat; simmer, uncovered, for 10 minutes or until sauce is reduced to 2 cups. Set aside.
2. Cut ribs into five serving-size pieces; sprinkle with salt and pepper. Place in a 5- or 6-qt. slow cooker. Pour sauce over ribs. Cover and cook on low for 6-8 hours or until meat is tender. Serve with sauce.

DID YOU KNOW?

Baby back ribs come from the blade and center section of the pork loin. They are called baby back ribs because they are smaller than spareribs.

ROOT BEER BBQ RIBS

OKTOBERFEST PORK ROAST

Oktoberfest Pork Roast

My mom used to make a version of this roast when I was growing up. It has all of our favorite fall flavors, such as apples, sauerkraut and red potatoes.

—TONYA SWAIN SEVILLE, OH

PREP: 35 MIN. • **COOK:** 8 HOURS
MAKES: 8 SERVINGS

- 16 **small red potatoes**
- 1 **can (14 ounces) sauerkraut, rinsed and well drained**
- 2 **large tart apples, peeled and cut into wedges**
- 1 **pound smoked kielbasa or Polish sausage, cut into 16 slices**
- 2 **tablespoons brown sugar**
- 1 **teaspoon caraway seeds**
- 1 **teaspoon salt, divided**
- 1 **teaspoon pepper, divided**
- 1 **boneless pork loin roast (3 pounds)**
- 3 **tablespoons canola oil**

1. Place potatoes in a greased 6-qt. slow cooker. Top with sauerkraut, apples and kielbasa. Sprinkle with brown sugar, caraway seeds, 1/2 teaspoon salt and 1/2 teaspoon pepper.
2. Cut roast in half; sprinkle with remaining salt and pepper. In a large skillet, brown meat in oil on all sides. Transfer to slow cooker.
3. Cover and cook on low for 8-10 hours or until meat and vegetables are tender. Skim fat and thicken cooking liquid if desired.

Texas Pork Burritos

I'm a fan of green enchilada sauce and pair it with many foods for amazing results. One of my kitchen experiments yielded these tasty pork burritos. The sauce, combined with a host of seasonings, gives the ribs a Lone Star twist.

—SALLY SIBTHORPE SHELBY TOWNSHIP, MI

PREP: 40 MIN. • **COOK:** 6½ HOURS
MAKES: 10 SERVINGS

- 1 **boneless pork shoulder butt roast (3 to 4 pounds), cubed**
- 1 **teaspoon salt**
- ½ **teaspoon pepper**
- 2 **tablespoons canola oil**
- 2 **cans (10 ounces each) green enchilada sauce**
- 1 **large onion, thinly sliced**
- 2 **medium carrots, thinly sliced**
- 2 **cans (2¼ ounces each) sliced ripe olives, drained**
- ½ **cup chicken broth**
- 2 **tablespoons ground cumin**
- 3 **garlic cloves, minced**
- 2 **teaspoons dried oregano**
- 2 **tablespoons all-purpose flour**
- 1 **cup (8 ounces) sour cream**
- ½ **cup minced fresh cilantro**
- 10 **flour tortillas (8 inches), warmed**
- 2 **cups (8 ounces) shredded Mexican cheese blend**

1. Sprinkle pork with salt and pepper. In a large skillet, brown meat in oil in batches. Transfer to a 3-qt. slow cooker. Combine the enchilada sauce, onion, carrots, olives, broth, cumin, garlic and oregano; pour over meat. Cover and cook on low for 6-8 hours or until meat is tender.
2. Combine flour and sour cream; stir into meat mixture. Cover and cook on high for 30 minutes or until thickened. Stir in cilantro.
3. Spoon 2/3 cup pork mixture onto each tortilla; top with about 3 tablespoons cheese. Roll up tightly.

TEXAS PORK BURRITOS

Saucy Pork Chops

I don't have a lot of time to cook, so I've come to rely on my slow cooker. I fix these tangy chops at least once a week. The meat's so tender, you can cut it with a fork.

—**JENNIFER RUBERG** TWO HARBORS, MN

PREP: 15 MIN. • **COOK:** 4 HOURS
MAKES: 4 SERVINGS

- 4 **bone-in pork loin chops (8 ounces each)**
- 1 **teaspoon garlic powder**
- ½ **teaspoon salt**
- ¼ **teaspoon pepper**
- 2 **tablespoons canola oil**
- 2 **cups ketchup**
- ½ **cup packed brown sugar**
- 1 **teaspoon liquid smoke, optional**

1. Sprinkle pork chops with garlic powder, salt and pepper. In a large skillet, brown chops in oil on both sides; drain.

2. In a small bowl, combine the ketchup, brown sugar and liquid smoke if desired. Pour half of the sauce into a 3-qt. slow cooker. Top with pork chops and remaining sauce. Cover and cook on low for 4-5 hours or until meat is tender.

SAUCY PORK CHOPS

Pork Tenderloin with Cran-Apple Sauerkraut

My pork tenderloin is perfect for an Oktoberfest celebration or any time in fall when apples are ripe for picking. Serve the meat and sauerkraut with a hearty dark bread, such as rye or pumpernickel, along with an ice cold beer. Delicious!

—**BARBARA LENTO** HOUSTON, PA

PREP: 25 MIN. • **COOK:** 2 HOURS + STANDING
MAKES: 4 SERVINGS

- ¼ **pound center-cut bacon strips, chopped**
- 1 **cup sliced leeks (white portion only)**
- 1 **cup cubed peeled sweet potato**
- 1 **tablespoon water**
- 1 **can (14 ounces) sauerkraut, rinsed and well drained**
- 1 **medium apple, peeled and finely chopped**
- ½ **cup frozen cranberries**
- ½ **cup sweet white wine or unsweetened apple juice**
- ¼ **cup packed brown sugar**
- 1 **teaspoon caraway seeds**
- ¾ **teaspoon salt, divided**
- 1 **pork tenderloin (1 pound)**
- ¼ **teaspoon pepper**

1. In a large skillet, cook bacon and leeks over medium heat 6-8 minutes or until bacon is crisp, stirring occasionally. Remove with a slotted spoon; drain on paper towels.

2. Place sweet potato and water in a large microwave-safe dish. Microwave, covered, on high for 2-3 minutes or until potatoes are almost tender; drain. Stir in bacon mixture, sauerkraut, apple, cranberries, wine, brown sugar, caraway seeds and ¼ teaspoon salt.

3. Transfer half of the sauerkraut mixture to a greased 4-qt. slow cooker. Sprinkle pork with pepper and remaining salt; place in slow cooker.

PORK TENDERLOIN WITH CRAN-APPLE SAUERKRAUT

Top with remaining sauerkraut mixture. Cook, covered, on low 2-3 hours or until pork is tender (a thermometer inserted in pork should read at least 145°).

4. Remove pork from slow cooker; tent with foil. Let stand 10 minutes before slicing. Serve pork with sauerkraut.

TOP TIP

Pork tenderloin thaws quickly, so it's an idaeal choice when you only have frozen meats in your freezer to select from. Thaw it using the "defrost" cycle of your microwave according to the manufacturer's directions.

Asian Pork Chops

I enjoy Asian food, and one day when I had pork chops on hand, I decided to put this spin on them. The sauce is sweet and tangy, and the meat is moist and tender.

—BETTY KERCHEVAL BELLEVUE, WA

PREP: 20 MIN. • **COOK:** 3 HOURS
MAKES: 4 SERVINGS

- 4 boneless pork loin chops (5 ounces each)
- ¼ teaspoon salt
- ⅛ teaspoon pepper
- 1 medium onion, chopped
- 1 medium green pepper, chopped
- 4 green onions, chopped
- ¼ cup packed brown sugar
- ¼ cup white wine or chicken broth
- ¼ cup soy sauce
- 1 tablespoon crystallized ginger, finely chopped
- 1½ teaspoons sesame oil
- 1 garlic clove, minced
- 2 tablespoons cornstarch
- 2 tablespoons cold water
  Hot cooked rice, optional

1. Sprinkle pork chops with salt and pepper. Place in a 3-qt. slow cooker. Add the onion, green pepper and green onions. In a small bowl, combine the brown sugar, wine, soy sauce, ginger, sesame oil and garlic; pour over chops. Cover and cook on low for 3-4 hours or until meat is tender.

2. Remove meat to a serving platter; keep warm. Skim fat from cooking juices; transfer to a small saucepan. Bring liquid to a boil. Combine cornstarch and water until smooth. Gradually stir into the pan. Bring to a boil; cook and stir for 2 minutes or until thickened. Serve with pork and rice if desired.

CANTONESE SWEET AND SOUR PORK

Cantonese Sweet and Sour Pork

Step away from the takeout menu. There will be no reason for delivery once you get a bite of my version of traditional sweet and sour pork. The tender veggies, juicy pork and flavorful sauce are delicious over steaming hot rice.

—NANCY TEWS ANTIGO, WI

PREP: 20 MIN. • **COOK:** 7½ HOURS
MAKES: 6 SERVINGS

- 1 can (15 ounces) tomato sauce
- 1 medium onion, halved and sliced
- 1 medium green pepper, cut into strips
- 1 can (4½ ounces) sliced mushrooms, drained
- 3 tablespoons brown sugar
- 4½ teaspoons white vinegar
- 2 teaspoons steak sauce
- 1 teaspoon salt
- 1½ pounds pork tenderloin, cut into 1-inch cubes
- 1 tablespoon olive oil
- 1 can (8 ounces) unsweetened pineapple chunks, drained
  Hot cooked rice

1. In a large bowl, combine the first eight ingredients; set aside.

2. In a large skillet, brown pork in oil in batches. Transfer to a 3- or 4-qt. slow cooker. Pour tomato sauce mixture over pork. Cover and cook on low for 7-8 hours or until meat is tender.

3. Add pineapple; cover and cook 30 minutes longer or until heated through. Serve with rice.

ASIAN PORK CHOPS

Pork Roast with Plum Sauce

The ginger, soy sauce and other seasonings in this Asian-inspired roast evoke the Far East. If you don't have plum jam, try apricot preserves instead.

—JEANNIE KLUGH LANCASTER, PA

PREP: 20 MIN. • **COOK:** 5 HOURS + STANDING
MAKES: 10 SERVINGS

- 1 boneless whole pork loin roast (4 pounds)
- 2 tablespoons canola oil
- 1 cup sherry
- 2 tablespoons dried thyme
- 2 tablespoons soy sauce
- 4 garlic cloves, minced
- 1 tablespoon ground mustard
- 1½ teaspoons ground ginger
- 1 teaspoon garlic salt
- ½ teaspoon salt
- ½ teaspoon pepper
- ½ cup plum jam
- 2 tablespoons cornstarch
- ¼ cup cold water

1. Cut roast in half. In a large skillet, brown roast in oil on all sides; drain. Transfer to a 4-qt. slow cooker.

2. In a small bowl, combine the sherry, thyme, soy sauce, garlic, mustard, ginger, garlic salt, salt and pepper; pour over pork. Cover and cook on low for 5 to 6 hours or until a meat is tender. Remove meat to a serving platter; keep warm. Let stand for 10-15 minutes before slicing.

3. Skim fat from cooking juices; transfer to a small saucepan. Add jam. Bring to a boil. Combine cornstarch and water until smooth. Gradually stir into the pan. Bring to a boil; cook and stir for 2 minutes or until thickened. Serve with gravy.

Tangy Lamb Tagine

Lamb stew is one of my favorite dishes. But I wanted to experiment and expand my cooking repertoire, so I got creative and combined lamb with Moroccan spices. The stew tastes even better served a day or two later, when the flavors have had a chance to blend.

—BRIDGET KLUSMAN OTSEGO, MI

PREP: 40 MIN. • **COOK:** 8 HOURS
MAKES: 8 SERVINGS

- 3 pounds lamb stew meat, cut into 1½-inch cubes
- 1 teaspoon salt
- 1 teaspoon pepper
- 4 tablespoons olive oil, divided
- 6 medium carrots, sliced
- 2 medium onions, chopped
- 6 garlic cloves, minced
- 2 teaspoons grated lemon peel
- ¼ cup lemon juice
- 1 tablespoon minced fresh gingerroot
- 1½ teaspoons ground cinnamon
- 1½ teaspoons ground cumin
- 1½ teaspoons paprika
- 2½ cups reduced-sodium chicken broth
- ¼ cup sweet vermouth
- ¼ cup honey
- ½ cup pitted dates, chopped
- ½ cup sliced almonds, toasted

1. Sprinkle lamb with salt and pepper. In a Dutch oven, brown meat in 2 tablespoons oil in batches. Using a slotted spoon, transfer to a 4- or 5-qt. slow cooker.

2. In the same skillet, saute the carrots, onions, garlic and lemon peel in remaining oil until crisp-tender. Add the lemon juice, ginger, cinnamon, cumin and paprika; cook and stir 2 minutes longer. Add to slow cooker.

3. Stir in the broth, vermouth, honey and dates. Cover and cook on low for 8-10 hours or until lamb is tender. Sprinkle with almonds.

TANGY LAMB TAGINE

APPLE-CINNAMON PORK LOIN

Apple-Cinnamon Pork Loin

An apple-cinnamon aroma fills the entire house while this pork loin slowly simmers. Boasting delectable autumn flavors, it's perfect when the days turn chilly. It tastes even better with creamy homemade mashed potatoes.
—**RACHEL SCHULTZ** LANSING, MI

PREP: 20 MIN. • **COOK:** 6 HOURS
MAKES: 6 SERVINGS

- 1 boneless pork loin roast (2 to 3 pounds)
- ½ teaspoon salt
- ¼ teaspoon pepper
- 1 tablespoon canola oil
- 3 medium apples, peeled and sliced, divided
- ¼ cup honey
- 1 small red onion, halved and sliced
- 1 tablespoon ground cinnamon
  Minced fresh parsley, optional

1. Sprinkle roast with salt and pepper. In a large skillet, brown roast in oil on all sides; cool slightly. With a paring knife, cut about sixteen 3-in.-deep slits in sides of roast; insert one apple slice into each slit.

2. Place half of the remaining apples in a 4-qt. slow cooker. Place roast over apples. Drizzle with honey; top with onion and remaining apples. Sprinkle with cinnamon.

3. Cover and cook on low for 6-8 hours or until meat is tender. Remove pork and apple mixture; keep warm.

4. Transfer cooking juices to a small saucepan. Bring to a boil; cook until liquid is reduced by half. Serve with pork and apple mixture. Sprinkle with parsley if desired.

Creamy Mushroom, Ham & Potatoes

Once folks try these potatoes, they always come back for more. I like this comforting main dish because it uses only seven ingredients and it is easy to prepare.
—**TRACI MEADOWS** MONETT, MO

PREP: 25 MIN. • **COOK:** 4 HOURS
MAKES: 4 SERVINGS

- 1 can (10¾ ounces) condensed cream of mushroom soup, undiluted
- ½ cup 2% milk
- 1 tablespoon dried parsley flakes
- 6 medium potatoes, peeled and thinly sliced
- 1 small onion, chopped
- 1½ cups cubed fully cooked ham
- 6 slices process American cheese

In a small bowl, combine the soup, milk and parsley. In a greased 3-qt. slow cooker, layer half of the potatoes, onion, ham, cheese and soup mixture. Repeat layers. Cover and cook on low for 4-5 hours or until potatoes are tender.

CREAMY MUSHROOM, HAM & POTATOES

Conga Lime Pork

PREP: 20 MIN. • **COOK:** 4 HOURS
MAKES: 6 SERVINGS

- 1 **teaspoon salt, divided**
- ½ **teaspoon pepper, divided**
- 1 **boneless pork shoulder butt roast (2 to 3 pounds)**
- 1 **tablespoon canola oil**
- 1 **large onion, chopped**
- 3 **garlic cloves, peeled and thinly sliced**
- ½ **cup water**
- 2 **chipotle peppers in adobo sauce, seeded and chopped**
- 2 **tablespoons molasses**
- 2 **cups broccoli coleslaw mix**
- 1 **medium mango, peeled and chopped**
- 2 **tablespoons lime juice**
- 1½ **teaspoons grated lime peel**
- 6 **prepared corn muffins, halved**

1. Sprinkle ¾ teaspoon salt and ¼ teaspoon pepper over roast. In a large skillet, brown pork in oil on all sides. Transfer meat to a 3- or 4-qt. slow cooker.

2. In the same skillet, saute onion until tender. Add garlic; cook 1 minute longer. Add water, chipotle peppers and molasses, stirring to loosen browned bits from pan. Pour over pork. Cover and cook on high for 4-5 hours or until meat is tender.

3. Remove roast; cool slightly. Skim fat from cooking juices. Shred pork with two forks and return to slow cooker; heat through. In a large bowl, combine the coleslaw mix, mango, lime juice, lime peel and remaining salt and pepper.

4. Place muffin halves cut side down on an ungreased baking sheet. Broil 4 in. from the heat for 2-3 minutes or until lightly toasted. Serve pork with muffins; top with slaw.

CONGA LIME PORK

EASY CITRUS HAM

PORK CHOPS WITH SCALLOPED POTATOES

Easy Citrus Ham

I created this recipe many years ago with items I had on hand. The succulent ham has a mild citrus flavor. It was so popular at a church social that I knew I had a keeper!

—SHEILA CHRISTENSEN SAN MARCOS, CA

PREP: 15 MIN. • **COOK:** 4 HOURS + STANDING
MAKES: 10-12 SERVINGS

- 1 **boneless fully cooked ham (3 to 4 pounds)**
- ½ **cup packed dark brown sugar**
- 1 **can (12 ounces) lemon-lime soda, divided**
- 1 **medium navel orange, thinly sliced**
- 1 **medium lemon, thinly sliced**
- 1 **medium lime, thinly sliced**
- 1 **tablespoon chopped crystallized ginger**

1. Cut ham in half; place in a 5-qt. slow cooker. In a small bowl, combine the brown sugar and ¼ cup soda; rub over ham. Top with orange, lemon and lime slices. Add the candied ginger and remaining soda to the slow cooker.

2. Cover and cook on low for 4-5 hours or until a meat thermometer reads 140°, basting occasionally with cooking juices. Let stand for 10 minutes before slicing.

Pork Chops with Scalloped Potatoes

My sister gave me a similar recipe for a casserole baked in the oven, but I altered it slightly to cook on the stovetop and in the slow cooker. Everyone who has tasted it loves it. This is a homey dinner that feels Sunday-special.

—ELIZABETH JOHNSTON GLENDALE, AZ

PREP: 30 MIN. • **COOK:** 8 HOURS
MAKES: 6 SERVINGS

- 4 **medium potatoes, peeled and thinly sliced**
- 6 **bone-in pork loin chops (7 ounces each)**
- 1 **tablespoon canola oil**
- 2 **large onions, sliced and separated into rings**
- 2 **teaspoons butter**
- 3 **tablespoons all-purpose flour**
- ¼ **teaspoon salt**
- ¼ **teaspoon pepper**
- 1 **can (14½ ounces) reduced-sodium chicken broth**
- 1 **cup fat-free milk**

1. Place potatoes in a 5- or 6-qt. slow cooker coated with cooking spray. In a large nonstick skillet, brown pork chops in oil in batches.

2. Place chops over potatoes. Saute onions in drippings until tender; place over chops. Melt butter in skillet. Combine the flour, salt, pepper and broth until smooth. Stir into pan. Add milk. Bring to a boil; cook and stir for 2 minutes or until thickened.

3. Pour sauce over onions. Cover and cook on low for 8-10 hours or until pork is tender. Skim fat and thicken cooking juices if desired.

SLOW-SIMMERING PASTA SAUCE

HOISIN PORK WRAPS

Slow-Simmering Pasta Sauce

Spaghetti with hot buttered garlic bread is my kids' top pick for dinner. Through trial and error, I came up with my own meat sauce. This is the popular result.

—**SAMANTHA VICARS** KENOSHA, WI

PREP: 20 MIN. • **COOK:** 6 HOURS
MAKES: 6 SERVINGS

- 1 **pound bulk Italian sausage**
- 1 **medium onion, chopped**
- 3 **garlic cloves, minced**
- 2 **cans (14½ ounces each) diced tomatoes, undrained**
- 1 **can (8 ounces) tomato sauce**
- 1 **can (6 ounces) tomato paste**
- 1 **tablespoon brown sugar**
- 2 **bay leaves**
- 2 **teaspoons dried oregano**
- 2 **teaspoons dried basil**
- 1 **teaspoon salt**
- ½ **teaspoon dried thyme**
- ¼ **cup minced fresh basil, divided**
  Hot cooked pasta

1. In a large skillet, cook sausage and onion over medium heat for 7-8 minutes or until sausage is no longer pink and onion is tender. Add garlic; cook 1 minute longer. Drain. Transfer to a 3-qt. slow cooker.

2. Stir in the tomatoes, tomato sauce, tomato paste, brown sugar, bay leaves, oregano, dried basil, salt and thyme. Cover and cook on low for 6-8 hours.

3. Discard bay leaves; stir in half of the fresh basil. Serve with pasta. Top with remaining basil.

Hoisin Pork Wraps

For a casual get-together, set a buffet with the pork, tortillas and the red cabbage slaw and have your guests make their own wraps.

—**LINDA WOO** DERBY, KS

PREP: 25 MIN. • **COOK:** 7 HOURS
MAKES: 15 SERVINGS

- 1 **boneless pork loin roast (3 pounds)**
- 1 **cup hoisin sauce, divided**
- 1 **tablespoon minced fresh gingerroot**
- 6 **cups shredded red cabbage**
- 1½ **cups shredded carrots**
- ¼ **cup thinly sliced green onions**
- 3 **tablespoons rice vinegar**
- 4½ **teaspoons sugar**
- 15 **flour tortillas (8 inches), warmed**

1. Cut roast in half. Combine ⅓ cup hoisin sauce and ginger; rub over pork. Transfer to a 3-qt. slow cooker. Cover and cook on low for 7-8 hours or until pork is tender.

2. Meanwhile, in a large bowl, combine the cabbage, carrots, onions, vinegar and sugar. Chill until serving.

3. Shred meat with two forks and return to the slow cooker; heat through. Place 2 teaspoons remaining hoisin sauce down the center of each tortilla; top with ⅓ cup shredded pork and ⅓ cup coleslaw. Roll up.

SPICED LAMB STEW WITH APRICOTS

Spiced Lamb Stew with Apricots

My family loves lamb, especially my son. During his first year of college, he claimed to be a vegetarian. When he came home, I had a pot of my lamb stew simmering in the kitchen. When my husband and I wanted to eat dinner, there were only a few shreds of meat left floating in the gravy—and my son confessed that he was the culprit!

—ARLENE ERLBACH MORTON GROVE, IL

PREP: 30 MIN. • **COOK:** 5 HOURS
MAKES: 5 SERVINGS

- 2 pounds lamb stew meat, cut into ¾-inch cubes
- 3 tablespoons butter
- 1½ cups chopped sweet onion
- ¾ cup dried apricots
- ½ cup orange juice
- ½ cup chicken broth
- 2 teaspoons paprika
- 2 teaspoons ground allspice
- 2 teaspoons ground cinnamon
- 1½ teaspoons salt
- 1 teaspoon ground cardamom
  Hot cooked couscous
  Chopped dried apricots, optional

1. In a large skillet, brown lamb in butter in batches. With a slotted spoon, transfer to a 3-qt. slow cooker. In the same skillet, saute onion in drippings until tender. Stir in the apricots, orange juice, broth and seasonings; pour over lamb.

2. Cover and cook on high for 5-6 hours or until meat is tender. Serve with couscous. Sprinkle with chopped apricots if desired.

Cajun Pork and Rice

After returning home from traveling, I found that my cupboards were a little bare. I pulled together the few ingredients that were in my fridge and pantry. To my surprise, the combo made a great meal boasting Cajun flavors. I have made it several times since.

—ALLISON GAPINSKI CARY, NC

PREP: 20 MIN. • **COOK:** 4 HOURS 10 MIN.
MAKES: 4 SERVINGS

- 1½ teaspoons ground cumin
- 1½ teaspoons chili powder
- 1½ pounds boneless pork loin chops
- 1 can (14½ ounces) petite diced tomatoes, undrained
- 1 small onion, finely chopped
- 1 celery rib, finely chopped
- 1 small carrot, shredded
- 1 garlic clove, minced
- ½ teaspoon Louisiana-style hot sauce
- ¼ teaspoon salt
- 1½ cups uncooked instant rice
- 1 cup reduced-sodium chicken broth
- 1 teaspoon olive oil
- 1 medium green pepper, julienned

1. Mix cumin and chili powder; sprinkle pork chops with 2 teaspoon spice mixture. Transfer to a 4-qt. slow cooker.

2. In a small bowl, mix tomatoes, onion, celery, carrot, garlic, hot sauce, salt and remaining spice mixture; pour over chops. Cook, covered, on low 4-5 hours or until meat is tender.

3. Stir in rice and chicken broth, breaking up pork into pieces. Cook, covered, on low 10-15 minutes longer or until rice is tender. In a small skillet, heat oil over medium-high heat. Add green pepper; cook and stir 5-7 minutes or until crisp-tender. Serve with pork mixture.

CAJUN PORK AND RICE

Harvest Butternut & Pork Stew

Cure your craving for something different with a savory stew that's tasty with warm bread. Edamame adds an interesting protein-packed touch.

—**ERIN CHILCOAT** CENTRAL ISLIP, NY

PREP: 20 MIN. • **COOK:** 7½ HOURS
MAKES: 6 SERVINGS (2 QUARTS)

- ⅓ cup plus 1 tablespoon all-purpose flour, divided
- 1 tablespoon paprika
- 1 teaspoon salt
- 1 teaspoon ground coriander
- 1½ pounds boneless pork shoulder butt roast, cut into 1-inch cubes
- 1 tablespoon canola oil
- 2¾ cups cubed peeled butternut squash
- 1 can (14½ ounces) diced tomatoes, undrained
- 1 cup frozen corn, thawed
- 1 medium onion, chopped
- 2 tablespoons cider vinegar
- 1 bay leaf
- 2½ cups reduced-sodium chicken broth
- 1⅔ cups frozen shelled edamame, thawed

1. In a large resealable plastic bag, combine ⅓ cup flour, paprika, salt and coriander. Add pork, a few pieces at a time, and shake to coat.
2. In a large skillet, brown pork in oil in batches; drain. Transfer to a 5-qt. slow cooker. Add the squash, tomatoes, corn, onion, vinegar and bay leaf. In a small bowl, combine broth and remaining flour until smooth; stir into slow cooker.
3. Cover and cook on low for 8-10 hours or until pork and vegetables are tender. Stir in edamame; cover and cook 30 minutes longer. Discard bay leaf.

HARVEST BUTTERNUT & PORK STEW

ITALIAN SAUSAGE AND VEGETABLES

Italian Sausage and Vegetables

What can be better than a complete meal-in-a-pot— one that is both healthy and delicious? This dish is wonderful served with a slice of hot garlic bread. I found the recipe in a magazine and made adjustments to suit myself.

—GINNY STUBY ALTOONA, PA

PREP: 20 MIN. • **COOK:** 5½ HOURS
MAKES: 6 SERVINGS

- 1¼ **pounds sweet or hot Italian turkey sausage links**
- 1 **can (28 ounces) diced tomatoes, undrained**
- 2 **medium potatoes, cut into 1-inch pieces**
- 4 **small zucchini, cut into 1-inch slices**
- 1 **medium onion, cut into wedges**
- ½ **teaspoon garlic powder**
- ¼ **teaspoon crushed red pepper flakes**
- ¼ **teaspoon dried oregano**
- ¼ **teaspoon dried basil**
- 1 **tablespoon dry bread crumbs**
- ¾ **cup shredded pepper jack cheese**

1. In a nonstick skillet, brown sausages over medium heat. Place in a 5-qt. slow cooker. Add vegetables and seasonings. Cover and cook on low for 5½ to 6½ hours or until a thermometer reads 165°.
2. Remove sausages and cut into 1-in. pieces; return to slow cooker. Stir in bread crumbs. Serve in bowls; sprinkle with cheese.

Creamy Garlic-Lemon Chicken

I needed an easy way to prepare my family's favorite meal, lemon chicken, and this recipe was it. It's a keeper. My entire family loves the rich dinner, and everyone who tries it asks for the recipe. I serve the chicken over a bed of rice or couscous and spoon some of the creamy sauce on top.

—NAN SLAUGHTER SAMMAMISH, WA

PREP: 15 MIN. • **COOK:** 3 HOURS
MAKES: 6 SERVINGS

- 1 **cup vegetable broth**
- 1½ **teaspoons grated lemon peel**
- 3 **tablespoons lemon juice**
- 2 **tablespoons capers, drained**
- 3 **garlic cloves, minced**
- ½ **teaspoon pepper**
- 6 **boneless skinless chicken breast halves (6 ounces each)**
- 2 **tablespoons butter**
- 2 **tablespoons all-purpose flour**
- ½ **cup heavy whipping cream**
  Hot cooked rice

1. In a small bowl, combine the first six ingredients. Place chicken in a 5-qt. slow cooker; pour broth mixture over chicken. Cook, covered, on low 3-4 hours or until chicken is tender.
2. Remove chicken from slow cooker; keep warm. In a large saucepan, melt butter over medium heat. Stir in flour until smooth; gradually whisk in cooking juices. Bring to a boil, stirring constantly; cook and stir 1-2 minutes or until thickened. Remove from heat and stir in cream. Serve chicken and rice with sauce.

CREAMY GARLIC-LEMON CHICKEN

Turkey Breast with Berry Compote

At our house, turkey is often on the menu because we enjoy it so much. We can have it all year around as this delicious dish is a great way to get all that yummy flavor without heating up the house; the berries make the perfect summer chutney.

—MARGARET BRACHER ROBERTSDALE, AL

PREP: 35 MIN. • **COOK:** 3 HOURS
MAKES: 12 SERVINGS (3¼ CUP COMPOTE)

- 1 teaspoon salt
- ½ teaspoon garlic powder
- ½ teaspoon dried thyme
- ½ teaspoon pepper
- 2 boneless turkey breast halves (2 pounds each)
- ⅓ cup water

COMPOTE

- 2 medium apples, peeled and finely chopped
- 2 cups fresh raspberries
- 2 cups fresh blueberries
- 1 cup white grape juice
- ¼ teaspoon crushed red pepper flakes
- ¼ teaspoon ground ginger

1. Mix salt, garlic powder, thyme and pepper; rub over turkey breasts. Place in a 5- or 6-qt. slow cooker. Pour water around turkey. Cook, covered, on low 3-4 hours (a thermometer inserted in turkey should read at least 165°).
2. Remove turkey from slow cooker; tent with foil. Let stand 10 minutes before slicing.
3. Meanwhile, in a large saucepan, combine compote ingredients. Bring to a boil. Reduce heat to medium; cook, uncovered, 15-20 minutes or until slightly thickened and apples are tender, stirring occasionally. Serve turkey with compote.

MANGO-PINEAPPLE CHICKEN TACOS

FREEZE IT Mango-Pineapple Chicken Tacos

I lived in the Caribbean as a child and the fresh tropical fruits in this delectable chicken entree bring me back to my childhood.

—LISSA NELSON PROVO, UT

PREP: 25 MIN. • **COOK:** 5 HOURS
MAKES: 16 SERVINGS

- 2 medium mangoes, peeled and chopped
- 1½ cups cubed fresh pineapple or canned pineapple chunks, drained
- 2 medium tomatoes, chopped
- 1 medium red onion, finely chopped
- 2 small Anaheim peppers, seeded and chopped
- 2 green onions, finely chopped
- 1 tablespoon lime juice
- 1 teaspoon sugar
- 4 pounds bone-in chicken breast halves, skin removed
- 3 teaspoons salt
- ¼ cup packed brown sugar
- 32 taco shells, warmed
- ¼ cup minced fresh cilantro

1. In a large bowl, combine the first eight ingredients. Place chicken in a 6-qt. slow cooker; sprinkle with salt and brown sugar. Top with mango mixture. Cover and cook on low for 5-6 hours or until chicken is tender.
2. Remove chicken; cool slightly. Strain cooking juices, reserving mango mixture and ½ cup juices. Discard remaining juices. When cool enough to handle, remove chicken from bones; discard bones.
3. Shred chicken with two forks. Return chicken and reserved mango mixture and cooking juices to slow cooker; heat through. Serve in taco shells; sprinkle with cilantro.
FREEZE OPTION *Freeze cooled meat mixture in freezer containers. To use, partially thaw in refrigerator overnight. Heat through in a saucepan, stirring occasionally and adding a little broth if necessary.*

Chicken & Mushroom Alfredo

Everyone in my family loves this dinner. You can add vegetables you have on hand to make it heartier, such as corn, peas or red bell pepper.

—**MONICA WERNER** ONTARIO, CA

PREP: 20 MIN. • **COOK:** 4 HOURS
MAKES: 4 SERVINGS

- 4 **bone-in chicken breast halves (12 to 14 ounces each), skin removed**
- 2 **tablespoons canola oil**
- 1 **can (10¾ ounces) condensed cream of chicken soup, undiluted**
- 1 **can (10¾ ounces) condensed cream of mushroom soup, undiluted**
- 1 **cup chicken broth**
- 1 **small onion, chopped**
- 1 **jar (6 ounces) sliced mushrooms, drained**
- ¼ **teaspoon garlic salt**
- ¼ **teaspoon pepper**
- 8 **ounces fettuccine**
- 1 **package (8 ounces) cream cheese, softened and cubed**
  Shredded Parmesan cheese, optional

1. In a large skillet, brown chicken in oil in batches. Transfer to a 4- or 5-qt. slow cooker. In a large bowl, combine the soups, broth, onion, mushrooms, garlic salt and pepper; pour over meat. Cover and cook on low for 4-5 hours or until chicken is tender.

2. Cook fettuccine according to package directions; drain. Remove chicken from slow cooker and keep warm. Turn slow cooker off and stir in cream cheese until melted. Serve with fettucine. Top with Parmesan cheese if desired.

CHICKEN & MUSHROOM ALFREDO

CARIBBEAN CHICKEN STEW

Caribbean Chicken Stew

I lived with a West Indian family for awhile and enjoyed watching them cook. I left out the oil and sugar this recipe originally called for, removed the chicken skin and used chicken sausage to lighten it up.

—**JOANNE IOVINO** KINGS PARK, NY

PREP: 25 MIN. + MARINATING • **COOK:** 6 HOURS
MAKES: 8 SERVINGS

- ¼ cup ketchup
- 3 garlic cloves, minced
- 1 tablespoon sugar
- 1 tablespoon hot pepper sauce
- 1 teaspoon browning sauce, optional
- 1 teaspoon dried basil
- 1 teaspoon dried thyme
- 1 teaspoon paprika
- ½ teaspoon salt
- ½ teaspoon dried oregano
- ½ teaspoon ground allspice
- ½ teaspoon pepper
- 8 bone-in chicken thighs (about 3 pounds), skin removed
- 1 pound fully cooked andouille chicken sausage links, sliced
- 1 medium onion, finely chopped
- 2 medium carrots, finely chopped
- 2 celery ribs, finely chopped

1. In a large resealable plastic bag, combine ketchup, garlic, sugar, pepper sauce and, if desired, browning sauce; stir in seasonings. Add chicken thighs, sausage and vegetables. Seal bag and turn to coat. Refrigerate 8 hours or overnight.

2. Transfer contents of bag to a 4- or 5-qt. slow cooker. Cook, covered, on low 6-8 hours or until chicken is tender.

Lemon Dill Chicken

Here, chicken gets a sunny treatment with help from lemon. The slow-cooked entree goes well with a side of noodles or a quick mixed green salad.

—**LORI LOCKREY** PICKERING, ON

PREP: 20 MIN. • **COOK:** 4 HOURS + STANDING
MAKES: 6 SERVINGS

- 2 medium onions, coarsely chopped
- 2 tablespoons butter, softened
- ¼ teaspoon grated lemon peel
- 1 broiler/fryer chicken (4 to 5 pounds)
- ¼ cup chicken stock
- 4 sprigs fresh parsley
- 4 fresh dill sprigs
- 3 tablespoons lemon juice
- 1 teaspoon salt
- 1 teaspoon paprika
- ½ teaspoon dried thyme
- ¼ teaspoon pepper

1. Place onions on bottom of a 6-qt. slow cooker. In a small bowl, mix butter and lemon peel.

2. Tuck wings under chicken; tie drumsticks together. With fingers, carefully loosen skin from chicken breast; rub butter mixture under the skin. Secure skin to underside of breast with toothpicks. Place chicken over onions, breast side up. Add stock, parsley and dill.

3. Drizzle lemon juice over the chicken; sprinkle with seasonings. Cook, covered, on low 4-5 hours (a thermometer inserted in thigh should read at least 175°).

4. Remove chicken from slow cooker; tent with foil. Let stand 15 minutes before carving.

LEMON DILL CHICKEN

CHICKEN CORN BREAD CASSEROLE

Chicken Corn Bread Casserole

I love this super-easy chicken dish because it tastes like Thanksgiving, but without all the hassle! It's a hearty, delicious meal for the fall and winter seasons.
—**NANCY BARKER** PEORIA, AZ

PREP: 40 MIN. • **COOK:** 3 HOURS
MAKES: 6 SERVINGS

- 5 **cups cubed corn bread**
- ¼ **cup butter, cubed**
- 1 **large onion, chopped (about 2 cups)**
- 4 **celery ribs, chopped (about 2 cups)**
- 3 **cups shredded cooked chicken**
- 1 **can (10¾ ounces) condensed cream of chicken soup, undiluted**
- 1 **can (10¾ ounces) condensed cream of mushroom soup, undiluted**
- ½ **cup reduced-sodium chicken broth**
- 1 **teaspoon poultry seasoning**
- ½ **teaspoon salt**
- ½ **teaspoon rubbed sage**
- ¼ **teaspoon pepper**

1. Preheat oven to 350°. Place bread cubes on an ungreased 15x10-in. baking pan. Bake 20-25 minutes or until toasted. Cool on baking pan.
2. In a large skillet, heat butter over medium-high heat. Add onion and celery; cook and stir 6-8 minutes or until tender. Transfer to a greased 4-qt. slow cooker. Stir in corn bread, chicken, soups, broth and seasonings.
3. Cook, covered, on low 3-4 hours or until heated through.

Chicken with Apple-Chardonnay Gravy

I create my own recipes by experimenting with various ingredients in the kitchen. I love this savory slow-cooker chicken dish because it's easy, affordable and fills the house with awesome aromas that make your mouth water.
—**THERESA RETELLE** APPLETON, WI

PREP: 20 MIN. • **COOK:** 6 HOURS
MAKES: 6 SERVINGS

- 6 **chicken leg quarters**
- ½ **teaspoon salt**
- ¼ **teaspoon pepper**
- 2 **large sweet apples, peeled and cut into wedges**
- 1 **large sweet onion, chopped**
- 2 **celery ribs, chopped**
- ½ **cup chardonnay**
- 1 **envelope brown gravy mix**
- 2 **large garlic cloves, minced**
- 1 **teaspoon each minced fresh oregano, rosemary and thyme**
  Hot mashed potatoes

1. Sprinkle chicken with salt and pepper. Place half of the chicken in a 5-qt. slow cooker. In a bowl, combine the apples, onion and celery; spoon half of the mixture over chicken. Repeat layers.
2. In the same bowl, whisk wine, gravy mix, garlic and herbs until blended; pour over top. Cover and cook on low for 6-8 hours or until chicken is tender.
3. Remove chicken to a serving platter; keep warm. Cool the apple mixture slightly; skim fat. In a blender, cover and process apple mixture in batches until smooth. Transfer to a saucepan and heat through over medium heat, stirring occasionally. Serve with chicken and mashed potatoes.

CHICKEN WITH APPLE-CHARDONNAY GRAVY

CHICKEN & BLACK BEAN SOFT TACOS

Chicken & Black Bean Soft Tacos

My husband and I love Mexican food, and these tacos have become one of our favorite meals. Try setting out the toppings in different bowls on the table so dinner guests and kids can assemble their own tacos.

—**LAURA RODRIGUEZ** WILLOUGHBY, OH

PREP: 20 MIN. • **COOK:** 4¼ HOURS
MAKES: 6 SERVINGS

- 1 **can (8 ounces) crushed pineapple**
- ½ **cup salsa**
- 2 **green onions, sliced**
- 1 **teaspoon grated lime peel**
- ¼ **cup lime juice**
- ½ **teaspoon chili powder**
- ¼ **teaspoon garlic powder**
- ¼ **teaspoon ground cumin**
- ⅛ **teaspoon each salt, cayenne pepper and pepper**
- 1 **pound boneless skinless chicken thighs**
- 1 **can (15 ounces) black beans, rinsed and drained**
- 12 **flour tortillas (6 inches), warmed**
  Toppings: shredded Mexican cheese blend, shredded lettuce and chopped avocado

1. In a small bowl, combine the first five ingredients; stir in seasonings. Place chicken in a 3-qt. slow cooker; add pineapple mixture. Cook, covered, on low 4-5 hours or until chicken is tender.
2. Remove chicken; cool slightly. Shred meat with two forks; return to slow cooker. Stir in beans. Cook, covered, on low 15-20 minutes longer or until heated through. Using a slotted spoon, serve chicken mixture in tortillas with toppings.

Chicken Thighs with Ginger-Peach Sauce

This sweet-and-sour main dish has become a favorite recipe to prepare on Sunday. It's easy to assemble and requires very little clean up, plus I have plenty of time to do other things!

—**LISA RENSHAW** KANSAS CITY, MO

PREP: 15 MIN. • **COOK:** 4 HOURS
MAKES: 10 SERVINGS

- 10 **boneless skinless chicken thighs (about 2½ pounds)**
- 1 **cup sliced peeled fresh or frozen peaches**
- 1 **cup golden raisins**
- 1 **cup peach preserves**
- ⅓ **cup chili sauce**
- 2 **tablespoons minced crystallized ginger**
- 1 **tablespoon reduced-sodium soy sauce**
- 1 **tablespoon minced garlic**
  Hot cooked rice, optional

1. Place chicken in a 4-qt. slow cooker coated with cooking spray. Top with peaches and raisins. In a small bowl, combine the preserves, chili sauce, ginger, soy sauce and garlic. Spoon over the top.
2. Cover and cook on low for 4-5 hours or until chicken is tender. Serve with rice if desired.

CHICKEN THIGHS WITH GINGER-PEACH SAUCE

PEPPERY CHICKEN WITH POTATOES

chicken. Place chicken over vegetables.

2. Cook, covered, on low 5-6 hours or until a thermometer inserted in thickest part of thigh reads 170°-175°. Remove chicken from slow cooker; tent with foil. Let stand 15 minutes before carving.

3. Transfer vegetables to a platter; keep warm. If desired, skim fat and thicken cooking juices for gravy. Serve with chicken.

Curry Chicken Stew

PREP: 15 MIN. • **COOK:** 4 HOURS
MAKES: 6 SERVINGS

- 2 **cans (14½ ounces each) chicken broth**
- 1 **can (10¾ ounces) condensed cream of chicken soup, undiluted**
- 1 **tub Knorr concentrated chicken stock**
- 4 **garlic cloves, minced**
- 1 **tablespoon curry powder**
- ¼ **teaspoon salt**
- ¼ **teaspoon cayenne pepper**
- ¼ **teaspoon pepper**
- 6 **boneless skinless chicken breasts (6 ounces each)**
- 1 **medium green pepper, cut into thin strips**
- 1 **medium onion, thinly sliced**
  Hot cooked rice
  Chopped fresh cilantro and chutney, optional

1. In a large bowl, combine the first eight ingredients. Place chicken, green pepper and onion in a 5- or 6-qt. slow cooker; pour broth mixture over top. Cook, covered, on low 4-5 hours or until chicken and vegetables are tender.

2. Remove chicken and cool slightly. Cut or shred meat into bite-size pieces and return to slow cooker; heat through. Serve with rice. If desired, top with cilantro and chutney.

Peppery Chicken with Potatoes

We like this recipe because while we go to church on Sundays the chicken cooks and is ready for us when we get home.

—**LORI DRAVES** HIGHLAND, WI

PREP: 20 MIN. • **COOK:** 5 HOURS + STANDING
MAKES: 4 SERVINGS

- 1 **pound red potatoes (about 6 medium), cut into wedges**
- 1 **large onion, chopped**
- 2 **teaspoons salt**
- 1 **teaspoon paprika**
- ½ **teaspoon onion powder**
- ½ **teaspoon garlic powder**
- ½ **teaspoon dried thyme**
- ½ **teaspoon white pepper**
- ½ **teaspoon cayenne pepper**
- ¼ **teaspoon pepper**
- 1 **broiler/fryer chicken (3½ to 4 pounds)**

1. Place potatoes and onion in a 6-qt. slow cooker. In a small bowl, mix seasonings. Tuck wings under chicken; tie drumsticks together. Rub seasoning mixture over outside and inside of

My grandma grew up in India and was pleased to pass down this recipe to my mother who then passed it down to me. The dish brings back fond memories of the family gathered around the table, enjoying a delicious meal and catching up on one another's day. I tweaked the ingredients a bit to fit my toddler's taste buds, but it's just as scrumptious.

—**TERESA FLOWERS** SACRAMENTO, CA

CURRY CHICKEN
STEW

Stuffed Turkey with Mojo Sauce

I love Latin food so I created a main course that combines wonderful spices and fresh ingredients. This is a traditional turkey recipe with a healthier twist because it uses chicken sausage instead of chorizo.

—MELISSA LAUER SAN ANTONIO, TX

PREP: 30 MIN. • **COOK:** 5 HOURS + STANDING
MAKES: 8 SERVINGS (ABOUT 1 CUP SAUCE)

- 1 medium green pepper, finely chopped
- 1 medium onion, finely chopped
- 2 garlic cloves, minced
- 2 teaspoons ground coriander
- 1 teaspoon ground cumin
- ⅛ teaspoon cayenne pepper
- 1 pound uncooked chicken sausage links, casings removed
- 1 fresh boneless turkey breast (4 pounds)
- ¼ teaspoon salt
- ¼ teaspoon pepper

MOJO SAUCE
- 1 cup orange juice
- ½ cup fresh cilantro leaves
- ¼ cup minced fresh oregano or 4 teaspoons dried oregano
- ¼ cup lime juice
- 4 garlic cloves, minced
- 1 teaspoon ground cumin
- ½ teaspoon pepper
- ¼ teaspoon salt
- ⅛ teaspoon cayenne pepper
- 1 cup olive oil

1. In a bowl, combine the first six ingredients. Crumble sausage over mixture and mix well.

2. With skin side down, pound turkey breast with a meat mallet to ½-in. thickness. Sprinkle with salt and pepper. Spread sausage mixture over turkey to within 1 in. of edges. Roll up jelly-roll style, starting with a short side; tie at 1½-in. to 2-in. intervals with kitchen string. Place in a 5-qt. oval slow cooker.

3. In a blender, combine the first nine sauce ingredients; cover and process until blended. While processing, gradually add oil in a steady stream. Pour over turkey.

4. Cover and cook on low for 5 hours or until a thermometer inserted in center reads 165°. Remove from slow cooker; cover and let stand for 10 minutes before slicing. Discard string.

5. Meanwhile, skim fat from cooking juices; transfer juices to a small saucepan. Bring to a boil; cook until liquid is reduced by half. Serve with turkey.

STUFFED TURKEY WITH MOJO SAUCE

DID YOU KNOW?

Mojo sauce is the Cuban favorite that features garlic, herbs and citrus—orange, lime, lemon or a combination of all three. The bold sauce complements many meats. It also works well on sandwiches and even grilled vegetables.

CHICKEN MERLOT WITH MUSHROOMS

Chicken Merlot with Mushrooms

A dear friend who liked cooking as much as I do shared this recipe with me, and I think of her every time I make it. Friends and family love it and request it often.
—**SHELLI MCWILLIAM** SALEM, OR

PREP: 10 MIN. • **COOK:** 5 HOURS
MAKES: 5 SERVINGS

- ¾ pound sliced fresh mushrooms
- 1 large onion, chopped
- 2 garlic cloves, minced
- 3 pounds boneless skinless chicken thighs
- 1 can (6 ounces) tomato paste
- ¾ cup chicken broth
- ¼ cup merlot or additional chicken broth
- 2 tablespoons quick-cooking tapioca
- 2 teaspoons sugar
- 1½ teaspoons dried basil
- ½ teaspoon salt
- ¼ teaspoon pepper
- 2 tablespoons grated Parmesan cheese
  Hot cooked pasta, optional

1. Place the mushrooms, onion and garlic in a 5-qt. slow cooker. Top with chicken.
2. In a small bowl, combine the tomato paste, broth, wine, tapioca, sugar, basil, salt and pepper. Pour over chicken. Cover and cook on low for 5-6 hours or until chicken is tender.
3. Sprinkle with cheese. Serve with pasta if desired.

Thai Chicken Thighs

Thanks to the slow cooker, a traditional Thai dish with peanut butter, jalapeno peppers and chili sauce becomes incredibly easy to make. If you want to crank up the spice a bit, use more jalapeno peppers.
—*TASTE OF HOME* TEST KITCHEN

PREP: 25 MIN. • **COOK:** 5 HOURS
MAKES: 8 SERVINGS

- 8 bone-in chicken thighs (about 3 pounds), skin removed
- ½ cup salsa
- ¼ cup creamy peanut butter
- 2 tablespoons lemon juice
- 2 tablespoons reduced-sodium soy sauce
- 1 tablespoon chopped seeded jalapeno pepper
- 2 teaspoons Thai chili sauce
- 1 garlic clove, minced
- 1 teaspoon minced fresh gingerroot
- 2 green onions, sliced
- 2 tablespoons sesame seeds, toasted
  Hot cooked basmati rice, optional

1. Place chicken in a 3-qt. slow cooker. In a small bowl, combine the salsa, peanut butter, lemon juice, soy sauce, jalapeno, Thai chili sauce, garlic and ginger; pour over chicken.
2. Cover and cook on low for 5-6 hours or until chicken is tender. Sprinkle with green onions and sesame seeds. Serve with rice if desired.
NOTE *Wear disposable gloves when cutting hot peppers; the oils can burn skin. Avoid touching your face.*

THAI CHICKEN THIGHS

AMAZING SLOW COOKER ORANGE CHICKEN

Turkey Leg Pot Roast

Well-seasoned turkey and tender veggies simmer into a meal-in-one that's ideal for a chilly night. Tender and satisfying, this recipe couldn't be easier!

—**RICK AND VEGAS PEARSON** CADILLAC, MI

PREP: 15 MIN. • **COOK:** 5 HOURS
MAKES: 3 SERVINGS

- 3 **medium potatoes, peeled and quartered**
- 2 **cups fresh baby carrots**
- 2 **celery ribs, cut into 2½-inch pieces**
- 1 **medium onion, peeled and quartered**
- 3 **garlic cloves, peeled and quartered**
- ½ **cup chicken broth**
- 3 **turkey drumsticks (12 ounces each), skin removed**
- 2 **teaspoons seasoned salt**
- 1 **teaspoon dried thyme**
- 1 **teaspoon dried parsley flakes**
- ¼ **teaspoon pepper**

In a greased 5-qt. slow cooker, combine the first six ingredients. Place drumsticks over vegetables. Sprinkle with the seasoned salt, thyme, parsley and pepper. Cover and cook on low for 5 to 5½ hours or until turkey is tender.

Amazing Slow Cooker Orange Chicken

Orange chicken is my favorite Chinese takeout food, but I know that it's very high in sodium and fat. So I got to work at home to make a healthier version. Now I have peace of mind knowing what ingredients are in it and that it's better for my family.

—**BARB MILLER** OAKDALE, MN

PREP: 25 MIN. • **COOK:** 4 HOURS
MAKES: 8 SERVINGS

- 1 **cup chicken stock**
- 1 **cup orange juice**
- 1 **cup orange marmalade**
- ½ **cup ketchup**
- ¼ **cup Dijon mustard**
- 2 **tablespoons brown sugar**
- 2 **tablespoons rice vinegar**
- 2 **tablespoons reduced-sodium soy sauce**
- 1 **tablespoon minced fresh gingerroot**
- 1 **teaspoon garlic powder**
- ¾ **teaspoon crushed red pepper flakes**
- 2 **tablespoons molasses, optional**
- 2 **pounds boneless skinless chicken breasts, cut into ¾-inch pieces**
- ½ **cup cornstarch**
- ¾ **teaspoon salt**
- ½ **teaspoon pepper**
- 1 **large sweet red pepper, cut into 1-inch pieces**
- 2 **cups fresh broccoli florets**
  Hot cooked rice
  Optional toppings: chopped green onions, peanuts and fresh cilantro

1. In a small bowl, combine the first 11 ingredients; stir in molasses if desired. In a 4-qt. slow cooker, combine chicken, cornstarch, salt and pepper; toss to coat. Top with red pepper. Pour stock mixture over top. Cover and cook on low for 4 hours or until the chicken is tender.
2. Stir in the broccoli. Cover and cook on high 30-40 minutes longer or until broccoli is crisp-tender. Serve with rice. Sprinkle with toppings of your choice.

TURKEY LEG POT ROAST

Spring-Thyme Chicken Stew

When my husband and I are in need of something warm and comforting, we make this stew. It reminds me of the days my mom would make chicken soup.

—**AMY CHASE** VANDERHOOF, BC

PREP: 15 MIN. • **COOK:** 7 HOURS
MAKES: 4 SERVINGS

- 1 **pound small red potatoes, halved**
- 1 **large onion, finely chopped**
- ¾ **cup shredded carrots**
- 3 **tablespoons all-purpose flour**
- 6 **garlic cloves, minced**
- 2 **teaspoons grated lemon peel**
- 2 **teaspoons dried thyme**
- ½ **teaspoon salt**
- ¼ **teaspoon pepper**
- 1½ **pounds boneless skinless chicken thighs, halved**
- 2 **cups reduced-sodium chicken broth**
- 2 **bay leaves**
- 2 **tablespoons minced fresh parsley**

1. Place potatoes, onion and carrots in a 3-qt. slow cooker. Sprinkle with flour, garlic, lemon peel, thyme, salt and pepper; toss to coat. Place chicken over top. Add broth and bay leaves.
2. Cook, covered, on low 7-9 hours or until chicken and vegetables are tender. Remove bay leaves. Sprinkle with parsley.

DID YOU KNOW?

The lid on your slow cooker seals in steam that cooks food. Unless the recipe instructs you to stir in or add ingredients, do not lift the lid. Every time you sneak a peek, the food will take longer to cook.

BUTTER & HERB TURKEY

Butter & Herb Turkey

My kids love turkey for dinner, and this easy recipe lets me make it whenever I want. No special occasion required. The meat is so tender it falls right off the bone.

—**ROCHELLE POPOVIC** SOUTH BEND, IN

PREP: 10 MIN. • **COOK:** 5 HOURS
MAKES: 12 SERVINGS (3 CUPS GRAVY)

- 1 **bone-in turkey breast (6 to 7 pounds)**
- 2 **tablespoons butter, softened**
- ½ **teaspoon dried rosemary, crushed**
- ½ **teaspoon dried thyme**
- ¼ **teaspoon garlic powder**
- ¼ **teaspoon pepper**
- 1 **can (14½ ounces) chicken broth**
- 3 **tablespoons cornstarch**
- 2 **tablespoons cold water**

1. Rub turkey with butter. Combine the rosemary, thyme, garlic powder and pepper; sprinkle over turkey. Place in a 6-qt. slow cooker. Pour broth over top. Cover and cook on low for 5-6 hours or until tender.
2. Remove turkey to a serving platter; keep warm. Skim fat from cooking juices; transfer to a small saucepan. Bring to a boil.
3. Combine cornstarch and water until smooth. Gradually stir into the pan. Bring to a boil; cook and stir for 2 minutes or until thickened. Serve with the turkey.

**APPLE
BALSAMIC CHICKEN**

Apple Balsamic Chicken

I just love the sweet and tart flavor that balsamic vinegar gives this dish. It's easy to prepare, and after cooking in the slow cooker, the chicken thighs are tender and flavorful.

—**JULI SNAER** ENID, OK

PREP: 15 MIN. • **COOK:** 4 HOURS
MAKES: 4 SERVINGS

- 4 **bone-in chicken thighs (about 1½ pounds), skin removed**
- ½ **cup chicken broth**
- ¼ **cup apple cider or juice**
- ¼ **cup balsamic vinegar**
- 2 **tablespoons lemon juice**
- ½ **teaspoon salt**
- ½ **teaspoon garlic powder**
- ½ **teaspoon dried thyme**
- ½ **teaspoon paprika**
- ½ **teaspoon pepper**
- 2 **tablespoons butter**
- 2 **tablespoons all-purpose flour**

1. Place chicken in a 1½-qt. slow cooker. In a small bowl, combine the broth, cider, vinegar, lemon juice and seasonings; pour over meat. Cover and cook on low for 4-5 hours or until chicken is tender.

2. Remove chicken; keep warm. Skim fat from cooking liquid. In a small saucepan, melt butter; stir in flour until smooth. Gradually add cooking liquid. Bring to a boil; cook and stir for 2-3 minutes or until thickened. Serve with chicken.

Slow Cooker Buffalo Chicken Lasagna

When I make this tasty lasagna at home, I use a whole bottle of buffalo wing sauce because my family likes it nice and spicy. Simply use less if you prefer, and increase the pasta sauce.

—**HEIDI PEPIN** SYKESVILLE, MD

PREP: 25 MIN. • **COOK:** 4 HOURS + STANDING
MAKES: 8 SERVINGS

- 1½ **pounds ground chicken**
- 1 **tablespoon olive oil**
- 1 **bottle (12 ounces) buffalo wing sauce**
- 1½ **cups meatless spaghetti sauce**
- 1 **carton (15 ounces) ricotta cheese**
- 2 **cups (8 ounces) shredded part-skim mozzarella cheese**
- 9 **no-cook lasagna noodles**
- 2 **medium sweet red peppers, chopped**
- ½ **cup crumbled blue cheese or feta cheese**
  Chopped celery and additional crumbled blue cheese, optional

1. In a Dutch oven, cook chicken in oil over medium heat until no longer pink; drain. Stir in wing sauce and spaghetti sauce. In a small bowl, mix ricotta and mozzarella cheeses.

2. Spread 1 cup sauce onto the bottom of an oval 6-qt. slow cooker. Layer with three noodles (breaking noodles to fit), 1 cup sauce, a third of the peppers and a third of the cheese mixture. Repeat the layers twice. Top with the remaining sauce; sprinkle with blue cheese.

3. Cover and cook on low for 4-5 hours or until noodles are tender. Let stand 15 minutes before serving. Top with celery and additional blue cheese if desired.

SLOW COOKER BUFFALO CHICKEN LASAGNA

Slow Cooker Rotisserie-Style Chicken

You wouldn't believe this golden brown chicken was made in the slow cooker. Packed with flavor, the meat is moist, the carrots are tender and the juices make a nice gravy.

—*TASTE OF HOME* TEST KITCHEN

PREP: 30 MIN. • **COOK:** 6 HOURS + STANDING
MAKES: 6 SERVINGS

- 4 teaspoons seasoned salt
- 4 teaspoons poultry seasoning
- 1 tablespoon paprika
- 1½ teaspoons onion powder
- 1½ teaspoons brown sugar
- 1½ teaspoons salt-free lemon-pepper seasoning
- ¾ teaspoon garlic powder
- 1 broiler/fryer chicken (4 pounds)
- 1 pound carrots, halved lengthwise and cut into 1½-inch lengths
- 2 large onions, chopped
- 2 tablespoons cornstarch

1. In a small bowl, combine the first seven ingredients. Carefully loosen skin from chicken breast; rub 1 tablespoon spice mixture under the skin. Rub remaining spice mixture over chicken. In another bowl, toss carrots and onions with cornstarch; transfer to a 6-qt. slow cooker. Place chicken on vegetables.

2. Cover and cook on low for 6-7 hours or until a thermometer inserted in thigh reads 180°. Remove chicken and vegetables to a serving platter; cover and let stand for 15 minutes before carving. Skim fat from cooking juices. Serve with chicken and vegetables.

SLOW COOKER ROTISSERIE-STYLE CHICKEN

TURKEY-MUSHROOM EGG ROLLS

FREEZE IT Turkey-Mushroom Egg Rolls

Ground turkey is simmered in a combo of hoisin, soy and sesame sauces along with fresh veggies for a sensational filling for egg rolls. The bites are a favorite appetizer with guests. I never have any leftovers, but I do have lots of requests for the recipe!
—**SARAH HERSE** BROOKLYN, NY

PREP: 1¼ HOURS • **COOK:** 4 HOURS
MAKES: 3½ DOZEN

1½ pounds ground turkey
½ pound sliced fresh mushrooms
2 medium leeks (white portion only), thinly sliced
3 celery ribs, thinly sliced
½ cup hoisin sauce
2 tablespoons minced fresh gingerroot
2 tablespoons rice vinegar
2 tablespoons reduced-sodium soy sauce
1 tablespoon packed brown sugar
1 tablespoon sesame oil
2 garlic cloves, minced
½ cup sliced water chestnuts, chopped
3 green onions, thinly sliced
42 egg roll wrappers
Oil for frying
Sweet-and-sour sauce or Chinese-style mustard, optional

1. In a large skillet, cook turkey over medium heat 8-10 minutes or until no longer pink, breaking into crumbles. Transfer to a 5-qt. slow cooker.

2. Stir in mushrooms, leeks, celery, hoisin sauce, ginger, vinegar, soy sauce, brown sugar, sesame oil and garlic. Cook, covered, on low 4-5 hours or until vegetables are tender. Stir water chestnuts and green onions into turkey mixture; cool slightly.

3. With one corner of an egg roll wrapper facing you, place 2 tablespoons filling just below center of wrapper. (Cover remaining wrappers with a damp paper towel until ready to use.) Fold bottom corner over filling; moisten remaining wrapper edges with water. Fold side corners toward center over filling. Roll egg roll up tightly, pressing at tip to seal. Repeat.

4. In an electric skillet, heat ¼ in. of oil to 375°. Fry egg rolls, a few at a time, 3-4 minutes or until golden brown, turning occasionally. Drain on paper towels. If desired, serve with sweet-and-sour sauce.

FREEZE OPTION *Cover and freeze unfried egg rolls on waxed paper-lined baking sheets until firm. Transfer to resealable plastic freezer bags; return to freezer. To use, fry egg rolls as recipe directs, increasing cooking time to 4-5 minutes.*

Casablanca Chutney Chicken

If you enjoy ethnic food, you'll love this dish. An array of spices and dried fruit slowly simmer with boneless chicken thighs for an aromatic and satisfying meal. To make it complete, serve over jasmine or basmati rice. Yum!

—ROXANNE CHAN ALBANY, CA

PREP: 25 MIN. • **COOK:** 7 HOURS
MAKES: 4 SERVINGS

- 1 **pound boneless skinless chicken thighs, cut into ¾-inch pieces**
- 1 **can (14½ ounces) chicken broth**
- ⅓ **cup finely chopped onion**
- ⅓ **cup chopped sweet red pepper**
- ⅓ **cup chopped carrot**
- ⅓ **cup chopped dried apricots**
- ⅓ **cup chopped dried figs**
- ⅓ **cup golden raisins**
- 2 **tablespoons orange marmalade**
- 1 **tablespoon mustard seed**
- 2 **garlic cloves, minced**
- ½ **teaspoon curry powder**
- ¼ **teaspoon crushed red pepper flakes**
- ¼ **teaspoon ground cumin**
- ¼ **teaspoon ground cinnamon**
- ¼ **teaspoon ground cloves**
- 2 **tablespoons minced fresh parsley**
- 2 **tablespoons minced fresh mint**
- 1 **tablespoon lemon juice**
- 4 **tablespoons chopped pistachios**

1. In a 3-qt. slow cooker, combine the first 16 ingredients. Cover and cook on low for 7-8 hours or until the chicken is tender.

2. Stir in the parsley, mint and lemon juice; heat through. Sprinkle each serving with pistachios.

CASABLANCA CHUTNEY CHICKEN

SUPER EASY TURKEY STROGANOFF

Super Easy Turkey Stroganoff

I have been making this tasty main course for 30-plus years. Our family loves turkey and I make it a lot, but this is our favorite. It's great served over cooked noodles, mashed potatoes or even polenta.

—CINDY ADAMS TRACY, CA

PREP: 20 MIN. • **COOK:** 6 HOURS
MAKES: 6 SERVINGS

- 4 **turkey thighs (about 4 pounds)**
- 1 **large onion, halved and thinly sliced**
- 1 **can (10¾ ounces) condensed cream of celery soup, undiluted**
- ⅓ **cup water**
- 3 **garlic cloves, minced**
- 2 **teaspoons dried tarragon**
- ½ **teaspoon salt**
- ½ **teaspoon pepper**
- ½ **cup sour cream**
  Hot cooked egg noodles

1. Place turkey and onion in a 5-qt. slow cooker. In a large bowl, whisk soup, water, garlic, tarragon, salt and pepper until blended; pour over top. Cook, covered, on low 6-8 hours or until meat is tender.

2. Remove turkey from slow cooker. When cool enough to handle, remove meat from bones; discard bones. Shred meat with two forks. Whisk sour cream into cooking juices; return meat to slow cooker. Serve with noodles.

Sunday Chicken Stew

I serve this classic dish on Sundays because so much of the prep work can be done in advance and I, too, can enjoy a leisurely day relaxing with my family. I prepare the vegetables Saturday night before bed. Then in the morning, I brown the chicken and assemble everything in the slow cooker before we leave for church.

—**DIANE HALFERTY** CORPUS CHRISTI, TX

PREP: 30 MIN. • **COOK:** 6½ HOURS
MAKES: 6 SERVINGS

- ½ **cup all-purpose flour**
- 1 **teaspoon salt**
- ½ **teaspoon white pepper**
- 1 **broiler/fryer chicken (3 pounds), cut up and skin removed**
- 2 **tablespoons canola oil**
- 3 **cups chicken broth**
- 6 **large carrots, cut into 1-inch pieces**
- 2 **celery ribs, cut into ½-inch pieces**
- 1 **large sweet onion, thinly sliced**
- 1 **teaspoon dried rosemary, crushed**
- 1½ **cups frozen peas**

DUMPLINGS

- 1 **cup all-purpose flour**
- 2 **teaspoons baking powder**
- ½ **teaspoon salt**
- ½ **teaspoon dried rosemary, crushed**
- 1 **egg, lightly beaten**
- ½ **cup 2% milk**

1. In a large resealable plastic bag, combine the flour, salt and pepper; add chicken, a few pieces at a time, and shake to coat. In a large skillet, brown chicken in oil; remove and keep warm. Gradually add broth to the skillet; bring to a boil.
2. In a 5-qt. slow cooker, layer carrots, celery and onion; sprinkle with rosemary. Add the chicken and hot broth. Cover and cook on low for 6-8 hours or until chicken and vegetables are tender and stew is bubbling.
3. Remove chicken; when cool enough to handle, remove meat from the bones and discard bones. Cut meat into bite-size pieces and return to the slow cooker. Stir in peas.

4. For dumplings, in a small bowl, combine the flour, baking powder, salt and rosemary. Combine the egg and milk; stir into dry ingredients. Drop by heaping teaspoonfuls onto simmering chicken mixture. Cover and cook on high for 25-30 minutes or until a toothpick inserted in a dumpling comes out clean (do not lift the cover while simmering).

Tuscan-Style Chicken

I found this Italian-style recipe in a magazine and tweaked it to my family's tastes. It's great with Italian bread and spinach salad with lemon vinaigrette.

—**MARY WATKINS** LITTLE ELM, TX

PREP: 25 MIN. • **COOK:** 6 HOURS
MAKES: 4 SERVINGS

- 2 **cans (14½ ounces each) Italian stewed tomatoes, undrained**
- 10 **small red potatoes (about 1 pound), quartered**
- 1 **medium onion, chopped**
- 1 **can (6 ounces) tomato paste**
- 2 **fresh rosemary sprigs**
- 4 **garlic cloves, minced**
- 1 **teaspoon olive oil**
- ½ **teaspoon dried basil**
- 1 **teaspoon Italian seasoning, divided**
- 1 **broiler/fryer chicken (3 to 4 pounds), cut up and skin removed**
- ½ **teaspoon salt**
- ½ **teaspoon pepper**
- 1 **jar (5¾ ounces) pimiento-stuffed olives, drained**

1. In a 5-qt. slow cooker, combine the first eight ingredients. Stir in ½ teaspoon Italian seasoning. Place chicken on top. Sprinkle with salt, pepper and remaining Italian seasoning. Top with olives.
2. Cover and cook on low for 6-7 hours or until chicken is tender. Discard rosemary sprigs before serving.

SUNDAY CHICKEN STEW

MEATY SLOW-COOKED JAMBALAYA

Meaty Slow-Cooked Jambalaya

This recipe makes a big batch. Stash some away in the freezer for those days when you don't feel like cooking.
—**DIANE SMITH** PINE MOUNTAIN, GA

PREP: 25 MIN. • **COOK:** 7¼ HOURS
MAKES: 12 SERVINGS (3½ QUARTS)

- 1 can (28 ounces) diced tomatoes, undrained
- 1 cup reduced-sodium chicken broth
- 1 large green pepper, chopped
- 1 medium onion, chopped
- 2 celery ribs, sliced
- ½ cup white wine or additional reduced-sodium chicken broth
- 4 garlic cloves, minced
- 2 teaspoons Cajun seasoning
- 2 teaspoons dried parsley flakes
- 1 teaspoon dried basil
- 1 teaspoon dried oregano
- ¾ teaspoon salt
- ½ to 1 teaspoon cayenne pepper
- 2 pounds boneless skinless chicken thighs, cut into 1-inch pieces
- 1 package (12 ounces) fully cooked andouille or other spicy chicken sausage links
- 2 pounds uncooked medium shrimp, peeled and deveined
- 8 cups hot cooked brown rice

1. In a large bowl, combine the first 13 ingredients. Place chicken and sausage in a 6-qt. slow cooker. Pour tomato mixture over top. Cook, covered, on low 7-9 hours or until chicken is tender.
2. Stir in shrimp. Cook, covered, 15-20 minutes longer or until shrimp turn pink. Serve with rice.

FREEZE IT Mandarin Turkey Tenderloin

My husband grew up in an area with lots of turkey farms nearby, so from an early age he learned to love dishes that use turkey. I serve this tasty dish when I have company over, as it requires no last-minute fussing.
—**LORIE MINER** KAMAS, UT

PREP: 15 MIN. • **COOK:** 4½ HOURS
MAKES: 8 SERVINGS

- 8 turkey breast tenderloins (4 ounces each)
- ½ teaspoon ground ginger
- ½ teaspoon crushed red pepper flakes
- 1 can (11 ounces) mandarin oranges, drained
- 1 cup sesame ginger marinade
- ½ cup chicken broth
- 1 package (16 ounces) frozen stir-fry vegetable blend, thawed
- 1 tablespoon sesame seeds, toasted
- 1 green onion, sliced
  Hot cooked rice, optional

1. Place turkey in a 3-qt. slow cooker. Sprinkle with ginger and pepper flakes. Top with oranges. In a small bowl, combine marinade and broth; pour over turkey. Cover and cook on low for 4-5 hours or until a meat thermometer reads 170°.
2. Stir vegetables into the slow cooker. Cover and cook 30 minutes longer or until vegetables are heated through.
3. Sprinkle with sesame seeds and green onion. Serve with rice if desired.
FREEZE OPTION *Cool turkey mixture. Freeze in freezer containers. To use, partially thaw in refrigerator overnight. Heat through slowly in a covered skillet until a thermometer inserted in turkey reads 165°, stirring occasionally and adding a little broth or water if necessary. Garnish as directed.*

MANDARIN TURKEY TENDERLOIN

Greek Shrimp Orzo

Looking for a new family favorite? Give this Greek specialty a try. It tastes delicious and reheats well. My husband would rather have "the orzo dish" than go out to eat at a restaurant.

—**MOLLY SEIDEL** EDGEWOOD, NM

PREP: 45 MIN. • **COOK:** 2 HOURS
MAKES: 6 SERVINGS

- 2 **cups uncooked orzo pasta**
- 2 **tablespoons minced fresh basil or 2 teaspoons dried basil**
- 3 **tablespoons olive oil, divided**
- 1½ **tablespoons chopped shallot**
- 2 **tablespoons butter**
- 1 **can (14½ ounces) diced tomatoes, drained**
- 2 **tablespoons minced fresh oregano or 2 teaspoons dried oregano**
- 3 **garlic cloves, minced**
- 1 **pound uncooked large shrimp, peeled and deveined**
- 1 **cup oil-packed sun-dried tomatoes, chopped**
- 2½ **cups (10 ounces) crumbled feta cheese**
- 1½ **cups pitted Greek olives**

1. Cook orzo according to package directions; rinse in cold water and drain. Transfer to a large bowl. Add basil and 1 tablespoon oil; toss to coat and set aside.
2. In a large skillet, saute shallot in butter and remaining oil until tender. Add the diced tomatoes, oregano and garlic; cook and stir for 1-2 minutes. Add shrimp and sun-dried tomatoes; cook and stir for 2-3 minutes or until shrimp turn pink.
3. Transfer to a greased 5-qt. slow cooker. Stir in the orzo mixture, cheese and olives. Cover and cook on low for 2-3 hours or until heated through.

VEGETARIAN CHILI OLE!

Vegetarian Chili Ole!

I combine the ingredients for this hearty chili the night before, start my trusty slow cooker in the morning and come home to a rich, spicy meal at night!

—**MARJORIE AU** HONOLULU, HI

PREP: 35 MIN. • **COOK:** 6 HOURS
MAKES: 7 SERVINGS

- 1 **can (16 ounces) kidney beans, rinsed and drained**
- 1 **can (15 ounces) black beans, rinsed and drained**
- 1 **can (14½ ounces) diced tomatoes, undrained**
- 1½ **cups frozen corn**
- 1 **large onion, chopped**
- 1 **medium zucchini, chopped**
- 1 **medium sweet red pepper, chopped**
- 1 **can (4 ounces) chopped green chilies**
- 1 **ounce Mexican chocolate, chopped**
- 1 **cup water**
- 1 **can (6 ounces) tomato paste**
- 1 **tablespoon cornmeal**
- 1 **tablespoon chili powder**
- ½ **teaspoon salt**
- ½ **teaspoon dried oregano**
- ½ **teaspoon ground cumin**
- ¼ **teaspoon hot pepper sauce, optional**
  Optional toppings: diced tomatoes, chopped green onions and crumbled queso fresco

1. In a 4-qt. slow cooker, combine the first nine ingredients. Combine the water, tomato paste, cornmeal, chili powder, salt, oregano, cumin and pepper sauce if desired until smooth; stir into slow cooker. Cover and cook on low for 6-8 hours or until vegetables are tender.
2. Serve with toppings of your choice.

Apple-Cranberry Multigrain Hot Cereal

While on my quest to lose 130 pounds, I made some changes in my diet, including reducing sugar and increasing my fiber and protein intake. These delicious grains are perfect because they are in line with my eating habits and my husband and kids love them as well. I set my slow cooker to start automatically overnight and a hearty breakfast is ready by the time we wake up in the morning.

—SHERISSE DAWE BLACK DIAMOND, AB

PREP: 10 MIN. • **COOK:** 4 HOURS
MAKES: 10 SERVINGS

- 2 **medium apples, peeled and chopped**
- 1 **cup sugar**
- 1 **cup fresh cranberries**
- ½ **cup wheat berries**
- ½ **cup quinoa, rinsed**
- ½ **cup oat bran**
- ½ **cup medium pearl barley**
- ½ **cup chopped walnuts**
- ½ **cup packed brown sugar**
- 1½ **to 2 teaspoons ground cinnamon**
- 6 **cups water**
  Milk

In a 3-qt. slow cooker, combine the first 11 ingredients. Cook, covered, on low 4-5 hours or until grains are tender. Serve with milk.

APPLE-CRANBERRY MULTIGRAIN HOT CEREAL

ENCHILADA PIE

Enchilada Pie

Stacked with layers of beans, vegetables and cheese, this mile-high pie will have you stuffed in no time. It's a great meatless addition to a fun fiesta night.

—JACQUELINE CORREA LANDING, NJ

PREP: 40 MIN. • **COOK:** 4 HOURS
MAKES: 8 SERVINGS

- 1 **package (12 ounces) frozen vegetarian meat crumbles**
- 1 **cup chopped onion**
- ½ **cup chopped green pepper**
- 2 **teaspoons canola oil**
- 1 **can (16 ounces) kidney beans, rinsed and drained**
- 1 **can (15 ounces) black beans, rinsed and drained**
- 1 **can (10 ounces) diced tomatoes and green chilies, undrained**
- ½ **cup water**
- 1½ **teaspoons chili powder**
- ½ **teaspoon ground cumin**
- ¼ **teaspoon pepper**
- 6 **whole wheat tortillas (8 inches)**
- 2 **cups (8 ounces) shredded reduced-fat cheddar cheese**

1. Cut three 25x3-in. strips of heavy-duty foil; crisscross so they resemble spokes of a wheel. Place strips on the bottom and up the sides of a 5-qt. slow cooker. Coat strips with cooking spray.

2. In a large saucepan, cook the meat crumbles, onion and green pepper in oil until vegetables are tender. Stir in both cans of beans, tomatoes, water, chili powder, cumin and pepper. Bring to a boil. Reduce heat; simmer, uncovered, for 10 minutes.

3. In prepared slow cooker, layer about a cup of bean mixture, one tortilla and ⅓ cup cheese. Repeat layers five times. Cover and cook on low for 4-5 hours or until heated through and cheese is melted.

4. Using foil strips as handles, remove the pie to a platter.

NOTE *Vegetarian meat crumbles are a nutritious protein source made from soy. Look for them in the natural foods freezer section.*

SPICY LENTIL & CHICKPEA STEW

Spicy Lentil & Chickpea Stew

A friend gave me the recipe for this chunky stew. I altered a few of the ingredients until I found a version my family loves. My son doesn't like anything too spicy, so I keep it on the mild side for him and add a sprinkle of extra spice in my bowl. My husband is a farmer and works long days outdoors. The dish is chock-full of hearty beans, lentils and veggies, so it's hearty enough to keep even him satisfied.

—**MELANIE MACFARLANE** BEDEQUE, PEI

PREP: 25 MIN. • **COOK:** 8 HOURS
MAKES: 8 SERVINGS (2¾ QUARTS)

- 2 **teaspoons olive oil**
- 1 **medium onion, thinly sliced**
- 1 **teaspoon dried oregano**
- ½ **teaspoon crushed red pepper flakes**
- 2 **cans (15 ounces each) chickpeas or garbanzo beans, rinsed and drained**
- 1 **cup dried lentils, rinsed**
- 1 **can (2¼ ounces) sliced ripe olives, drained**
- 3 **teaspoons smoked paprika**
- 4 **cups vegetable broth**
- 4 **cans (8 ounces each) no-salt-added tomato sauce**
- 4 **cups fresh baby spinach**
- ¾ **cup fat-free plain yogurt**

1. In a small skillet, heat oil over medium-high heat. Add onion, oregano and pepper flakes; cook and stir 8-10 minutes or until onion is tender. Transfer to a 5- or 6-qt. slow cooker.
2. Add chickpeas, lentils, olives and paprika; stir in broth and tomato sauce. Cook, covered, on low 8-10 hours or until lentils are tender. Stir in spinach. Top servings with yogurt.

Carrot Cake Oatmeal

Start your day off with a bowl of my warm breakfast cereal. It will keep you full all morning and give you a healthy serving of fruits and veggies. Garnish with ground walnuts or pecans for extra crunch.

—**DEBBIE KAIN** COLORADO SPRINGS, CO

PREP: 10 MIN. • **COOK:** 6 HOURS
MAKES: 8 SERVINGS

- 4½ **cups water**
- 1 **can (20 ounces) crushed pineapple, undrained**
- 2 **cups shredded carrots**
- 1 **cup steel-cut oats**
- 1 **cup raisins**
- 2 **teaspoons ground cinnamon**
- 1 **teaspoon pumpkin pie spice**
  Brown sugar, optional

In a 4-qt. slow cooker coated with cooking spray, combine the first seven ingredients. Cover and cook on low for 6-8 hours or until oats are tender and liquid is absorbed. Sprinkle with brown sugar if desired.

CARROT CAKE OATMEAL

Slow Cooker Frittata Provencal

Take your taste buds on a trip with this frittata inspired by French flavors. It's a lovely choice for when you have guests for brunch or when you want something special on a holiday morning.

—**CONNIE EATON** PITTSBURGH, PA

PREP: 30 MIN. • **COOK:** 3 HOURS
MAKES: 6 SERVINGS

- ½ **cup water**
- 1 **tablespoon olive oil**
- 1 **medium Yukon Gold potato, peeled and sliced**
- 1 **small onion, thinly sliced**
- ½ **teaspoon smoked paprika**
- 12 **eggs**
- 1 **teaspoon minced fresh thyme or ¼ teaspoon dried thyme**
- 1 **teaspoon hot pepper sauce**
- ½ **teaspoon salt**
- ¼ **teaspoon pepper**
- 1 **log (4 ounces) fresh goat cheese, coarsely crumbled, divided**
- ½ **cup chopped soft sun-dried tomatoes (not packed in oil)**

1. Layer two 24-in. pieces of aluminum foil; starting with a long side, fold up foil to create a 1-in. wide strip. Shape strip into a coil to make a rack for bottom of a 6-qt. oval slow cooker. Add water to slow cooker; set foil rack in water.

2. In a large skillet, heat oil over medium-high heat. Add potato and onion; cook and stir 5-7 minutes or until potato is lightly browned. Stir in paprika. Transfer to a greased 1½-qt. baking dish (dish must fit in slow cooker).

3. In a large bowl, whisk eggs, thyme, pepper sauce, salt and pepper; stir in 2 ounces cheese. Pour over potato mixture. Top with tomatoes and remaining goat cheese. Place dish on foil rack.

4. Cook, covered, on low 3 hours or until eggs are set and a knife inserted near the center comes out clean.

NOTE *This recipe was tested with sun-dried tomatoes that are ready-to-use without soaking. When using other sun-dried tomatoes that are not oil-packed, cover with boiling water and let stand until soft. Drain before using.*

Simple Poached Salmon

My kind of recipe is one that is healthy and nearly effortless. This one is great as the salmon always cooks to perfection!

—**ERIN CHILCOAT** CENTRAL ISLIP, NY

PREP: 10 MIN. • **COOK:** 1½ HOURS
MAKES: 4 SERVINGS

- 2 **cups water**
- 1 **cup white wine**
- 1 **medium onion, sliced**
- 1 **celery rib, sliced**
- 1 **medium carrot, sliced**
- 2 **tablespoons lemon juice**
- 3 **fresh thyme sprigs**
- 1 **fresh rosemary sprig**
- 1 **bay leaf**
- ½ **teaspoon salt**
- ¼ **teaspoon pepper**
- 4 **salmon fillets (1¼ inches thick and 6 ounces each)**
  Lemon wedges

1. In a 3-qt. slow cooker, combine the first 11 ingredients. Cook, covered, on low 45 minutes.

2. Carefully place fillets in liquid; add additional warm water (120° to 130°) to cover if needed. Cook, covered, 45-55 minutes or just until fish flakes easily with a fork (a thermometer inserted in fish should read at least 145°). Remove fish from cooking liquid. Serve warm or cold with lemon wedges.

SIMPLE POACHED SALMON

VEGETARIAN STUFFED PEPPERS

Vegetarian Stuffed Peppers

These meatless peppers are an updated version of my mom's, which were a favorite when I was growing up in New York. The flavor and aroma bring back fond memories of her and our home.

—MELISSA MCCABE LONG BEACH, CA

PREP: 30 MIN. • **COOK:** 3½ HOURS
MAKES: 6 SERVINGS

- 2 **cups cooked brown rice**
- 3 **small tomatoes, chopped**
- 1 **cup frozen corn, thawed**
- 1 **small sweet onion, chopped**
- ¾ **cup cubed Monterey Jack cheese**
- 1 **can (4¼ ounces) chopped ripe olives**
- ⅓ **cup canned black beans, rinsed and drained**
- ⅓ **cup canned red beans, rinsed and drained**
- 4 **fresh basil leaves, thinly sliced**
- 3 **garlic cloves, minced**
- 1 **teaspoon salt**
- ½ **teaspoon pepper**
- 6 **large sweet peppers**
- ¾ **cup meatless spaghetti sauce**
- ½ **cup water**
- 4 **tablespoons grated Parmesan cheese, divided**

1. Place the first 12 ingredients in a large bowl; mix lightly to combine. Cut and discard tops from sweet peppers; remove seeds. Fill peppers with rice mixture.

2. In a small bowl, mix spaghetti sauce and water; pour half of the mixture into an oval 5-qt. slow cooker. Add filled peppers. Top with remaining sauce. Sprinkle with 2 tablespoons Parmesan cheese.

3. Cook, covered, on low 3½ to 4 hours or until heated through and peppers are tender. Sprinkle with remaining Parmesan cheese.

ROSEMARY COD STEW

Rosemary Cod Stew

I love fish and chowder, so this stew hits the spot. It's made without cream or whole milk for a healthier touch. Top servings with a little grated cheddar cheese for added richness and flavor.

—JANE WHITTAKER PENSACOLA, FL

PREP: 25 MIN. • **COOK:** 6½ HOURS
MAKES: 8 SERVINGS (3 QUARTS)

- 1 **pound potatoes (about 2 medium), peeled and finely chopped**
- 1 **package (10 ounces) frozen corn, thawed**
- 1½ **cups frozen lima beans, thawed**
- 1 **large onion, finely chopped**
- 1 **celery rib, finely chopped**
- 1 **medium carrot, finely chopped**
- 4 **garlic cloves, minced**
- 1 **bay leaf**
- 1 **teaspoon lemon-pepper seasoning**
- 1 **teaspoon dried parsley flakes**
- 1 **teaspoon dried rosemary, crushed**
- ½ **teaspoon salt**
- 1½ **cups vegetable or chicken broth**
- 1 **can (10¾ ounces) condensed cream of celery soup, undiluted**
- ½ **cup white wine or additional vegetable broth**
- 1 **pound cod fillets, cut into 1-inch pieces**
- 1 **can (14½ ounces) diced tomatoes, undrained**
- 1 **can (12 ounces) fat-free evaporated milk**

1. In a 5-qt. slow cooker, combine the first 15 ingredients. Cook, covered, on low 6-8 hours or until potatoes are tender.

2. Remove bay leaf. Stir in cod, tomatoes and milk; cook, covered, 30-35 minutes longer or until fish just begins to flake easily with a fork.

Slow-Cooked Blueberry French Toast

Your slow cooker can be your best friend on a busy morning. Get this recipe going, run some errands and come back to the aroma of French toast ready to eat.

—**ELIZABETH LORENZ** PERU, IN

PREP: 30 MIN. + CHILLING • **COOK:** 3 HOURS
MAKES: 12 SERVINGS (2 CUPS SYRUP)

- 8 **eggs**
- ½ **cup plain yogurt**
- ⅓ **cup sour cream**
- 1 **teaspoon vanilla extract**
- ½ **teaspoon ground cinnamon**
- 1 **cup 2% milk**
- ⅓ **cup maple syrup**
- 1 **loaf (1 pound) French bread, cubed**
- 1½ **cups fresh or frozen blueberries**
- 12 **ounces cream cheese, cubed**

BLUEBERRY SYRUP
- 1 **cup sugar**
- 2 **tablespoons cornstarch**
- 1 **cup cold water**
- ¾ **cup fresh or frozen blueberries, divided**
- 1 **tablespoon butter**
- 1 **tablespoon lemon juice**

1. In a large bowl, whisk eggs, yogurt, sour cream, vanilla and cinnamon. Gradually whisk in milk and maple syrup until blended.
2. Place half of the bread in a greased 5- or 6-qt. slow cooker; layer with half of the blueberries, cream cheese and egg mixture. Repeat layers. Refrigerate, covered, overnight.
3. Remove from refrigerator 30 minutes before cooking. Cook, covered, on low 3-4 hours or until a knife inserted near the center comes out clean.
4. For syrup, in a small saucepan, mix sugar and cornstarch; stir in water until smooth. Stir in ¼ cup blueberries. Bring to a boil; cook and stir until berries pop, about 3 minutes. Remove from heat; stir in butter, lemon juice and remaining berries. Serve warm with French toast.

Bayou Gulf Shrimp Gumbo

My gumbo skips the traditional hard-to-find spices but still delivers the same authentic seafood flavor renowned in the Louisiana bayou and beyond.

—**WOLFGANG HANAU** WEST PALM BEACH, FL

PREP: 35 MIN. • **COOK:** 5 HOURS
MAKES: 6 SERVINGS

- ½ **pound bacon strips, chopped**
- 3 **celery ribs, chopped**
- 1 **medium onion, chopped**
- 1 **medium green pepper, chopped**
- 2 **garlic cloves, minced**
- 2 **bottles (8 ounces each) clam juice**
- 1 **can (14½ ounces) diced tomatoes, undrained**
- 2 **tablespoons Worcestershire sauce**
- 1 **teaspoon kosher salt**
- 1 **teaspoon dried marjoram**
- 2 **pounds uncooked large shrimp, peeled and deveined**
- 2½ **cups frozen sliced okra, thawed**
  Hot cooked rice

1. In a large skillet, cook bacon over medium heat until crisp. Remove to paper towels with a slotted spoon; drain, reserving 2 tablespoons drippings. Saute the celery, onion, green pepper and garlic in drippings until tender.
2. Transfer to a 4-qt. slow cooker. Stir in the bacon, clam juice, tomatoes, Worcestershire sauce, salt and marjoram. Cover and cook on low for 4 hours.
3. Stir in shrimp and okra. Cover and cook 1 hour longer or until shrimp turn pink and okra is heated through. Serve with rice.

**SLOW-COOKED
BLUEBERRY FRENCH TOAST**

VEGETARIAN RED BEAN CHILI

Vegetarian Red Bean Chili

This red bean chili is healthy, tastes great and gets raves from die-hard meat lovers. I top bowls with shredded cheddar cheese.

—**CONNIE BARNETT** ATHENS, GA

PREP: 10 MIN. • **COOK:** 5 HOURS
MAKES: 6 SERVINGS (2 QUARTS)

- 1 can (16 ounces) red beans, rinsed and drained
- 2 cans (8 ounces each) no-salt-added tomato sauce
- 2 cups water
- 1 can (14½ ounces) diced tomatoes, undrained
- 1 package (12 ounces) frozen vegetarian meat crumbles
- 1 large onion, chopped
- 1 to 2 tablespoons chili powder
- 1 tablespoon ground cumin
- 2 garlic cloves, minced
- 1 teaspoon pepper
- ½ teaspoon salt
- ½ teaspoon cayenne pepper
  Sour cream and shredded cheddar cheese, optional

In a 4-qt. slow cooker, combine all ingredients. Cover and cook on low for 5-6 hours or until heated through. Serve with sour cream and cheddar cheese if desired.

NOTE *Vegetarian meat crumbles are a nutritious protein source made from soy. Look for them in the natural foods freezer section.*

Corn Bread-Topped Frijoles

My family loves this flavorful meatless dish. The Southwestern mixture of beans, peppers, tomatoes and seasonings bubbling beneath warm corn bread is unforgettable. It's also economical; one batch makes several servings.

—**SUZANNE CALDWELL** ARTESIA, NM

PREP: 20 MIN. • **COOK:** 3 HOURS
MAKES: 8 SERVINGS

- 1 medium onion, chopped
- 1 medium green pepper, chopped
- 1 tablespoon canola oil
- 2 garlic cloves, minced
- 1 can (16 ounces) kidney beans, rinsed and drained
- 1 can (15 ounces) pinto beans, rinsed and drained
- 1 can (14½ ounces) diced tomatoes, undrained
- 1 can (8 ounces) tomato sauce
- 1 teaspoon chili powder
- ½ teaspoon pepper
- ⅛ teaspoon hot pepper sauce

CORN BREAD TOPPING

- 1 cup all-purpose flour
- 1 cup yellow cornmeal
- 1 tablespoon sugar
- 1½ teaspoons baking powder
- ½ teaspoon salt
- 2 eggs, lightly beaten
- 1¼ cups fat-free milk
- 1 can (8¼ ounces) cream-style corn
- 3 tablespoons canola oil

1. In a large skillet, saute onion and green pepper in oil until tender. Add garlic; cook 1 minute longer. Transfer to a greased 5-qt. slow cooker.

2. Stir in the beans, tomatoes, tomato sauce, chili powder, pepper and pepper sauce. Cover and cook on high for 1 hour.

3. In a large bowl, combine the flour, cornmeal, sugar, baking powder and salt. Combine the eggs, milk, corn and oil; add to dry ingredients and mix well. Spoon evenly over bean mixture.

4. Cover and cook on high for 2 hours or until a toothpick inserted near the center of corn bread comes out clean.

CORN BREAD-TOPPED FRIJOLES

SLOW-COOKED FRUITED OATMEAL WITH NUTS

VEGGIE LASAGNA

Slow-Cooked Fruited Oatmeal with Nuts

The beauty of this recipe is that you can set your slow cooker to work its magic overnight. In the morning, you'll have a hot breakfast ready to serve your clan.

—**TRISHA KRUSE** EAGLE, ID

PREP: 15 MIN. • **COOK:** 6 HOURS
MAKES: 6 SERVINGS

- 3 **cups water**
- 2 **cups old-fashioned oats**
- 2 **cups chopped apples**
- 1 **cup dried cranberries**
- 1 **cup fat-free milk**
- 2 **teaspoons butter, melted**
- 1 **teaspoon pumpkin pie spice**
- 1 **teaspoon ground cinnamon**
- 6 **tablespoons chopped almonds, toasted**
- 6 **tablespoons chopped pecans, toasted**
  Additional fat-free milk

1. In a 3-qt. slow cooker coated with cooking spray, combine the first eight ingredients. Cover and cook on low for 6-8 hours or until liquid is absorbed.
2. Spoon oatmeal into bowls. Sprinkle with almonds and pecans; drizzle with additional milk if desired.

Veggie Lasagna

Here's a "veggie-licious" alternative to traditional baked lasagna. I use chunky spaghetti sauce for extra heartiness.

—**LAURA DAVISTER** LITTLE SUAMICO, WI

PREP: 25 MIN. • **COOK:** 3½ HOURS
MAKES: 2 SERVINGS

- ½ **cup shredded part-skim mozzarella cheese**
- 3 **tablespoons 1% cottage cheese**
- 2 **tablespoons grated Parmesan cheese**
- 2 **tablespoons egg substitute**
- ½ **teaspoon Italian seasoning**
- ⅛ **teaspoon garlic powder**
- ¾ **cup meatless spaghetti sauce**
- ½ **cup sliced zucchini**
- 2 **no-cook lasagna noodles**
- 4 **cups fresh baby spinach**
- ½ **cup sliced fresh mushrooms**

1. In a small bowl, combine the first six ingredients. Spread 1 tablespoon spaghetti sauce on the bottom of a 1½-qt. slow cooker coated with cooking spray. Top with half of the zucchini and a third of the cheese mixture.
2. Break noodles into 1-in. pieces; sprinkle half of the noodles over cheese mixture. Spread with 1 tablespoon sauce. Top with half of the spinach and half of the mushrooms. Repeat layers. Top with remaining cheese mixture and spaghetti sauce.
3. Cover and cook on low for 3½ to 4 hours or until noodles are tender.

SWEET POTATO LENTIL STEW

BUFFALO SHRIMP MAC & CHEESE

Sweet Potato Lentil Stew

Everyone enjoys the rich and bold blend of flavors in this stew. It's perfect in fall, just after the weather turns cool. You can serve it alone or with meat or poultry. Either way, I guarantee you'll love it!

—**HEATHER GRAY** LITTLE ROCK, AR

PREP: 5 MIN. • **COOK:** 5 HOURS
MAKES: 6 SERVINGS

- 4 cups vegetable broth
- 1¼ pounds sweet potatoes, peeled and cubed (about 3 cups)
- 1½ cups dried lentils, rinsed
- 3 medium carrots, cut into chunks
- 1 medium onion, chopped
- 4 garlic cloves, minced
- ½ teaspoon ground cumin
- ¼ teaspoon ground ginger
- ¼ teaspoon cayenne pepper
- ¼ cup minced fresh cilantro
- ¼ teaspoon salt

In a 3-qt. slow cooker, combine the first nine ingredients. Cover and cook on low for 5-6 hours or until vegetables are tender. Stir in cilantro and salt.

Buffalo Shrimp Mac & Cheese

You can't beat this rich, creamy and slightly spicy shrimp and pasta. It's a fun twist on classic mac and cheese.

—**ROBIN HAAS** CRANSTON, RI

PREP: 15 MIN. • **COOK:** 3½ HOURS
MAKES: 6 SERVINGS

- 2 cups 2% milk
- 1 cup half-and-half cream
- 2 tablespoons Louisiana-style hot sauce
- 1 tablespoon butter
- 1 teaspoon ground mustard
- ½ teaspoon onion powder
- ¼ teaspoon white pepper
- ¼ teaspoon ground nutmeg
- 2 cups (8 ounces) finely shredded cheddar cheese
- 1 cup (4 ounces) shredded Gouda or Swiss cheese
- 1½ cups uncooked elbow macaroni
- ¾ pound frozen cooked salad shrimp, thawed
- 1 cup (4 ounces) crumbled blue cheese
- 2 tablespoons minced fresh chives
- 2 tablespoons minced fresh parsley
  Additional Louisiana-style hot sauce, optional

1. In a 3-qt. slow cooker, combine the first eight ingredients; stir in shredded cheeses and macaroni. Cook, covered, on low 3 to 3½ hours or until macaroni is almost tender.
2. Stir in shrimp and blue cheese; cook, covered, 30-35 minutes longer or until heated through. Just before serving, stir in chives, parsley and, if desired, additional hot sauce.

BLACK-EYED PEAS & HAM

Cheddar Creamed Corn

I brought this super-easy recipe to a school potluck, and it was gone in no time. I've been asked to bring it to every function since.

—JESSICA MAXWELL ENGLEWOOD, NJ

PREP: 10 MIN. • **COOK:** 3 HOURS
MAKES: 9 SERVINGS

- 2 packages (one 16 ounces, one 12 ounces) frozen corn, thawed
- 1 package (8 ounces) cream cheese, cubed
- ¾ cup shredded cheddar cheese
- ¼ cup butter, melted
- ¼ cup heavy whipping cream
- ½ teaspoon salt
- ¼ teaspoon pepper

In a 3- or 4-qt. slow cooker, combine all ingredients. Cook, covered, on low 3 to 3½ hours or until cheese is melted and corn is tender. Stir just before serving.

CHEDDAR CREAMED CORN

Black-Eyed Peas & Ham

Add some Southern flair to your next meal with these slow-cooked black-eyed peas.

—DAWN FRIHAUF FORT MORGAN, CO

PREP: 20 MIN. • **COOK:** 6 HOURS
MAKES: 12 SERVINGS (¾ CUP EACH)

- 1 package (16 ounces) dried black-eyed peas, rinsed and sorted
- ½ pound fully cooked boneless ham, finely chopped
- 1 medium onion, finely chopped
- 1 medium sweet red pepper, finely chopped
- 5 bacon strips, cooked and crumbled
- 1 large jalapeno pepper, seeded and finely chopped
- 2 garlic cloves, minced
- 1½ teaspoons ground cumin
- 1 teaspoon reduced-sodium chicken bouillon granules
- ½ teaspoon salt
- ½ teaspoon cayenne pepper
- ¼ teaspoon pepper
- 6 cups water
  Minced fresh cilantro, optional
  Hot cooked rice

In a 6-qt. slow cooker, combine the first 13 ingredients. Cover and cook on low for 6-8 hours or until peas are tender. Sprinkle with cilantro if desired. Serve with rice.

NOTE *Wear disposable gloves when cutting hot peppers; the oils can burn skin. Avoid touching your face.*

Butternut Squash with Whole Grains

Fresh thyme really shines in this hearty slow-cooked side dish featuring nutritious whole grains, vitamin-packed spinach and winter butternut squash.

—*TASTE OF HOME* TEST KITCHEN

PREP: 15 MIN. • **COOK:** 4 HOURS
MAKES: 12 SERVINGS (¾ CUP EACH)

- 1 **cup whole grain brown and red rice blend**
- 1 **can (14½ ounces) vegetable broth**
- 1 **medium onion, chopped**
- ½ **cup water**
- 3 **garlic cloves, minced**
- 2 **teaspoons minced fresh thyme or ½ teaspoon dried thyme**
- ½ **teaspoon salt**
- ¼ **teaspoon pepper**
- 1 **medium butternut squash (about 3 pounds), cut into ½-inch cubes**
- 1 **package (6 ounces) fresh baby spinach**

In a 4-qt slow cooker, combine the first nine ingredients. Cover and cook on low for 4-5 hours or until grains are tender. Just before serving, stir in spinach.

EASY BEANS & POTATOES WITH BACON

DID YOU KNOW?

Baby spinach is harvested shortly after planting, usually 15-30 days. It has small flat leaves that are tender in texture and have a sweet taste. Most supermarkets carry it either in bulk, so you can choose the amount you need, or in several different-size cellophane bags. It can be eaten either raw or cooked.

---

⑤INGREDIENTS Easy Beans & Potatoes with Bacon

I came up with this recipe because I love the tasty combination of green beans and bacon. It's great when you're having guests over, because you can start it in the slow cooker and then turn your attention to prepping the rest of the meal.

—**BARBARA BRITTAIN** SANTEE, CA

PREP: 15 MIN. • **COOK:** 6 HOURS
MAKES: 10 SERVINGS

- 8 **bacon strips, chopped**
- 1½ **pounds fresh green beans, trimmed and cut into 2-inch pieces (about 4 cups)**
- 4 **medium potatoes, peeled and cubed (½ inch)**
- 1 **small onion, halved and sliced**
- ¼ **cup reduced-sodium chicken broth**
- ½ **teaspoon salt**
- ¼ **teaspoon pepper**

1. In a large skillet, cook bacon over medium heat until crisp, stirring occasionally. Remove to paper towels with a slotted spoon; drain, reserving 1 tablespoon drippings. Cover and refrigerate bacon until serving.

2. In a 5-qt. slow cooker, combine the remaining ingredients; stir in reserved drippings. Cover and cook on low for 6-8 hours or until potatoes are tender. Stir in bacon; heat through.

Tzimmes

Tzimmes is a sweet Eastern European Jewish dish consisting of a variety of fruits and vegetables, with or without meat. I follow tradition and toss it with honey and cinnamon. As it slowly cooks, the flavors blend for an amazing taste.

—LISA RENSHAW KANSAS CITY, MO

PREP: 20 MIN. • **COOK:** 5 HOURS
MAKES: 12 SERVINGS (⅔ CUP EACH)

- ½ **medium butternut squash, peeled and cubed**
- 2 **medium sweet potatoes, peeled and cubed**
- 6 **medium carrots, sliced**
- 2 **medium tart apples, peeled and sliced**
- 1 **cup chopped sweet onion**
- 1 **cup chopped dried apricots**
- 1 **cup golden raisins**
- ½ **cup orange juice**
- ¼ **cup honey**
- 2 **tablespoons finely chopped crystallized ginger**
- 3 **teaspoons ground cinnamon**
- 3 **teaspoons pumpkin pie spice**
- 2 **teaspoons grated orange peel**
- 1 **teaspoon salt**
  Vanilla yogurt, optional

1. Place the first seven ingredients in a 5- or 6-qt. slow cooker. Combine the orange juice, honey, ginger, cinnamon, pie spice, orange peel and salt; pour over top and mix well.

2. Cover and cook on low for 5-6 hours or until vegetables are tender. Dollop servings with yogurt if desired.

Garlic Green Beans with Gorgonzola

I updated this favorite holiday side dish by adding a touch of white wine, fresh thyme and green onions. It's delicious, easy to make and my family loves it.

—NANCY HEISHMAN LAS VEGAS, NV

PREP: 20 MIN. • **COOK:** 3 HOURS
MAKES: 10 SERVINGS

- 2 **pounds fresh green beans, trimmed and halved**
- 1 **can (8 ounces) sliced water chestnuts, drained**
- 4 **green onions, chopped**
- 5 **bacon strips, cooked and crumbled, divided**
- ⅓ **cup white wine or chicken broth**
- 2 **tablespoons minced fresh thyme or 2 teaspoons dried thyme**
- 4 **garlic cloves, minced**
- 1½ **teaspoons seasoned salt**
- 1 **cup (8 ounces) sour cream**
- ¾ **cup crumbled Gorgonzola cheese**

1. Place green beans, water chestnuts, green onions and ¼ cup cooked bacon in a 4-qt. slow cooker. In a small bowl, mix wine, thyme, garlic and seasoned salt; pour over top. Cook, covered, on low 3-4 hours or until green beans are crisp-tender. Drain liquid from beans.

2. Just before serving, stir in sour cream; sprinkle with cheese and remaining bacon.

TZIMMES

GARLIC GREEN BEANS
WITH GORGONZOLA

PARSLEY SMASHED POTATOES

Onion-Garlic Hash Browns

Quick to assemble, these hash browns are one of my go-to sides. Stir in extra hot sauce if you like. I top my finished dish with a sprinkling of shredded cheddar cheese.

—CINDI BOGER ARDMORE, AL

PREP: 20 MIN. • **COOK:** 3 HOURS
MAKES: 12 SERVINGS (½ CUP EACH)

- 1 large red onion, chopped
- 1 small sweet red pepper, chopped
- 1 small green pepper, chopped
- ¼ cup butter, cubed
- 1 tablespoon olive oil
- 4 garlic cloves, minced
- 1 package (30 ounces) frozen shredded hash brown potatoes
- ½ teaspoon salt
- ½ teaspoon pepper
- 3 drops hot pepper sauce, optional
- 2 teaspoons minced fresh parsley

1. In a large skillet, saute onion and peppers in butter and oil until crisp-tender. Add garlic; cook 1 minute longer. Stir in the hash browns, salt, pepper and pepper sauce if desired.
2. Transfer to a 5-qt. slow cooker coated with cooking spray. Cover and cook on low for 3-4 hours or until heated through. Sprinkle with parsley before serving.

Parsley Smashed Potatoes

I like mashed potatoes but hate all the work it takes to make them from scratch. So I came up with this simple side dish that my slow cooker makes even easier. The best part is I can use the leftover broth for soup the next day!

—KATIE HAGY BLACKSBURG, SC

PREP: 20 MIN. • **COOK:** 6 HOURS
MAKES: 8 SERVINGS

- 16 small red potatoes (about 2 pounds)
- 1 celery rib, sliced
- 1 medium carrot, sliced
- ¼ cup finely chopped onion
- 2 cups chicken broth
- 1 tablespoon minced fresh parsley
- 1½ teaspoons salt, divided
- 1 teaspoon pepper, divided
- 1 garlic clove, minced
- 2 tablespoons butter, melted
  Additional minced fresh parsley

1. Place potatoes, celery, carrot and onion in a 4-qt. slow cooker. In a small bowl, mix broth, parsley, 1 teaspoon salt, ½ teaspoon pepper and garlic; pour over vegetables. Cook, covered, on low 6-8 hours or until potatoes are tender.
2. Transfer potatoes from slow cooker to a 15x10x1-in. pan; discard cooking liquid and vegetables. Using the bottom of a measuring cup, flatten potatoes slightly. Transfer to a large bowl; drizzle with butter. Sprinkle with remaining salt and pepper; toss to coat. Sprinkle with additional parsley.

ONION-GARLIC HASH BROWNS

HONEY-BUTTER PEAS AND CARROTS

Honey-Butter Peas and Carrots

This classic vegetable combination is even more delectable with a handful of flavor enhancers. Simmering for hours allows the ingredients to meld for maximum richness.
—**THERESA KREYCHE** TUSTIN, CA

PREP: 15 MIN. • **COOK:** 5¼ HOURS
MAKES: 12 SERVINGS (½ CUP EACH)

- 1 pound carrots, sliced
- 1 large onion, chopped
- ¼ cup water
- ¼ cup butter, cubed
- ¼ cup honey
- 4 garlic cloves, minced
- 1 teaspoon salt
- 1 teaspoon dried marjoram
- ⅛ teaspoon white pepper
- 1 package (16 ounces) frozen peas

In a 3-qt. slow cooker, combine the first nine ingredients. Cook, covered, on low 5 hours. Stir in the peas. Cook, covered, on high 15-25 minutes or until the vegetables are tender.

Pecan-Coconut Sweet Potatoes

Looking for a yummy twist on sweet potato casserole? Slow-cook the spuds with toasted pecans, coconut and a few other ingredients. Then sprinkle with mini marshmallows, and you're done!
—**REBECCA CLARK** WARRIOR, AL

PREP: 20 MIN. • **COOK:** 5 HOURS
MAKES: 6 SERVINGS

- ¼ cup packed brown sugar
- 2 tablespoons flaked coconut
- 2 tablespoons chopped pecans, toasted
- 1 teaspoon vanilla extract
- ½ teaspoon salt
- ¼ teaspoon ground cinnamon
- 2 pounds sweet potatoes, peeled and cut into ¾-inch cubes
- 1 tablespoon butter, melted
- ½ cup miniature marshmallows

1. In a small bowl, mix the first six ingredients. Place sweet potatoes in a 3-qt. slow cooker coated with cooking spray; sprinkle with brown sugar mixture. Drizzle with butter.

2. Cook, covered, on low 5-6 hours or until the sweet potatoes are tender. Turn off slow cooker. Sprinkle the marshmallows over potatoes; let stand, covered, 5 minutes before serving.

⑤INGREDIENTS Italian Mushrooms

You need just four ingredients for this rich and flavorful side dish that's perfect with beef and mashed potatoes.
—**KIM REICHERT** ST. PAUL, MN

PREP: 10 MIN. • **COOK:** 4 HOURS
MAKES: 6 SERVINGS

- 1 pound medium fresh mushrooms
- 1 large onion, sliced
- ½ cup butter, melted
- 1 envelope Italian salad dressing mix

In a 3-qt. slow cooker, layer mushrooms and onion. Combine butter and salad dressing mix; pour over vegetables. Cover and cook on low for 4-5 hours or until vegetables are tender. Serve with a slotted spoon.

ITALIAN MUSHROOMS

Slow Cooker Mushroom Rice Pilaf

A few modifications to our dear Great-Aunt Bernice's easy mushroom rice pilaf recipe have made this a mandatory dish for potlucks, barbecues and family get-togethers. It'll become a slow cooker favorite in your household, too.

—AMY WILLIAMS RIALTO, CA

PREP: 20 MIN. • **COOK:** 3 HOURS
MAKES: 6 SERVINGS

- 1 **cup medium grain rice**
- ¼ **cup butter**
- 6 **green onions, chopped**
- 2 **garlic cloves, minced**
- ½ **pound sliced baby portobello mushrooms**
- 2 **cups warm water**
- 4 **teaspoons beef base**

1. In a large skillet, saute rice in butter until lightly browned. Add green onions and garlic; cook and stir until tender. Stir in mushrooms.

2. Transfer to a 1½-qt. slow cooker. In a small bowl, whisk water and beef base; pour over rice mixture. Cover and cook on low for 3 to 3½ hours or until rice is tender and liquid is absorbed. Fluff with a fork.

NOTE *Look for beef base near the broth and bouillon.*

Black Bean Potato au Gratin

Black beans and vegetables add protein, fiber and extra flavor to this luxurious side dish, and the slow cooker makes it easy. If you want a Southwestern twist, toss in a handful or two of chopped cooked ham or chorizo sausage and replace the peas with one cup of corn.

—ERIN CHILCOAT CENTRAL ISLIP, NY

PREP: 25 MIN. • **COOK:** 8 HOURS
MAKES: 6 SERVINGS

BLACK BEAN POTATO AU GRATIN

- 2 **cans (15 ounces each) black beans, rinsed and drained**
- 1 **can (10¾ ounces) condensed cream of mushroom soup, undiluted**
- 1 **medium sweet red pepper, chopped**
- 1 **cup frozen peas**
- 1 **cup chopped sweet onion**
- 1 **celery rib, thinly sliced**
- 2 **garlic cloves, minced**
- 1 **teaspoon dried thyme**
- ¼ **teaspoon coarsely ground pepper**
- 1½ **pounds medium red potatoes, cut into ¼-inch slices**
- 1 **teaspoon salt**
- 1 **cup (4 ounces) shredded cheddar cheese**

In a large bowl, combine the beans, soup, red pepper, peas, onion, celery, garlic, thyme and pepper. Spoon half of mixture into a greased 3- or 4-qt. slow cooker. Layer with half of the potatoes, salt and cheese. Repeat layers. Cover and cook on low for 8-10 hours or until potatoes are tender.

SLOW COOKER MUSHROOM RICE PILAF

Rich & Creamy Mashed Potatoes

It's a cinch to jazz up instant mashed potatoes with sour cream and cream cheese. For a special touch, sprinkle the perfect-for-party-time potatoes with chopped fresh chives, canned French-fried onions or fresh grated Parmesan cheese.

—DONNA BARDOCZ HOWELL, MI

PREP: 15 MIN. • **COOK:** 2 HOURS
MAKES: 10 SERVINGS

- 3¾ cups boiling water
- 1½ cups 2% milk
- 1 package (8 ounces) cream cheese, softened
- ½ cup butter, cubed
- ½ cup sour cream
- 4 cups mashed potato flakes
- 1 teaspoon garlic salt
- ¼ teaspoon pepper
  Minced fresh parsley, optional

In a greased 4-qt. slow cooker, whisk the boiling water, milk, cream cheese, butter and sour cream until smooth. Stir in the potato flakes, garlic salt and pepper. Cover and cook on low for 2-3 hours or until heated through. Sprinkle with parsley if desired.

Glazed Spiced Carrots

Glazed carrots are a classic side dish for special occasions. This recipe is easy to put together, and people really enjoy it.

—TASTE OF HOME TEST KITCHEN

PREP: 10 MIN. • **COOK:** 6 HOURS
MAKES: 6 SERVINGS

- 2 pounds fresh baby carrots
- ½ cup peach preserves
- ¼ cup packed brown sugar
- ½ cup butter, melted
- 1 teaspoon vanilla extract
- ½ teaspoon ground cinnamon
- ¼ teaspoon salt
- ⅛ teaspoon ground nutmeg
- 2 tablespoons cornstarch
- 2 tablespoons water
  Toasted chopped pecans, optional

1. Place carrots in a 3-qt. slow cooker. Combine the preserves, brown sugar, butter, vanilla, cinnamon, salt and nutmeg. Combine cornstarch and water until smooth; stir into preserve mixture. Pour over carrots.

2. Cover and cook on low for 6-8 hours or until tender. Stir carrots; sprinkle with pecans if desired.

Scalloped Potatoes & Ham

I adapted an oven recipe to simmer in the slow cooker while I'm out. It's ready to serve when I get back, making it a keeper!

—JONI HILTON ROCKLIN, CA

PREP: 25 MIN. • **COOK:** 8 HOURS
MAKES: 16 SERVINGS (¾ CUP EACH)

- 1 can (10¾ ounces) condensed cheddar cheese soup, undiluted
- 1 can (10¾ ounces) condensed cream of mushroom soup, undiluted
- 1 cup 2% milk
- 10 medium potatoes, peeled and thinly sliced
- 3 cups cubed fully cooked ham
- 2 medium onions, chopped
- 1 teaspoon paprika
- 1 teaspoon pepper

1. In a small bowl, combine the soups and milk. In a greased 5-qt. slow cooker, layer half of the potatoes, ham, onions and soup mixture. Repeat layers. Sprinkle with paprika and pepper.

2. Cover and cook on low for 8-10 hours or until potatoes are tender.

SCALLOPED POTATOES & HAM

POTLUCK CANDIED SWEET POTATOES

Potluck Candied Sweet Potatoes

I love bringing this traditional Southern staple to potlucks and gatherings, so I found a way to prepare it in the slow cooker, which makes it easier to tote. It's hard to go wrong with candied sweet potatoes—folks rave about them!

—**DEIRDRE COX** KANSAS CITY, MO

PREP: 20 MIN. • **COOK:** 5 HOURS
MAKES: 12 SERVINGS (¾ CUP EACH)

- 1 **cup packed brown sugar**
- 1 **cup sugar**
- 8 **medium sweet potatoes, peeled and cut into ½-inch slices**
- ¼ **cup butter, melted**
- 2 **teaspoons vanilla extract**
- ¼ **teaspoon salt**
- 2 **tablespoons cornstarch**
- 2 **tablespoons cold water**
  Minced fresh parsley, optional

1. In a small bowl, combine sugars. In a greased 5-qt. slow cooker, layer a third of the sweet potatoes; sprinkle with a third of the sugar mixture. Repeat layers twice. In a small bowl, combine the butter, vanilla and salt; drizzle over potatoes. Cover and cook on low for 5-6 hours or until sweet potatoes are tender.

2. Using a slotted spoon, transfer potatoes to a serving dish; keep warm. Pour cooking juices into a small saucepan; bring to a boil. In a small bowl, combine cornstarch and water until smooth; stir into pan. Return to a boil, stirring constantly; cook and stir for 1-2 minutes or until thickened. Spoon over sweet potatoes.

3. Sprinkle with parsley if desired.

Slow Cooker Ratatouille

Not only does this classic recipe make a phenomenal side dish, you can also serve it with sliced French bread for a warm and easy appetizer. Try it in the summer with garden-fresh vegetables.

—**JOLENE WALTERS** NORTH MIAMI, FL

PREP: 20 MIN. + STANDING • **COOK:** 3 HOURS
MAKES: 10 SERVINGS

- 1 **large eggplant, peeled and cut into 1-inch cubes**
- 2 **teaspoons salt, divided**
- 3 **medium tomatoes, chopped**
- 3 **medium zucchini, halved lengthwise and sliced**
- 2 **medium onions, chopped**
- 1 **large green pepper, chopped**
- 1 **large sweet yellow pepper, chopped**
- 1 **can (6 ounces) pitted ripe olives, drained and chopped**
- 1 **can (6 ounces) tomato paste**
- ½ **cup minced fresh basil**
- 2 **garlic cloves, minced**
- ½ **teaspoon pepper**
- 2 **tablespoons olive oil**

1. Place eggplant in a colander over a plate; sprinkle with 1 teaspoon salt and toss. Let stand for 30 minutes. Rinse and drain well. Transfer to a 5-qt. slow cooker coated with cooking spray.

2. Stir in the tomatoes, zucchini, onions, green and yellow peppers, olives, tomato paste, basil, garlic, pepper and remaining salt. Drizzle with oil. Cover and cook on high for 3-4 hours or until vegetables are tender.

SLOW COOKER RATATOUILLE

Green Beans with Bacon and Tomatoes

Here's a side you can easily double or triple to serve larger crowds. You can substitute garlic salt for the seasoned salt.

—**CATHY BELL** JOPLIN, MO

PREP: 15 MIN. • **COOK:** 4½ HOURS
MAKES: 12 SERVINGS (¾ CUP)

- 1 package (14 ounces) thick-sliced bacon strips, chopped
- 1 large red onion, chopped
- 2 packages (16 ounces each) frozen cut green beans
- 1 can (28 ounces) petite diced tomatoes, undrained
- ¼ cup packed brown sugar
- 1 tablespoon seasoned pepper
- ½ teaspoon seasoned salt
- 1 can (16 ounces) red beans, rinsed and drained

1. In a large skillet, cook bacon over medium heat until partially cooked but not crisp, stirring occasionally. Remove with a slotted spoon; drain on paper towels. Discard drippings, reserving 2 tablespoons. Add onion to drippings; cook and stir over medium-high heat until tender.

2. In a 4- or 5-qt. slow cooker, combine green beans, tomatoes, brown sugar, pepper, salt, bacon and onion. Cook, covered, on low 4 hours. Stir in red beans. Cook 30 minutes longer or until heated through.

TOP TIP

Instead of frying bacon, line a baking pan with aluminum foil, place strips of bacon on it and bake in the oven at 350° for 30 minutes or until the bacon is crisp. The pan cleans easily, and there's no stovetop spattering.

SWEET & SPICY BEANS

Maple-Walnut Sweet Potatoes

Sweet potatoes with dried cherries and walnuts is a fantastic flavor combo.

—**SARAH HERSE** BROOKLYN, NY

PREP: 15 MIN. • **COOK:** 5 HOURS
MAKES: 12 SERVINGS (¾ CUP EACH)

- 4 pounds sweet potatoes (about 8 medium)
- ¾ cup coarsely chopped walnuts, divided
- ½ cup packed light brown sugar
- ½ cup dried cherries, coarsely chopped
- ½ cup maple syrup
- ¼ cup apple cider or juice
- ¼ teaspoon salt

1. Peel and cut sweet potatoes lengthwise in half; cut crosswise into ½-in. slices. Place in a 5-qt. slow cooker. Add ½ cup walnuts, brown sugar, cherries, syrup, cider and salt; toss to combine.

2. Cook, covered, on low 5-6 hours or until potatoes are tender. Sprinkle with remaining walnuts.

Sweet & Spicy Beans

My husband and I love this sweet and savory dish, which you can serve as a side or as a dip. When you fill up a corn "scoop" chip, the party starts in your mouth!

—**SONDRA POPE** MOORESVILLE, NC

PREP: 10 MIN. • **COOK:** 5 HOURS
MAKES: 12 SERVINGS (⅔ CUP EACH)

- 1 can (16 ounces) kidney beans, rinsed and drained
- 1 can (15¼ ounces) whole kernel corn, drained
- 1 can (15 ounces) garbanzo beans or chickpeas, rinsed and drained
- 1 can (15 ounces) black beans, rinsed and drained
- 1 can (15 ounces) chili with beans
- 1 cup barbecue sauce
- 1 cup salsa
- ⅓ cup packed brown sugar
- ¼ teaspoon hot pepper sauce
  Chopped green onions, optional

In a 4- or 5-qt. slow cooker, combine the first nine ingredients. Cover and cook on low for 5-6 hours. Top with green onions if desired.

Ranch Potatoes

I've been serving this comforting potato and bacon side dish to my family for years, and they still ask for it! Give it a try—your crew will be hooked, too.

—**LYNN IRELAND** LEBANON, WI

PREP: 15 MIN. • **COOK:** 7 HOURS
MAKES: 10 SERVINGS

- 6 **bacon strips, chopped**
- 2½ **pounds small red potatoes, cubed**
- 1 **package (8 ounces) cream cheese, softened**
- 1 **can (10¾ ounces) condensed cream of potato soup, undiluted**
- ¼ **cup 2% milk**
- 1 **envelope buttermilk ranch salad dressing mix**
- 3 **tablespoons thinly sliced green onions**

1. In a large skillet, cook bacon over medium heat until crisp, stirring occasionally. Remove with a slotted spoon; drain on paper towels. Drain drippings, reserving 1 tablespoon.

2. Place potatoes in a 3-qt. slow cooker. In a bowl, beat cream cheese, soup, milk, dressing mix and reserved drippings until blended; stir into potatoes. Sprinkle with bacon.

3. Cook, covered, on low 7-8 hours or until potatoes are tender. Top with green onions.

TOP TIP

When a recipe calls for thinly sliced green onions, cut them with a kitchen scissors instead of a knife. If the recipe calls for quite a few, grab a bunch at one time and snip away. This method is easy and fast, and you're done before you know it. It also saves you from having to wash a cutting board after chopping.

RANCH POTATOES

HARVARD BEETS

Harvard Beets

Fresh beets are delicious when combined with aromatic spice and a hint of orange. These have the perfect balance of sweet and sour flavors.

—*TASTE OF HOME* TEST KITCHEN

PREP: 15 MIN. • COOK: 7 HOURS
MAKES: 6 SERVINGS

- 2 **pounds small fresh beets, peeled and halved**
- ½ **cup sugar**
- ¼ **cup packed brown sugar**
- 2 **tablespoons cornstarch**
- ½ **teaspoon salt**
- ¼ **cup orange juice**
- ¼ **cup cider vinegar**
- 2 **tablespoons butter**
- 1½ **teaspoons whole cloves**

1. Place beets in a 3-qt. slow cooker. In a small bowl, combine the sugar, brown sugar, cornstarch and salt. Stir in orange juice and vinegar. Pour over beets; dot with butter. Place cloves on a double thickness of cheesecloth; bring up corners of cloth and tie with string to form a bag. Place bag in slow cooker.
2. Cover and cook on low for 7-8 hours or until tender. Discard spice bag.

Bacon & Sausage Stuffing

My mother's stuffing recipe inspired me to come up with this version. It smells like heaven while it's cooking, and people never seem to get enough of it.

—**SCOTT RUGH** PORTLAND, OR

PREP: 25 MIN. • COOK: 4 HOURS + STANDING
MAKES: 20 SERVINGS (¾ CUP EACH)

- 1 **pound bulk pork sausage**
- 1 **pound thick-sliced bacon strips, chopped**
- ½ **cup butter, cubed**
- 1 **large onion, chopped**
- 3 **celery ribs, sliced**
- 10½ **cups unseasoned stuffing cubes**
- 1 **cup sliced fresh mushrooms**
- 1 **cup chopped fresh parsley**
- 4 **teaspoons dried sage leaves**
- 4 **teaspoons dried thyme**
- 6 **eggs**
- 2 **cans (10¾ ounces each) condensed cream of chicken soup, undiluted**
- 1¼ **cups chicken stock**

1. In a large skillet, cook sausage over medium heat for 6-8 minutes or until no longer pink, breaking into crumbles. Remove with a slotted spoon; drain on paper towels. Discard drippings.
2. Add bacon to pan; cook over medium heat until crisp. Remove to paper towels to drain. Discard drippings. Wipe out pan. In same pan, heat butter over medium-high heat. Add onion and celery; cook and stir 6-8 minutes or until tender. Remove from heat.
3. In a large bowl, combine stuffing cubes, sausage, bacon, onion mixture, mushrooms, parsley, sage and thyme. In a small bowl, whisk eggs, soup and stock; pour over stuffing mixture and toss to coat.
4. Transfer to a greased 6-qt. slow cooker. Cook, covered, on low 4-5 hours or until a thermometer reads 160°. Remove lid; let stand 15 minutes before serving.

BACON & SAUSAGE STUFFING

BUTTERSCOTCH-PECAN BREAD PUDDING

Butterscotch-Pecan Bread Pudding

Bread pudding fans are sure to love this rich and delectable version. Complete each serving with whipped cream and warm butterscotch ice cream topping.

—**LISA M. VARNER** EL PASO, TX

PREP: 15 MIN. • **COOK:** 3 HOURS
MAKES: 8 SERVINGS

- 9 cups cubed day-old white bread (about 8 slices)
- ½ cup chopped pecans
- ½ cup butterscotch chips
- 4 eggs
- 2 cups half-and-half cream
- ½ cup packed brown sugar
- ½ cup butter, melted
- 1 teaspoon vanilla extract
  Whipped cream and butterscotch ice cream topping

1. Place bread, pecans and butterscotch chips in a greased 4-qt. slow cooker. In a large bowl, whisk eggs, cream, brown sugar, melted butter and vanilla until blended. Pour over bread mixture; stir gently to combine.

2. Cook, covered, on low 3-4 hours or until a knife inserted in center comes out clean. Serve warm with whipped cream and butterscotch topping.

Warm Rocky Road Cake

I love eating this cake while it's warm; it reminds me of moist lava cake. Brimming with chocolate, pecans and marshmallows, this dish will be an instant favorite.

—**SCARLETT ELROD** NEWNAN, GA

PREP: 20 MIN. • **COOK:** 3 HOURS
MAKES: 16 SERVINGS

- 1 package German chocolate cake mix (regular size)
- 1 package (3.9 ounces) instant chocolate pudding mix
- 1 cup (8 ounces) sour cream
- ⅓ cup butter, melted
- 3 eggs
- 1 teaspoon vanilla extract
- 3¾ cups 2% milk, divided
- 1 package (3.4 ounces) cook-and-serve chocolate pudding mix
- 1½ cups miniature marshmallows
- 1 cup (6 ounces) semisweet chocolate chips
- ½ cup chopped pecans, toasted
  Vanilla ice cream, optional

1. In a large bowl, combine the first six ingredients; add 1¼ cups milk. Beat on low speed 30 seconds. Beat on medium 2 minutes. Transfer to a greased 4- or 5-qt. slow cooker. Sprinkle cook-and-serve pudding mix over batter.

2. In a small saucepan, heat remaining milk until bubbles form around sides of pan; gradually pour over dry pudding mix.

3. Cook, covered, on high 3-4 hours or until a toothpick inserted in cake portion comes out with moist crumbs.

4. Turn off slow cooker. Sprinkle marshmallows, chocolate chips and pecans over cake; let stand, covered, 5 minutes or until marshmallows begin to melt. Serve warm. If desired, top with ice cream.

NOTE *To toast nuts, spread in a 15x10x1-in. baking pan. Bake at 350° for 5-10 minutes or until lightly browned, stirring occasionally. Or, spread in a dry nonstick skillet and heat over low heat until lightly browned, stirring occasionally.*

WARM ROCKY ROAD CAKE

CHERRY & SPICE RICE PUDDING

Cherry & Spice Rice Pudding

Cinnamon and cherries sweeten the deal in this homey dessert. If you've never tried rice pudding, I recommend this recipe. You'll be hooked.

—DEB PERRY TRAVERSE CITY, MI

PREP: 10 MIN. • **COOK:** 2 HOURS
MAKES: 12 SERVINGS

- 4 **cups cooked long grain rice**
- 1 **can (12 ounces) evaporated milk**
- 1 **cup 2% milk**
- ⅓ **cup sugar**
- ¼ **cup water**
- ¾ **cup dried cherries**
- 3 **tablespoons butter, softened**
- 2 **teaspoons vanilla extract**
- ½ **teaspoon ground cinnamon**
- ¼ **teaspoon ground nutmeg**

1. In a large bowl, combine the rice, evaporated milk, milk, sugar and water. Stir in the remaining ingredients. Transfer to a 3-qt. slow cooker coated with cooking spray.
2. Cover and cook on low for 2-3 hours or until mixture is thickened. Stir lightly before serving. Serve warm or cold. Refrigerate leftovers.

Blueberry Grunt

Blueberry lovers won't be able to get enough of this easy and old-fashioned treat. Serve it warm with vanilla ice cream.

—CLEO GONSKE REDDING, CA

PREP: 20 MIN. • **COOK:** 2½ HOURS
MAKES: 6 SERVINGS

- 4 **cups fresh or frozen blueberries**
- ¾ **cup sugar**
- ½ **cup water**
- 1 **teaspoon almond extract**

DUMPLINGS
- 2 **cups all-purpose flour**
- 4 **teaspoons baking powder**
- 1 **teaspoon sugar**
- ½ **teaspoon salt**
- 1 **tablespoon cold butter**
- 1 **tablespoon shortening**
- ¾ **cup 2% milk**
  Vanilla ice cream, optional

1. Place blueberries, sugar, water and extract in a 3-qt. slow cooker; stir to combine. Cook, covered, on high 2-3 hours or until bubbly.
2. For dumplings, in a small bowl, whisk flour, baking powder, sugar and salt. Cut in butter and shortening until crumbly. Add milk; stir just until a soft dough forms.
3. Drop dough by tablespoonfuls on top of hot blueberry mixture. Cook, covered, 30 minutes longer or until a toothpick inserted in center of dumplings comes out clean. If desired, serve warm with ice cream.

BLUEBERRY GRUNT

[FREEZE IT] Apple-Pear Compote

Everyone loves the refreshing and sweet taste of apples and pears, so this fruit-packed compote is great for potlucks and other get-togethers. I like to toss in raisins or chopped nuts, and for a more adult flavor, I add ⅓ cup brandy or rum.

—NANCY HEISHMAN LAS VEGAS, NV

PREP: 20 MIN. • **COOK:** 3¼ HOURS
MAKES: 8 CUPS

- 5 medium apples, peeled and chopped
- 3 medium pears, chopped
- 1 medium orange, thinly sliced
- ½ cup dried cranberries
- ½ cup packed brown sugar
- ½ cup maple syrup
- ⅓ cup butter, cubed
- 2 tablespoons lemon juice
- 2 teaspoons ground cinnamon
- 1 teaspoon ground ginger
- 5 tablespoons orange juice, divided
- 4 teaspoons cornstarch
  Sweetened whipped cream and toasted chopped pecans, optional

1. In a 4- or 5-qt. slow cooker, combine the first 10 ingredients. Stir in 2 tablespoons orange juice. Cook, covered, on low 3-4 hours or until fruit is tender.

2. In a small bowl, mix cornstarch and remaining orange juice until smooth; gradually stir into fruit mixture. Cook, covered, on high 15-20 minutes longer or until sauce is thickened. If desired, top with whipped cream and pecans.

FREEZE OPTION *Freeze cooled compote in freezer containers. To use, partially thaw in refrigerator overnight. Heat through in a saucepan, stirring occasionally and adding a little orange juice if necessary.*

APPLE-PEAR COMPOTE

APPLE PIE OATMEAL DESSERT

Apple Pie Oatmeal Dessert

This warm and comforting dessert stirs up memories of time spent with my family around the kitchen table. Serve this dish with sweetened whipped cream or vanilla ice cream.

—CAROL GREER EARLVILLE, IL

PREP: 15 MIN. • **COOK:** 4 HOURS
MAKES: 6 SERVINGS

- 1 cup quick-cooking oats
- ½ cup all-purpose flour
- ⅓ cup packed brown sugar
- 2 teaspoons baking powder
- 1½ teaspoons apple pie spice
- ¼ teaspoon salt
- 3 eggs
- 1⅔ cups 2% milk, divided
- 1½ teaspoons vanilla extract
- 3 medium apples, peeled and finely chopped
  Vanilla ice cream, optional

1. In a large bowl, whisk oats, flour, brown sugar, baking powder, pie spice and salt. In a small bowl, whisk eggs, 1 cup milk and vanilla until blended. Add to oat mixture, stirring just until moistened. Fold in apples.

2. Transfer to a greased 3-qt. slow cooker. Cook, covered, on low 4-5 hours or until apples are tender and top is set.

3. Stir in remaining milk. Serve warm or cold with ice cream if desired.

Slow Cooker Baked Apples

Coming home to these irresistible apples on a dreary, cold day always puts a smile on my face. I love that my slow cooker makes them a cinch to prepare.

—**EVANGELINE BRADFORD** ERLANGER, KY

PREP: 25 MIN. • **COOK:** 4 HOURS
MAKES: 6 SERVINGS

- 6 medium tart apples
- ½ cup raisins
- ⅓ cup packed brown sugar
- 1 tablespoon grated orange peel
- 1 cup water
- 3 tablespoons thawed orange juice concentrate
- 2 tablespoons butter

1. Core apples and peel top third of each if desired. Combine the raisins, brown sugar and orange peel; spoon into apples. Place in a 5-qt. slow cooker.
2. Pour water around apples. Drizzle with orange juice concentrate. Dot with butter. Cover and cook on low for 4-5 hours or until apples are tender.

AMARETTO CHERRIES WITH DUMPLINGS

SLOW COOKER BAKED APPLES

Amaretto Cherries with Dumplings

Treat everyone to a dessert of comfort food—warm tart cherries drizzled with amaretto and topped with fluffy dumplings. A scoop of vanilla ice cream is the perfect finishing touch.

—***TASTE OF HOME*** TEST KITCHEN

PREP: 15 MIN. • **COOK:** 7¾ HOURS
MAKES: 6 SERVINGS

- 2 cans (14½ ounces each) pitted tart cherries
- ¾ cup sugar
- ¼ cup cornstarch
- ⅛ teaspoon salt
- ¼ cup amaretto or ½ teaspoon almond extract

DUMPLINGS
- 1 cup all-purpose flour
- ¼ cup sugar
- 1 teaspoon baking powder
- ½ teaspoon grated lemon peel
- ⅛ teaspoon salt
- ⅓ cup 2% milk
- 3 tablespoons butter, melted
  Vanilla ice cream, optional

1. Drain cherries, reserving ¼ cup juice. Place cherries in a 3-qt. slow cooker.
2. In a small bowl, mix the sugar, cornstarch and salt; stir in reserved juice until smooth. Stir into cherries. Cook, covered, on high 7 hours. Drizzle amaretto over cherry mixture.
3. For dumplings, in a small bowl, whisk flour, sugar, baking powder, lemon peel and salt. In another bowl, whisk milk and melted butter. Add to flour mixture; stir just until moistened.
4. Drop by tablespoonfuls on top of hot cherry mixture. Cook, covered, 45 minutes or until a toothpick inserted in center of dumplings comes out clean. If desired, serve warm with ice cream.

**CHOCOLATE-COVERED
CHERRY PUDDING CAKE**

Chocolate-Covered Cherry Pudding Cake

My grandfather cherished the chocolate-covered cherries we brought him for Christmas every year. After he passed away, I created this rich recipe in his honor. It's delicious served with whipped topping.

—MEREDITH COE CHARLOTTESVILLE, VA

PREP: 20 MIN. • **COOK:** 2 HOURS + STANDING
MAKES: 8 SERVINGS

- ½ **cup reduced-fat sour cream**
- 2 **tablespoons canola oil**
- 1 **tablespoon butter, melted**
- 2 **teaspoons vanilla extract**
- 1 **cup all-purpose flour**
- ¼ **cup sugar**
- ¼ **cup packed brown sugar**
- 3 **tablespoons baking cocoa**
- 2 **teaspoon baking powder**
- ½ **teaspoon ground cinnamon**
- ⅛ **teaspoon salt**
- 1 **cup fresh or frozen pitted dark sweet cherries, thawed**
- 1 **cup fresh or frozen pitted tart cherries, thawed**
- ⅓ **cup 60% cacao bittersweet chocolate baking chips**

PUDDING
- ½ **cup packed brown sugar**
- 2 **tablespoons baking cocoa**
- 1¼ **cups hot water**

1. In a large bowl, beat the sour cream, oil, butter and vanilla until blended. Combine the flour, sugars, cocoa, baking powder, cinnamon and salt. Add to sour cream mixture just until combined. Stir in cherries and chips. Pour into a 3-qt. slow cooker coated with cooking spray.

2. In a small bowl, combine brown sugar and cocoa. Stir in hot water until blended. Pour over the batter (do not stir). Cover and cook on high for 2 to 2½ hours or until set. Let stand for 15 minutes. Serve warm.

Bananas Foster

The flavors of caramel, rum and walnut naturally complement fresh bananas in this classic dessert!

—CRYSTAL BRUNS ILIFF, CO

PREP: 10 MIN. • **COOK:** 2 HOURS
MAKES: 5 SERVINGS

- 5 **medium firm bananas**
- 1 **cup packed brown sugar**
- ¼ **cup butter, melted**
- ¼ **cup rum**
- 1 **teaspoon vanilla extract**
- ½ **teaspoon ground cinnamon**
- ⅓ **cup chopped walnuts**
- ⅓ **cup flaked coconut**
    Vanilla ice cream or sliced pound cake

1. Cut bananas in half lengthwise, then widthwise; layer in the bottom of a 1½-qt. slow cooker. Combine the brown sugar, butter, rum, vanilla and cinnamon; pour over bananas. Cover and cook on low for 1½ hours or until heated through.

2. Sprinkle with walnuts and coconut; cook 30 minutes longer. Serve with ice cream or pound cake.

BANANAS FOSTER

Old-Fashioned Tapioca

My family loves old-fashioned tapioca, but traditional recipes require too much babysitting at the stove. So I developed this simpler version that lets us enjoy the dessert without all the fuss.

—**RUTH PETERS** BEL AIR, MD

PREP: 10 MIN. • **COOK:** 4½ HOURS
MAKES: 18 SERVINGS (½ CUP EACH)

8 cups 2% milk
1 cup pearl tapioca
1 cup plus 2 tablespoons sugar
⅛ teaspoon salt
4 eggs
1½ teaspoons vanilla extract
   Sliced fresh strawberries and
     whipped cream, optional

1. In a 4- to 5-qt. slow cooker, combine the milk, tapioca, sugar and salt. Cover and cook on low for 4-5 hours.
2. In a large bowl, beat the eggs; stir in a small amount of hot tapioca mixture. Return all to the slow cooker, stirring to combine. Cover and cook 30 minutes longer or until a thermometer reads 160°. Stir in vanilla.
3. Serve with strawberries and whipped cream if desired.

Maple Creme Brulee

The slow cooker is the perfect cooking vessel for the classic dessert, creme brulee. The maple custard is smooth and creamy, and the crunchy brown sugar topping can't be beat.

—**TASTE OF HOME** TEST KITCHEN

PREP: 20 MIN. • **COOK:** 2 HOURS + CHILLING
MAKES: 3 SERVINGS

1⅓ cups heavy whipping cream
3 egg yolks
½ cup packed brown sugar
¼ teaspoon ground cinnamon
½ teaspoon maple flavoring

TOPPING
1½ teaspoons sugar
1½ teaspoons brown sugar

1. In a small saucepan, heat cream until bubbles form around sides of pan. In a small bowl, whisk the egg yolks, brown sugar and cinnamon. Remove cream from the heat; stir a small amount of hot cream into egg mixture. Return all to the pan, stirring constantly. Stir in maple flavoring.
2. Transfer to three 6-oz. ramekins or custard cups. Place in a 6-qt. slow cooker; add 1 in. of boiling water to slow cooker. Cover and cook on high for 2 to 2½ hours or until centers are just set (mixture will jiggle). Carefully remove ramekins from slow cooker; cool for 10 minutes. Cover and refrigerate for at least 4 hours.
3. For topping, combine sugar and brown sugar. If using a creme brulee torch, sprinkle custards with sugar mixture. Heat sugar with the torch until caramelized. Serve immediately.
4. If broiling the custards, place ramekins on a baking sheet; let stand at room temperature for 15 minutes. Sprinkle with sugar mixture. Broil 8 in. from the heat for 3-5 minutes or until sugar is caramelized. Refrigerate for 1-2 hours or until firm.

MAPLE CREME BRULEE

PINK GRAPEFRUIT CHEESECAKE

Pink Grapefruit Cheesecake

Cheesecake made in a slow cooker? It's true! I experimented a few times to turn this iconic dessert into a slow-cooker classic. Try any one of the three topping variations. You'll be amazed at the results!

—**KRISTA LANPHIER** MILWAUKEE, WI

PREP: 20 MIN. • **COOK:** 2 HOURS + CHILLING
MAKES: 6 SERVINGS

- ¾ cup graham cracker crumbs
- 1 tablespoon plus ⅔ cup sugar, divided
- 1 teaspoon grated grapefruit peel
- ¼ teaspoon ground ginger
- 2½ tablespoons butter, melted
- 2 packages (8 ounces each) cream cheese, softened
- ½ cup sour cream
- 2 tablespoons pink grapefruit juice
- 2 eggs, lightly beaten

1. Place a greased 6-in. springform pan on a double thickness of heavy-duty foil (about 12 in. square). Wrap foil securely around pan. Pour 1 in. water in a 6-qt. slow cooker. Layer two 24-in. pieces of aluminum foil. Starting with a long side, fold up foil to create a 1-in.-wide strip; roll into a coil. Place in slow cooker to form a rack for the cheesecake.

2. In a small bowl, mix cracker crumbs, 1 tablespoon sugar, peel and ginger; stir in butter. Press onto bottom and about 1 in. up sides of prepared pan.

3. In a large bowl, beat cream cheese and remaining sugar until smooth. Beat in sour cream and grapefruit juice. Add eggs and beat on low speed just until combined.

4. Pour into crust. Place springform pan on top of coil. Cover slow cooker with a double layer of paper towels; place lid securely over towels. Cook, covered, on high 2 hours. Do not remove lid; turn off the slow cooker and let cheesecake stand, covered, in slow cooker 1 hour. The center of the cheesecake will be just set and the top will appear dull.

5. Remove springform pan from slow cooker; remove foil from pan. Cool cheesecake on a wire rack 1 hour. Loosen sides from pan with a knife. Refrigerate overnight, covering when completely cooled. Remove rim from the pan.

CITRUS TOPPING *Top cheesecake with orange and grapefruit sections (from half an orange and half a grapefruit) and kumquat slices. Add sugared cranberries (recipe below) if desired.*

CHOCOLATE & PECAN TOPPING *Melt 2 ounces semisweet chocolate with 1 teaspoon shortening and stir until smooth; drizzle over cheesecake. Top with glazed pecans.*

SUGARED CRANBERRY TOPPING *Lightly mist ½ cup fresh cranberries with water; toss with 2 tablespoons sugar. Arrange over cheesecake; top with orange peel curls.*

NOTE *Six-inch springform pans are available at* wilton.com.

CHERRY PEAR BUCKLE

Cherry Pear Buckle

While watching a popular cooking show, I was inspired to experiement and make my own version of the recipe the cooks were demonstrating. When the enticing aromas of this down-home dessert drift from the kitchen, your clan will come running!

—**SHERRI MELOTIK** OAK CREEK, WI

PREP: 10 MIN. • **COOK:** 3 HOURS
MAKES: 6 SERVINGS

- 2 cans (15 ounces each) sliced pears, drained
- 1 can (21 ounces) cherry pie filling
- ¼ teaspoon almond extract
- 1 package yellow cake mix (regular size)
- ¼ cup old-fashioned oats
- ¼ cup sliced almonds
- 1 tablespoon brown sugar
- ½ cup butter, melted
  Vanilla ice cream, optional

1. In a greased 5-qt. slow cooker, combine pears and pie filling; stir in extract. In a large bowl, combine cake mix, oats, almonds and brown sugar; stir in melted butter. Sprinkle over fruit.

2. Cook, covered, on low 3-4 hours or until topping is golden brown. If desired, serve with ice cream.

ELVIS' PUDDING CAKE

Elvis' Pudding Cake

I love the flavors of peanut butter and banana together, and my pudding cake is just like eating an Elvis sandwich...only sweeter! Banana chips add a surprisingly crunchy texture—find them near the dried fruit in your grocery store.

—LISA RENSHAW KANSAS CITY, MO

PREP: 10 MIN. • **COOK:** 3 HOURS + STANDING
MAKES: 12 SERVINGS

- 3 **cups cold 2% milk**
- 1 **package (3.4 ounces) instant banana cream pudding mix**
- 1 **package banana cake mix (regular size)**
- ½ **cup creamy peanut butter**
- 2 **cups peanut butter chips**
- 1 **cup chopped dried banana chips**

1. In a small bowl, whisk milk and pudding mix for 2 minutes. Let stand for 2 minutes or until soft-set. Transfer to a greased 5-qt. slow cooker.
2. Prepare cake mix batter according to package directions, adding peanut butter before mixing. Pour over pudding. Cover and cook on low for 3 to 3½ hours or until a toothpick inserted near the center comes out with moist crumbs.
3. Sprinkle with peanut butter chips; cover and let stand for 15-20 minutes or until partially melted. Top with banana chips.

Cinnamon-Apple Brown Betty

If I had to define the "Betty" of Apple Brown Betty, she'd be a smart and thrifty Southern gal with a knack for creating simple, soul-comforting desserts. In this sweet dish, spiced apples are slow-cooked between layers of cinnamon-raisin bread cubes for a modern twist on the traditional oven-baked classic.

—HEATHER DEMERITTE SCOTTSDALE, AZ

PREP: 15 MIN. • **COOK:** 2 HOURS
MAKES: 6 SERVINGS

- 5 **medium tart apples, cubed**
- 2 **tablespoons lemon juice**
- 1 **cup packed brown sugar**
- 1 **teaspoon ground cinnamon**
- ¼ **teaspoon ground nutmeg**
- 6 **cups cubed day-old cinnamon-raisin bread (about 10 slices)**
- 6 **tablespoons butter, melted**
  Sweetened whipped cream, optional

1. In a large bowl, toss apples with lemon juice. In a small bowl, mix brown sugar, cinnamon and nutmeg; add to apple mixture and toss to coat. In a large bowl, drizzle butter over bread cubes; toss to coat.
2. Place 2 cups bread cubes in a greased 3- or 4-qt. slow cooker. Layer with half of the apple mixture and 2 cups bread cubes. Repeat layers. Cook, covered, on low 2-3 hours or until apples are tender. Stir before serving. If desired, top with whipped cream.

CINNAMON-APPLE BROWN BETTY

MOLTEN MOCHA CAKE

The first time I made my chocolate cake, my husband and daughter declared it a keeper. In fact, my daughter now claims it's one of her all-time favorites. I also shared the cake with my next door neighbor's son, who liked it so much that he ate the whole thing without telling anyone about it!
—**AIMEE FORTNEY** FAIRVIEW, TN

Molten Mocha Cake

PREP: 10 MIN. • **COOK:** 2½ HOURS
MAKES: 4 SERVINGS

- 4 **eggs**
- 1½ **cups sugar**
- ½ **cup butter, melted**
- 3 **teaspoons vanilla extract**
- 1 **cup all-purpose flour**
- ½ **cup baking cocoa**
- 1 **tablespoon instant coffee granules**
- ¼ **teaspoon salt**
   Fresh raspberries or sliced fresh strawberries and vanilla ice cream, optional

1. In a large bowl, beat eggs, sugar, butter and vanilla until blended. In another bowl, whisk flour, cocoa, coffee granules and salt; gradually beat into egg mixture.
2. Transfer to greased 1½-qt. slow cooker. Cook, covered, on low 2½ to 3 hours or until a toothpick comes out with moist crumbs. If desired, serve warm cake with berries and ice cream.

PEAR-BLUEBERRY GRANOLA

Pear-Blueberry Granola

The colorful mixture of pears, blueberries and granola in this dish make it a great breakfast, but you'll love it even more as a dessert with vanilla ice cream on top.

—LISA WORKMAN BOONES MILL, VA

PREP: 15 MIN. • **COOK:** 3 HOURS
MAKES: 10 SERVINGS

- 5 medium pears, peeled and thinly sliced
- 2 cups fresh or frozen unsweetened blueberries
- ½ cup packed brown sugar
- ⅓ cup apple cider or unsweetend apple juice
- 1 tablespoon all-purpose flour
- 1 tablespoon lemon juice
- 2 teaspoons ground cinnamon
- 2 tablespoons butter
- 3 cups granola without raisins

In a 4-qt. slow cooker, combine the first seven ingredients. Dot with butter. Sprinkle granola over top. Cover and cook on low for 3-4 hours or until fruit is tender.

Very Vanilla Slow Cooker Cheesecake

Cinnamon and vanilla give this cheesecake so much flavor, and making it in the slow cooker creates a silky, smooth texture that's hard to resist.

—KRISTA LANPHIER MILWAUKEE, WI

PREP: 40 MIN. • **COOK:** 2 HOURS + CHILLING
MAKES: 6 SERVINGS

- ¾ cup graham cracker crumbs
- 1 tablespoon sugar plus ⅔ cup sugar, divided
- ¼ teaspoon ground cinnamon
- 2½ tablespoons butter, melted
- 2 packages (8 ounces each) cream cheese, softened
- ½ cup sour cream
- 2 to 3 teaspoons vanilla extract
- 2 eggs, lightly beaten

TOPPING
- 2 ounces semisweet chocolate, chopped
- 1 teaspoon shortening
  Toasted sliced almonds

1. Grease a 6-in. springform pan; place on a double thickness of heavy-duty foil (about 12 in. square). Wrap foil securely around pan.

2. Pour 1 in. water into a 6-qt. slow cooker. Layer two 24-in. pieces of aluminum foil. Starting with a long side, roll up foil to make a 1-in.-wide strip; shape into a circle. Place in bottom of slow cooker to make a rack.

3. In a small bowl, mix cracker crumbs, 1 tablespoon sugar and cinnamon; stir in butter. Press onto bottom and about 1 in. up sides of prepared pan.

4. In a large bowl, beat cream cheese and remaining sugar until smooth. Beat in sour cream and vanilla. Add eggs; beat on low speed just until combined. Pour into crust.

5. Place springform pan on foil circle without touching slow cooker sides. Cover slow cooker with a double layer of white paper towels; place lid securely over towels. Cook, covered, on high 2 hours.

6. Do not remove lid; turn off slow cooker and let cheesecake stand, covered, in slow cooker 1 hour.

7. Remove springform pan from slow cooker; remove foil around pan. Cool cheesecake on a wire rack 1 hour longer. Loosen sides from pan with a knife. Refrigerate overnight, covering when completely cooled.

8. For topping, in a microwave, melt chocolate and shortening; stir until smooth. Cool slightly. Remove rim from springform pan. Pour chocolate mixture over cheesecake; sprinkle with almonds.

VERY VANILLA SLOW COOKER CHEESECAKE

BREAD PUDDING WITH BOURBON SAUCE

Bread Pudding with Bourbon Sauce

There's nothing I like better than this soothing bread pudding on a cold, wintry day. The bourbon sauce makes the dessert taste special, but you won't believe how easy it is to prepare.

—**HOPE JOHNSON** YOUNGWOOD, PA

PREP: 20 MIN. • **COOK:** 3 HOURS
MAKES: 6 SERVINGS

- 3 eggs
- 1¼ cups 2% milk
- ½ cup sugar
- 3 teaspoons vanilla extract
- ½ teaspoon ground cinnamon
- ¼ teaspoon ground nutmeg
- ⅛ teaspoon salt
- 4½ cups cubed day-old brioche or egg bread
- 1¼ cups raisins

BOURBON SAUCE
- ¼ cup butter, cubed
- ½ cup sugar
- ¼ cup light corn syrup
- 3 tablespoons bourbon

1. In a large bowl, whisk the first seven ingredients; stir in bread and raisins. Transfer to a greased 4-qt. slow cooker. Cover and cook on low for 3 hours.

2. In a small saucepan, heat butter. Stir in sugar and corn syrup; bring to a boil. Reduce heat; cook and stir until sugar is dissolved. Remove from the heat; stir in bourbon. Serve warm with bread pudding.

(5) INGREDIENTS Chocolate Peanut Drops

I received this fun recipe from a friend, who got it from her sister, and between the three of us we've handed it out everywhere! The chocolaty candies couldn't be easier to make and depending on the size of your spoon, you can get at least several dozen candies from one recipe. It's so and great for gifts.

—**ANITA BELL** HERMITAGE, TN

PREP: 20 MIN. • **COOK:** 1½ HOURS + STANDING
MAKES: ABOUT 11 DOZEN

- 4 ounces German sweet chocolate, chopped
- 1 package (12 ounces) semisweet chocolate chips
- 4 packages (10 to 12 ounces each) white baking chips
- 2 jars (16 ounces each) lightly salted dry roasted peanuts

1. In a 6-qt. slow cooker, layer ingredients in order listed (do not stir). Cover and cook on low for 1½ hours. Stir to combine. (If chocolate is not melted, cover and cook 15 minutes longer; stir. Repeat in 15-minute increments until chocolate is melted.)

2. Drop mixture by rounded tablespoonfuls onto waxed paper. Let stand until set. Store in an airtight container at room temperature.

Caramel Pears

The crystallized ginger and cinnamon add an enticing flavor to this decadent dessert made with fresh pears.

—**TASTE OF HOME** TEST KITCHEN

PREP: 15 MIN. • **COOK:** 2 HOURS
MAKES: 6 SERVINGS

- 6 medium pears, peeled and sliced
- ¾ cup packed brown sugar
- ¼ cup heavy whipping cream
- 2 teaspoons lemon juice
- 2 tablespoons butter, melted
- 1 tablespoon chopped crystallized ginger
- 1 teaspoon cornstarch
- ½ teaspoon ground cinnamon
  Grilled pound cake, whipped topping and sliced almonds

In a 1½-qt. slow cooker, combine the first eight ingredients. Cover and cook on low for 2-3 hours or until heated through. Serve warm over pound cake. Top with whipped topping; sprinkle with almonds.

CHOCOLATE PEANUT DROPS

GLAZED CINNAMON APPLES

TROPICAL COMPOTE DESSERT

Glazed Cinnamon Apples

If you're craving something comforting and sweet, this warm and yummy apple dessert, flavored with cinnamon and nutmeg, will hit the spot.

—**MEGAN MAZE** OAK CREEK, WI

PREP: 20 MIN. • **COOK:** 3 HOURS
MAKES: 7 SERVINGS

- 6 **large tart apples**
- 2 **tablespoons lemon juice**
- ½ **cup packed brown sugar**
- ½ **cup sugar**
- 2 **tablespoons all-purpose flour**
- 1 **teaspoon ground cinnamon**
- ¼ **teaspoon ground nutmeg**
- 6 **tablespoons butter, melted**
  Vanilla ice cream

1. Peel, core and cut each apple into eight wedges; transfer to a 3-qt. slow cooker. Drizzle with lemon juice. Combine the sugars, flour, cinnamon and nutmeg; sprinkle over apples. Drizzle with butter.

2. Cover and cook on low for 3-4 hours or until apples are tender. Serve in dessert dishes with ice cream.

Tropical Compote Dessert

This sweet and colorful fruit compote is perfect with an egg casserole at a brunch To make a grown-up version of this recipe, use brandy instead of the extra tropical fruit juice.

—**TASTE OF HOME TEST KITCHEN**

PREP: 15 MIN. • **COOK:** 2¼ HOURS
MAKES: 6 SERVINGS

- 1 **jar (23½ ounces) mixed tropical fruit**
- 1 **jalapeno pepper, seeded and chopped**
- ¼ **cup sugar**
- 1 **tablespoon chopped crystallized ginger**
- ¼ **teaspoon ground cinnamon**
- 1 **can (15 ounces) mandarin oranges, drained**
- 1 **jar (6 ounces) maraschino cherries, drained**
- 1 **medium firm banana, sliced**
- 6 **individual round sponge cakes**
- 6 **tablespoons flaked coconut, toasted**

1. Drain tropical fruit, reserving ¼ cup liquid. Combine tropical fruit and jalapeno in a 1½-qt. slow cooker. Combine the sugar, ginger, cinnamon and reserved juice; pour over fruit. Cover and cook on low for 2 hours. Stir in the mandarin oranges, cherries and banana; cook 15 minutes longer.

2. Place sponge cakes on dessert plates; top with compote. Sprinkle with coconut.

NOTE *Wear disposable gloves when cutting hot peppers; the oils can burn skin. Avoid touching your face.*

CRUNCHY CANDY CLUSTERS

SLOW COOKER
APPLE PUDDING CAKE

(5) INGREDIENTS Crunchy Candy Clusters

My family expects these bite-size clusters to be on the cookie and candy platter during the holidays. These treats so good, and so easy to make, that you'll be tempted to enjoy them all year long.

—**FAYE O'BRYAN** OWENSBORO, KY

PREP: 15 MIN. • **COOK:** 1 HOUR
MAKES: 6½ DOZEN

- 2 **pounds white candy coating, coarsely chopped**
- 1½ **cups peanut butter**
- ½ **teaspoon almond extract, optional**
- 4 **cups Cap'n Crunch cereal**
- 4 **cups crisp rice cereal**
- 4 **cups miniature marshmallows**

1. Place candy coating in a 5-qt. slow cooker. Cover and cook on high for 1 hour. Add peanut butter. Stir in extract if desired.
2. In a large bowl, combine the cereals and marshmallows. Stir in the peanut butter mixture until well coated. Drop by tablespoonfuls onto waxed paper. Let stand until set. Store at room temperature.

Slow Cooker Apple Pudding Cake

A satisfying dessert like this is a superb treat on a chilly night. It separates into three layers—apples, cake and sauce—and is easy to eat served in a bowl.

—**ELLEN SCHROEDER** REEDSBURG, WI

PREP: 15 MIN. • **COOK:** 2 HOURS
MAKES: 10 SERVINGS

- 2 **cups all-purpose flour**
- ⅔ **cup plus ¼ cup sugar, divided**
- 3 **teaspoons baking powder**
- 1 **teaspoon salt**
- ½ **cup cold butter**
- 1 **cup 2% milk**
- 2 **medium tart apples, peeled and chopped**
- 1½ **cups orange juice**
- ½ **cup honey**
- 2 **tablespoons butter, melted**
- 1 **teaspoon ground cinnamon**
- 1⅓ **cups sour cream**
- ¼ **cup confectioners' sugar**

1. In a small bowl, combine the flour, ⅔ cup sugar, baking powder and salt. Cut in butter until mixture resembles coarse crumbs. Stir in milk just until moistened. Spread into the bottom of a greased 4- or 5-qt. slow cooker; sprinkle apples over batter.
2. In a small bowl, combine the orange juice, honey, melted butter, cinnamon and remaining sugar; pour over apples. Cover and cook on high for 2-3 hours or until apples are tender.
3. In a small bowl, combine sour cream and confectioners' sugar. Serve with warm pudding cake.

Spiced Poached Pears

Looking for a healthy dessert that is sure to impress? These poached pears make a pretty addition to a formal dinner. The recipe may look intimidating, but I promise it's easy, and you can prepare it in advance. Another reason to love your slow cooker!

—**JILL MANT** DENVER, CO

PREP: 25 MIN. • **COOK:** 4 HOURS
MAKES: 8 SERVINGS

- 1½ **cups dry red wine or cranberry juice**
- ⅓ **cup packed brown sugar**
- 2 **tablespoons dried cherries**
- 1 **tablespoon ground cinnamon**
- 1 **whole star anise**
- 1 **dried Sichuan peppercorn, optional**
- 4 **ripe Bosc pears**
- **GANACHE**
- 6 **ounces bittersweet chocolate, chopped**
- ¼ **cup heavy whipping cream**
- **TOPPINGS**
- 2 **tablespoons pine nuts**
- **Fresh blackberries**
- **Sweetened whipped cream, optional**

1. In a 3-qt. slow cooker, mix wine, brown sugar, cherries, cinnamon, star anise and, if desired, peppercorn until blended. Peel and cut pears lengthwise in half. Remove cores, leaving a small well in the center of each. Arrange pears in wine mixture.

2. Cook, covered, on low 4-5 hours or until pears are almost tender. Discard star anise and peppercorn.

3. Place chocolate in a small bowl. In a small saucepan, bring cream just to a boil. Pour over chocolate; stir with a whisk until smooth.

4. To serve, remove pears to dessert dishes; drizzle with some of the poaching liquid. Spoon ganache into wells of pears. Top with pine nuts and blackberries. If desired, serve with whipped cream.

WARM APPLE-CRANBERRY DESSERT

Warm Apple-Cranberry Dessert

My family can't get enough of this apple-cranberry combo. I like that this dessert practically makes itself.

—**MARY JONES** WILLIAMSTOWN, WV

PREP: 20 MIN. • **COOK:** 2 HOURS
MAKES: 10 SERVINGS

- 5 **large apples, peeled and sliced**
- 1 **cup fresh or frozen cranberries, thawed**
- ¾ **cup packed brown sugar, divided**
- 2 **tablespoons lemon juice**
- ½ **cup all-purpose flour**
- **Dash salt**
- ⅓ **cup cold butter**
- **Vanilla ice cream**
- **Toasted chopped pecans**

1. In a greased 5-qt. slow cooker, combine apples, cranberries, ¼ cup brown sugar and lemon juice. In a small bowl, mix flour, salt and remaining brown sugar; cut in butter until crumbly. Sprinkle over fruit mixture.

2. Cook, covered, on high 2 to 2½ hours or until apples are tender. Serve with ice cream and pecans.

SPICED POACHED PEARS

Soups

FROM ALL-TIME CLASSICS TO NEW CHANGE-OF-PACE FAVORITES, IT'S A SNAP
TO LADLE OUT COMFORT WITH THESE SIMMERING SPECIALTIES.

GERMAN SOUP
PAGE 231

CRAB CORN CHOWDER
PAGE 269

**YELLOW TOMATO SOUP WITH
GOAT CHEESE CROUTONS**
PAGE 281

CHEESEBURGER PARADISE SOUP

Stuffed Pepper Soup

I'm a cook at a restaurant, and some of us were talking about stuffed peppers one day. That's when we decided to combine similar ingredients into a soup. The customers loved our creation.

—**KRISTA MUDDIMAN** MEADVILLE, PA

PREP: 15 MIN. • **COOK:** 30 MIN.
MAKES: 10 SERVINGS (2½ QUARTS)

- 2 **pounds ground beef**
- 2 **quarts water**
- 1 **can (28 ounces) tomato sauce**
- 1 **can (28 ounces) diced tomatoes, undrained**
- 2 **cups cooked long grain rice**
- 2 **cups chopped green peppers**
- ¼ **cup packed brown sugar**
- 2 **teaspoons salt**
- 2 **teaspoons beef bouillon granules**
- 1 **teaspoon pepper**

In a Dutch oven, cook beef over medium heat until no longer pink; drain. Stir in the remaining ingredients; bring to a boil. Reduce heat; cover and simmer for 30-40 minutes or until peppers are tender.

Cheeseburger Paradise Soup

I've never met a person who didn't enjoy this creamy soup, and it's hearty enough to serve as a main course with bread or rolls.

—**NADINA IADIMARCO** BURTON, OH

PREP: 30 MIN. • **COOK:** 25 MIN.
MAKES: 14 SERVINGS (ABOUT 3½ QUARTS)

- 6 **medium potatoes, peeled and cubed**
- 1 **small carrot, grated**
- 1 **small onion, chopped**
- ½ **cup chopped green pepper**
- 2 **tablespoons chopped seeded jalapeno pepper**
- 3 **cups water**
- 2 **tablespoons plus 2 teaspoons beef bouillon granules**
- 2 **garlic cloves, minced**
- ⅛ **teaspoon pepper**
- 2 **pounds ground beef**
- ½ **pound sliced fresh mushrooms**
- 2 **tablespoons butter**
- 5 **cups 2% milk, divided**
- 6 **tablespoons all-purpose flour**
- 1 **package (16 ounces) process cheese (Velveeta), cubed Crumbled cooked bacon**

1. In a Dutch oven, bring the first nine ingredients to a boil. Reduce heat; cover and simmer for 10-15 minutes or until potatoes are tender.
2. Meanwhile, in a large skillet, cook beef and mushrooms in butter over medium heat until meat is no longer pink; drain. Add to soup. Stir in 4 cups milk; heat through.
3. In a small bowl, combine flour and remaining milk until smooth; gradually stir into soup. Bring to a boil; cook and stir for 2 minutes or until thickened. Reduce heat; stir in cheese until melted. Garnish with bacon.
NOTE *Wear disposable gloves when cutting hot peppers; the oils can burn skin. Avoid touching your face.*

STUFFED PEPPER SOUP

Asian Vegetable-Beef Soup

My husband is Korean-American, and I enjoy working Asian flavors into our menu. I put this tasty soup together one night with what I found in our fridge. Everyone loved it!

—**MOLLIE LEE** ROCKWALL, TX

PREP: 30 MIN. • **COOK:** 1¾ HOURS
MAKES: 6 SERVINGS

- 1 **pound beef stew meat, cut into 1-inch cubes**
- 1 **tablespoon canola oil**
- 2 **cups water**
- 1 **cup beef broth**
- ¼ **cup sherry or additional beef broth**
- ¼ **cup reduced-sodium soy sauce**
- 6 **green onions, chopped**
- 3 **tablespoons brown sugar**
- 2 **garlic cloves, minced**
- 1 **tablespoon minced fresh gingerroot**
- 2 **teaspoons sesame oil**
- ¼ **teaspoon cayenne pepper**
- 1½ **cups sliced fresh mushrooms**
- 1½ **cups julienned carrots**
- 1 **cup sliced bok choy**
- 1½ **cups uncooked long grain rice**
   Chive blossoms, optional

1. In a large saucepan, brown meat in oil on all sides; drain. Add the water, broth, sherry, soy sauce, onions, brown sugar, garlic, ginger, sesame oil and cayenne. Bring to a boil. Reduce heat; cover and simmer for 1 hour.

2. Stir in mushrooms, carrots and bok choy; cover and simmer 20-30 minutes longer or until vegetables are tender. Meanwhile, cook rice according to package directions.

3. Divide rice among six soup bowls, ¾ cup in each; top each with 1 cup of soup. Garnish with chive blossoms if desired.

TOMATO SPINACH SOUP

Tomato Spinach Soup

I first sampled this soup in a restaurant. After some experimenting with ingredients and seasonings, I finally found a combo my family preferred more than the original.

—**ERNA KETCHUM** SAN JOSE, CA

PREP: 15 MIN. • **COOK:** 45 MIN.
MAKES: 8-10 SERVINGS (2½ QUARTS)

- 2 **large yellow onions, cubed**
- 2 **tablespoons olive oil**
- 1 **can (28 ounces) diced tomatoes, undrained**
- 1 **quart water**
- 4 **beef bouillon cubes**
- 1 **cup sliced fresh mushrooms**
- ¾ **teaspoon Italian seasoning**
- ½ **teaspoon dried basil**
- ½ **teaspoon salt**
- ⅛ **teaspoon pepper**
- 4 **cups loosely packed spinach leaves**
   Grated Parmesan or shredded cheddar cheese, optional

In a Dutch oven or soup kettle, saute onions in oil over medium heat for 10 minutes or until tender. Add the next eight ingredients; bring to a boil. Reduce heat; cover and simmer for 30 minutes. Stir in spinach; simmer for 3-5 minutes or until tender. Garnish individual servings with cheese if desired.

Meat and Potato Soup

Potatoes and roast beef come together in this rich and savory medley. The result is a well-balanced, flavorful dish perfect for the fall.

—TASTE OF HOME TEST KITCHEN

START TO FINISH: 30 MIN.
MAKES: 6 SERVINGS (2 QUARTS)

- 4 **cups water**
- 3 **cups cubed cooked beef chuck roast**
- 4 **medium red potatoes, cubed**
- 4 **ounces sliced fresh mushrooms**
- ½ **cup chopped onion**
- ¼ **cup ketchup**
- 2 **teaspoons beef bouillon granules**
- 2 **teaspoons cider vinegar**
- 1 **teaspoon brown sugar**
- 1 **teaspoon Worcestershire sauce**
- ⅛ **teaspoon ground mustard**
- 1 **cup coarsely chopped fresh spinach**

In a Dutch oven, combine the first 11 ingredients. Bring to a boil. Reduce heat; cover and simmer for 14-18 minutes or until potatoes are tender. Stir in spinach; cook 1-2 minutes longer or until tender.

Hamburger Soup

Oregano really shines in this hearty and satisfying dish. It smells so delicious while it's cooking, and it makes a great dinner. Leftovers are perfect for lunch the next day. You could use lima beans instead of the green beans if you'd like.

—TRACI WYNNE DENVER, PA

PREP: 10 MIN. • **COOK:** 40 MIN.
MAKES: 10 SERVINGS (3¾ QUARTS)

- 1 **pound ground beef**
- 1 **medium onion, chopped**
- ½ **large green pepper, diced**
- 4 **garlic cloves, minced**
- 8 **cups beef broth**

HAMBURGER SOUP

- 2 **cans (14½ ounces each) Italian stewed tomatoes**
- 1 **package (9 ounces) frozen cut green beans**
- 1 **can (8 ounces) tomato sauce**
- 1 **cup ditalini or other small pasta**
- 1 **tablespoon Worcestershire sauce**
- 2 **teaspoons dried oregano**
- 1 **teaspoon dried basil**
- ½ **teaspoon pepper**

1. In a Dutch oven, cook the beef, onion and green pepper over medium heat until meat is no longer pink. Add garlic; cook 1 minute longer. Drain.
2. Stir in the remaining ingredients. Bring to a boil. Reduce heat; cover and simmer for 30 minutes or until vegetables and pasta are tender.

DID YOU KNOW?

Ditalini is a tiny tube-shaped pasta. It's great in soups because it cooks quickly. Many soup recipes that call for ditalini don't require boiling the pasta first. Simply add it to the soup and bring it all to a boil.

MEAT AND POTATO SOUP

Beefy Vegetable Soup

Tender beef stew meat, carrots and other veggies make a hearty and tasty dish! A little steak sauce and garlic powder season the broth perfectly.

—**JIMMY OSMON** UPPER DARBY, PA

PREP: 20 MIN. • **COOK:** 1 HOUR 50 MIN.
MAKES: 9 SERVINGS (ABOUT 3¼ QUARTS)

- 1½ pounds beef stew meat
- 1 tablespoon canola oil
- 2 cans (14½ ounces each) reduced-sodium beef broth
- 1½ cups water
- 2 tablespoons reduced-sodium soy sauce
- 3 medium potatoes, cubed (about 1 pound)
- 3 medium carrots, cubed
- 3 celery ribs, chopped
- 2 tablespoons Worcestershire sauce
- 2 tablespoons steak sauce
- 1 tablespoon garlic powder
- ½ teaspoon salt
- ¼ teaspoon dried oregano
- ⅛ teaspoon ground nutmeg
- ⅛ teaspoon pepper
- 2 cups fresh corn or frozen corn
- 1¾ cups frozen cut green beans

1. In a Dutch oven, cook beef over medium heat in oil until no longer pink; drain. Add the broth, water and soy sauce. Bring to a boil. Reduce heat; cover and simmer for 1 hour.

2. Add the potatoes, carrots, celery, Worcestershire sauce, steak sauce and seasonings. Bring to a boil. Reduce heat; cover soup and simmer for 30-40 minutes or until the vegetables are just tender.

3. Add corn and beans. Bring to a boil. Reduce heat; cover and simmer for 5-10 minutes longer or until vegetables are tender.

German Soup

My sister-in-law shared her recipe with me—it's a nice thick soup. It does call for quite a few ingredients, but the taste is worth it!

—**GUDRUN BRAKER** BURNETT, WI

PREP: 15 MIN. • **COOK:** 35 MIN.
MAKES: 16 SERVINGS (4 QUARTS)

- 1½ pounds ground beef
- 2 medium onions, diced
- 2 tablespoons beef bouillon granules
- 1 cup water
  Salt and pepper to taste
- ½ to 1 teaspoon garlic powder
- 1 bay leaf
- 1 can (46 ounces) tomato or vegetable juice
- 3 celery ribs, diced
- 6 medium carrots, sliced
- 3 medium potatoes, peeled and diced
- 3 cups shredded cabbage
- 1 small green pepper, chopped
- 1 can (15¼ ounces) whole kernel corn, drained
- 1 can (8½ ounces) peas, drained
- 1 can (8 ounces) cut green beans, drained

1. In a Dutch oven, cook beef and onions over medium heat until meat is no longer pink; drain.

2. Dissolve bouillon in water; add to the beef mixture. Add the salt, pepper, garlic, bay leaf, tomato juice, celery, carrots, potatoes, cabbage and green pepper.

3. Simmer, uncovered, for 25 minutes or until vegetables are tender. Stir in the corn, peas and beans; heat through. Discard bay leaf before serving.

GERMAN SOUP

CABBAGE SOUP

Hearty Hamburger Soup

At family get-togethers, our children always request this spirit-warming soup along with a fresh loaf of homemade bread and tall glasses of milk. It has robust flavor and plenty of fresh-tasting vegetables, and it's easy to stir together.

—**BARBARA BROWN** JANESVILLE, WI

PREP: 10 MIN. • **COOK:** 30 MIN.
MAKES: 8 SERVINGS (2 QUARTS)

- 1 **pound ground beef**
- 4 **cups water**
- 1 **can (14½ ounces) diced tomatoes, undrained**
- 3 **medium carrots, sliced**
- 2 **medium potatoes, peeled and cubed**
- 1 **medium onion, chopped**
- ½ **cup chopped celery**
- 4 **teaspoons beef bouillon granules**
- 1½ **teaspoons salt**
- ¼ **teaspoon pepper**
- ¼ **teaspoon dried oregano**
- 1 **cup cut fresh or frozen green beans**

1. In a large saucepan, brown beef; drain. Add the next 10 ingredients; bring to a boil.

2. Reduce heat; cover and simmer for 15 minutes or until potatoes and carrots are tender. Add beans. Cover and simmer 15 minutes longer or until the beans are tender.

TOP TIP

When I have time, I chop a few stalks of celery or a few onions. After I sautee them in butter, I spoon them into ice cube trays, freeze them and pop the frozen "veggie cubes" into a labeled freezer bag to store. They are an invaluable addition to soups and casseroles when I'm in a hurry.
—**SALLY B.** NELIGH, NE

Cabbage Soup

My husband was never very fond of cabbage—until the first time he tried this recipe from my aunt. Now it's a cherished staple at our house.

—**NANCY STEVENS** MORRISON, IL

PREP: 15 MIN. • **COOK:** 25 MIN.
MAKES: 20 SERVINGS (5 QUARTS)

- 1 **medium head cabbage, chopped**
- 1 **cup chopped celery**
- 1 **cup chopped onion**
- 8 **cups water**
- 1 **teaspoon beef bouillon granules**
- 1 **tablespoon salt**
- 2 **teaspoons pepper**
- 1½ **pounds ground beef, browned and drained**
- 2 **cans (15 ounces each) tomato sauce**
- 1 **tablespoon brown sugar**
- ¼ **cup ketchup**

In a stockpot, cook the cabbage, celery and onion in water until tender. Add bouillon, salt, pepper, beef and tomato sauce. Bring to a boil; reduce heat and simmer 10 minutes. Stir in brown sugar and ketchup; simmer another 10 minutes to allow flavors to blend.

HEARTY HAMBURGER SOUP

FLAVORFUL TACO SOUP

Flavorful Taco Soup

You'll get a kick out of this fun Southwest-inspired soup. Feel free to dunk your tortilla chips right into it!

—**SANDI LEE** HOUSTON, TX

PREP: 10 MIN. • **COOK:** 35 MIN.
MAKES: 4 CUPS

- ½ **pound lean ground beef (90% lean)**
- 1 **can (15 ounces) pinto beans, rinsed and drained**
- 1 **can (10 ounces) diced tomatoes with mild green chilies, undrained**
- 1 **can (8¾ ounces) whole kernel corn, drained**
- 1½ **cups water**
- 2 **tablespoons taco seasoning**
- 4½ **teaspoons ranch salad dressing mix**
- ½ **medium ripe avocado, peeled and cubed**
- 2 **tablespoons shredded cheddar cheese**
- 2 **teaspoons minced fresh cilantro Tortilla chips**

1. In a large saucepan, cook beef over medium heat until no longer pink; drain. Stir in the beans, tomatoes, corn, water, taco seasoning and the salad dressing mix. Bring to a boil. Reduce heat; cover and simmer for 30 minutes to allow flavors to blend.
2. Spoon into bowls; top with avocado, cheese and cilantro. Serve with chips.

Lasagna Soup

All the traditional flavors of lasagna come together in this heartwarming meal-in-a-bowl.

—**SHERYL OLENICK** DEMAREST, NJ

START TO FINISH: 30 MIN.
MAKES: 8 SERVINGS (2¾ QUARTS)

- 1 **pound lean ground beef (90% lean)**
- 1 **large green pepper, chopped**
- 1 **medium onion, chopped**
- 2 **garlic cloves, minced**
- 2 **cans (14½ ounces each) diced tomatoes, undrained**
- 2 **cans (14½ ounces each) reduced-sodium beef broth**
- 1 **can (8 ounces) tomato sauce**
- 1 **cup frozen corn**
- ¼ **cup tomato paste**
- 2 **teaspoons Italian seasoning**
- ¼ **teaspoon pepper**
- 2½ **cups uncooked spiral pasta**
- ½ **cup shredded Parmesan cheese**

1. In a large saucepan, cook beef, green pepper and onion over medium heat 6-8 minutes or until meat is no longer pink, breaking up beef into crumbles. Add garlic; cook 1 minute longer. Drain.
2. Stir in tomatoes, broth, tomato sauce, corn, tomato paste, Italian seasoning and pepper. Bring to a boil. Stir in pasta. Return to a boil. Reduce heat; simmer, covered, 10-12 minutes or until pasta is tender. Sprinkle with cheese.

LASAGNA SOUP

Ravioli Soup

My family craves pasta, which inspired me to create my rich, delicious soup. We really enjoy the flavorful tomato base and tender, cheese-filled ravioli.

—SHELLEY WAY CHEYENNE, WY

PREP: 20 MIN. • **COOK:** 45 MIN.
MAKES: 10 SERVINGS (2½ QUARTS)

- 1 **pound ground beef**
- 2 **cups water**
- 2 **cans (one 28 ounces, one 14½ ounces) crushed tomatoes**
- 1 **can (6 ounces) tomato paste**
- 1½ **cups chopped onions**
- ¼ **cup minced fresh parsley**
- 2 **garlic cloves, minced**
- ¾ **teaspoon dried basil**
- ½ **teaspoon sugar**
- ½ **teaspoon dried oregano**
- ½ **teaspoon onion salt**
- ½ **teaspoon salt**
- ¼ **teaspoon pepper**
- ¼ **teaspoon dried thyme**
- 1 **package (9 ounces) refrigerated cheese ravioli**
- ¼ **cup grated Parmesan cheese**
  Additional minced fresh parsley, optional

In a Dutch oven, cook beef over medium heat until no longer pink; drain. Add the water, tomatoes, tomato paste, onions, parsley, garlic, basil, sugar, oregano, onion salt, salt, pepper and thyme; bring to a boil. Reduce heat; cover and simmer for 30 minutes. Cook ravioli according to package directions; drain. Add to soup and heat through. Stir in the Parmesan cheese. Sprinkle soup with additional parsley if desired.

EASY VEGETABLE BEEF SOUP

Easy Vegetable Beef Soup

Chase away winter's chill with spoonfuls of stick-to-your-ribs soup. It features a rich flavor and is full of nutritious vegetables and chunks of steak.

—BRIGITTE SCHULTZ BARSTOW, CA

PREP: 5 MIN. • **COOK:** 30 MIN.
MAKES: 7 SERVINGS

- 1 **pound beef top sirloin steak, cut into ½-inch cubes**
- ¼ **teaspoon pepper, divided**
- 2 **teaspoons olive oil**
- 2 **cans (14½ ounces each) beef broth**
- 2 **cups cubed peeled potatoes**
- 1¼ **cups water**
- 2 **medium carrots, sliced**
- 1 **tablespoon onion soup mix**
- 1 **tablespoon dried basil**
- ½ **teaspoon dried tarragon**
- 2 **tablespoons cornstarch**
- ½ **cup white wine or additional beef broth**

1. Sprinkle steak with ⅛ teaspoon pepper. In a Dutch oven, brown steak in batches in oil over medium heat. Add the broth, potatoes, water, carrots, onion soup mix, basil, tarragon and remaining pepper; bring to a boil. Reduce heat; cover and simmer for 20-25 minutes or until vegetables are tender.

2. In a small bowl, combine the cornstarch and wine until smooth; stir into soup. Bring to a boil; cook and stir for 2 minutes or until thickened.

FREEZE IT Zesty Hamburger Soup

When it is a soup day, turn to this one. The zip from the jalapenos and green chilies should perk you right up.

—KELLY MILAN LAKE JACKSON, TX

START TO FINISH: 30 MIN.
MAKES: 10 SERVINGS (3¾ QUARTS)

- 1 **pound ground beef**
- 2 **cups sliced celery**
- 1 **cup chopped onion**
- 2 **teaspoons minced garlic**
- 4 **cups water**
- 2 **medium red potatoes, peeled and cubed**
- 2 **cups frozen corn**
- 1½ **cups uncooked small shell pasta**
- 4 **pickled jalapeno slices**
- 4 **cups V8 juice**
- 2 **cans (10 ounces each) diced tomatoes with green chilies**
- 1 **to 2 tablespoons sugar**

1. In a Dutch oven, cook beef, celery and onion over medium heat until meat is no longer pink. Add garlic; cook 1 minute longer. Drain. Stir in water, potatoes, corn, pasta and jalapeno.
2. Bring to a boil. Reduce heat; cover and simmer 10-15 minutes or until pasta is tender. Stir in the remaining ingredients. Cook and stir until heated through.
FREEZE OPTION *Cool soup and transfer to freezer containers. Freeze up to 3 months. To use, thaw in the refrigerator overnight. Transfer to a saucepan. Cover and cook over medium heat until heated through.*

ZESTY HAMBURGER SOUP

BEEF BARLEY SOUP

Beef Barley Soup

Barley soup is a popular menu item in our house throughout the year. Everyone savors the flavor.

—**ELIZABETH KENDALL** CAROLINA BEACH, NC

PREP: 20 MIN. • **COOK:** 1 HOUR 50 MIN.
MAKES: 9 SERVINGS (2¼ QUARTS)

- 1 pound beef top round steak, cut into ½-inch cubes
- 1 tablespoon canola oil
- 3 cans (14½ ounces each) beef broth
- 2 cups water
- ⅓ cup medium pearl barley
- 1 teaspoon salt
- ⅛ teaspoon pepper
- 1 cup chopped carrots
- ½ cup chopped celery
- ¼ cup chopped onion
- 3 tablespoons minced fresh parsley
- 1 cup frozen peas

1. In a Dutch oven, brown beef in oil; drain. Stir in the broth, water, barley, salt and pepper. Bring to a boil. Reduce heat; cover and simmer for 1 hour.
2. Add the carrots, celery, onion and parsley; cover and simmer for 45 minutes or until meat and vegetables are tender. Stir in peas; heat through.

Flavorful French Onion Soup

This satisfying soup truly complements any roast beef dinner. Serve it as a first course to get mouths watering. Or set it alongside a salad for a light meal.

—*TASTE OF HOME* TEST KITCHEN

PREP: 20 MIN. • **COOK:** 1¾ HOURS
MAKES: 11 SERVINGS (ABOUT 2½ QUARTS)

- ¼ cup butter, cubed
- 2½ pounds onions, thinly sliced
- 3 tablespoons brown sugar
- 1 teaspoon pepper
- 3 tablespoons all-purpose flour
- 8 cups beef broth
- 1 cup dry red wine or additional beef broth
- ¼ cup steak sauce

HOMEMADE CROUTONS

- 3 cups cubed French bread
- 2 tablespoons olive oil
- 2 tablespoons butter, melted
- ½ teaspoon dried oregano
- ½ teaspoon dried basil
- ¼ teaspoon salt
- ¼ teaspoon pepper
- ¾ cup shredded Swiss cheese

1. In a Dutch oven, melt butter. Add the onions, brown sugar and pepper; cook over low heat until onion are lightly browned, about 1 hour.
2. Sprinkle onions with flour; stir to blend. Gradually stir in broth. Add wine and steak sauce. Bring to a boil. Reduce heat; cover and simmer for 45 minutes.
3. Meanwhile, preheat oven to 375°. In a large bowl, toss bread cubes with oil and butter. Combine oregano, basil, salt and pepper; sprinkle over bread and toss to coat.
4. Transfer to an ungreased 15x10-in. baking pan. Bake 10-12 minutes or until golden brown. Garnish soup with croutons and cheese.

FLAVORFUL FRENCH ONION SOUP

Think "steak dinner in a bowl" when eating this satisfying soup. It makes great cold-weather fare and packs a welcome chili-powder kick!

—**LISA RENSHAW** KANSAS CITY, MO

Spicy Steak House Soup

PREP: 10 MIN. • **COOK:** 35 MIN.
MAKES: 2 SERVINGS

- ¼ **pound beef tenderloin, cut into ¼-inch pieces**
- ¼ **cup chopped onion**
- ¼ **teaspoon salt**
- 2 **teaspoons olive oil**
- 1½ **cups cubed peeled Yukon Gold potatoes**
- 1 **cup reduced-sodium beef broth**
- ¼ **cup steak sauce**
- ¾ **teaspoon chili powder**
- ¼ **teaspoon ground cumin**
- ⅛ **teaspoon cayenne pepper**
- 2 **tablespoons minced fresh parsley**

In a large nonstick saucepan, saute the beef, onion and salt in oil for 4-5 minutes or until meat is no longer pink. Stir in the potatoes, broth, steak sauce, chili powder, cumin and the cayenne. Bring to a boil. Reduce heat; cover and simmer for 30-35 minutes or until potatoes are tender. Garnish with parsley.

Beefy Mushroom Soup

Here's a tasty way to use leftover roast or steak and get a delicious supper on the table in about a half hour. Its heartwarming flavor is sure to please.

—**GINGER ELLSWORTH** CALDWELL, ID

START TO FINISH: 30 MIN.
MAKES: 3 CUPS

- 1 **medium onion, chopped**
- ½ **cup sliced fresh mushrooms**
- 2 **tablespoons butter**
- 2 **tablespoons all-purpose flour**
- 2 **cups reduced-sodium beef broth**
- ⅔ **cup cubed cooked roast beef**
- ½ **teaspoon garlic powder**
- ¼ **teaspoon paprika**
- ¼ **teaspoon pepper**
- ⅛ **teaspoon salt**
  Dash hot pepper sauce
- ¼ **cup shredded part-skim mozzarella cheese, optional**

1. In a large saucepan, saute onion and mushrooms in butter until onion is tender; remove with a slotted spoon and set aside. In a small bowl, whisk flour and broth until smooth; gradually add to the pan. Bring to a boil; cook and stir for 1-2 minutes or until thickened.
2. Add the roast beef, garlic powder, paprika, pepper, salt, pepper sauce and onion mixture; cook and stir until heated through. Garnish with cheese if desired.

TOP TIP

It's a snap to pair soup with a sandwich, green salad or loaf of bread, but why not think outside the box and jazz up your soup menus? Try offering an assortment of bagels or a fruit medley alongside soup. You can also pair many soups with a slice of quiche, a baked potato, a taco or burrito, or even cooked shrimp.

SPICY STEAK HOUSE SOUP

Grandmother's Chowder

Nothing can compare to homemade soup, especially when this is the delicious result! Winter days seem a little warmer when I prepare my savory chowder.

—**DULYSE MOLNAR** OSWEGO, NY

PREP: 20 MIN. • **COOK:** 30 MIN.
MAKES: 14 SERVINGS (3½ QUARTS)

- 1 **pound ground beef**
- 1 **medium onion, chopped**
- 12 **medium potatoes, peeled and cubed**
- 3 **cups water**
  Salt and pepper to taste
- 2 **cups whole milk**
- 1 **can (15¼ ounces) whole kernel corn, drained**
- 2 **teaspoons dried parsley flakes**
- 1 **cup (8 ounces) sour cream**

1. In a Dutch oven, cook beef and onion over medium heat until meat is no longer pink; drain. Add the potatoes, water, salt and pepper; bring to a boil. Reduce heat; cover and simmer for 15-20 minutes or until potatoes are tender.

2. Stir in the milk, corn and parsley; cook for 5 minutes or until heated through. Add a small amount of hot soup to sour cream. Gradually return all to pan, stirring constantly. Heat through but do not boil.

Couscous Meatball Soup

This soup is easy, healthy, full of flavor and a great way to warm you up!

—**JONATHAN PACE** SAN FRANCISCO, CA

PREP: 25 MIN. • **COOK:** 40 MIN.
MAKES: 10 SERVINGS (2½ QUARTS)

- 1 **pound lean ground beef (90% lean)**
- 2 **teaspoons dried basil**
- 2 **teaspoons dried oregano**
- ½ **teaspoon salt**
- 1 **large onion, finely chopped**

COUSCOUS MEATBALL SOUP

- 2 **teaspoons canola oil**
- 8 **cups chopped collard greens**
- 8 **cups chopped fresh kale**
- 2 **cartons (32 ounces each) vegetable stock**
- 1 **tablespoon white wine vinegar**
- ½ **teaspoon crushed red pepper flakes**
- ¼ **teaspoon pepper**
- 1 **package (8.8 ounces) pearl (Israeli) couscous**

1. In a small bowl, combine the beef, basil, oregano and salt. Shape into ½-in. balls. In a large nonstick skillet coated with cooking spray, brown meatballs; drain. Remove meatballs and set aside.

2. In the same skillet, brown onion in oil. Add greens and kale; cook 6-7 minutes longer or until wilted.

3. In a Dutch oven, combine the greens mixture, meatballs, stock, vinegar, pepper flakes and pepper. Bring to a boil. Reduce heat; cover and simmer for 10 minutes. Return to a boil. Stir in couscous. Reduce heat; cover and simmer for 10-15 minutes or until couscous is tender, stirring once.

SAUSAGE WILD RICE SOUP

Sausage Wild Rice Soup

Turn to my big-batch recipe the next time you need to feed a crowd. Brimming with wild rice and sausage, the soup makes a hearty meal.

—TONYA SCHAFFER HURON, SD

PREP: 35 MIN. • **COOK:** 1 HOUR
MAKES: 5 QUARTS (13 SERVINGS)

- 9 cups water, divided
- 1 cup uncooked wild rice
- 2 pounds bulk Italian sausage
- 2 large onions, chopped
- 2 teaspoons olive oil
- 6 garlic cloves, minced
- 3 cartons (32 ounces each) chicken broth
- 1 can (28 ounces) diced tomatoes, undrained
- 1 can (6 ounces) tomato paste
- 2 teaspoons dried basil
- 2 teaspoons dried oregano
- 1 package (6 ounces) fresh baby spinach, coarsely chopped
- ½ teaspoon salt
- ½ teaspoon pepper

1. In a large saucepan, bring 3 cups water to a boil. Stir in rice. Reduce heat; cover and simmer for 55-60 minutes or until tender.

2. Meanwhile, in a stockpot, cook sausage over medium heat until no longer pink; drain. Remove and set aside. In the same pan, saute onions in oil until tender. Add garlic; cook 1 minute longer. Stir in the broth, tomatoes, tomato paste, basil, oregano and remaining water. Return sausage to the pan. Bring to a boil. Reduce heat; simmer, uncovered, for 20 minutes.

3. Stir in the spinach, salt, pepper and wild rice; heat through.

Jamaican Ham and Bean Soup

"Island vacation in a bowl" is the best way to describe this hearty soup. A splash of lime juice and a hint of jerk seasoning add a tropical flair.

—MARY LOU TIMPSON COLORADO CITY, AZ

START TO FINISH: 25 MIN.
MAKES: 7 SERVINGS (2¾ QUARTS)

- 1 small onion, chopped
- 1 tablespoon canola oil
- 3 cups cubed fully cooked ham
- 2 cans (16 ounces each) vegetarian refried beans
- 1 can (14½ ounces) chicken broth
- 1 can (11 ounces) Mexicorn, drained
- 1 can (7 ounces) white or shoepeg corn, drained
- 1 can (4 ounces) chopped green chilies
- ½ cup salsa
- 1 teaspoon Caribbean jerk seasoning
- 1 can (2¼ ounces) sliced ripe olives, drained
- ⅓ cup lime juice
  Sour cream and lime slices

1. In a Dutch oven, saute onion in oil for 3-4 minutes or until tender. Stir in ham, refried beans, broth, corn, chilies, salsa and jerk seasoning; bring to a boil. Reduce heat; simmer, uncovered, for 5 minutes stirring occasionally.

2. Stir in the olives and lime juice; heat through. Garnish servings with sour cream and lime slices.

JAMAICAN HAM AND BEAN SOUP

Hearty Bean Soup

Here's a real crowd-pleaser. I like to serve it with fresh corn bread. No one can believe how quick and easy it is to make.

—**NELDA CAMERON** CLEVELAND, TX

START TO FINISH: 30 MIN.
MAKES: 10 SERVINGS (2½ QUARTS)

- 1 large onion, chopped
- ½ cup chopped green pepper
- 2 tablespoons butter
- 2 garlic cloves, minced
- 2 cans (15½ ounces each) great northern beans, rinsed and drained
- 2 cans (15 ounces each) pinto beans, rinsed and drained
- 2 cans (11½ ounces each) condensed bean with bacon soup, undiluted
- 2 cups diced fully cooked ham
- 2 cups water
- 2 tablespoons canned diced jalapeno peppers

In a small skillet, saute onion and green pepper in butter for 3 minutes. Add the garlic; cook 1 minute longer. Transfer to a Dutch oven or soup kettle. Stir in the remaining ingredients. Cover and cook over medium-low heat for 20 minutes or until heated through, stirring occasionally.

SAUSAGE LENTIL SOUP

Sausage Lentil Soup

I found this recipe in a men's magazine and decided to lighten it up. I ate a lot of it when I was pregnant because it's delicious and loaded with fiber, vitamins and iron. It uses low-fat ingredients without sacrificing any of the flavor of the original.

—**SUZANNE DABKOWSKI** BLYTHEWOOD, SC

PREP: 25 MIN. • **COOK:** 40 MIN.
MAKES: 6 SERVINGS

- 1 medium onion, chopped
- 1 celery rib, chopped
- ¼ pound reduced-fat smoked sausage, halved and thinly sliced
- 1 medium carrot, halved and thinly sliced
- 2 garlic cloves, minced
- 2 cans (14½ ounces each) reduced-sodium chicken broth
- ⅓ cup water
- 1 cup dried lentils, rinsed
- ½ teaspoon dried oregano
- ¼ teaspoon ground cumin
- ¼ teaspoon pepper
- 1 can (14½ ounces) stewed tomatoes, cut up
- 1 tablespoon Worcestershire sauce
- 1 cup chopped fresh spinach

1. In a large saucepan coated with cooking spray, cook and stir onion and celery over medium-high heat for 2 minutes. Add the sausage, carrot and garlic; cook 2-3 minutes longer or until onion is tender.

2. Stir in the broth, water, lentils, oregano, cumin and pepper. Bring to a boil. Reduce heat; cover and simmer for 25-30 minutes or until lentils and vegetables are tender.

3. Stir in the tomatoes, Worcestershire sauce and spinach; cook until heated through and spinach is wilted.

Meatball Veggie Soup

A little bit of this thick and satisfying soup goes a long way, so it's terrific to take to potlucks. Be sure to bring copies of the recipe, too!

—JANICE THOMPSON LANSING, MI

PREP: 20 MIN. • **COOK:** 45 MIN.
MAKES: 22 SERVINGS (5¾ QUARTS)

- 2 eggs
- 1 cup soft bread crumbs
- 1 teaspoon salt
- ½ teaspoon pepper
- 1 pound lean ground beef (90% lean)
- 1 pound ground pork
- ½ pound ground turkey
- 4 cups beef broth
- 1 can (46 ounces) tomato juice
- 2 cans (14½ ounces each) stewed tomatoes
- 8 cups shredded cabbage
- 1 cup thinly sliced celery
- 1 cup thinly sliced carrots
- 8 green onions, sliced
- ¾ cup uncooked long grain rice
- 2 teaspoons dried basil
- 3 tablespoons minced fresh parsley
- 2 tablespoons soy sauce

1. In a large bowl, combine the eggs, bread crumbs, salt and pepper. Crumble meat over mixture and mix well. Shape into 1-in. balls.
2. In a stockpot, bring broth to a boil. Carefully add the meatballs. Add the tomato juice, tomatoes, vegetables, rice and basil. Bring to a boil. Reduce heat; cover and simmer for 30 minutes.
3. Add the parsley and soy sauce. Simmer, uncovered, for 10 minutes or until meatballs are no longer pink and vegetables are tender.

Hominy Sausage Soup

I serve my soup with cheese nachos as a starter to a Southwest-style lunch. I follow it up with chicken or beef taco salad.

—JESSIE GUNN STEPHENS SHERMAN, TX

PREP: 10 MIN. • **COOK:** 25 MIN.
MAKES: 2 SERVINGS

HOMINY SAUSAGE SOUP

- ¼ pound bulk pork sausage
- 1 teaspoon cumin seeds
- ⅛ teaspoon ground coriander
- ⅛ teaspoon cayenne pepper
- 2 cups reduced-sodium chicken broth
- ¾ cup canned hominy, rinsed and drained
- 1 to 2 tablespoons chopped jalapeno pepper
- ¼ teaspoon pepper
- 1 tablespoon minced fresh cilantro

1. Crumble sausage into a small skillet. Cook over medium heat for 3-4 minutes or until no longer pink; drain. In a small saucepan, toast cumin seeds over medium heat for 2-3 minutes or until browned. Add coriander and cayenne; cook and stir for 30 seconds.
2. Add the broth, hominy, jalapeno, pepper and sausage. Bring to a boil. Reduce heat; simmer, uncovered, for 12-15 minutes to allow flavors to blend. Stir in cilantro.
NOTE *Wear disposable gloves when cutting hot peppers; the oils can burn skin. Avoid touching your face.*

MEATBALL VEGGIE SOUP

FREEZE IT Hot Italian Sausage Soup

I'm the part owner of a small tavern, and on Saturdays we offer soups and deli sandwiches free of charge. Our patrons love this one loaded with zesty sausage and an array of veggies. A hint of brown sugar balances the heat with a little sweetness, making it a real crowd-pleaser.

—DAN BUTE OTTAWA, IL

START TO FINISH: 25 MIN.
MAKES: 4 SERVINGS

- 1 pound bulk hot Italian sausage
- 1 can (14½ ounces) Italian stewed tomatoes
- 1 can (8 ounces) tomato sauce
- 1 cup frozen Italian vegetables
- ¾ cup julienned green, sweet red and/or yellow pepper
- ¼ cup chopped onion
- ¼ cup white wine or chicken broth
- 1 teaspoon brown sugar
- 1 teaspoon minced fresh parsley
- ½ teaspoon Italian seasoning
- ⅛ teaspoon salt
- ⅛ teaspoon pepper

1. In a large skillet, cook sausage over medium heat until no longer pink.
2. Meanwhile, in a large saucepan, combine the remaining ingredients. Bring to a boil. Reduce heat; cover and simmer for 10 minutes or until vegetables are tender.
3. Drain sausage; add to soup and heat through.
FREEZE OPTION *Cool soup and transfer to freezer containers. Freeze up to 3 months. To use, thaw in the refrigerator overnight. Transfer to a saucepan. Cover and cook over medium heat until heated through.*

Makeover Cheesy Ham 'n' Potato Soup

This better-for-you version calls for lean ham, broccoli, fat-free milk and reduced-fat cheese. Additional potatoes, whipped in the food processor, and dry milk powder maintain the soup's thick, creamy texture.

—TASTE OF HOME TEST KITCHEN

START TO FINISH: 30 MIN.
MAKES: 7 SERVINGS

- 2¼ cups cubed potatoes
- 1½ cups water
- 1½ cups cubed fully cooked lean ham
- 1 large onion, chopped
- 2 teaspoons canola oil
- ¼ cup nonfat dry milk powder
- 3 tablespoons all-purpose flour
- ¼ teaspoon pepper
- 3 cups fat-free milk
- 1½ cups (6 ounces) finely shredded reduced-fat cheddar cheese
- 1 cup frozen broccoli florets, thawed and chopped

1. In a saucepan, bring potatoes and water to a boil. Cover and cook for 10-15 minutes or until tender. Drain, reserving 1 cup cooking liquid. In a blender or food processor, process reserved liquid and ¼ cup cooked potatoes until smooth; set aside. Set remaining potatoes aside.
2. In a large saucepan, saute ham and onion in oil until onion is tender. In a bowl, combine milk powder, flour, pepper, milk and processed potato mixture until smooth. Stir into ham and onion. Bring to a boil; cook and stir for 2 minutes or until thickened.
3. Reduce heat to low. Add the cheese, broccoli and reserved potatoes; cook and stir over low heat until cheese is melted and heated through. Serve immediately.

MAKEOVER CHEESY
HAM 'N' POTATO SOUP

Sausage Kale Soup

This zesty Italian soup is sure to become a favorite with your guests—just as it has with mine. The spicier the sausage, the better the dish.

—**NANCY DYER** GROVER, OK

PREP: 35 MIN. • **COOK:** 20 MIN.
MAKES: 8 SERVINGS (2 QUARTS)

- 1 pound uncooked Italian sausage links
- ¾ cup chopped onion
- 1 bacon strip, diced
- 2 garlic cloves, minced
- 2 cups water
- 1 can (14½ ounces) chicken broth
- 2 cups diced potatoes
- 2 cups thinly sliced fresh kale
- ⅓ cup heavy whipping cream

1. Preheat oven to 325°. Place the sausages in a ungreased 15x10x1-in. baking pan; pierce casings. Bake 15-20 minutes or until fully cooked. Drain; set aside to cool.

2. Meanwhile, in a saucepan, saute onion and bacon 3 minutes or until onion is tender. Add garlic; saute 1 minute. Add water, broth and potatoes; bring to a boil. Reduce heat; cover and simmer 20 minutes or until potatoes are tender.

3. Cut sausages in half lengthwise, then into ¼-in. slices. Add kale, cream and sausage to soup; heat through (do not boil).

TOP TIP

You can snip the bottoms off of thin, tender kale stems with kitchen shears. If the stems are thick, however, they should be removed: place each leaf on a cutting board, fold it in half lengthwise and carefully slice away the stem.

SAUSAGE KALE SOUP

Cannellini & Sausage Soup

This soup will warm you from head to toe. Add a dash of ground ginger and Greek seasoning for a little something extra.

—**PAULINE WHITE** EL CAJON, CA

START TO FINISH: 30 MIN.
MAKES: 6 SERVINGS

- 12 **ounces beef summer or smoked sausage, cut into ½-inch pieces**
- 4½ **cups vegetable broth**
- 2 **cans (15 ounces each) cannellini or white kidney beans, rinsed and drained**
- 4 **cups coarsely chopped Chinese or napa cabbage**
- 3 **green onions, chopped**
- ¼ **teaspoon salt**
- ¼ **teaspoon pepper**

In a large saucepan, cook and stir sausage over medium heat until lightly browned; drain. Add the remaining ingredients; bring to a boil. Reduce the heat; simmer for 5-10 minutes or until the cabbage is tender and the flavors are blended.

CANNELLINI & SAUSAGE SOUP

KIELBASA POTATO SOUP

Kielbasa Potato Soup

Here's a dinner that takes just a few minutes to throw together. While it simmers, make a side salad or warm up some rye bread for a country-style meal.

—**BEVERLEE DEBERRY** HEMPSTEAD, TX

PREP: 15 MIN. • **COOK:** 20 MIN.
MAKES: 2 SERVINGS

- 1 **medium leek, (white portion only), halved and sliced**
- 1 **tablespoon butter**
- 1¾ **cups chicken broth**
- 1 **medium potato, peeled and diced**
- ⅓ **pound fully cooked kielbasa or Polish sausage, cut into bite-size pieces**
- ¼ **cup heavy whipping cream**
- ⅛ **teaspoon each caraway and cumin seeds, toasted**
- ⅓ **cup thinly sliced fresh spinach**

1. In a large saucepan, saute leek in butter until tender. Add broth and potato; bring to a boil. Reduce heat; cover and simmer for 15-20 minutes or until potato is tender.

2. Stir in the sausage, cream, caraway and cumin; heat through (do not boil). Just before serving, add the spinach.

PORK NOODLE SOUP

BEAN, CHICKEN AND SAUSAGE SOUP

Pork Noodle Soup

My daughter created this soup when she needed to use up some leftover pork. Add more water if you prefer a thinner soup or less water for a noodle dish. It's good with mushroom-flavored ramen noodles, too.
—**ELEANOR NISKA** TWIN FALLS, ID

START TO FINISH: 30 MIN.
MAKES: 10 SERVINGS (2½ QUARTS)

- ½ cup chopped celery
- ½ cup chopped onion
- 1 tablespoon olive oil
- ½ teaspoon minced garlic
- 7 cups water
- 1½ cups cut fresh asparagus (1-inch pieces)
- ½ cup chopped cabbage
- 1½ teaspoons minced fresh parsley
- ¾ teaspoon dried tarragon
  Dash cayenne pepper, optional
- 2 packages (3 ounces each) pork ramen noodles
- 2 cups cubed cooked pork

1. In a Dutch oven, saute celery and onion in oil until tender. Add garlic; cook 1 minute longer. Stir in the water, asparagus, cabbage, parsley, tarragon and cayenne if desired. Bring to a boil.
2. Coarsely crush the noodles. Add the noodles with the contents of the seasoning packets to the pan. Bring to a boil. Reduce heat; simmer, uncovered, for 3-5 minutes or until the noodles and vegetables are tender. Add pork; heat through.

Bean, Chicken and Sausage Soup

When I was paging through a magazine, I saw this recipe and it sparked my creativity. I've had fun experimenting with different ingredients throughout the years. My husband thinks this version is the best.
—**LINDA JOHNSON** SEVIERVILLE, TN

PREP: 10 MIN. • **COOK:** 70 MIN.
MAKES: 18 SERVINGS (4½ QUARTS)

- 1½ pounds bulk Italian sausage
- 2 cups chopped onion
- 6 bacon strips, diced
- 2 quarts water
- 2 cans (14½ ounces each) diced tomatoes, undrained
- 2 bay leaves
- 2 teaspoons garlic powder
- 1 teaspoon each dried thyme, savory and salt
- ½ teaspoon each dried basil, oregano and pepper
- 4 cups cubed cooked chicken
- 2 cans (15 to 16 ounces each) great northern beans, rinsed and drained

1. In a heavy 8-qt. Dutch oven, cook the sausage, onion and bacon over medium-high heat until sausage is not longer pink; drain. Add the water, tomatoes and seasonings. Cover and simmer for 30 minutes.
2. Add chicken and beans. Simmer, uncovered, for 30-45 minutes. Discard bay leaves.

GREEN BEAN SOUP

FARMHOUSE HAM CHOWDER

Green Bean Soup

My great-grandmother was the first in our family to make this veggie-filled soup. It's been a favorite ever since. I make it whenever I crave something warm and soothing. I use my own homegrown beans, carrots, onions and potatoes.

—ELVIRA BECKENHAUER OMAHA, NE

PREP: 15 MIN. • **COOK:** 30 MIN.
MAKES: 6 SERVINGS

- 4 **cups water**
- 2 **cups fresh green beans, cut into 2-inch pieces**
- 1½ **cups cubed peeled potatoes**
- 1 **cup cubed fully cooked ham**
- ½ **cup thinly sliced carrot**
- 1 **medium onion, diced**
- 1 **bay leaf**
- 1 **sprig fresh parsley**
- 1 **sprig fresh savory or ¼ teaspoon dried savory**
- 1 **teaspoon beef bouillon granules**
- ¼ **teaspoon pepper**
- ½ **teaspoon salt, optional**

In a large saucepan or soup kettle, combine all the ingredients. Bring to a boil. Reduce heat; cover and simmer for 20 minutes or until vegetables are tender. Before serving, remove bay leaf and parsley and savory sprigs.

Farmhouse Ham Chowder

Leftover ham, hash browns and a bounty of vegetables add body to this nourishing chowder, but the ranch dressing is the secret, zesty addition. A little smoked Gouda adds a nice touch, too.

—LISA RENSHAW KANSAS CITY, MO

PREP: 10 MIN. • **COOK:** 30 MIN.
MAKES: 8 SERVINGS (2 QUARTS)

- ½ **cup finely chopped onion**
- ½ **cup finely chopped celery**
- ½ **cup chopped sweet red pepper**
- 2 **tablespoons butter**
- ¼ **cup all-purpose flour**
- 1 **envelope ranch salad dressing mix**
- 4¼ **cups milk**
- 2 **cups frozen cubed hash brown potatoes, thawed**
- 2 **cups frozen corn, thawed**
- 2 **cups cubed fully cooked ham**
- 1 **teaspoon minced fresh thyme or ¼ teaspoon dried thyme**
- ½ **cup shredded smoked Gouda cheese**

1. In a large saucepan, saute the onion, celery and red pepper in butter until crisp-tender. Stir in flour and dressing mix until blended; gradually stir in milk. Bring to a boil; cook and stir for 2 minutes or until thickened.

2. Add the potatoes, corn, ham and thyme. Bring to a boil. Reduce heat; simmer, uncovered, for 8-10 minutes to allow flavors to blend. Stir in cheese until blended.

BUTTERNUT & BEAN SOUP

FREEZE IT Butternut & Bean Soup

PREP: 20 MIN. • **COOK:** 40 MIN.
MAKES: 12 SERVINGS (4½ QUARTS)

- 1 **pound bulk Italian sausage**
- 1 **medium onion, chopped**
- 1 **medium sweet red pepper, chopped**
- 4 **garlic cloves, minced**
- 1 **large butternut squash (about 5 pounds), peeled, seeded and cut into 1-inch pieces**
- 1 **package (16 ounces) frozen corn, divided**
- 4 **cups water**
- 1 **tablespoon chicken base**
- 2 **cans (15½ ounces each) great northern beans, rinsed and drained**
- 2 **cans (14½ ounces each) fire-roasted diced tomatoes, undrained**
- 1 **teaspoon salt**
- ¼ **teaspoon pepper**
  Heavy whipping cream and minced fresh parsley, optional

1. In a stockpot, cook sausage, onion and red pepper over medium heat 9-11 minutes or until sausage is no longer pink and onion is tender, breaking up sausage into crumbles. Add garlic; cook 1 minute longer. Remove with a slotted spoon; discard drippings.

2. Add squash, 1½ cups corn, water and chicken base to same pan; bring to a boil. Reduce heat; simmer, covered, 15-20 minutes or until squash is tender.

3. Remove soup from heat; cool slightly. Process in batches in a blender until smooth. Return to pot. Add beans, tomatoes, salt, pepper, sausage mixture and remaining corn; heat through. If desired, drizzle servings with cream and sprinkle with parsley.

FREEZE OPTION *Cool soup and transfer to freezer containers. Freeze up to 3 months. To use, partially thaw in refrigerator overnight. Heat through in a saucepan, stirring occasionally and adding a little water if necessary.*

Ham 'n' Chickpea Soup

Chock-full of ham, vegetables, chickpeas and orzo, this soup is loaded with flavor.
—**LINDA ARNOLD** EDMONTON, AB

PREP: 15 MIN. • **COOK:** 25 MIN.
MAKES: 4 SERVINGS

- ½ **cup uncooked orzo pasta**
- 1 **small onion, chopped**
- 2 **teaspoons canola oil**
- 1 **cup cubed fully cooked lean ham**
- 2 **garlic cloves, minced**
- 1 **teaspoon dried rosemary, crushed**
- 1 **teaspoon rubbed sage**
- 2 **cups reduced-sodium beef broth**
- 1 **can (14½ ounces) diced tomatoes, undrained**
- 1 **can (15 ounces) chickpeas or garbanzo beans, rinsed and drained**
- 4 **tablespoons shredded Parmesan cheese**
- 1 **tablespoon minced fresh parsley**

1. Cook orzo according to package directions. Meanwhile, in a large saucepan, saute onion in oil for 3 minutes. Add the ham, garlic, rosemary and sage; saute 1 minute longer. Stir in broth and tomatoes. Bring to a boil. Reduce heat; simmer, uncovered, for 10 minutes.

2. Drain orzo; stir into soup. Add chickpeas; heat through. Sprinkle each serving with cheese and parsley.

HAM 'N' CHICKPEA SOUP

WINTER COUNTRY SOUP

White Bean Soup

Parmesan crisps make a zippy topping for this rich, full-flavored soup. We love the Italian sausage garnish.

—**LINDA MIRANDA** WAKEFIELD, RI

PREP: 15 MIN. • **COOK:** 20 MIN.
MAKES: 2 SERVINGS

- ¼ **cup shredded Parmesan cheese**
  Cayenne pepper
- ¼ **pound bulk Italian sausage**
- 2 **tablespoons chopped onion**
- 1 **teaspoon olive oil**
- 1 **garlic clove, minced**
- 1 **can (15 ounces) white kidney**
  or cannellini beans, rinsed and
  drained
- 1 **cup chicken broth**
- ¼ **cup heavy whipping cream**
- 2 **teaspoons sherry, optional**
- 1 **teaspoon minced fresh parsley**
- ⅛ **teaspoon salt**
- ⅛ **teaspoon dried thyme**

1. Spoon Parmesan cheese into six mounds 3 in. apart on a parchment paper-lined baking sheet. Spread into 1½-in. circles. Sprinkle with a dash of cayenne. Bake at 400° for 5-6 minutes or until light golden brown. Cool.

2. In a saucepan, cook sausage and onion in oil over medium heat until meat is no longer pink; drain. Remove and keep warm.

3. In the same pan, saute garlic for 1-2 minutes or until tender. Stir in the beans, broth, cream, sherry if desired, parsley, salt, thyme and a dash of cayenne. Bring to a boil. Reduce heat; simmer, uncovered, for 12-15 minutes or until heated through. Cool slightly.

4. Transfer to a blender; cover and process on high until almost blended. Pour into soup bowls; sprinkle with sausage mixture and Parmesan crisps.

Winter Country Soup

My soup will warm you up on the chilliest of winter nights. With smoked sausage, beans and other vegetables, this dish is a hearty way start to dinner or is a satisfying light meal all by itself.

—**JEANNETTE SABO** LEXINGTON PARK, MD

PREP: 15 MIN. • **COOK:** 40 MIN.
MAKES: 12 SERVINGS (3 QUARTS)

- 1 **package (14 ounces) smoked**
  sausage, cut into ¼-inch slices
- 1 **large sweet red pepper, cut into**
  ½-inch pieces
- 8 **shallots, chopped**
- 1 **tablespoon butter**
- 8 **cups chopped fresh kale**
- 8 **cups vegetable broth**
- 3 **cups frozen corn**
- 1 **can (15½ ounces) great northern**
  beans, rinsed and drained
- ½ **teaspoon cayenne pepper**
- ¼ **teaspoon pepper**
- ¾ **cup uncooked orzo pasta**

1. In a Dutch oven, saute the sausage, red pepper and shallots in butter until vegetables are tender.

2. Add kale; cover and cook for 2-3 minutes or until kale is wilted. Stir in the broth, corn, beans, cayenne and pepper. Bring to a boil. Reduce heat; simmer, uncovered, for 20 minutes. Return to a boil. Stir in orzo. Cook 8-10 minutes longer or until pasta is tender.

Italian Vegetable Soup

Here's a chunky soup that will become a favorite. It takes only 25 minutes to make, and then you can sit down to enjoy spoonfuls of comfort.

—**JANET FRIEMAN** KENOSHA, WI

START TO FINISH: 25 MIN.
MAKES: 6-8 SERVINGS (2 QUARTS)

- 1 **pound bulk Italian sausage**
- 1 **medium onion, sliced**
- 1½ **cups water**
- 1 **can (15 ounces) garbanzo beans or chickpeas, rinsed and drained**
- 1 **can (14½ ounces) diced tomatoes, undrained**
- 1 **can (14½ ounces) beef broth**
- 2 **medium zucchini, cut into ¼-inch slices**
- ½ **teaspoon dried basil**
  Grated Parmesan cheese

1. In a large saucepan, cook sausage and onion over medium heat until meat is no longer pink; drain. Stir in the water, beans, tomatoes, broth, zucchini and basil.

2. Bring to a boil. Reduce heat and simmer for 5 minutes or until the zucchini is tender. Garnish with the Parmesan cheese.

DID YOU KNOW?

The two most common types of Italian sausage are hot and sweet. Hot Italian sausage contains red pepper flakes. Italian Vegetable Soup—and any other recipe in this cookbook that calls for Italian sausage—is referring to the sweet kind. Recipes using hot Italian sausage specifically call for it.

ITALIAN VEGETABLE SOUP

TURKEY-SWEET POTATO SOUP

Turkey-Sweet Potato Soup

A batch of this soup brings the nostalgic flavors and heartwarming feel of the holidays at any time of year. When I have time to slow-cook it, my whole house takes on a wonderful aroma.

—RADINE KELLOGG FAIRVIEW, IL

PREP: 20 MIN. • **COOK:** 30 MIN.
MAKES: 4 SERVINGS

- 2 **medium sweet potatoes, peeled and cubed**
- 2 **cups water**
- 2 **teaspoons sodium-free chicken bouillon granules**
- 1 **can (14¾ ounces) cream-style corn**
- 1 **tablespoon minced fresh sage**
- ¼ **teaspoon pepper**
- 1 **tablespoon cornstarch**
- 1 **cup 2% milk**
- 2 **cups cubed cooked turkey breast**

1. In a large saucepan, combine the potatoes, water and bouillon; bring to a boil. Reduce heat; cook, covered, 10-15 minutes or until potatoes are tender.
2. Stir in corn, sage and pepper; heat through. In a small bowl, mix the cornstarch and milk until smooth; stir into soup. Bring to a boil; cook and stir 1-2 minutes or until thickened. Stir in turkey; heat through.

Stuffing Dumpling Soup

I've always loved turkey, dumplings and stuffing, so I combined them and added a punch of Creole flavor. My family loves it, even my little ones. It's got some kick, but a dollop of sour cream cools it down.

—RELINA SHIRLEY RENO, NV

PREP: 20 MIN. • **COOK:** 25 MIN.
MAKES: 5 SERVINGS

- 1 **cup sliced fresh mushrooms**
- 1 **medium onion, chopped**
- 1 **tablespoon olive oil**
- 3 **garlic cloves, minced**
- 4 **cups reduced-sodium chicken broth**
- 1½ **cups chopped fresh carrots**
- 2 **teaspoons Creole seasoning**
- 2 **eggs**
- ½ **cup all-purpose flour**
- 2 **cups cooked stuffing**
- 2 **cups cubed cooked turkey**
- 1½ **cups cut fresh green beans**

1. In a Dutch oven, saute mushrooms and onion in oil until tender. Add garlic; cook 1 minute longer. Add the broth, carrots and Creole seasoning. Bring to a boil. Reduce heat; simmer, uncovered for 5-8 minutes or until carrots are tender.
2. Meanwhile, in a large bowl, whisk eggs and flour until smooth. Crumble stuffing over mixture; mix well. If necessary, add water, 1 teaspoon a time, until mixture holds its shape.
3. Add the turkey and green beans to soup; return to a boil. Drop stuffing mixture by heaping tablespoonfuls onto simmering soup. Cover and simmer for 8-10 minutes or until a toothpick inserted in a dumpling comes out clean (do not lift the cover while simmering).
NOTE *The following spices may be substituted for 1 teaspoon Creole seasoning: ¼ teaspoon each salt, garlic powder and paprika; and a pinch each of dried thyme, ground cumin and cayenne pepper.*

STUFFING DUMPLING SOUP

Matzo Ball Soup

A variety of winter vegetables gives the broth for this classic Jewish soup an amazing flavor. A few green onions may be substituted for the leek.

—TASTE OF HOME TEST KITCHEN

PREP: 25 MIN. + CHILLING • **COOK:** 2 HOURS
MAKES: 8 SERVINGS (2 QUARTS)

- 10 **cups water**
- 12 **garlic cloves, peeled**
- 3 **medium carrots, cut into chunks**
- 3 **small turnips, peeled and cut into chunks**
- 2 **medium onions, cut into wedges**
- 2 **medium parsnips, peeled and cut into chunks**
- 1 **medium leek (white portion only), sliced**
- ¼ **cup minced fresh parsley**
- 2 **tablespoons snipped fresh dill**
- 1 **teaspoon salt**
- 1 **teaspoon pepper**
- ¾ **teaspoon ground turmeric**

MATZO BALLS

- 3 **eggs, separated**
- 3 **tablespoons water or chicken broth**
- 3 **tablespoons rendered chicken fat**
- 1½ **teaspoons salt, divided**
- ¾ **cup matzo meal**
- 8 **cups water**

1. For broth, in a stockpot, combine the first 12 ingredients. Bring to a boil. Reduce heat; cover and simmer for 2 hours.

2. Meanwhile, in a large bowl, beat the egg yolks on high speed for 2 minutes or until thick and lemon-colored. Add the water, chicken fat and ½ teaspoon salt. In another bowl, beat egg whites on high until stiff peaks form; fold into yolk mixture. Fold in the matzo meal. Cover and refrigerate for at least 1 hour or until thickened.

3. In another stockpot, bring water to a boil; add remaining salt. Drop eight rounded tablespoonfuls of matzo ball dough into boiling water. Reduce heat; cover and simmer for 20-25 minutes or until a toothpick inserted into a matzo ball comes out clean (do not lift cover while simmering).

4. Strain broth, discarding vegetables and seasonings. Carefully remove matzo balls from water with a slotted spoon; place one matzo ball in each soup bowl. Add broth.

Veggie Chowder

When the weather turns brisk, we enjoy soothing foods like this hearty chowder. It's easy to prepare, and the aroma will make your mouth water.

—SHEENA HOFFMAN NORTH VANCOUVER, BC

PREP: 10 MIN. • **COOK:** 35 MIN.
MAKES: 4 SERVINGS

- 4 **bacon strips, diced**
- ½ **cup chopped onion**
- 2 **medium red potatoes, cubed**
- 2 **small carrots, halved lengthwise and thinly sliced**
- 1 **cup water**

VEGGIE CHOWDER

- 1½ **teaspoons chicken bouillon granules**
- 2 **cups whole milk**
- 1⅓ **cups frozen corn**
- ¼ **teaspoon pepper**
- 2 **tablespoons all-purpose flour**
- ¼ **cup cold water**
- 1¼ **cups shredded cheddar cheese**

1. In a large saucepan, cook bacon over medium heat until crisp. Remove to paper towels with a slotted spoon; drain, reserving 2 teaspoons drippings.

2. Saute onion in drippings until tender. Add the potatoes, carrots, water and bouillon. Bring to a boil. Reduce heat; cover and simmer for 15-20 minutes or until the vegetables are almost tender.

3. Stir in the milk, corn and pepper. Cook 5 minutes longer. Combine flour and cold water until smooth; gradually stir into soup. Bring to a boil; cook and stir for 1-2 minutes or until thickened. Remove from the heat; stir in cheese until melted. Sprinkle with bacon.

FIESTA SWEET
POTATO SOUP

Fiesta Sweet Potato Soup

Here's a simple soup with plenty of chunky ingredients and just a little flavor kick. Loaded with sweet potatoes, black beans and chicken sausage, it tastes even better the next day.

—GILDA LESTER MILLSBORO, DE

START TO FINISH: 30 MIN.
MAKES: 6 SERVINGS (2¼ QUARTS)

- 1 package (9 ounces) fully cooked spicy chicken sausage links, chopped
- 2 medium sweet potatoes, peeled and cubed
- 1 large onion, chopped
- 1 small green pepper, diced
- 2 tablespoons olive oil
- 2 teaspoons ground cumin
- 2 cans (14½ ounces each) reduced-sodium chicken broth
- 1 can (14½ ounces) diced tomatoes with mild green chilies, undrained
- 1 can (15 ounces) black beans, rinsed and drained
- 2 tablespoons minced fresh cilantro Sour cream and thinly sliced green onions

1. In a large saucepan, saute the sausage, sweet potatoes, onion and pepper in oil until onion is tender. Add cumin; cook 1 minute longer. Stir in the broth, tomatoes and beans. Bring to a boil. Reduce heat; cover and simmer for 10 minutes or until potatoes are tender. Stir in cilantro.

2. Garnish servings with sour cream and green onions.

FREEZE IT Cider Turkey Soup

Save the turkey carcass from your Thanksgiving dinner to create the homemade broth for this soup. Apple cider gives the broth a bit of sweetness.

—TASTE OF HOME TEST KITCHEN

PREP: 15 MIN. • **COOK:** 2½ HOURS
MAKES: 15 SERVINGS (3¾ QUARTS)

- 1 leftover turkey carcass (from a 12-pound turkey)
- 3½ quarts water
- 4 cups apple cider or juice
- 2 celery ribs, cut into 2-inch pieces
- 1 large onion, cut into wedges
- 1 large apple, cut into wedges
- 1 large carrot, cut into 2-inch pieces
- 8 sprigs fresh thyme
- 2 sprigs fresh sage

SOUP

- 3 cups shredded cooked turkey breast
- 2 cups cooked long grain and wild rice
- 2 large carrots, shredded
- 1 large onion, chopped
- 1 cup chopped celery
- 1 teaspoon salt
- ½ teaspoon dried thyme
- ¼ teaspoon pepper

1. Place the first nine ingredients in a stockpot. Slowly bring to a boil over low heat; cover and simmer for 1½ hours.

2. Discard the carcass. Strain broth through a cheesecloth-lined colander; discard vegetables and herbs. If using immediately, skim fat. Or cool, then refrigerate for 8 hours or overnight.

3. Remove fat from surface before using. Broth may be refrigerated for up to 3 days or frozen for 4-6 months.

4. Place the soup ingredients in a stockpot; add broth. Bring to a boil. Reduce heat; cover and simmer for 30 minutes or until the vegetables are tender.

FREEZE OPTION *Cool the soup and transfer to freezer containers. Freeze up to 3 months. To use, thaw soup in the refrigerator overnight. Transfer to a saucepan. Cover and cook over medium heat until heated through.*

FREEZE IT Broccoli Beer Cheese Soup

This soup tastes just as wonderful without the beer, making a great broccoli cheese soup. I always make extra and pop individual servings in the freezer.
—**LORI LEE** BROOKSVILLE, FL

PREP: 15 MIN. • **COOK:** 40 MIN.
MAKES: 12 SERVINGS (3 QUARTS)

- 5 celery ribs, finely chopped
- 3 medium carrots, finely chopped
- 1 small onion, finely chopped
- 3 tablespoons butter
- 4 cans (14½ ounces each) chicken broth
- 4 cups fresh broccoli florets, chopped
- ¼ cup chopped sweet red pepper
- 1 teaspoon salt
- ½ teaspoon pepper
- ½ cup all-purpose flour
- ½ cup water
- 3 cups (12 ounces) shredded cheddar cheese
- 1 package (8 ounces) cream cheese, cubed
- 1 bottle (12 ounces) beer or nonalcoholic beer
  Optional toppings: cooked and crumbled bacon, chopped green onions, shredded cheddar cheese, sour cream and salad croutons

1. In a Dutch oven, saute celery, carrots and onion in butter until almost tender; add broth, broccoli, red pepper, salt and pepper. Combine flour and water until smooth; stir into pan. Bring to a boil. Reduce heat; simmer, uncovered, 30-40 minutes or until thickened and vegetables are tender.
2. Stir in cheeses and beer; cook until heated through and cheese is melted, stirring occasionally (do not boil). Serve with toppings of your choice.
FREEZE OPTION *Cool soup; transfer to freezer containers. Freeze for up to 3 months. To use, thaw soup in the refrigerator overnight. Transfer to a saucepan. Cover soup and cook over medium-low heat until heated through, stirring occasionally (do not boil).*

FREEZE IT Turkey Sausage Bean Soup

Every generation since my great-grandmother has made this hearty soup. I've tweaked it a bit to add some of my current favorites like celery root. Serve it with a side salad and some artisan bread for a wonderful dinner.
—**TERREL PORTER-SMITH** LOS OSOS, CA

PREP: 15 MIN. • **COOK:** 25 MIN.
MAKES: 8 SERVINGS (2 QUARTS)

- 4 Italian turkey sausage links, casings removed
- 1 large onion, chopped
- 1 cup chopped fennel bulb
- 1 cup chopped peeled celery root or turnip
- 1 can (14½ ounces) no-salt-added diced tomatoes, undrained
- 3 cups water
- 4 bay leaves
- 1 tablespoon reduced-sodium beef base
- 2 teaspoons Italian seasoning
- ½ teaspoon pepper
- 2 cans (15 ounces each) white kidney or cannellini beans, rinsed and drained
  Shaved Parmesan cheese, optional

1. In a Dutch oven, cook sausage, onion, fennel and celery root over medium heat 4-5 minutes or until sausage is no longer pink, breaking into crumbles; drain. Stir in tomatoes, water, bay leaves, beef base, Italian seasoning and pepper.
2. Bring to a boil. Reduce heat; simmer, covered, 20 minutes or until vegetables are tender. Stir in beans; heat through. Remove bay leaves. If desired, top servings with cheese.
FREEZE OPTION *Cool soup without cheese and transfer to freezer containers. Freeze up to 3 months. To use, partially thaw in refrigerator overnight. Heat through in a saucepan, stirring soup occasionally. If desired, top with cheese.*

TURKEY SAUSAGE BEAN SOUP

Coconut Curry Chicken Soup

Similar to a Vietnamese pho rice noodle soup, coconut curry chicken soup packs big flavor and a bit of heat. The crisp raw vegetables help cool things down.

—MONNIE NORASING MANSFIELD, TX

PREP: 20 MIN. • **COOK:** 35 MIN.
MAKES: 6 SERVINGS

- 2 **cans (13.66 ounces each) coconut milk**
- ⅓ **to ½ cup red curry paste**
- 1 **package (8.8 ounces) thin rice noodles**
- 2 **cans (14½ ounces each) chicken broth**
- ¼ **cup packed brown sugar**
- 2 **tablespoons fish sauce or soy sauce**
- ¾ **teaspoon garlic salt**
- 3 **cups shredded rotisserie chicken**
- 1½ **cups shredded cabbage**
- 1½ **cups shredded carrots**
- ¾ **cup bean sprouts**
  Fresh basil and cilantro leaves

1. In a Dutch oven, bring coconut milk to a boil. Cook, uncovered, 10-12 minutes or until liquid is reduced to 3 cups. Stir in curry paste until completely dissolved.

2. Meanwhile, prepare noodles according to package directions.

3. Add broth, brown sugar, fish sauce and garlic salt to curry mixture; return to a boil. Reduce heat; simmer, uncovered, for 10 minutes, stirring soup occasionally. Stir in chicken; heat through.

4. Drain noodles; divide among six large soup bowls. Ladle soup over noodles; top servings with vegetables, basil and cilantro.

NOTE *This recipe was tested with Thai Kitchen Red Curry Paste.*

COCONUT CURRY CHICKEN SOUP

Lemony Mushroom Orzo Soup

My grandmother used to make a similar classic Greek soup, *avgolemono*, every Sunday after church. Here's my version of her recipe. The kids and I came up with this variation while experimenting with different ingredients. I think my *yia-yia* would be proud.

—**NICK HAROS** STROUDSBURG, PA

PREP: 10 MIN. • **COOK:** 25 MIN.
MAKES: 8 SERVINGS (2¾ QUARTS)

- 2 **tablespoons butter**
- 1 **pound sliced fresh button mushrooms**
- 1 **pound sliced fresh baby portobello mushrooms**
- 1 **celery rib, sliced**
- 2 **cartons (32 ounces each) chicken broth**
- 2 **teaspoons chicken bouillon granules**
- 1½ **cups uncooked orzo pasta**
- 2 **eggs**
- ¼ **cup lemon juice**
- ¼ **teaspoon pepper**
  Minced fresh parsley

1. In a Dutch oven, heat butter over medium-high heat. Add mushrooms and celery; cook and stir 6-7 minutes or until tender. Add broth and bouillon; bring to a boil. Stir in orzo; return to a boil. Cook, uncovered, 7-9 minutes or until orzo is al dente, stirring occasionally. Remove from heat; let stand 5 minutes.
2. Meanwhile, in a large bowl, whisk the eggs, lemon juice and pepper. Gradually whisk in 1½ cups of the hot broth; return all to pan, stirring constantly. Cook over medium heat until broth is slightly thickened, stirring occasionally. (Do not allow to boil.) Top servings with parsley.

WHITE BEAN SOUP WITH ESCAROLE

White Bean Soup with Escarole

My recipe card for this winter warmer has become well worn because I make it so often. The soup uses kitchen staples and is packed with healthy ingredients. If I can't find escarole, I use fresh spinach instead.

—**GINA SAMOKAR** NORTH HAVEN, CT

PREP: 15 MIN. • **COOK:** 35 MIN.
MAKES: 8 SERVINGS (2 QUARTS)

- 1 **tablespoon olive oil**
- 1 **small onion, chopped**
- 5 **garlic cloves, minced**
- 3 **cans (14½ ounces each) reduced-sodium chicken broth**
- 1 **can (14½ ounces) diced tomatoes, undrained**
- ½ **teaspoon Italian seasoning**
- ¼ **teaspoon crushed red pepper flakes**
- 1 **cup uncooked whole wheat orzo pasta**
- 1 **bunch escarole or spinach, coarsely chopped (about 8 cups)**
- 1 **can (15 ounces) white kidney or cannellini beans, rinsed and drained**
- ¼ **cup grated Parmesan cheese**

1. In a Dutch oven, heat oil over medium heat. Add onion and garlic; cook and stir until tender. Add broth, tomatoes, Italian seasoning and pepper flakes; bring to a boil. Reduce heat; simmer, uncovered, 15 minutes.
2. Stir in orzo and escarole. Return to a boil; cook 12-14 minutes or until orzo is tender. Add the beans; heat through, stirring occasionally. Sprinkle servings with cheese.

Authentic Cajun Gumbo

I learned to cook in Louisiana and love Cajun cuisine. This chicken oyster gumbo is one of my favorites.

—**PAUL MORRIS** KELSO, WA

PREP: 1 HOUR + SIMMERING • **COOK:** 45 MIN.
MAKES: 20 SERVINGS (1¼ CUPS EACH)

- 6 **quarts water**
- 1 **chicken (5 pounds), cut up**
- 2 **large onions, quartered**
- 4 **celery ribs, cut into 3-inch pieces**
- 6 **garlic cloves, coarsely chopped**
- 2 **tablespoons salt**
- 1 **teaspoon garlic powder**
- ½ **teaspoon poultry seasoning**
- ½ **teaspoon cayenne pepper**
- ½ **teaspoon pepper**
- ¼ **teaspoon white pepper**
- 1 **cup canola oil**
- 1½ **cups all-purpose flour**
- 1 **large onion, finely chopped**
- 1 **pound fully cooked andouille sausage links, chopped**
- 2 **pounds sliced okra**
- 2 **pints shucked oysters**
- 3 **tablespoons gumbo file powder**
  Hot cooked rice

1. Place the first 11 ingredients in a stockpot; bring to a boil. Reduce heat; cover and simmer for 1½ hours.

2. Remove chicken and allow to cool. Strain broth, discarding vegetables; skim fat. Remove meat from bones; cut chicken into bite-size pieces and set aside. Discard bones.

3. In the same pan, cook and stir oil and flour over medium heat until caramel-colored, about 14 minutes (do not burn). Add finely chopped onion; cook and stir 2 minutes longer. Gradually stir in broth. Bring to a boil.

4. Carefully stir in sausage and reserved chicken. Reduce heat; simmer, uncovered, for 10 minutes. Stir in okra and oysters. Simmer, uncovered, 10-15 minutes longer or just until okra is tender. Stir in file powder. Serve with rice.

NOTE *Gumbo file powder, used to thicken and flavor Creole recipes, is available in spice shops. If you don't want to use gumbo file powder, combine 2 tablespoons each cornstarch and cold water until smooth. Gradually stir into gumbo. Bring to a boil; cook and stir for 2 minutes or until thickened.*

HUNGARIAN MUSHROOM SOUP

Hungarian Mushroom Soup

You'll think you're eating at a fine restaurant when you taste this creamy mushroom soup. It's so delicious!

—**SANDY VAUGHN** CENTRAL POINT, OR

PREP: 20 MIN. • **COOK:** 30 MIN.
MAKES: 4 SERVINGS

- 1 **large sweet onion, chopped**
- ¼ **cup butter, cubed**
- ¾ **pound sliced fresh mushrooms**
- 3 **tablespoons all-purpose flour**
- 1 **tablespoon paprika**
- 1 **teaspoon dill weed**
- ¾ **teaspoon salt**
- ¼ **teaspoon coarsely ground pepper**
- 1 **can (14½ ounces) chicken broth**
- 1 **cup 2% milk**
- 1 **tablespoon soy sauce**
- ½ **cup sour cream**
- 2 **teaspoons lemon juice**

1. In a large saucepan, saute onion in butter for 2 minutes. Add mushrooms; cook 4-5 minutes longer or until mushrooms are tender.

2. Stir in the flour, paprika, dill, salt and pepper until blended. Gradually stir in the broth, milk and soy sauce. Bring mixture to a boil; cook and stir 2 minutes or until thickened. Reduce heat; cover and simmer for 15 minutes.

3. Just before serving, stir in sour cream and lemon juice (do not boil).

AUTHENTIC CAJUN GUMBO

Turkey Meatball Soup

I made up this recipe myself to take advantage of the abundance of locally available fresh vegetables. It's an economical yet hearty main dish that my husband and kids enjoy year-round.
—**LORA REHM** ENDICOTT, NY

PREP: 30 MIN. • **COOK:** 20 MIN.
MAKES: 6 SERVINGS

- ½ cup dry bread crumbs
- 3 tablespoons milk
- 1 egg, lightly beaten
- ½ teaspoon salt
- 1¼ pounds ground turkey
- 2½ cups water
- 1 can (14½ ounces) stewed tomatoes
- 2 medium zucchini, halved and sliced
- 2 small carrots, thinly sliced
- ⅔ cup frozen corn
- ½ cup cut fresh green beans or frozen cut green beans
- 2 teaspoons chicken bouillon granules
- 1 teaspoon dried basil
- ¼ teaspoon pepper

1. In a large bowl, combine the bread crumbs, milk, egg and salt. Crumble turkey over mixture and mix well. Shape into ½-in. balls. In a nonstick skillet over medium heat, brown meatballs in batches; drain if necessary.
2. In a large saucepan, combine the remaining ingredients. Bring to a boil. Carefully add meatballs. Reduce heat; cover and simmer for 20-25 minutes or until vegetables are tender.

DID YOU KNOW?

Not all ground turkey is the same. If you want to cut down on calories, look for labels that say ground turkey breast (instead of ground turkey, which may contain light and dark meat) or lean ground turkey.

Italian Wedding Soup

You don't have to be Italian to love this easy-to-make soup. It's a popular mainstay in our house and makes a great meal when served with hot crusty Italian bread.
—**MARY SHEETZ** CARMEL, IN

PREP: 30 MIN. • **COOK:** 40 MIN.
MAKES: 9 SERVINGS (2¼ QUARTS)

- 2 eggs, lightly beaten
- ½ cup dry bread crumbs
- ¼ cup minced fresh parsley
- 2 tablespoons grated Parmesan cheese
- 1 tablespoon raisins, finely chopped
- 3 garlic cloves, minced
- ¼ teaspoon crushed red pepper flakes
- ½ pound lean ground beef (90% lean)
- ½ pound bulk spicy pork sausage
- 2 cartons (32 ounces each) reduced-sodium chicken broth
- ½ teaspoon pepper
- 1½ cups cubed rotisserie chicken
- ⅔ cup uncooked acini di pepe pasta
- ½ cup fresh baby spinach, cut into thin strips
  Shredded Parmesan cheese, optional

1. In a large bowl, combine the first seven ingredients. Crumble beef and sausage over mixture and mix well. Shape into ½-in. balls.
2. In a Dutch oven, brown meatballs in small batches; drain. Add the broth and pepper; bring to a boil. Reduce heat; simmer, uncovered, for 10 minutes. Stir in chicken and pasta; cook soup 5-7 minutes longer or until pasta is tender. Stir in spinach; cook until wilted. Sprinkle soup with shredded Parmesan cheese if desired.

ITALIAN WEDDING SOUP

CHICKEN GNOCCHI PESTO SOUP

ASIAN CHICKEN NOODLE SOUP

Chicken Gnocchi Pesto Soup

I created this quick and easy soup after tasting a similar one at a restaurant.
—**DEANNA SMITH** DES MOINES, IA

START TO FINISH: 25 MIN.
MAKES: 4 SERVINGS

- 1 jar (15 ounces) roasted garlic Alfredo sauce
- 2 cups water
- 2 cups cubed rotisserie chicken
- 1 teaspoon Italian seasoning
- ¼ teaspoon salt
- ¼ teaspoon pepper
- 1 package (16 ounces) potato gnocchi
- 3 cups coarsley chopped fresh spinach
- 4 teaspoons prepared pesto

In a large saucepan, combine the first six ingredients; bring to a gentle boil, stirring occasionally. Stir in gnocchi and spinach; cook 3-8 minutes or until the gnocchi float. Top each serving with pesto.
NOTE *Look for potato gnocchi in the pasta or frozen foods section.*

Asian Chicken Noodle Soup

One night I didn't have any noodles for my chicken soup, so I gave it an Asian twist with wonton wrappers. It was great! Don't skip the celery leaves—they bring great flavor to this recipe.
—**NOELLE MYERS** GRAND FORKS, ND

PREP: 15 MIN. • **COOK:** 40 MIN.
MAKES: 10 SERVINGS (2½ QUARTS)

- 1½ pounds boneless skinless chicken breasts, cut into 1-inch cubes
- 1 tablespoon sesame oil
- 3 medium carrots, sliced
- 2 celery ribs, chopped
- 1 medium onion, chopped
- 6 cups chicken broth
- ⅓ cup teriyaki sauce
- ¼ cup chili garlic sauce
- 1 package (12 ounces) wonton wrappers, cut into ¼-inch strips
- 2 cups sliced fresh shiitake mushrooms
- ⅓ cup chopped celery leaves
- ¼ cup minced fresh basil
- 2 tablespoons minced fresh cilantro
- 2 green onions, sliced

1. In a Dutch oven, cook chicken in oil over medium heat until no longer pink. Remove and keep warm. In the same pan, saute the carrots, celery and onion until tender. Stir in the broth, teriyaki sauce, garlic sauce and the chicken. Bring to a boil. Reduce heat; simmer, uncovered, for 20 minutes.
2. Add the wonton strips, mushrooms, celery leaves, basil and cilantro. Cook and stir for 4-5 minutes or until the wonton strips and mushrooms are tender. Sprinkle with green onions.

SOUTH-OF-THE-BORDER CHOWDER

SAUSAGE PIZZA SOUP

South-of-the-Border Chowder

This filling soup loaded with potatoes comes together in no time. The tasty combination of sweet corn and pearl onions, smoky bacon and lots of spice creates a zesty Southwestern flavor.

—TONYA BURKHARD DAVIS, IL

START TO FINISH: 20 MIN.
MAKES: 10 SERVINGS (2½ QUARTS)

- ½ **cup chopped onion**
- 4 **bacon strips, diced**
- 2 **tablespoons all-purpose flour**
- ½ **teaspoon ground cumin**
- ½ **teaspoon chili powder**
- ⅛ **teaspoon garlic powder**
- 1 **package (32 ounces) frozen cubed hash brown potatoes**
- 2 **cans (14½ ounces each) chicken broth**
- 1 **can (14¾ ounces) cream-style corn**
- 1 **can (11 ounces) Mexicorn, drained**
- 1 **can (4 ounces) chopped green chilies**
- ¼ **cup pearl onions**
  Sour cream and minced fresh cilantro, optional

1. In a Dutch oven, saute onion and bacon until onion is tender and bacon is crisp. Stir in the flour, cumin, chili powder and garlic powder. Bring to a boil; cook and stir for 1 minute or until thickened.
2. Stir in the hash browns, broth, cream corn, Mexicorn, chilies and pearl onions. Bring to a boil. Reduce heat; simmer, uncovered, for 10 minutes or until heated through. Garnish with sour cream and cilantro if desired.

Sausage Pizza Soup

If you love pizza but are trying to watch your calories, try this healthy alternative. You won't believe how delicious it is.

—BETH SHERER MILWAUKEE, WI

PREP: 10 MIN. • **COOK:** 25 MIN.
MAKES: 4 SERVINGS

- ½ **pound Italian turkey sausage links, casings removed**
- 1 **medium zucchini, sliced**
- 1 **cup sliced fresh mushrooms**
- 1 **small onion, chopped**
- 1 **can (14½ ounces) no-salt-added diced tomatoes**
- 1 **cup water**
- 1 **cup reduced-sodium chicken broth**
- 1 **teaspoon dried basil**
- ¼ **teaspoon pepper**
  Minced fresh basil and crushed red pepper flakes, optional

In a large saucepan, cook the sausage, zucchini, mushrooms and onion over medium heat until the meat is no longer pink; drain. Add the tomatoes, water, broth, dried basil and pepper. Bring to a boil. Reduce the heat; simmer, uncovered, for 15 minutes. Sprinkle with fresh basil and pepper flakes if desired.

CARL'S CHICKEN NOODLE SOUP

Carl's Chicken Noodle Soup

I like lots of chunky vegetables in my chicken noodle soup. Feel free to make substitutions with whatever you have on hand. Add a crusty loaf of warm bread for a satisfying meal.

—**CARL BATES** PLEASANTON, CA

PREP: 30 MIN. • **COOK:** 50 MIN.
MAKES: 10 SERVINGS (4 QUARTS)

- 1 **pound boneless skinless chicken breast halves, cut into ½-inch pieces**
- 1 **medium onion, chopped**
- 2 **teaspoons olive oil**
- 2 **garlic cloves, minced**
- 2 **cans (49½ ounces each) chicken broth**
- 2 **cups frozen sliced okra, thawed**
- 3 **celery ribs, sliced**
- 1½ **cups cut fresh green beans**
- 3 **medium carrots, sliced**
- 1 **can (8¾ ounces) whole kernel corn, drained**
- 2 **tablespoons dried parsley flakes**
- 2 **teaspoons Italian seasoning**
- 2 **bay leaves**
- ½ **teaspoon salt**
- ½ **teaspoon pepper**
- 3½ **cups uncooked egg noodles**

1. In a Dutch oven, saute chicken and onion in oil until chicken is no longer pink. Add garlic; cook 1 minute longer. Add the broth, okra, celery, beans, carrots, corn, parsley, Italian seasoning, bay leaves, salt and pepper. Bring to a boil. Reduce heat; cover and simmer for 30 minutes or until the vegetables are tender.

2. Stir in noodles; cook 5-7 minutes longer or until tender. Discard bay leaves.

Wild Rice Turkey Soup

Our family loves this soup on a cold night. If you prefer something a little less rich, replace the half-and-half with milk.

—**BARBARA SCHMID** CAVALIER, ND

PREP: 10 MIN. • **COOK:** 1¼ HOURS
MAKES: 8 SERVINGS (2¾ QUARTS)

- 1 **cup uncooked wild rice**
- 7 **cups chicken broth, divided**
- ½ **pound sliced fresh mushrooms**
- 1 **medium onion, chopped**
- 1 **celery rib, chopped**
- ¼ **cup butter, cubed**
- ½ **cup all-purpose flour**
- ½ **teaspoon salt**
- ½ **teaspoon ground mustard**
- ½ **teaspoon poultry seasoning**
- ¼ **teaspoon pepper**
- 4 **cups cubed cooked turkey**
- 2 **cups half-and-half cream**

1. In a large saucepan, bring the rice and 3 cups broth to a boil. Reduce heat; cover and simmer for 50-60 minutes or until rice is tender.

2. In a Dutch oven, saute the mushrooms, onion and celery in butter until tender. Stir in flour and seasonings until blended. Gradually add remaining broth. Bring to a boil; cook and stir for 2 minutes or until thickened. Stir in the turkey, cream and cooked rice; heat through (do not boil).

WILD RICE TURKEY SOUP

FREEZE IT Minestrone with Turkey

I have fond memories of my mom making this dish when I was a little girl. I loved it then and still love it today.

—ANGELA GOODMAN KANEOHE, HI

START TO FINISH: 30 MIN.
MAKES: 6 SERVINGS (2 QUARTS)

- 1 tablespoon olive oil
- 1 medium onion, chopped
- 1 medium carrot, sliced
- 1 celery rib, sliced
- 1 garlic clove, minced
- 4 cups chicken broth or homemade turkey stock
- 1 can (14½ ounces) diced tomatoes, undrained
- ⅔ cup each frozen peas, corn and cut green beans, thawed
- ½ cup uncooked elbow macaroni
- 1 teaspoon salt
- ¼ teaspoon dried basil
- ¼ teaspoon dried oregano
- ¼ teaspoon pepper
- 1 bay leaf
- 1 cup cubed cooked turkey
- 1 small zucchini, halved lengthwise and cut into ¼-inch slices
- ¼ cup grated Parmesan cheese, optional

1. In a Dutch oven, heat the oil over medium-high heat. Add onion, carrot and celery; cook and stir until tender. Add garlic; cook 1 minute longer. Add broth, vegetables, macaroni and the seasonings. Bring to a boil.

2. Reduce heat; simmer, uncovered, 5 minutes or until macaroni is al dente. Stir in turkey and zucchini; cook until zucchini is crisp-tender. Discard bay leaf. If desired, sprinkle servings with cheese.

FREEZE OPTION *Cool the soup and transfer to freezer containers. Freeze up to 3 months. To use, thaw in the refrigerator overnight. Transfer to a saucepan. Cover and cook over medium heat until heated through. Serve with cheese if desired.*

MINESTRONE WITH TURKEY

THREE-CHEESE FRENCH ONION SOUP

Three-Cheese French Onion Soup

Here's a satisfying soup that's fantastic on any autumn or winter day. The blend of Swiss, Parmesan and mozzarella gives it a richness onion soup lovers will enjoy.

—GINA BERRY CHANHASSEN, MN

START TO FINISH: 30 MIN.
MAKES: 7 SERVINGS

- 2 large red onions, thinly sliced
- ¼ cup butter, cubed
- 2 cans (14½ ounces each) chicken broth
- 3 cups water
- 1 envelope onion soup mix
- 1 teaspoon pepper
- 1 teaspoon Worcestershire sauce
- ½ teaspoon garlic powder
- 7 slices French bread (¾ inch thick)
- ½ cup shredded Swiss cheese
- ½ cup shredded part-skim mozzarella cheese
- ¼ cup grated Parmesan cheese

1. In a Dutch oven, saute onions in butter until tender. Add broth, water, soup mix, pepper, Worcestershire sauce and garlic powder. Bring to a boil. Reduce heat; cover and simmer for 5 minutes.

2. Meanwhile, place bread slices on an ungreased baking sheet. Sprinkle with Swiss and mozzarella cheeses. Broil 4 in. from the heat for 1-2 minutes or until cheese is melted.

3. Ladle soup into serving bowls; top each with a toast slice. Sprinkle with Parmesan cheese.

Chunky Turkey Soup

This hearty, chunky soup is the perfect way to use up your Turkey Day leftovers. Combining the earthy flavors of curry and cumin, this is one that no one will mistake for canned soup.

—JANE SCANLON MARCO ISLAND, FL

PREP: 20 MIN. + SIMMERING • **COOK:** 40 MIN.
MAKES: 12 SERVINGS (1⅓ CUPS EACH)

- 1 **leftover turkey carcass (from a 12- to 14-pound turkey)**
- 4½ **quarts water**
- 1 **medium onion, quartered**
- 1 **medium carrot, cut into 2-inch pieces**
- 1 **celery rib, cut into 2-inch pieces**

SOUP

- 2 **cups shredded cooked turkey**
- 4 **celery ribs, chopped**
- 2 **cups frozen corn**
- 2 **medium carrots, sliced**
- 1 **large onion, chopped**
- 1 **cup uncooked orzo pasta**
- 2 **tablespoons minced fresh parsley**
- 4 **teaspoons chicken bouillon granules**
- 1 **teaspoon salt**
- 1 **teaspoon curry powder**
- ½ **teaspoon ground cumin**
- ½ **teaspoon pepper**

1. Place the turkey carcass in a stockpot; add the water, onion, carrot and celery. Slowly bring to a boil over low heat; cover and simmer for 1½ hours.

2. Discard the carcass. Strain broth through a cheesecloth-lined colander. If using immediately, skim fat. Or cool, then refrigerate for 8 hours or overnight; remove fat from surface before using. (Broth may be refrigerated for up to 3 days or frozen for 4-6 months.)

3. Place the soup ingredients in a stockpot; add the broth. Bring to a boil. Reduce heat; cover and simmer for 30 minutes or until pasta and vegetables are tender.

Roasted Garlic Butternut Soup

My soup is lower in fat than others of its kind. Yet it's still creamy and full of flavor.

—ROBIN HAAS CRANSTON, RI

PREP: 35 MIN. • **COOK:** 20 MIN.
MAKES: 9 SERVINGS (2¼ QUARTS)

- 1 **whole garlic bulb**
- 1 **teaspoon olive oil**
- 1 **medium butternut squash (3 pounds), peeled and cubed**
- 1 **medium sweet potato, peeled and cubed**
- 1 **large onion, chopped**
- 2 **tablespoons butter**
- 3¾ **cups water**
- 1 **can (14½ ounces) reduced-sodium chicken broth**
- 1 **teaspoon paprika**
- ½ **teaspoon pepper**
- ¼ **teaspoon salt**
- 9 **tablespoons crumbled blue cheese**

1. Preheat oven to 425°. Remove papery outer skin from garlic (do not peel or separate cloves). Cut top off garlic bulb. Brush with oil; wrap in heavy-duty foil. Bake 30-35 minutes or until softened. Cool for 10-15 minutes.

2. Meanwhile, in a Dutch oven, saute squash, sweet potato and onion in butter until crisp-tender. Add the water, broth, paprika, pepper and salt; squeeze softened garlic into pan. Bring to a boil. Reduce heat; cover soup and simmer 20-25 minutes or until the vegetables are tender. Cool slightly.

3. In a food processor, process soup in batches until smooth. Return all to pan and heat through. Ladle into bowls; top with blue cheese.

ROASTED GARLIC BUTTERNUT SOUP

FREEZE IT Southwest Turkey Soup

Ground turkey and a handful of other ingredients are all that's required for this satisfying bowl that's spiced with salsa, green chilies and chili powder. It's perfect for busy weeknights in the winter.

—GENISE KRAUSE STURGEON BAY, WI

START TO FINISH: 30 MIN.
MAKES: 6 SERVINGS (2½ QUARTS)

- 1 **pound ground turkey**
- 1 **tablespoon olive oil**
- 2 **cans (16 ounces each) kidney beans, rinsed and drained**
- 2 **cans (14½ ounces each) chicken broth**
- 2 **cups frozen corn**
- 1 **cup salsa**
- 1 **can (4 ounces) chopped green chilies**
- 1 **to 2 tablespoons chili powder**
  Sour cream and minced fresh cilantro

1. In a Dutch oven, cook turkey in oil over medium heat until meat is no longer pink; drain.

2. Add the beans, broth, corn, salsa, chilies and chili powder. Bring to a boil. Reduce heat; cover and simmer for 10-15 minutes to allow flavors to blend. Serve with sour cream and cilantro.

FREEZE OPTION *Cool the soup and transfer to freezer containers. Freeze for up to 3 months. To use, partially thaw soup in the refrigerator overnight. Heat through in a saucepan, stirring occasionally and adding a little broth or water if necessary. Allow soup to cool before adding sour cream and cilantro.*

SOUTHWEST TURKEY SOUP

Italian Chicken Sausage Soup

Bursting with fabulous Italian flavors, this hearty soup is sure to chase away winter's chills. Serve with some crusty rolls for a satisfying dinner.

—**CHERYL RAVESI** MILFORD, MA

PREP: 15 MIN. • **COOK:** 40 MIN.
MAKES: 6 SERVINGS (2½ QUARTS)

- 1 **package (12 ounces) fully cooked Italian chicken sausage links, halved lengthwise and sliced**
- 1 **medium onion, chopped**
- 1 **tablespoon olive oil**
- 3 **garlic cloves, minced**
- 2 **cans (15 ounces each) white kidney or cannellini beans, rinsed and drained**
- 2 **cans (14½ ounces each) no-salt-added diced tomatoes**
- 2 **medium zucchini, quartered and sliced**
- 1 **can (14½ ounces) reduced-sodium chicken broth**
- 8 **ounces whole fresh mushrooms, quartered**
- 1 **cup water**
- ¼ **cup prepared pesto**
- ¼ **cup dry red wine or additional reduced-sodium chicken broth**
- 1 **tablespoon balsamic vinegar**
- 1 **teaspoon minced fresh oregano or ¼ teaspoon dried oregano**
- ½ **teaspoon pepper**
  Grated Parmesan cheese

1. In a Dutch oven, cook sausage and onion in oil until sausage is browned. Add garlic; cook 1 minute longer.
2. Stir in the beans, tomatoes, zucchini, broth, mushrooms, water, pesto, wine, vinegar, oregano and pepper. Bring to a boil. Reduce heat; simmer, uncovered, for 25-30 minutes or until vegetables are tender. Sprinkle with cheese.

OLD-FASHIONED TURKEY NOODLE SOUP

Old-Fashioned Turkey Noodle Soup

Make the most of leftover turkey with a delicious homemade soup. Roasting the turkey bones, garlic and vegetables adds a rich flavor without added fat.

—*TASTE OF HOME* **TEST KITCHEN**

PREP: 3½ HOURS + CHILLING • **COOK:** 45 MIN.
MAKES: 10 SERVINGS (ABOUT 4 QUARTS)

BROTH
- 1 **leftover turkey carcass (from a 12- to 14-pound turkey)**
- 2 **cooked turkey wings, meat removed**
- 2 **cooked turkey drumsticks, meat removed**
- 1 **turkey neck bone**
- 1 **medium unpeeled onion, cut into wedges**
- 2 **small unpeeled carrots, cut into chunks**
- 6 **to 8 garlic cloves, peeled**
- 4 **quarts plus 1 cup cold water, divided**

SOUP
- 3 **quarts water**
- 5 **cups uncooked egg noodles**
- 2 **cups diced carrots**
- 2 **cups diced celery**
- 3 **cups cubed cooked turkey**
- ¼ **cup minced fresh parsley**
- 2½ **teaspoons salt**
- 2 **teaspoons dried thyme**
- 1 **teaspoon pepper**

1. Place the leftover turkey carcass, bones from wings and drumsticks, neck bone, onion, carrots and garlic in a 15x10x1-in. baking pan coated with cooking spray. Bake, uncovered, at 400° for 1 hour, turning once.
2. Transfer the carcass, bones and vegetables to an 8-qt. stockpot. Add 4 qts. cold water; set aside. Pour the remaining cold water into baking pan, stirring to loosen browned bits. Add to pot. Bring to a boil. Reduce heat; cover and simmer for 3-4 hours.
3. Cool slightly. Strain broth; discard bones and vegetables. Set stockpot in an ice-water bath until broth cools, stirring occasionally. Cover pot and refrigerate overnight.
4. Skim fat from broth. Cover and bring to a boil. Reduce the heat to a simmer. Meanwhile, in a Dutch oven, bring 3 qts. water to a boil. Add noodles and carrots; cook for 4 minutes. Add celery; cook 5-7 minutes longer or until noodles and vegetables are tender. Drain; add to simmering broth. Add cubed turkey; heat through. Stir in the parsley, salt, thyme and pepper.

HALIBUT CHOWDER

Halibut Chowder

I'm a teacher, and I love to cook and entertain. Several times a year, I invite my colleagues and their spouses to a dinner party, when I always serve this rich and creamy chowder. People love it for the chunks of fish, potatoes and carrots.

—**TERESA LUECK** ONAMIA, MN

PREP: 25 MIN. • **COOK:** 30 MIN.
MAKES: 12 SERVINGS (3 QUARTS)

- 4 **celery ribs, chopped**
- 3 **medium carrots, chopped**
- 1 **large onion, chopped**
- ½ **cup butter, cubed**
- ½ **cup all-purpose flour**
- ¼ **teaspoon white pepper**
- 2 **cups 2% milk**
- 1 **can (14½ ounces) chicken broth**
- ¼ **cup water**
- 1 **tablespoon chicken base**
- 3 **medium potatoes, peeled and chopped**
- 1 **can (15¼ ounces) whole kernel corn, drained**
- 3 **bay leaves**
- 2 **cups half-and-half cream**
- 2 **tablespoons lemon juice**
- 1 **pound halibut or other whitefish fillets, cut into 1-inch pieces**
- 1 **cup salad croutons**
- ¾ **cup grated Parmesan cheese**
- ½ **cup minced chives**

1. In a large saucepan, saute the celery, carrots and onion in butter until tender. Stir in flour and pepper until blended; gradually add the milk, broth, water and chicken base. Bring to a boil; cook and stir for 2 minutes or until thickened.

2. Add the potatoes, corn and bay leaves. Return to a boil. Reduce heat; cover and simmer for 15-20 minutes or until potatoes are tender.

3. Stir in cream and lemon juice; return to a boil. Add halibut. Reduce heat; simmer, uncovered, for 7-11 minutes or until fish flakes easily with a fork. Discard bay leaves.

4. Garnish servings with croutons, cheese and chives.

NOTE *Look for chicken base near the broth and bouillon.*

Crab Soup with Sherry

This comforting soup is a staple in the South. It has a smooth texture and the perfect hint of sherry.

—**REGINA HUGGINS** SUMMERVILLE, SC

PREP: 15 MIN. • **COOK:** 30 MIN.
MAKES: 6 SERVINGS

- 1 **pound fresh or frozen crabmeat, thawed**
- 6 **tablespoons sherry or chicken broth**
- 1 **small onion, grated**
- ¼ **cup butter, cubed**
- ¼ **cup all-purpose flour**
- ½ **teaspoon salt**
- 2 **cups 2% milk**
- 2 **chicken bouillon cubes**
- 3 **cups half-and-half cream**
- 2 **tablespoons minced fresh parsley**

1. In a small bowl, combine crabmeat and sherry; set aside.

2. In a large saucepan, saute onion in butter until tender. Stir in flour and salt until blended; gradually add milk and bouillon. Bring to a boil; cook and stir for 2 minutes or until thickened. Stir in cream and crab mixture; heat through. Sprinkle servings with parsley.

CRAB SOUP WITH SHERRY

Country Fish Chowder

You'll think you're on Cape Cod when you taste this thick, wholesome chowder. It's one of my husband's favorites. I have customized the basic recipe over the years to include the ingredients he loves most.

—LINDA LAZAROFF HEBRON, CT

PREP: 15 MIN. • **COOK:** 25 MIN.
MAKES: 8-10 SERVINGS (2½ QUARTS)

- 1 cup chopped onion
- 4 bacon strips, chopped
- 3 cans (12 ounces each) evaporated milk
- 1 can (15¼ ounces) whole kernel corn, undrained
- 1 can (6½ ounces) chopped clams, undrained
- 3 medium potatoes, peeled and cubed
- 3 tablespoons butter
- 1 teaspoon salt
- ¾ teaspoon pepper
- 1 pound fish fillets (haddock, cod or flounder), cooked and broken into pieces
  Crumbled cooked bacon, optional
  Minced chives, optional

In a large saucepan, cook onion and bacon over medium heat until onion is tender; drain. Add milk, corn, clams, potatoes, butter, salt and pepper. Cover and cook over medium heat, stirring occasionally, until potatoes are tender, about 20 minutes. Stir in fish and heat through. Ladle into bowls. If desired, top with bacon and chives.

CRAB CORN CHOWDER

Crab Corn Chowder

Is life too busy these days to make a homemade soup? Think again! You'll be spooning out steamy bowls of my satisfying chowder in no time. Canned corn and crab blend beautifully in this creamy, colorful creation. It's one of the best I've ever tasted.

—SARAH MCCLANAHAN RALEIGH, NC

PREP: 15 MIN. • **COOK:** 20 MIN.
MAKES: 8 SERVINGS (2 QUARTS)

- 3 teaspoons chicken bouillon granules
- 2 cups boiling water
- 6 bacon strips, diced
- ⅓ cup each diced sweet red, yellow and orange peppers
- ½ cup chopped onion
- ¼ cup all-purpose flour
- 3 cups half-and-half cream
- 2 cans (14¾ ounces each) cream-style corn
- 1½ teaspoons seasoned salt
- ½ teaspoon dried basil
- ¼ to ½ teaspoon cayenne pepper
- 2 cans (6 ounces each) crabmeat, drained, flaked and cartilage removed or 2 cups imitation crabmeat, flaked
- ½ cup minced chives

1. Dissolve bouillon in water; set aside. In a Dutch oven, cook bacon over medium heat until crisp. Remove bacon to paper towels to drain, reserving drippings.

2. In the same pan, saute peppers and onion in drippings until tender. Stir in flour. Gradually stir in bouillon mixture. Bring to a boil; cook and stir for 2 minutes or until thickened.

3. Reduce heat; gradually stir in cream and corn. Add the seasoned salt, basil and cayenne. Cook until heated through, stirring occasionally (do not boil). Stir in the crab. Garnish each serving with bacon and chives.

CREAMY SEAFOOD BISQUE

Creamy Seafood Bisque

My deceptively simple bisque makes a special first course or even a casual meal with a salad or bread. I like to top bowlfuls with shredded Parmesan cheese and green onions.

—WANDA ALLENDE ORLANDO, FL

PREP: 25 MIN. • **COOK:** 25 MIN.
MAKES: 8 SERVINGS (2½ QUARTS)

- ½ cup butter, cubed
- 1 medium red onion, chopped
- 1 cup sliced fresh mushrooms
- 2 garlic cloves, minced
- ½ cup all-purpose flour
- 1 teaspoon salt
- 1 teaspoon coarsely ground pepper
- 2 tablespoons tomato paste
- 1 carton (32 ounces) chicken broth
- 2 cups whole baby clams, drained
- ½ pound uncooked medium shrimp, peeled and deveined
- 2 cups lump crabmeat, drained
- 2 cups heavy whipping cream
- ½ cup shredded Parmesan cheese
- 2 green onions, thinly sliced

1. In a Dutch oven, heat butter over medium-high heat. Add red onion and mushrooms; saute for 4-5 minutes or until tender. Add garlic; cook 1 minute longer. Stir in flour, salt and pepper until blended; add tomato paste. Gradually whisk in broth; bring to a boil. Reduce heat; cover and simmer for 5 minutes.

2. Add clams and shrimp; return to a boil. Reduce heat; simmer, uncovered, 5-10 minutes longer or until shrimp turn pink, stirring occasionally. Stir in crab and cream; heat through (do not boil). Serve with cheese and green onions.

Thai Shrimp Soup

This tasty, crowd-pleasing soup comes together in minutes, and I like the fact that the ingredients are available in my town's small grocery store.

—JESSIE GREARSON-SAPAT FALMOUTH, ME

PREP: 20 MIN. • **COOK:** 20 MIN.
MAKES: 8 SERVINGS (2 QUARTS)

- 1 medium onion, chopped
- 1 tablespoon olive oil
- 3 cups reduced-sodium chicken broth
- 1 cup water
- 1 tablespoon brown sugar
- 1 tablespoon minced fresh gingerroot
- 1 tablespoon fish sauce or soy sauce
- 1 tablespoon red curry paste
- 1 lemon grass stalk
- 1 pound uncooked large shrimp, peeled and deveined
- 1½ cups frozen shelled edamame
- 1 can (13.66 ounces) light coconut milk
- 1 can (8¾ ounces) whole baby corn, drained and cut in half
- ½ cup bamboo shoots
- ¼ cup fresh basil leaves, torn
- ¼ cup minced fresh cilantro
- 2 tablespoons lime juice
- 1½ teaspoons grated lime peel
- 1 teaspoon curry powder

1. In a Dutch oven, saute onion in oil until tender. Add the broth, water, brown sugar, ginger, fish sauce, curry paste and lemon grass. Bring to a boil. Reduce heat; carefully stir in shrimp and edamame. Cook, uncovered, for 5-6 minutes or until shrimp turn pink.

2. Add the coconut milk, corn, bamboo shoots, basil, cilantro, lime juice, lime peel and curry powder; heat through. Discard lemon grass.

THAI SHRIMP SOUP

SHRIMP BLITZ

Shrimp Blitz

This refreshing chilled soup hits the spot on a hot summer day. I like to make it for special-occasion luncheons as well as casual dinners with friends.

—JEANNETTE AIELLO PLACERVILLE, CA

PREP: 15 MIN. + CHILLING
MAKES: 8 SERVINGS (2 QUARTS)

- 1 **bottle (8 ounces) clam juice**
- 1 **package (8 ounces) cream cheese, softened**
- 1 **bottle (32 ounces) tomato juice**
- 1 **package (5 ounces) frozen cooked salad shrimp, thawed**
- 1 **medium ripe avocado, peeled and diced**
- ½ **cup chopped cucumber**
- ⅓ **cup chopped green onions**
- 2 **tablespoons red wine vinegar**
- 2 **teaspoons sugar**
- 1 **teaspoon dill weed**
- 1 **garlic clove, minced**
- ½ **teaspoon salt**
- ¼ **teaspoon hot pepper sauce**
- ⅛ **teaspoon pepper**

In a blender, combine clam juice and cream cheese; cover and process until smooth. Pour into a large serving bowl. Stir in the remaining ingredients. Cover and chill for at least 4 hours.

Shrimp Egg Drop Soup

Who knew that egg drop soup could be so easy? All it takes is three simple steps to achieve this restaurant-quality soup with the perfect blend of veggies and shrimp.

—TASTE OF HOME TEST KITCHEN

START TO FINISH: 30 MIN.
MAKES: 4 SERVINGS

- 4 **teaspoons cornstarch**
- ½ **teaspoon soy sauce**
- ⅛ **teaspoon ground ginger**
- 1½ **cups water, divided**
- 2 **cans (14½ ounces each) chicken broth**
- 1½ **cups frozen home-style egg noodles**
- 1 **cup frozen broccoli florets, thawed and coarsely chopped**
- ½ **cup julienned carrot**
- 1 **egg, lightly beaten**
- ½ **pound cooked medium shrimp, peeled and deveined**

1. In a small bowl, combine the cornstarch, soy sauce, ginger and ½ cup cold water; set aside.

2. In a large saucepan, combine broth and remaining water. Bring to a simmer; add noodles. Cook, uncovered, for 15 minutes. Add broccoli and carrot; simmer 3-4 minutes longer or until noodles are tender.

3. Drizzle beaten egg into hot soup, stirring constantly. Stir cornstarch mixture and add to the pan. Bring to a boil; cook and stir for 2 minutes or until slightly thickened. Add shrimp; heat through.

SHRIMP EGG DROP SOUP

HEARTY FISH SOUP

Hearty Fish Soup

I'm usually pressed for time, so I avoid recipes that require lots of preparation. This chunky soup is convenient because it calls for frozen vegetables, frozen hash browns and canned tomatoes already seasoned with herbs.

—**DEBORAH GROFF** LIVE OAK, TX

PREP: 15 MIN. • **COOK:** 20 MIN.
MAKES: 4 CUPS

- 2 **small shallots, chopped**
- 1 **small garlic clove, minced**
- 1 **can (14½ ounces) diced tomatoes with basil, oregano and garlic, undrained**
- 1½ **cups chicken broth**
- ¾ **cup frozen mixed vegetables**
- ½ **cup frozen cubed hash brown potatoes**
- 1 **teaspoon seafood seasoning**
- ¼ **teaspoon sugar**
- ¼ **teaspoon ground allspice**
  Dash cayenne pepper
- 2 **bay leaves**
- 1 **halibut fillet (6 ounces), cut into bite-size pieces**

1. In a large saucepan coated with cooking spray, saute shallots and garlic until tender. Add the tomatoes, broth, mixed vegetables, hash browns, seafood seasoning, sugar, allspice, cayenne and bay leaves. Bring to a boil. Reduce heat; simmer, uncovered, for 5 minutes or until vegetables are tender.
2. Add halibut; simmer 2-3 minutes longer or until fish turns opaque. Just before serving, discard bay leaves.

LAUREN'S BOUILLABAISSE

Lauren's Bouillabaisse

Bouillabaisse is a traditional fish stew that originated in the French Mediterranean port of Marseille. My version brims with an assortment of seafood. I serve it with savory sourdough croutons.

—**LAUREN COVAS** NEW BRUNSWICK, NJ

PREP: 30 MIN. • **COOK:** 20 MIN.
MAKES: 12 SERVINGS

- ⅔ **cup chopped roasted sweet red pepper, drained**
- ¼ **cup reduced-fat mayonnaise**

CROUTONS

- 6 **slices sourdough bread**
- 1 **garlic clove, halved**

BOUILLABAISSE

- 1 **medium onion, chopped**
- 1 **tablespoon olive oil**
- 2 **garlic cloves, minced**
- 2 **plum tomatoes, chopped**
- ½ **teaspoon saffron threads or 2 teaspoons ground turmeric**
- 3½ **cups cubed red potatoes**
- 2½ **cups thinly sliced fennel bulb**
- 1 **carton (32 ounces) reduced-sodium chicken broth**
- 3 **cups clam juice**
- 2 **teaspoons dried tarragon**
- 24 **fresh littleneck clams**
- 24 **fresh mussels, scrubbed and beards removed**
- 1 **pound red snapper fillet, cut into 2-inch pieces**
- ¾ **pound uncooked large shrimp, peeled and deveined**
- ¼ **cup minced fresh parsley**

1. Place red pepper and mayonnaise in a food processor; cover and process until smooth. Refrigerate until serving.
2. For croutons, rub one side of each bread slice with garlic; discard garlic. Cut bread slices in half. Place on an ungreased baking sheet. Bake at 400 for 4-5 minutes on each side or until lightly browned.
3. In a stockpot, saute onion in oil until tender. Add garlic; cook 1 minute longer. Reduce heat; stir in tomatoes and saffron. Add the potatoes, fennel, broth, clam juice and tarragon. Bring to a boil. Reduce the heat; simmer, uncovered, for 10-12 minutes or until potatoes are almost tender.
4. Add the clams, mussels, snapper and shrimp. Cook bouillabaisse, stirring occasionally, for 10-15 minutes or until clams and mussels open and fish flakes easily with a fork. Discard any unopened clams or mussels. Spoon into bowls; sprinkle with parsley. Spread pepper mayo over croutons; serve with bouillabaisse.

Andouille-Shrimp Cream Soup

Try my variation on a creamy southern Louisiana corn stew. The bold flavor of andouille sausage blends beautifully with the shrimp and subtle spices.

—JUDY ARMSTRONG PRAIRIEVILLE, LA

PREP: 20 MIN. • **COOK:** 30 MIN.
MAKES: 7 SERVINGS

- ½ **pound fully cooked andouille sausage links, thinly sliced**
- 1 **medium onion, chopped**
- 2 **celery ribs, thinly sliced**
- 1 **medium sweet red pepper, chopped**
- 1 **medium green pepper, chopped**
- 1 **jalapeno pepper, seeded and chopped**
- ¼ **cup butter, cubed**
- 3 **garlic cloves, minced**
- 2 **cups fresh or frozen corn, thawed**
- 4 **plum tomatoes, chopped**
- 1 **cup vegetable broth**
- 2 **tablespoons minced fresh thyme or 2 teaspoons dried thyme**
- 1 **teaspoon chili powder**
- ½ **teaspoon salt**
- ½ **teaspoon pepper**
- ¼ **to ½ teaspoon cayenne pepper**
- 1 **pound uncooked medium shrimp, peeled and deveined**
- 1 **cup heavy whipping cream**

1. In a large skillet, saute the first six ingredients in butter until vegetables are tender. Add garlic; cook 1 minute longer. Add the corn, tomatoes, broth, thyme, chili powder, salt, pepper and cayenne. Bring to a boil. Reduce heat; simmer, uncovered, for 10 minutes.
2. Stir in shrimp and cream. Bring to a gentle boil. Simmer, uncovered, for 8-10 minutes or until shrimp turn pink. **NOTE** *Wear disposable gloves when cutting hot peppers; the oils can burn skin. Avoid touching your face.*

COCONUT SHRIMP CHOWDER

Coconut Shrimp Chowder

After eating a coconut soup at a Thai restaurant, I added coconut milk to my fish chowder recipe. The fresh, simple ingredients allow the seafood to shine.

—MICHALENE BASKETT DECATUR, GA

START TO FINISH: 30 MIN.
MAKES: 5 SERVINGS

- 1 **medium onion, chopped**
- 2 **teaspoons canola oil**
- ¼ **teaspoon cayenne pepper**
- 2 **cups chicken broth**
- 1 **package (10 ounces) frozen corn**
- ¼ **teaspoon salt**
- ¼ **teaspoon pepper**
- 1 **can (13.66 ounces) coconut milk**
- 1 **pound uncooked medium shrimp, peeled and deveined**
- ¼ **cup lime juice**
- 2 **tablespoons minced fresh cilantro**
- 1 **medium ripe avocado, peeled and cubed**

1. In a large saucepan, saute onion in oil until tender. Add pepper. Stir in the broth, corn, salt and pepper. Bring to a boil. Reduce heat; simmer, uncovered, for 5 minutes. Remove from the heat and stir in coconut milk. Cool slightly.
2. In a food processor, process soup in batches until blended. Return all to pan. Add shrimp; cook and stir over medium heat for 5-6 minutes or until shrimp turn pink. Stir in lime juice and cilantro. Garnish servings with avocado.

ANDOUILLE-SHRIMP CREAM SOUP

Veggie Salmon Chowder

I created this chowder using up odds and ends in my fridge. It's become a mainstay.
—**LIV VORS** PETERBOROUGH, ON

START TO FINISH: 30 MIN.
MAKES: 2 SERVINGS

- 1 medium sweet potato, peeled and cut into ½-inch cubes
- 1 cup reduced-sodium chicken broth
- ½ cup fresh or frozen corn
- ½ small onion, chopped
- 2 garlic cloves, minced
- 1½ cups fresh spinach, torn
- ½ cup flaked smoked salmon fillet
- 1 teaspoon pickled jalapeno slices, chopped
- 1 tablespoon cornstarch
- ½ cup 2% milk
- 1 tablespoon minced fresh cilantro
  Dash pepper

1. In a large saucepan, combine the first five ingredients; bring to a boil. Reduce heat; simmer, covered, 8-10 minutes or until potato is tender.
2. Stir in spinach, salmon and jalapeno; cook 1-2 minutes or until spinach is wilted. In a small bowl, mix cornstarch and milk until smooth; stir into soup. Bring to a boil; cook and stir 2 minutes or until thickened. Stir in cilantro and pepper.

DID YOU KNOW?

Smoked salmon is fresh salmon that has been processed with cold or hot smoking. Cold-smoked salmon or lox has been brined or cured in salt and/or sugar, then smoked at 70-90 degrees. Hot-smoked salmon has been processed for several hours at 120-180 degrees. Hot-smoked salmon is commonly thicker than lox, usually the whole fillet.

VEGGIE SALMON CHOWDER

Quick Shrimp Gumbo

This hearty gumbo is a favorite. I've made it with all shrimp or with all turkey sausage, both with equally good results. Cooking it in the microwave speeds up prep time.

—MRS. LEO MERCHANT JACKSON, MS

START TO FINISH: 20 MIN.
MAKES: 4 SERVINGS

- 1 **cup finely chopped onion**
- 3 **garlic cloves, minced**
- 1 **teaspoon canola oil**
- ½ **pound reduced-fat cooked kielbasa or Polish sausage, halved and cut into ¼-inch slices**
- 1½ **cups chopped green pepper**
- 1 **can (14½ ounces) diced tomatoes, undrained**
- 1 **cup reduced-sodium chicken broth**
- 1 **bay leaf**
- 1 **teaspoon Italian seasoning**
- ½ **teaspoon salt**
- ½ **teaspoon chili powder**
- ¼ **teaspoon pepper**
- ⅛ **teaspoon hot pepper sauce**
- ¾ **pound uncooked medium shrimp, peeled and deveined**
- ½ **cup uncooked instant rice**
  Lemon slices, optional

1. In a large saucepan, saute onion and garlic in oil for 2 minutes or until crisp-tender. Stir in sausage; cook and stir for 2 minutes or until sausage begins to brown. Add green pepper; cook and stir for 2 minutes or until crisp-tender. Stir in the tomatoes, broth, seasonings and hot pepper sauce. Bring to a boil.

2. Cook, uncovered, for 2 minutes or until heated through. Stir in shrimp. Cook 3-4 minutes longer or until shrimp turn pink. Stir in rice. Remove from the heat.

3. Cover and let stand for 5 minutes or until rice is tender. Discard bay leaf. Serve with lemon slices if desired.

Tomato Clam Chowder

Steaming bowls of this Manhattan-style clam chowder are a special treat on a cold night or any time you're craving something different.

—WEDA MOSELLIE PHILLIPSBURG, NJ

PREP: 20 MIN. • **COOK:** 35 MIN.
MAKES: 11 SERVINGS (2¾ QUARTS)

- 5 **to 6 medium potatoes, peeled and diced**
- 6 **bacon strips, diced**
- 1 **small onion, finely chopped**
- 2 **celery ribs, chopped**
- 1 **garlic clove, minced**
- 2 **cans (6 ounces each) minced clams**
- 2 **cups water**
- 1 **can (15 ounces) tomato sauce**
- 1 **can (14½ ounces) diced tomatoes, undrained**
- ½ **to 1 teaspoon pepper**
- ¼ **teaspoon salt**
- 2 **teaspoons minced fresh parsley**

1. Place the potatoes in a Dutch oven and cover with water. Bring to a boil. Reduce heat; cover and cook for 10-15 minutes or until tender.

2. Meanwhile, in a large skillet, cook bacon over medium heat until crisp. Using a slotted spoon, remove to paper towels; drain, reserving 2 tablespoons drippings. In the drippings, saute the onion and celery until tender. Add garlic; cook 1 minute longer.

3. Drain clams, reserving liquid; set clams aside. Drain potatoes and return to the pan. Add the onion mixture, bacon and reserved clam liquid. Stir in the water, tomato sauce, tomatoes, pepper and salt. Bring to a boil. Reduce heat; simmer, uncovered, for 30-35 minutes or until heated through. Add clams and parsley; simmer 5 minutes longer.

TOMATO CLAM CHOWDER

SCALLOP & SHRIMP CHOWDER

Scallop & Shrimp Chowder

Shrimp and scallops make this rich, cheesy chowder extra special. Garnish with crispy bacon and it becomes irresistible.

—*TASTE OF HOME* TEST KITCHEN

PREP: 15 MIN. • **COOK:** 20 MIN.
MAKES: 6 SERVINGS

- 6 **bacon strips, chopped**
- 2 **celery ribs, finely chopped**
- ½ **cup chopped sweet orange pepper**
- 1 **small onion, finely chopped**
- 2 **garlic cloves, minced**
- ¼ **cup all-purpose flour**
- 1 **can (14½ ounces) chicken broth**
- 2 **cups 2% milk**
- 2 **medium red potatoes, cubed**
- 1 **teaspoon seafood seasoning**
- ¼ **teaspoon salt**
- ½ **pound uncooked medium shrimp, peeled and deveined**
- ½ **pound bay scallops**
- 1½ **cups (6 ounces) shredded cheddar cheese**

1. In a large saucepan, cook bacon over medium heat until crisp. Remove to paper towels with a slotted spoon; drain, reserving 2 tablespoons drippings.

2. In the drippings, saute the celery, orange pepper and onion until crisp-tender. Add garlic; cook 1 minute longer. Stir in flour until blended; gradually add broth and milk. Bring to a boil; cook and stir for 1 minute or until thickened.

3. Add the potatoes, seafood seasoning and salt; return to a boil. Reduce heat; cover and simmer for 10-15 minutes or until potatoes are tender.

4. Add shrimp and scallops; cook and stir for 3-4 minutes or until shrimp turn pink and scallops are opaque. Stir in cheese until melted. Garnish each serving with bacon.

Cream of Mussel Soup

Every New England cook has her or his own version of mussel soup, depending on the regional herbs and cooking customs. Feel free to start with my recipe, and develop your unique variation.

—**DONNA NOEL** GRAY, ME

PREP: 35 MIN. • **COOK:** 10 MIN.
MAKES: 5 SERVINGS

- 3 **pounds fresh mussels (about 5 dozen), scrubbed, beards removed**
- 2 **medium onions, finely chopped**
- 2 **celery ribs, finely chopped**
- 1 **cup water**
- 1 **cup white wine or chicken broth**
- 1 **bottle (8 ounces) clam juice**
- ¼ **cup minced fresh parsley**
- 2 **garlic cloves, minced**
- ¼ **teaspoon salt**
- ¼ **teaspoon pepper**
- 1 **cup half-and-half cream**

1. Tap mussels; discard any that do not close. Set aside. In a stockpot, combine the onions, celery, water, wine or broth, clam juice, parsley, garlic, salt and pepper.

2. Bring to a boil. Reduce heat; add mussels. Cover and simmer for 5-6 minutes or until mussels have opened. Remove mussels with a slotted spoon, discarding any unopened mussels; set aside opened mussels and keep warm.

3. Cool cooking liquid slightly. In a blender, cover and process cooking liquid in batches until blended. Return all to pan. Add cream and reserved mussels; heat through (do not boil).

CREAM OF MUSSEL SOUP

CARROT BROCCOLI SOUP

Carrot Broccoli Soup

This soup is a staple at our house. It's fast, easy and filled to the brim with carrots and broccoli. Even picky eaters like it.

—**SANDY SMITH** LONDON, ON

PREP: 15 MIN. • **COOK:** 20 MIN.
MAKES: 4 SERVINGS

- 1 medium onion, chopped
- 2 medium carrots, chopped
- 2 celery ribs, chopped
- 1 tablespoon butter
- 3 cups fresh broccoli florets
- 3 cups fat-free milk, divided
- ¾ teaspoon salt
- ½ teaspoon dried thyme
- ⅛ teaspoon pepper
- 3 tablespoons all-purpose flour

1. In a large saucepan coated with cooking spray, cook the onion, carrots and celery in butter for 3 minutes. Add broccoli; cook 3 minutes longer. Stir in 2¾ cups milk, salt, thyme and pepper.
2. Bring to a boil. Reduce heat; cover and simmer for 5-10 minutes or until vegetables are tender. Combine the flour and remaining milk until smooth; gradually stir into soup. Bring to a boil; cook 2 minutes longer or until thickened.

Garlic-Basil Tortellini Soup

Serve this with a sandwich or in a big bowl for a main-dish meal.

—**LINDA KEES** BOISE, ID

START TO FINISH: 25 MIN.
MAKES: 4 SERVINGS

- 2 garlic cloves, minced
- 1 teaspoon butter
- 2 cans (14½ ounces each) reduced-sodium vegetable broth or chicken broth
- ½ cup water
- ⅓ cup minced fresh basil
- ¼ teaspoon pepper
- 2½ cups frozen cheese tortellini
- 1 can (19 ounces) white kidney beans or cannellini beans, rinsed and drained
- 2 tablespoons balsamic vinegar
- ¼ cup shredded Parmesan cheese

In a large saucepan, saute garlic in butter until tender. Stir in the broth, water, basil and pepper. Bring to a boil. Stir in tortellini. Reduce heat; simmer, uncovered, for about 3 minutes or until tortellini begins to float. Stir in beans and vinegar; heat through. Sprinkle with Parmesan cheese.

⑤INGREDIENTS # Cool as a Cucumber Soup

Chilled soups make a refreshing appetizer or side on a hot summer day. The bright bursts of dill in my soup provide a pleasant contrast to the mild flavor of cucumber.

—**DEIRDRE COX** KANSAS CITY, MO

PREP: 15 MIN. + STANDING
MAKES: 5 SERVINGS

- 1 pound cucumbers, peeled, seeded and sliced
- ½ teaspoon salt
- 1½ cups fat-free plain yogurt
- 1 green onion, coarsely chopped
- 1 garlic clove, minced
- 4½ teaspoons snipped fresh dill
  Additional chopped green onion and snipped fresh dill

1. In a colander set over a bowl, toss cucumbers with salt. Let stand for 30 minutes. Squeeze and pat dry.
2. Place the cucumbers, yogurt, onion and garlic in a food processor; cover and process until smooth. Stir in dill. Serve immediately in chilled bowls. Garnish with additional onion and dill.

COOL AS A CUCUMBER SOUP

Broccoli Cheese Soup

When my husband and I visit fresh-food stands, we often come home with more vegetables than we can eat. I lightened up this tarragon-flavored soup to use up the broccoli we brought.

—MARGE HILL GLENSIDE, PA

PREP: 20 MIN. • **COOK:** 35 MIN. + COOLING
MAKES: 4 SERVINGS

- ½ cup chopped sweet onion
- 3 garlic cloves, minced
- 2 tablespoons all-purpose flour
- 1 can (14½ ounces) reduced-sodium vegetable broth or chicken broth
- 4 cups fresh broccoli florets
- ¼ to ½ teaspoon dried tarragon
- ¼ teaspoon dried thyme
- ⅛ teaspoon pepper
- 1½ cups 1% milk
- 1¼ cups shredded reduced-fat cheddar cheese, divided

1. In a large nonstick saucepan coated with cooking spray, saute onion until tender. Add garlic; cook 1 minute longer. Stir in flour until blended. Gradually whisk in broth. Bring to a boil; cook and stir for 1-2 minutes or until slightly thickened.

2. Add the broccoli, tarragon, thyme and pepper; return to a boil. Reduce heat; cover and simmer for 10 minutes or until broccoli is tender. Add milk; cook, uncovered, 5 minutes longer. Remove from the heat; cool to room temperature.

3. In a blender, process soup in batches until smooth. Return all to the pan; heat through. Reduce heat. Add 1 cup of cheese; stir just until melted. Serve immediately. Garnish with remaining cheese.

CHILLED SUMMER BERRY BISQUE

Chilled Summer Berry Bisque

A blend of yogurt and spices thickens this cold blueberry soup and tempers the sweetness. It makes an attractive and healthy first course for a summer menu.

—ARLENE KNICK NEWPORT NEWS, VA

PREP: 20 MIN. + CHILLING
MAKES: 8 SERVINGS

- 4½ cups fresh or frozen blueberries, thawed, divided
- 1 cup unsweetened apple juice
- 1 cup orange juice
- ¼ cup honey
- 2 teaspoons minced fresh gingerroot
- 1 teaspoon grated orange peel
- ¼ teaspoon ground cinnamon
- ⅛ teaspoon ground nutmeg
- 2 cups (16 ounces) plain yogurt
  Fresh mint leaves

1. In a large saucepan, combine 4 cups blueberries, apple juice, orange juice, honey, ginger, orange peel, cinnamon and nutmeg. Bring to a boil, stirring occasionally. Cool slightly.

2. In a blender, process blueberry mixture and yogurt in batches until smooth. Refrigerate until chilled. Just before serving, garnish with mint and remaining blueberries.

HEARTY QUINOA & CORN CHOWDER

Hearty Quinoa & Corn Chowder

My grandmother lived in the Appalachian Mountains and served straight-from-the-garden corn and beans. I gave her dish a modern twist by adding quinoa and herbs.

—**KARI NAPIER** LOUISVILLE, KY

PREP: 25 MIN. + STANDING • **COOK:** 15 MIN.
MAKES: 14 SERVINGS (¾ CUP EACH)

- 3 **medium sweet red peppers**
- 1 **cup quinoa, rinsed**
- 1 **tablespoon butter**
- 1 **tablespoon olive oil**
- 1 **medium onion, chopped**
- 2 **garlic cloves, minced**
- ⅓ **cup all-purpose flour**
- 4 **cups vegetable stock**
- 2 **cups heavy whipping cream**
- 6 **medium ears sweet corn, kernels removed (about 4 cups) or 2 packages (10 ounces) frozen corn, thawed**
- 1 **can (15 ounces) pinto beans, rinsed and drained**
- 2 **tablespoons minced fresh parsley**
- ½ **teaspoon minced fresh thyme**
- 1½ **teaspoons salt**
- ½ **teaspoon pepper**

1. Broil peppers 4 in. from the heat until skins blister, about 5 minutes. With tongs, rotate peppers a quarter turn. Broil and rotate until all sides are blistered and blackened. Immediately place peppers in a large bowl; cover and let stand for 20 minutes.

2. Peel off and discard charred skin. Remove stems and seeds. Finely chop peppers.

3. Meanwhile, in a Dutch oven, cook and stir quinoa over medium-high heat for 3-5 minutes or until lightly toasted; remove from the pan.

4. In the same pan, heat butter and oil over medium-high heat. Add onion; cook and stir until tender. Add garlic; cook 1 minute longer. Stir in flour until blended. Gradually whisk in stock and cream.

5. Add the corn, beans, roasted peppers and quinoa; bring to a boil, stirring frequently. Reduce heat; simmer, uncovered, for 15-20 minutes or until quinoa is tender, stirring occasionally. Stir in the remaining ingredients.

Curried Sweet Potato Soup

I serve this cream soup as a fabulous first course for special dinners. I double the recipe because family and friends usually ask for seconds.

—**PAULA MARCHESI** LENHARTSVILLE, PA

PREP: 30 MIN. • **COOK:** 45 MIN.
MAKES: 8 SERVINGS

- 1 **medium onion, chopped**
- 2 **tablespoons butter**
- 2 **teaspoons curry powder**
- 2 **teaspoons minced fresh gingerroot**
- ½ **teaspoon salt**
- 2 **pounds sweet potatoes, peeled and cubed**
- 1 **can (14½ ounces) vegetable broth**
- 1¼ **cups water**
- 1 **can (13.66 ounces) coconut milk**
- ¾ **cup half-and-half cream**
- ⅓ **cup minced fresh cilantro**
  Optional garnishes: minced fresh cilantro, toasted flaked coconut and toasted chopped pecans

1. In a large saucepan, saute onion in butter until tender. Stir in the curry, gingerroot and salt; cook 1 minute longer. Stir in the potatoes, broth and water. Bring to a boil. Reduce heat; cover and simmer for 15-20 minutes or until sweet potatoes are tender. Cool slightly.

2. In a blender, process soup in batches until smooth. Return all to the pan. Stir in the coconut milk, cream and cilantro; heat through. Garnish with cilantro, coconut and pecans if desired.

CURRIED SWEET POTATO SOUP

Vegetarian Polka Dot Stew

Here's a speedy and satisfying version of traditional minestrone. Its name is derived from the polka-dot shapes of the black beans, couscous and sliced baby carrots.

—TEAGAN O'TOOLE BOSTON, MA

START TO FINISH: 30 MIN.
MAKES: 5 SERVINGS

- 2 **cups water**
- 1 **cup uncooked pearl (Israeli) couscous**
- 2 **medium carrots, sliced**
- 1 **plum tomato, chopped**
- ¼ **cup chopped onion**
- 1 **garlic clove, minced**
- 2 **cans (19 ounces each) ready-to-serve tomato soup**
- 1 **can (15 ounces) black beans, rinsed and drained**
- 1 **package (10 ounces) frozen chopped spinach, thawed and squeezed dry**
- 1 **tablespoon minced fresh basil or 1 teaspoon dried basil**
- ½ **teaspoon salt**
- ½ **teaspoon dried oregano**
- ½ **teaspoon dried marjoram**
- ¼ **teaspoon pepper**
  Shredded Parmesan cheese

In a large saucepan, bring water to a boil. Stir in the couscous, carrots, tomato, onion and garlic. Bring to a boil. Reduce heat; simmer, uncovered, for 10-15 minutes or until tender and water is absorbed. Stir in the remaining ingredients; heat through. Sprinkle with cheese.
NOTE *You may substitute 1 cup quick-cooking barley for the couscous if desired.*

YELLOW TOMATO SOUP WITH GOAT CHEESE CROUTONS

Yellow Tomato Soup with Goat Cheese Croutons

Get your next dinner party off to an impressive start with this savory cream soup. Guests will love the roasted tomato flavor and crispy croutons. You can also grill the tomatoes once the weather turns warm.

—PATTERSON WATKINS PHILADELPHIA, PA

PREP: 45 MIN. • **COOK:** 30 MIN.
MAKES: 6 SERVINGS

- 3 **pounds yellow tomatoes, halved (about 9 medium)**
- 2 **tablespoons olive oil, divided**
- 4 **garlic cloves, minced, divided**
- 1 **teaspoon salt**
- 1 **teaspoon pepper**
- 1 **teaspoon minced fresh rosemary**
- 1 **teaspoon minced fresh thyme**
- 1 **large onion, chopped**
- 1 **cup vegetable broth**
- ½ **cup milk**
- ½ **cup heavy whipping cream**

CROUTONS
- 12 **slices French bread baguette (½ inch thick)**
- 1 **tablespoon olive oil**
- 2 **tablespoons prepared pesto**
- ½ **cup crumbled goat cheese**
- 1 **teaspoon pepper**

1. Place tomatoes, cut side down, in a greased 15x10x1-in. baking pan; brush with 1 tablespoon oil. Sprinkle with 2 teaspoons garlic and the salt, pepper, rosemary and thyme.
2. Bake at 400° for 25-30 minutes or until tomatoes are tender and skins are charred. Cool slightly. Discard tomato skins. In a blender, process tomatoes until blended.
3. In a large saucepan, saute onion in remaining oil until tender. Add remaining garlic; saute 1 minute longer. Add broth and milk; bring to a boil. Carefully stir in tomato puree. Simmer, uncovered, for 15 minutes to allow flavors to blend. Stir in cream; heat through (do not boil).
4. Meanwhile, for croutons, place bread on a baking sheet and brush with oil. Bake for 5-6 minutes or until golden brown. Spread with pesto and sprinkle with goat cheese and pepper. Bake 2 minutes longer. Ladle soup into bowls and top with croutons.

Ginger Butternut Squash Bisque

This soup suits both my husband's tastes and mine. I like that it's meatless, and he likes that it's a meal on its own. The couple who introduced us to each other made it for us on a cold night, and we've been hooked ever since.

—CARA MCDONALD WINTER PARK, CO

PREP: 25 MIN. • **BAKE:** 40 MIN. + COOLING
MAKES: 6 SERVINGS

- 1 medium butternut squash (about 3 pounds)
- 1 tablespoon olive oil
- 2 medium carrots, finely chopped
- 1 medium onion, chopped
- 2 garlic cloves, minced
- 2 teaspoons minced fresh gingerroot
- 2 teaspoons curry powder
- 1 can (14½ ounces) vegetable broth
- 1 can (13.66 ounces) coconut milk
- 1 teaspoon salt
- ½ teaspoon pepper
- 2 cups hot cooked brown rice
- ¼ cup flaked coconut, toasted
- ¼ cup salted peanuts, coarsely chopped
- ¼ cup minced fresh cilantro

1. Preheat oven to 400°. Cut squash lengthwise in half; remove and discard seeds. Place squash in a greased shallow roasting pan, cut side down. Roast 40-45 minutes or until squash is tender. Cool slightly.

2. In a large saucepan, heat oil over medium heat. Add carrots and onion; cook and stir until tender. Add garlic, ginger and curry powder; cook and stir 1 minute longer. Add broth; bring to a boil. Reduce heat; simmer, uncovered, 10-12 minutes or until carrots are tender.

3. Scoop pulp from squash; discard skins. Add squash, coconut milk, salt and pepper to carrot mixture; bring just to a boil, stirring occasionally. Remove from heat; cool slightly. Process in batches in a blender until smooth.

4. Return to pan; heat through. Top servings with rice, coconut, peanuts and cilantro.

NOTE *To toast coconut, spread in a dry skillet; cook and stir over low heat until lightly browned.*

Chilled Melon Soup

Looking for something to put pizazz in a summer luncheon? Try this pretty, refreshing soup with a kick of cayenne pepper to get the conversation going.

—MARY LOU TIMPSON COLORADO CITY, AZ

PREP: 25 MIN. + CHILLING
MAKES: 6 SERVINGS

- ¾ cup orange juice
- 1 cup (8 ounces) plain yogurt
- 1 medium cantaloupe, peeled, seeded and cubed
- 1 tablespoon honey
- ¼ teaspoon salt
- ¼ teaspoon ground nutmeg
- ⅛ teaspoon cayenne pepper
- 6 mint sprigs

Place the orange juice, yogurt and cantaloupe in a blender; cover and process until pureed. Add the honey, salt, nutmeg and cayenne; cover and process until smooth. Refrigerate for at least 1 hour before serving. Garnish with mint sprigs.

GINGER BUTTERNUT SQUASH BISQUE

CHEESE-TOPPED VEGETABLE SOUP

Cheese-Topped Vegetable Soup

Just-picked garden flavor makes this hearty vegetable soup a summer staple. It warms the soul.

—**ANNA MINEGAR** ZOLFO SPRINGS, FL

PREP: 15 MIN. • **COOK:** 25 MIN.
MAKES: 4 CUPS

- 1 can (28 ounces) Italian stewed tomatoes
- 1½ cups water
- 1 can (8¾ ounces) whole kernel corn, drained
- ¾ cup chopped sweet red pepper
- ⅔ cup chopped red onion
- ⅔ cup chopped green pepper
- ¼ cup minced fresh basil
- 1 garlic clove, minced
- ½ teaspoon salt
- ¼ teaspoon pepper
- ½ cup salad croutons
- ¼ cup shredded part-skim mozzarella cheese

1. In a large saucepan, combine the first 10 ingredients. Bring to a boil. Reduce heat; simmer, uncovered, for 20-25 minutes or until heated through and vegetables are tender.
2. Ladle the soup into ovenproof bowls. Top each with croutons and cheese. Broil 6 in. from the heat until cheese is melted.

Watermelon Gazpacho

My refreshing gazpacho is delightfully simple and elegant. Serve as a side or with pita and hummus for a meal.

—**NICOLE DEELAH** NASHVILLE, TN

START TO FINISH: 25 MIN.
MAKES: 4 SERVINGS

- 4 cups cubed watermelon, seeded, divided
- 2 tablespoons lime juice
- 1 tablespoon grated lime peel
- 1 teaspoon minced fresh gingerroot
- 1 teaspoon salt
- 1 cup chopped tomato
- ½ cup chopped cucumber
- ½ cup chopped green pepper
- ¼ cup minced fresh cilantro
- 2 tablespoons chopped green onion
- 1 tablespoon finely chopped seeded jalapeno pepper

1. Puree 3 cups watermelon in a blender. Cut remaining watermelon into ½-inch pieces; set aside.
2. In a large bowl, combine the watermelon puree, lime juice, lime peel, ginger and salt. Stir in the tomato, cucumber, green pepper, cilantro, onion, jalapeno and cubed watermelon. Chill until serving.
NOTE *Wear disposable gloves when cutting hot peppers; the oils can burn skin. Avoid touching your face.*

TOP TIP

Here's an easy way to cut and seed a jalapeno pepper: Cut off the top and then slice the pepper in half lengthwise; use a small melon baller to scrape out the seeds and membranes.

WATERMELON GAZPACHO

FREEZE IT (5) INGREDIENTS

Roasted Tomato Soup

Just before the first frost, we gather up all of the tomatoes left in my mom's garden to create this flavor-packed soup. It may seem like a lot of garlic, but it becomes mellow and almost sweet once it's roasted. It's delicious with grilled cheese sandwiches or toasted bread spread with pesto.

—**KAITLYN LERDAHL** MADISON, WI

PREP: 25 MIN. • **COOK:** 40 MIN.
MAKES: 6 SERVINGS

- 15 **large tomatoes (5 pounds), seeded and quartered**
- ¼ **cup plus 2 tablespoons canola oil, divided**
- 8 **garlic cloves, minced**
- 1 **large onion, chopped**
- 2 **cups water**
- 1 **teaspoon salt**
- ½ **teaspoon crushed red pepper flakes, optional**
- ½ **cup heavy whipping cream**
  Fresh basil leaves, optional

1. Preheat oven to 400°. Place tomatoes in a greased 15x10x1-in. baking pan. Combine ¼ cup oil and garlic; drizzle over tomatoes. Toss to coat. Bake 15-20 minutes or until softened, stirring occasionally. Remove and discard skins.

2. Meanwhile, in a Dutch oven, saute onion in remaining oil until tender. Add tomatoes, water, salt and, if desired, pepper flakes. Bring to a boil. Reduce heat; cover and simmer 30 minutes or until flavors are blended. Cool slightly.

3. In a blender, process soup in batches until smooth. Return to pan. Stir in cream and heat through.

FREEZER OPTION *Cool soup and transfer to freezer containers. Freeze up to 3 months. To use, thaw in the refrigerator overnight. Place in a large saucepan; heat through. Garnish with basil if desired.*

ROASTED TOMATO SOUP

ASPARAGUS SOUP WITH LEMON CREME FRAICHE

Asparagus Soup with Lemon Creme Fraiche

Here is a definite winner—a silky smooth, fresh asparagus soup. Serve it warm or chilled depending on the weather.

—**FERN VITENSE** TIPTON, IA

PREP: 25 MIN. • **COOK:** 25 MIN.
MAKES: 6 SERVINGS

- 1 tablespoon butter
- 1 tablespoon olive oil
- 1 small onion, chopped
- 4 cups cut fresh asparagus (1-inch pieces)
- 3 medium red potatoes, peeled and cubed
- 2 cans (14½ ounces each) vegetable broth
- 2 teaspoons grated lemon peel
- ½ teaspoon salt
- ½ teaspoon pepper
- ½ teaspoon ground coriander
- ¼ teaspoon ground ginger

GARNISH
- ¼ cup minced chives
- ¼ cup creme fraiche or sour cream
- 1 tablespoon lemon juice
- ½ teaspoon grated lemon peel

1. In a large saucepan, heat butter and oil over medium-high heat. Add onion; cook and stir until tender. Add asparagus and potatoes; cook 3 minutes longer. Stir in broth, lemon peel and seasonings. Bring to a boil. Reduce heat; simmer, covered, 15-20 minutes or until potatoes are tender.
2. Cool slightly. Process soup in batches in a blender until smooth. Return all to pan and heat through. Combine garnish ingredients; serve with soup.

Tomato Tortellini Soup

Here's a flavorful pasta soup that tastes homemade all the way. No one will guess you "cheated" with convenience items. Toss in extra tortellini to make it heartier.

—**SANDRA FICK** LINCOLN, NE

START TO FINISH: 25 MIN.
MAKES: 10 SERVINGS (2½ QUARTS)

- 1 package (9 ounces) refrigerated cheese tortellini
- 2 cans (10¾ ounces each) reduced-sodium condensed tomato soup, undiluted
- 2 cups vegetable broth
- 2 cups 2% milk
- 2 cups half-and-half cream
- ½ cup chopped oil-packed sun-dried tomatoes
- 1 teaspoon onion powder
- 1 teaspoon garlic powder
- 1 teaspoon dried basil
- ½ teaspoon salt
- ½ cup shredded Parmesan cheese
  Additional shredded Parmesan cheese, optional

1. Cook tortellini according to package directions.
2. Meanwhile, in a Dutch oven, combine the soup, broth, milk, cream, tomatoes and seasonings. Heat through, stirring frequently. Drain tortellini; carefully add to soup. Stir in cheese. Sprinkle each serving with additional cheese if desired.

TOMATO TORTELLINI SOUP

CARROT SOUP

Carrot Soup

Fat-free half-and-half gives velvety flair to this colorful recipe. It makes a nice change of pace from tomato soup.

—**BARBARA RICHARD** HOUSTON, OH

PREP: 20 MIN. • **COOK:** 35 MIN.
MAKES: 6 SERVINGS

- ¾ **cup finely chopped onion**
- 3 **garlic cloves, minced**
- 2 **teaspoons olive oil**
- 3 **cans (14½ ounces each) reduced-sodium vegetable broth or chicken broth**
- 6 **cups sliced carrots (about 2½ pounds)**
- ¾ **cup cubed peeled potatoes**
- 1 **teaspoon salt**
- 1 **teaspoon dried thyme**
- ¼ **teaspoon pepper**
- 1 **bay leaf**
- 1 **cup fat-free half-and-half**

1. In a large saucepan, saute onion and garlic in oil until tender. Add the broth, carrots, potatoes, salt, thyme, pepper and bay leaf. Bring to a boil. Reduce heat; cover and simmer for 20-30 minutes or until vegetables are very tender.

2. Remove from the heat; cool slightly. Discard bay leaf. In a blender, puree carrot mixture in batches. Return to the pan. Stir in half-and-half; heat through (do not boil).

Christmas Tortellini & Spinach Soup

START TO FINISH: 25 MIN.
MAKES: 6 SERVINGS

- 2 **cans (14½ ounces each) vegetable broth**
- 1 **package (9 ounces) refrigerated cheese tortellini or tortellini of your choice**
- 1 **can (15 ounces) white kidney or cannellini beans, rinsed and drained**
- 1 **can (14½ ounces) Italian diced tomatoes, undrained**
- ¼ **teaspoon salt**
- ⅛ **teaspoon pepper**
- 3 **cups fresh baby spinach**
- 3 **tablespoons minced fresh basil**
- ¼ **cup shredded Asiago cheese**

1. In a large saucepan, bring broth to a boil. Add tortellini; reduce heat. Simmer, uncovered, for 5 minutes. Stir in the beans, tomatoes, salt and pepper; return to a simmer. Cook 4-5 minutes longer or until tortellini are tender.

2. Stir in spinach and basil; cook until spinach is wilted. Top servings with cheese.

The first time I made this soup was in the summer, but when I saw its bright red and green colors, I thought that it would make a perfect first course for Christmas dinner.
—**MARIETTA SLATER** JUSTIN, TX

CHRISTMAS TORTELLINI & SPINACH SOUP

Spicy Peanut Soup

After enjoying a similar Thai-inspired soup at a cafe, I duplicated it at home. You could also add chicken or rice.

—**LISA MEREDITH** ST. PAUL, MN

PREP: 35 MIN. • **COOK:** 20 MIN.
MAKES: 7 SERVINGS

- 2 **medium carrots, chopped**
- 1 **small onion, chopped**
- 2 **tablespoons olive oil**
- 2 **garlic cloves, minced**
- 1 **large sweet potato, peeled and cubed**
- ½ **cup chunky peanut butter**
- 2 **tablespoons red curry paste**
- 2 **cans (14½ ounces each) vegetable broth**
- 1 **can (14½ ounces) fire-roasted diced tomatoes, undrained**
- 1 **bay leaf**
- 1 **fresh thyme sprig**
- ½ **teaspoon pepper**
- ½ **cup unsalted peanuts**

1. In a large saucepan, cook carrots and onion in oil over medium heat for 2 minutes. Add garlic; cook 1 minute longer.

2. Stir in sweet potato; cook 2 minutes longer. Stir in peanut butter and curry paste until blended. Add the broth, tomatoes, bay leaf, thyme and pepper.

3. Bring to a boil. Reduce heat; cover and simmer for 15-20 minutes or until sweet potatoes and carrots are tender. (Soup will appear curdled.) Discard bay leaf and thyme sprig. Stir soup until blended. Sprinkle with peanuts.

ITALIAN SAUSAGE BEAN SOUP

Southwest Bean Soup

I created this nutritious recipe while trying to lose weight. My calorie-conscious friends say it's the best soup they've ever eaten. Cilantro and vegetables give it a lively, satisfying flavor.

—**MARIANNE BROWN** GLENDALE, AZ

PREP: 15 MIN. • **COOK:** 30 MIN.
MAKES: 13 SERVINGS (3¼ QUARTS)

- 1 **large onion, chopped**
- 1 **medium green pepper, chopped**
- 3 **garlic cloves, minced**
- 3 **cans (14½ ounces each) reduced-sodium beef broth**
- 2 **cans (15 ounces each) black beans, rinsed and drained**
- 1 **can (28 ounces) diced tomatoes, undrained**
- 2 **cans (4 ounces each) chopped green chilies**
- 1 **cup frozen corn**
- 1½ **teaspoons chili powder**
- 1 **teaspoon ground cumin**
- ½ **cup minced fresh cilantro**

1. In a large nonstick saucepan coated with cooking spray, cook and stir onion and green pepper over medium heat until almost tender. Add garlic; cook 1 minute longer.

2. Stir in the broth, beans, tomatoes, chilies, corn, chili powder and cumin. Bring to a boil. Reduce heat; cover and simmer for 20 minutes. Stir in cilantro.

SOUTHWEST BEAN SOUP

Italian Sausage Bean Soup

During the frigid months, you'll often find me putting on a big pot of this soothing soup. I love that I can turn my attention to other tasks while the soup cooks.

—**GLENNA REIMER** GIG HARBOR, WA

PREP: 20 MIN. • **COOK:** 1½ HOURS
MAKES: 8 SERVINGS (3 QUARTS)

- 1 **pound bulk Italian sausage**
- 1 **medium onion, finely chopped**
- 3 **garlic cloves, sliced**
- 4 **cans (14½ ounces each) reduced-sodium chicken broth**
- 2 **cans (15 ounces each) pinto beans, rinsed and drained**
- 1 **can (14½ ounces) diced tomatoes, undrained**
- 1 **cup medium pearl barley**
- 1 **large carrot, sliced**
- 1 **celery rib, sliced**
- 1 **teaspoon minced fresh sage**
- ½ **teaspoon minced fresh rosemary or ⅛ teaspoon dried rosemary, crushed**
- 6 **cups chopped fresh kale**

1. In a Dutch oven, cook sausage and onion over medium heat until meat is no longer pink. Add garlic; cook 1 minute longer. Drain.

2. Stir in the broth, beans, tomatoes, barley, carrot, celery, sage and rosemary. Bring to a boil. Reduce heat; cover and simmer for 45 minutes.

3. Stir in the kale; return to a boil. Reduce heat; cover and simmer for 25-30 minutes or until the vegetables are tender.

Pasta and White Bean Soup With Sun-Dried Tomatoes

This is my go-to recipe when I'm in the mood for filling comfort foods like soup and pasta. Vegetarians will love it because it's hearty but not too heavy.

—MARY SWARTZ PALM DESERT, CA

PREP: 20 MIN. + SOAKING COOK 1¼ HOURS
MAKES: 6 SERVINGS (2 QUARTS)

- 1 cup dried great northern beans
- 2 cups finely chopped onions
- 2 medium carrots, chopped
- ½ cup sliced fennel bulb or celery
- ¼ cup olive oil
- 4 garlic cloves, minced
- ¾ teaspoon crushed red pepper flakes
- 2 bay leaves
- 4 cans (14½ ounces each) chicken or vegetable broth
- 2 cups uncooked bow tie pasta
- ½ cup oil-packed sun-dried tomatoes, chopped
- ¼ cup minced fresh parsley
- ½ teaspoon salt
  Shredded Parmesan cheese, optional

1. Rinse and sort beans; soak according to package directions. Drain and rinse beans; discard liquid and set beans aside.

2. In a Dutch oven, saute onions, carrots and fennel in oil until tender. Add garlic, pepper flakes and bay leaves; cook 1 minute. Add broth and beans.

3. Bring to a boil. Reduce heat; cover and simmer until beans are almost tender, about 1 hour. Stir in pasta, tomatoes, parsley and salt. Bring to a boil. Reduce heat; cover and simmer 15 minutes or until beans and pasta are tender. Discard bay leaves. Serve with cheese if desired.

LENTIL SOUP

Lentil Soup

I first tasted this soup at a friend's house. Now it's my favorite, especially on a cool, crisp autumn night here in Colorado.

—CATHERINE ROWE BERTHOUD, CO

PREP: 10 MIN. • **COOK:** 1 HOUR
MAKES: 6 SERVINGS

- ½ pound bulk Italian sausage
- 1 large onion, finely chopped
- 1 small green pepper, finely chopped
- 1 small carrot, finely chopped
- 1 large garlic clove, finely minced
- 1 bay leaf
- 2 cans (14½ ounces each) chicken broth
- 1 can (14½ ounces) diced tomatoes, undrained
- 1 cup water
- ¾ cup dried lentils, rinsed
- ¼ cup country-style or regular Dijon mustard

In a Dutch oven, cook sausage over medium heat until no longer pink. Drain fat and crumble sausage; return to Dutch oven along with remaining ingredients, except mustard. Simmer, covered, 1 hour or until lentils and vegetables are tender. Stir in mustard. Remove and discard the bay leaf before serving.

DID YOU KNOW?

Grown all over the world, lentils are the edible seeds (also sometimes called pulses) that grow inside the pods of leguminous plants. They vary in size and shape as well as color. Lentils are low in fat and high in protein and fiber, making them a great substitute for meat. They cook quickly and often boast flavors that are mild, nutty or earthy.

Bart's Black Bean Soup

Try this 10-minute soup for a super-fast dinner that everyone will love. Stir in hot salsa for a spicy alternative.

—**SHARON ULLYOT** LONDON, ON

START TO FINISH: 10 MIN.
MAKES: 4 SERVINGS

- 1 can (15 ounces) black beans, rinsed and drained
- 1½ cups chicken broth
- ¾ cup chunky salsa
- ½ cup canned whole kernel corn, drained
  Dash hot pepper sauce
- 2 teaspoons lime juice
- 1 cup (4 ounces) shredded cheddar cheese
- 2 tablespoons chopped green onions

In a microwave-safe bowl, combine the first five ingredients. Cover and microwave on high for 2 minutes or until heated through. Pour into four serving bowls; drizzle each with lime juice. Sprinkle with cheese and green onions.

NOTE *This recipe was tested in a 1,100-watt microwave.*

Moroccan Chickpea Stew

When I served this spicy stew to guests, including three vegetarians, they were thrilled with the abundance of squash, potatoes, tomatoes and zucchini. The recipe is definitely a keeper!

—**CINDY BEBERMAN** ORLAND PARK, IL

PREP: 20 MIN. • **COOK:** 30 MIN.
MAKES: 9 SERVINGS (ABOUT 2 QUARTS)

- 1 large onion, finely chopped
- 2 tablespoons olive oil
- 1 tablespoon butter

MOROCCAN CHICKPEA STEW

- 2 garlic cloves, minced
- 2 teaspoons ground cumin
- 1 cinnamon stick (3 inches)
- ½ teaspoon chili powder
- 4 cups vegetable broth
- 2 cups cubed peeled butternut squash
- 1 can (15 ounces) chickpeas or garbanzo beans, rinsed and drained
- 1 can (14½ ounces) diced tomatoes, undrained
- 1 medium red potato, cut into 1-inch cubes
- 1 medium sweet potato, peeled and cut into 1-inch cubes
- 1 medium lemon, thinly sliced
- ¼ teaspoon salt
- 2 small zucchini, cubed
- 3 tablespoons minced fresh cilantro

1. In a Dutch oven, saute onion in oil and butter until tender. Add the garlic, cumin, cinnamon stick and chili powder; saute 1 minute longer.
2. Stir in the broth, squash, chickpeas, tomatoes, potatoes, lemon and salt. Bring to a boil. Reduce heat; cover and simmer for 15-20 minutes or until potatoes and squash are almost tender.
3. Add zucchini; return to a boil. Reduce heat; cover and simmer for 5-8 minutes or until vegetables are tender. Discard cinnamon stick and lemon slices. Stir in cilantro.

BART'S BLACK BEAN SOUP

FREEZE IT Chunky Sausage Lentil Soup

Lentils are an inexpensive, nutritious power food. We love this soup. It freezes and reheats well, too.

—**DLEE SCAR** E. HANOVER, NJ

PREP: 30 MIN. • **COOK:** 25 MIN.
MAKES: 10 SERVINGS (3½ QUARTS)

- 8 cups water
- 1 package (16 ounces) dried lentils, rinsed
- 1 package (19½ ounces) Italian turkey sausage links, casings removed and crumbled
- 2 medium onions, chopped
- 2 celery ribs, chopped
- 2 medium carrots, cut into ¼-inch slices
- 6 garlic cloves, minced
- 3 cans (14½ ounces each) reduced-sodium beef broth
- 1 can (28 ounces) crushed tomatoes
- 1 medium red potato, diced
- 1½ teaspoons dried thyme
- 1½ teaspoons coarsely ground pepper
  Salad croutons, optional

1. In a large saucepan, bring water and lentils to a boil. Reduce heat; cover and simmer for 18-22 minutes or until lentils are tender. Drain. Meanwhile, in a Dutch oven, cook the sausage, onions, celery and carrots over medium heat until meat is no longer pink and vegetables are tender; drain. Add garlic; cook 2 minutes longer.

2. Stir in the broth, tomatoes, potato, thyme and pepper. Bring to a boil. Reduce heat; simmer, uncovered, for 15-20 minutes or until potato is tender. Stir in lentils; heat through. Serve with croutons if desired.

FREEZE OPTION *Reserving croutons for later, freeze cooled soup in freezer containers. Freeze up to 3 months. To use, partially thaw in refrigerator overnight. Heat through in a saucepan, stirring occasionally and adding a little broth or water if necessary. Top each serving with croutons if desired.*

Spiced-Up Healthy Soup

My spiced-up soup is low in fat and filled with a bounty of good-for-you ingredients.

—**DIANE TAYMAN** DIXON/GRAND DETOUR, IL

PREP: 15 MIN. • **COOK:** 40 MIN.
MAKES: 14 SERVINGS (3½ QUARTS)

- 1 medium onion, chopped
- ⅓ cup medium pearl barley
- 2 tablespoons canola oil
- 4 garlic cloves, minced
- 5 cans (14½ ounces each) reduced-sodium chicken broth
- 2 boneless skinless chicken breast halves (4 ounces each)
- 1 cup dried lentils, rinsed
- 1 jar (16 ounces) picante sauce
- 1 can (15 ounces) garbanzo beans or chickpeas, rinsed and drained
- ½ cup minced fresh cilantro
- 8 cups chopped fresh spinach

1. In a Dutch oven, saute onion and barley in oil until onion is tender. Add garlic; cook 1 minute longer. Add the broth, chicken and lentils; bring to a boil. Reduce heat; cover and simmer for 15 minutes or until chicken is no longer pink. Remove chicken and set aside.

2. Add the picante sauce, garbanzo beans and cilantro to soup; cover and simmer 10 minutes longer or until barley and lentils are tender.

3. Shred chicken with two forks. Add spinach and chicken to soup. Simmer, uncovered, for 5 minutes or until spinach is wilted.

SPICED-UP HEALTHY SOUP

HEARTY ITALIAN WHITE BEAN SOUP

Hearty Italian White Bean Soup

This soup is so satisfying that it's hard to believe it is actually good for you, too. With lots of beans and potatoes, a bowlful even hits the spot with die-hard meat lovers.

—TINA KRUMMEL ELKINS, AR

START TO FINISH: 30 MIN.
MAKES: 6 SERVINGS

- 1 tablespoon olive oil
- 1 medium potato, peeled and cut into ½-inch cubes
- 2 medium carrots, chopped
- 1 medium onion, chopped
- 2 celery ribs, chopped
- 1 medium zucchini, chopped
- 1 teaspoon finely chopped seeded jalapeno pepper
- 1 can (15½ ounces) navy beans, rinsed and drained
- 2 to 2½ cups vegetable or chicken broth
- 1 can (8 ounces) tomato sauce
- 2 tablespoons minced fresh parsley or 2 teaspoons dried parsley flakes
- 1½ teaspoons minced fresh thyme or ½ teaspoon dried thyme

1. In a Dutch oven, heat oil over medium-high heat. Add potato and carrots; cook and stir 3 minutes. Add onion, celery, zucchini and jalapeno; cook and stir 3-4 minutes or until vegetables are crisp-tender.

2. Stir in remaining ingredients; bring to a boil. Reduce heat; simmer, covered, 12-15 minutes or until vegetables are tender.

NOTE *Wear disposable gloves when cutting hot peppers; the oils can burn skin. Avoid touching your face.*

SPLIT PEA SOUP

Split Pea Soup

Try this recipe for a new spin on traditional split pea soup. The flavor is peppery rather than smoky, and the corned beef is an unexpected, tasty change of pace.

—BARBARA LINK RANCHO CUCAMONGA, CA

PREP: 15 MIN. • **COOK:** 1½ HOURS
MAKES: 12 SERVINGS (3 QUARTS)

- 1 package (16 ounces) dried split peas
- 8 cups water
- 2 medium potatoes, peeled and cubed
- 2 large onions, chopped
- 2 medium carrots, chopped
- 2 cups cubed cooked corned beef or ham
- ½ cup chopped celery
- 5 teaspoons chicken bouillon granules
- 1 teaspoon dried marjoram
- 1 teaspoon poultry seasoning
- 1 teaspoon rubbed sage
- ½ to 1 teaspoon pepper
- ½ teaspoon dried basil
- ½ teaspoon salt, optional

In a Dutch oven, combine all ingredients; bring to a boil. Reduce heat; cover and simmer for 1¼ to 1½ hours or until peas and vegetables are tender.

Lentil Soup for the Soul

My boyfriend and I are vegetarians, and I like to experiment with new meatless dishes. This is one of our favorites on brisk fall or winter evenings.

—**ATHENA RUSSELL** FLORENCE, SC

PREP: 20 MIN. • **COOK:** 30 MIN.
MAKES: 3 SERVINGS

- ⅓ **cup chopped peeled parsnip**
- ⅓ **cup diced peeled potato**
- ¼ **cup chopped green onions**
- ¼ **cup chopped leek (white portion only)**
- ¼ **cup chopped carrot**
- ¼ **cup chopped celery**
- 2 **teaspoons olive oil**
- 1 **can (14½ ounces) vegetable broth**
- 1 **cup no-salt-added diced tomatoes**
- ⅓ **cup dried lentils, rinsed**
- ¼ **cup dry red wine or additional vegetable broth**
- 1 **teaspoon Worcestershire sauce**
- 1 **bay leaf**
- ⅓ **cup minced fresh cilantro**

1. In a large saucepan, saute the parsnip, potato, onions, leek, carrot and celery in oil for 3 minutes. Add the broth, tomatoes, lentils, wine, Worcestershire sauce and bay leaf. Bring to a boil. Reduce heat; cover and simmer for 25-30 minutes or until lentils are tender.

2. Just before serving, discard bay leaf; stir in cilantro.

Southwestern Bean Chowder

The heat from the spices and green chilies doesn't stop my young kids from enjoying this soup. In fact, they like it as much as my husband and I do. I use white kidney beans because they have a terrific texture.

—**JULI MEYERS** HINESVILLE, GA

PREP: 20 MIN. • **COOK:** 35 MIN.
MAKES: 8 SERVINGS (2 QUARTS)

- 2 **cans (15 ounces each) white kidney or cannellini beans, rinsed and drained, divided**
- 1 **medium onion, chopped**
- ¼ **cup chopped celery**
- ¼ **cup chopped green pepper**

SOUTHWESTERN BEAN CHOWDER

- 1 **tablespoon olive oil**
- 2 **garlic cloves, minced**
- 3 **cups vegetable broth**
- 1½ **cups frozen corn, thawed**
- 1 **medium carrot, shredded**
- 1 **can (4 ounces) chopped green chilies**
- 1 **tablespoon ground cumin**
- ½ **teaspoon chili powder**
- 4½ **teaspoons cornstarch**
- 2 **cups 2% milk**
- 1 **cup (4 ounces) shredded cheddar cheese**
  Minced fresh cilantro and additional shredded cheddar cheese, optional

1. In a small bowl, mash one can beans with a fork; set aside.

2. In a Dutch oven, saute the onion, celery and pepper in oil until tender. Add garlic; cook 1 minute longer. Stir in the mashed beans, broth, corn, carrot, chilies, cumin, chili powder and remaining beans. Bring to a boil. Reduce heat; simmer, uncovered, for 20 minutes.

3. Combine cornstarch and milk until smooth. Stir into bean mixture. Bring to a boil; cook and stir for 2 minutes or until thickened. Stir in cheese until melted. Serve with cilantro and additional cheese if desired.

LENTIL SOUP FOR THE SOUL

LIMA BEAN OKRA SOUP

Lima Bean Okra Soup

The combination of beans and vegetables with a hint of sweet spices gives this soup a unique flavor. Every serving is loaded with color and a lots of vitamins to keep you healthy when it's cold outside.

—CLARA COULSON MINNEY
WASHINGTON COURT HOUSE, OH

PREP: 20 MIN. • **COOK:** 15 MIN.
MAKES: 7 SERVINGS

- 1 **medium green pepper, chopped**
- 1 **medium onion, chopped**
- ¼ **teaspoon whole cloves**
- 1 **tablespoon butter**
- 3 **cups vegetable broth**
- 3 **cups chopped tomatoes**
- 2½ **cups sliced fresh or frozen okra, thawed**
- 1 **cup frozen lima beans, thawed**
- ½ **cup fresh or frozen corn, thawed**
- ½ to 1 **teaspoon salt**
- ¼ to ½ **teaspoon ground allspice**
- ¼ **teaspoon pepper**
- ⅛ **teaspoon cayenne pepper**

1. In a large saucepan, saute the green pepper, onion and cloves in butter until vegetables are tender. Discard cloves.
2. Stir in the remaining ingredients. Bring to a boil. Reduce heat; cover and simmer for 15-20 minutes or until beans are tender.

TOP TIP

I use okra in soups and many other recipes, so I keep some on hand in the freezer. I wash fresh okra, blanch it, cool it quickly, then drain it well on paper towel. I slice it, arrange the slices on a baking sheet and freeze. Once frozen, the okra can easily be transferred to heavy-duty resealable plastic bags for long-term storage.
—MAXINE B. LA QUINTA, CA

MEATLESS LENTIL SOUP

SPILL-THE-BEANS
MINESTRONE

Meatless Lentil Soup

My husband and I have been married for many years, and throughout that time this soup has been one of his special recipe requests. On cold days, I pack it in his lunch along with homemade biscuits and butter.

—**JANET CHASE** BERRIEN SPRINGS, MI

PREP: 15 MIN. • **COOK:** 35 MIN.
MAKES: 8 SERVINGS (3 QUARTS)

- 2 **large carrots, halved and sliced**
- 2 **celery ribs, sliced**
- 1 **medium onion, chopped**
- 10 **cups water**
- 1 **package (16 ounces) dried lentils, rinsed**
- 4 **small red potatoes, diced**
- 2 **bay leaves**
- 2 **teaspoons salt**
- 1 **teaspoon pepper**

1. In a large nonstick saucepan coated with cooking spray, cook carrots, celery and onion over medium heat for 5 minutes.

2. Stir in the water, lentils, potatoes, bay leaves, salt and pepper. Bring to a boil. Reduce heat; cover and simmer for 30-35 minutes or until lentils are tender. Discard bay leaves.

Spill-the-Beans Minestrone

Chock-full of vegetables and vitamins, this hearty soup is a meal in itself. It makes a great vegetarian dish, but also tastes delicious with turkey kielbasa if you like meat. Serve it with crusty bread or breadsticks so you can soak up every savory drop.

—**REUBEN TSUJIMURA** WALLA WALLA, WA

PREP: 20 MIN. • **COOK:** 20 MIN.
MAKES: 6 SERVINGS

- 1 **medium onion, chopped**
- 1 **tablespoon olive oil**
- 2 **garlic cloves, minced**
- 2 **cans (14½ ounces each) reduced-sodium chicken broth or vegetable broth**
- 1 **can (16 ounces) kidney beans, rinsed and drained**
- 1 **can (15 ounces) garbanzo beans or chickpeas, rinsed and drained**
- 1 **can (14½ ounces) stewed tomatoes, cut up**
- 2 **cups chopped fresh kale**
- ½ **cup water**
- ½ **cup uncooked small pasta shells**
- 1 **teaspoon Italian seasoning**
- ¼ **teaspoon crushed red pepper flakes**
- 6 **teaspoons shredded Parmesan cheese**

In a large saucepan, saute onion in oil until onion is tender. Add garlic; cook 1 minute longer. Add the broth, beans, tomatoes, kale, water, pasta, Italian seasoning and pepper flakes. Bring to a boil. Reduce heat; cover and simmer for 10-15 minutes or until pasta is tender. Sprinkle each serving with cheese.

ITALIAN-STYLE LENTIL SOUP

**SAUSAGE &
CANNELLINI BEAN SOUP**

Italian-Style Lentil Soup

Lentils are a staple at my house. I like to add them to homemade spaghetti sauce. But this flavorful soup is my favorite way to use lentils.

—**RACHEL GREENAWALT KELLER** ROANOKE, VA

PREP: 15 MIN. • **COOK:** 40 MIN.
MAKES: 6 SERVINGS

- 2 **medium onions, chopped**
- 2 **celery ribs, thinly sliced**
- 1 **medium carrot, chopped**
- 2 **teaspoons olive oil**
- 5¼ **cups water**
- 1 **cup dried lentils, rinsed**
- ¼ **cup minced fresh parsley**
- 1 **tablespoon reduced-sodium beef bouillon granules**
- ½ **teaspoon pepper**
- 1 **can (6 ounces) tomato paste**
- 2 **tablespoons white vinegar**
- 2 **teaspoons brown sugar**
- ½ **teaspoon salt**
- 2 **tablespoons shredded Parmesan cheese**

1. In a large saucepan coated with cooking spray, saute the onions, celery and carrot in oil until almost tender. Stir in the water, lentils, parsley, bouillon and pepper. Bring to a boil. Reduce heat; cover and simmer for 20-25 minutes or until lentils are tender, stirring occasionally.

2. Stir in the tomato paste, vinegar, brown sugar and salt; heat through. Sprinkle each serving with cheese.

Sausage & Cannellini Bean Soup

Here's my version of a dish from a famous Chicago restaurant. I think it rivals the original. I cook this at least once a week. I like to take some with me for lunch the next day; it's tasty and healthy.

—**MARILYN MCGINNIS** PEORIA, AZ

START TO FINISH: 30 MIN.
MAKES: 4 SERVINGS

- 3 **Italian turkey sausage links (4 ounces each), casings removed**
- 1 **medium onion, chopped**
- 2 **garlic cloves, minced**
- 1 **can (15 ounces) cannellini or white kidney beans, rinsed and drained**
- 1 **can (14½ ounces) reduced-sodium chicken broth**
- 1 **cup water**
- ¼ **cup white wine or additional reduced-sodium chicken broth**
- ¼ **teaspoon pepper**
- 1 **bunch escarole or spinach, chopped**
- 4 **teaspoons shredded Parmesan cheese**

1. Cook the sausage and onion in a large saucepan over medium heat until meat is no longer pink; drain. Add garlic; cook 1 minute longer.

2. Stir in the beans, broth, water, wine and pepper. Bring to a boil. Add the escarole; heat through. Sprinkle with cheese.

Autumn Chili

A touch of baking cocoa gives my chili a rich flavor without adding sweetness. When I was growing up in the North, we served chili over rice. But after I married a Texan, I began including chopped onions, shredded cheese and, of course, corn bread on the side.
—**AUDREY BYRNE** LILLIAN, TX

PREP: 10 MIN. • **COOK:** 20 MIN. + SIMMERING
MAKES: 4 SERVINGS

- 1 **large onion, chopped**
- 2 **cans (16 ounces each) kidney beans, rinsed and drained**
- 2 **cans (14½ ounces each) diced tomatoes, undrained**
- 2 **cups cooked and crumbled ground beef**
- 1 **can (8 ounces) tomato sauce**
- 1 **medium green pepper**
- 3 **tablespoons chili powder**
- 1 **tablespoon ground cumin**
- 2 **garlic cloves, minced**
- 1 **teaspoon baking cocoa**
- 1 **teaspoon dried oregano**
- 1 **teaspoon Worcestershire sauce, optional**
   Salt and pepper to taste

In a large saucepan coated with cooking spray, saute onion until tender. Add the remaining ingredients; bring to a boil. Reduce heat; cover and simmer for 2 hours, stirring occasionally.

Thick & Chunky Beef Chili

Hearty, flavorful ingredients and a thick sauce make this a satisfying meal that's sure to win you compliments on your cooking. It's a great way to serve a crowd during the big game.
—*TASTE OF HOME* TEST KITCHEN

PREP: 30 MIN. • **COOK:** 3 HOURS
MAKES: 4 QUARTS

- 12 **ounces center-cut bacon, diced**
- 2 **pounds beef stew meat, cut into ¼-inch cubes**
- 2 **medium onions, chopped**
- 4 **garlic cloves, minced**
- 3 **cans (14½ ounces each) no-salt-added diced tomatoes, undrained**
- 1 **cup barbecue sauce**
- 1 **cup chili sauce**
- ½ **cup honey**
- 4 **teaspoons reduced-sodium beef bouillon granules**
- 1 **bay leaf**
- 1 **tablespoon chili powder**
- 1 **tablespoon baking cocoa**
- 1 **tablespoon Worcestershire sauce**
- 1 **tablespoon Dijon mustard**
- 1½ **teaspoons ground cumin**
- ¼ **teaspoon cayenne powder, optional**
- 3 **cans (16 ounces each) kidney beans, rinsed and drained**
   Shredded reduced-fat cheddar cheese, optional

1. In a large Dutch oven, cook bacon until crisp; remove to paper towels to drain. Reserve 3 tablespoons drippings.
2. Brown beef in drippings. Add onion; cook until onions are tender. Add garlic; cook 1 minute longer. Return bacon to pan. Stir in the next 12 ingredients.
3. Bring to a boil. Reduce heat; cover and simmer until meat is tender, about 3 hours.
4. Add beans and heat through. Discard bay leaf. Garnish with cheese if desired.

AUTUMN CHILI

SWEET POTATO &
BLACK BEAN CHILI

Sweet Potato &
Black Bean Chili

My whole family enjoys this vegetarian chili, and especially my daughter. I love it because it's easy to make and has a great flavor.

—**JOY PENDLEY** ORTONVILLE, MI

PREP: 25 MIN. • **COOK:** 35 MIN.
MAKES: 8 SERVINGS (2 QUARTS)

- 3 **large sweet potatoes, peeled and cut into ½-inch cubes**
- 1 **large onion, chopped**
- 1 **tablespoon olive oil**
- 2 **tablespoons chili powder**
- 3 **garlic cloves, minced**
- 1 **teaspoon ground cumin**
- ¼ **teaspoon cayenne pepper**
- 2 **cans (15 ounces each) black beans, rinsed and drained**
- 1 **can (28 ounces) diced tomatoes, undrained**
- ¼ **cup brewed coffee**
- 2 **tablespoons honey**
- ½ **teaspoon salt**
- ¼ **teaspoon pepper**
- ½ **cup shredded reduced-fat Monterey Jack cheese or reduced-fat Mexican cheese blend**

1. In a nonstick Dutch oven coated with cooking spray, saute sweet potatoes and onion in oil until crisp-tender. Add the chili powder, garlic, cumin and cayenne; cook 1 minute longer. Stir in the beans, tomatoes, coffee, honey, salt and pepper.

2. Bring to a boil. Reduce heat; cover and simmer for 30-35 minutes or until sweet potatoes are tender. Sprinkle with cheese.

Zesty Steak Chili

This full-flavored, medium-hot, Texas-style chili tastes even better the second day after the flavors have blended.

—**MICHELLE SMITH** RUNNING SPRINGS, CA

PREP: 40 MIN. • **COOK:** 2 HOURS
MAKES: 20 SERVINGS

- 4 **pounds beef top round steak, cut into 1-inch cubes**
- 4 **garlic cloves, minced**
- ¼ **cup canola oil**
- 3 **cups chopped onion**
- 2¾ **cups water, divided**
- 2 **cups sliced celery**
- 3 **cans (14½ ounces each) diced tomatoes, undrained**
- 2 **cans (15 ounces each) no-salt-added tomato sauce**
- 1 **jar (16 ounces) salsa**
- 3 **tablespoons chili powder**
- 2 **teaspoons ground cumin**
- 2 **teaspoons dried oregano**
- 1 **teaspoon salt, optional**
- 1 **teaspoon pepper**
- ¼ **cup all-purpose flour**
- ¼ **cup yellow cornmeal**
  Shredded reduced-fat cheddar cheese, reduced-fat sour cream, sliced green onions and sliced ripe olives, optional

1. In a Dutch oven over medium-high heat, saute steak and garlic in oil until browned. Add onion; cook and stir for 5 minutes. Stir in 2 cups water and next nine ingredients; bring to a boil.

2. Reduce heat; cover and simmer 2 hours or until tender. Combine flour, cornmeal and remaining water; stir until smooth. Bring chili to a boil. Add flour mixture; cook and stir 2 minutes or until thickened. If desired, garnish with reduced-fat cheese, reduced-fat sour cream, onions and olives.

ZESTY STEAK CHILI

SHRIMP 'N' BLACK BEAN CHILI

Shrimp 'n' Black Bean Chili

It's not spicy, but this chili is sure to warm you up on cold winter nights. The recipe calls for precooked shrimp and canned goods, so it's a cinch to prepare.

—**ELIZABETH HUNT** KIRBYVILLE, TX

START TO FINISH: 25 MIN.
MAKES: 6 SERVINGS

- ½ cup chopped onion
- ½ cup chopped green pepper
- 1 tablespoon canola oil
- 1 can (15 ounces) black beans, rinsed and drained
- 1 can (14½ ounces) diced tomatoes, undrained
- 1 cup chicken broth
- ⅓ cup picante sauce
- 1 teaspoon ground cumin
- ½ teaspoon dried basil
- 1 pound cooked medium shrimp, peeled and deveined
  Hot cooked rice, optional

1. In a large saucepan, saute onion and green pepper in oil for 4-5 minutes or until crisp-tender. Stir in the beans, tomatoes, broth, picante sauce, cumin and basil. Reduce heat; simmer, uncovered, for 10-15 minutes or until heated through.
2. Add shrimp; simmer 3-4 minutes longer or until heated through. Serve with rice if desired.

Spicy Pork Chili

This Southwestern chili, loaded with white beans and cubes of pork, has plenty of bite. But if it's not spicy enough for you, top it with shredded jalapeno jack cheese and finely diced onions.

—**LARRY LAATSCH** SAGINAW, MI

PREP: 10 MIN. • **COOK:** 1½ HOURS
MAKES: 15 SERVINGS

- 1½ pounds pork tenderloin, cubed
- 2 large onions, diced
- 4 celery ribs, diced
- 2 tablespoons butter
- 6 cans (15½ ounces each) great northern beans, rinsed and drained
- 4 cans (14½ ounces each) chicken broth
- 2 cups water
- 2 jalapeno peppers, seeded and chopped
- 2 teaspoons chili powder
- ½ teaspoon each white pepper, cayenne pepper, ground cumin and black pepper
- 2 garlic cloves, minced
- ½ teaspoon salt
- ¼ teaspoon dried parsley flakes
- ¼ teaspoon hot pepper sauce, optional
- 1 cup (4 ounces) shredded Monterey Jack cheese

1. In a Dutch oven, brown pork in butter in batches. Remove and keep warm.
2. In the same pan, saute onions and celery in butter until tender. Stir in the beans, broth, water, jalapenos, spices, garlic, salt, parsley, pork and, if desired, hot pepper sauce. Bring to a boil. Reduce heat; cover and simmer for 45 to 60 minutes or until pork is tender.
3. Uncover; simmer 30-40 minutes longer or until chili reaches desired consistency. Sprinkle with cheese.
NOTE *Wear disposable gloves when cutting hot peppers; the oils can burn skin. Avoid touching your face.*

SPICY PORK CHILI

Roasted Vegetable Chili

I suggest serving this delicious and satisfying dish with corn chips, cheese, sour cream and a small salad. To save time, purchase vegetables that have already been pre-washed and diced.

—**HANNAH BARRINGER** LOUDON, TN

PREP: 35 MIN. • **COOK:** 30 MIN.
MAKES: 13 SERVINGS (5 QUARTS)

- 1 **medium butternut squash, peeled and cut into 1-inch pieces**
- 3 **large carrots, sliced**
- 2 **medium zucchini, cut into 1-inch pieces**
- 2 **tablespoons olive oil, divided**
- 1½ **teaspoons ground cumin**
- 2 **medium green peppers, diced**
- 1 **large onion, chopped**
- 3 **cans (14½ ounces each) reduced-sodium chicken broth**
- 3 **cans (14½ ounces each) diced tomatoes, undrained**
- 2 **cans (15 ounces each) cannellini or white kidney beans, rinsed and drained**
- 1 **cup water**
- 1 **cup salsa**
- 3 **teaspoons chili powder**
- 6 **garlic cloves, minced**

1. Place the squash, carrots and zucchini in a 15x10x1-in. baking pan. Combine 1 tablespoon oil and cumin; drizzle over vegetables and toss to coat. Bake, uncovered, at 450° for 25-30 minutes or until tender, stirring once.

2. Meanwhile, in a stockpot, saute green peppers and onion in remaining oil for 3-4 minutes or until tender. Stir in the broth, tomatoes, beans, water, salsa, chili powder and garlic. Bring to a boil. Reduce heat; simmer, uncovered, for 10 minutes.

3. Stir in roasted vegetables. Return to a boil. Reduce heat; simmer, uncovered, for 5-10 minutes or until heated through.

KIELBASA CHILI

FREEZE IT **5** INGREDIENTS

Kielbasa Chili

This has the classic flavors of a chili dog in a bowl. I make it when I need a hot, hearty meal in a hurry. It's also great for parties and football games.

—**AUDRA DUVALL** LAS VEGAS, NV

START TO FINISH: 20 MIN.
MAKES: 7 SERVINGS

- 1 **pound smoked kielbasa or Polish sausage, halved and sliced**
- 2 **cans (14½ ounces each) diced tomatoes, undrained**
- 1 **can (15 ounces) chili with beans**
- 1 **can (8¾ ounces) whole kernel corn, drained**
- 1 **can (2¼ ounces) sliced ripe olives, drained**

In a Dutch oven coated with cooking spray, saute kielbasa until browned. Stir in the remaining ingredients. Bring to a boil. Reduce heat; simmer, uncovered, for 4-5 minutes or until heated through.

FREEZE OPTION *Cool chili and transfer to freezer containers. Freeze up to 3 months. To use, thaw in the refrigerator. Place in a saucepan; heat through.*

Kids' Favorite Chili

This sweet and easy chili is sure to warm the whole family up on those chilly fall nights. The recipe has been in my family for three generations.

—**TERRI KEENEY** GREELEY, CO

START TO FINISH: 25 MIN.
MAKES: 4 SERVINGS

- 1 **pound ground turkey**
- ½ **cup chopped onion**
- 1 **can (15¾ ounces) pork and beans**
- 1 **can (14½ ounces) diced tomatoes, undrained**
- 1 **can (10¾ ounces) condensed tomato soup, undiluted**
- 1 **tablespoon brown sugar**
- 1 **tablespoon chili powder**

In a large saucepan, cook turkey and onion over medium heat until meat is no longer pink; drain. Stir in the remaining ingredients. Bring to a boil. Reduce heat; cover and simmer for 15-20 minutes or until heated through.

Award-Winning Chuck Wagon Chili

Sprinkle in additional chili powder for an extra-spicy kick—but make sure you've got a cool drink close by!

—EUGENE JARZAB JR. PHOENIX, AZ

PREP: 30 MIN. • **COOK:** 80 MIN.
MAKES: 6 SERVINGS

- 1 **boneless beef chuck roast (3 pounds), cut into ½-inch cubes**
- 1 **pound pork stew meat, cut into ½-inch cubes**
- ⅓ **cup chili powder, divided**
- 4 **tablespoons canola oil, divided**
- 1 **large onion, finely chopped**
- 1 **celery rib, finely chopped**
- 3 **garlic cloves, minced**
- 1 **tablespoon chopped canned green chilies**
- 1 **carton (32 ounces) beef broth**
- ¾ **cup beer**
- ¾ **cup tomato sauce**
- 2 **tablespoons grated dark chocolate**
- 3 **teaspoons ground cumin**
- 1 **teaspoon dried oregano**
- ½ **teaspoon salt**
- ½ **teaspoon ground mustard**
- ½ **teaspoon cayenne pepper**

1. Sprinkle beef and pork with half of the chili powder. In a Dutch oven, brown meat in batches in 2 tablespoons oil; drain and set aside. In the same pan, saute onion and celery in remaining oil until crisp-tender. Add the garlic, chilies and remaining chili powder; cook 1 minute longer.

2. Stir in the broth, beer, tomato sauce, chocolate, cumin, oregano, salt, mustard, cayenne and meat. Bring to a boil. Reduce heat; simmer, uncovered, for 1 to 1½ hours or until meat is tender.

AWARD-WINNING CHUCK WAGON CHILI

Chipotle-Black Bean Chili

I love soup weather, and this chili is ideal to warm you up when there's a nip in the air. The whole can of chipotles in adobo sauce gives it some heat. Cut back on the amount if you prefer a milder level of spice.

—**KARLA SHEELEY** WORDEN, IL

PREP: 20 MIN. • **COOK:** 1¼ HOURS
MAKES: 10 SERVINGS (3 QUARTS)

- 1 **tablespoon Creole seasoning**
- 1 **beef top sirloin steak (2 pounds), cut into ½-inch cubes**
- 3 **tablespoons olive oil**
- 1 **large sweet onion, chopped**
- 3 **chipotle peppers in adobo sauce, seeded and finely chopped**
- 2 **tablespoons minced garlic**
- ⅓ **cup masa harina**
- 2 **tablespoons chili powder**
- 2 **tablespoons Worcestershire sauce**
- 1 **tablespoon ground cumin**
- 1 **teaspoon ground cinnamon**
- ¼ **teaspoon salt**
- ¼ **teaspoon cayenne pepper**
- 4 **cups reduced-sodium beef broth**
- 1 **can (28 ounces) diced tomatoes, undrained**
- 3 **cans (15 ounces each) black beans, rinsed and drained**
  Shredded cheddar cheese and/or finely chopped red onion, optional

1. Place Creole seasoning in a large resealable plastic bag. Add beef, a few pieces at a time, and shake to coat.
2. In a Dutch oven, saute beef in oil in batches. Stir in the onion, chipotle peppers and garlic. Cook 3 minutes longer or until onion is tender. Drain.
3. Stir in the masa harina, chili powder, Worcestershire sauce, cumin, cinnamon, salt and cayenne. Cook and stir for 3-5 minutes. Stir in broth and tomatoes. Bring to a boil. Reduce heat; simmer, uncovered, for 45 minutes or until beef is tender.

4. Stir in beans; heat through. Garnish with cheddar cheese and/or red onion if desired.
NOTE *Wear disposable gloves when cutting hot peppers; the oils can burn skin. Avoid touching your face.*

Hearty Meatless Chili

Years ago, I came across a recipe for plain chili. I adjusted the spices, reduced the oil and added vegetables to give it a beautiful color. Dozens of folks have enjoyed the results and asked for the recipe since.

—**LOIS BEACH** COLLEGE STATION, TX

PREP: 20 MIN. • **COOK:** 55 MIN.
MAKES: 8 SERVINGS (2½ QUARTS)

- 1 **small onion, chopped**
- 1 **tablespoon olive oil**
- 3 **garlic cloves, minced**
- 2 **medium zucchini, finely chopped**
- 2 **medium carrots, finely chopped**
- 3 **tablespoons cornmeal**
- 2 **tablespoons chili powder**
- 2 **tablespoons paprika**
- 1 **tablespoon sugar**
- ½ **teaspoon ground cumin**
- ¼ **to ½ teaspoon cayenne pepper**
- 2 **cans (one 28 ounces, one 14½ ounces) diced tomatoes, undrained**
- 2 **cans (15 ounces each) pinto beans, rinsed and drained**
- 1 **can (16 ounces) kidney beans, rinsed and drained**

GARNISH
- 8 **tablespoons fat-free sour cream**
- 8 **tablespoons thinly sliced green onions**
- 8 **teaspoons minced fresh cilantro**

1. In a Dutch oven, saute onion in oil until tender. Add garlic; cook 1 minute longer. Stir in zucchini and carrots. Add the cornmeal, chili powder, paprika, sugar, cumin and cayenne; cook and stir for 1 minute.
2. Stir in tomatoes and beans. Bring to a boil. Reduce heat; cover and simmer for 45 minutes. Garnish each serving with sour cream, green onions and cilantro.

HEARTY MEATLESS CHILI

Lime Chicken Chili

Lime juice gives this chili a tart twist. Canned tomatoes and beans make preparation a snap. Serve with toasted tortilla strips on top for a little crunch.

—**DIANE RANDAZZO** SINKING SPRING, PA

PREP: 25 MIN. • **COOK:** 40 MIN.
MAKES: 6 SERVINGS

- 1 **medium onion, chopped**
- 1 **each medium sweet yellow, red and green pepper, chopped**
- 2 **tablespoons olive oil**
- 3 **garlic cloves, minced**
- 1 **pound ground chicken**
- 1 **tablespoon all-purpose flour**
- 1 **tablespoon baking cocoa**
- 1 **tablespoon ground cumin**
- 1 **tablespoon chili powder**
- 2 **teaspoons ground coriander**
- ½ **teaspoon salt**
- ½ **teaspoon garlic pepper blend**
- ¼ **teaspoon pepper**
- 2 **cans (14½ ounces each) diced tomatoes, undrained**
- ¼ **cup lime juice**
- 1 **teaspoon grated lime peel**
- 1 **can (15 ounces) white kidney or cannellini beans, rinsed and drained**
- 2 **flour tortillas (8 inches), cut into ¼-inch strips**
- 6 **tablespoons reduced-fat sour cream**

1. In a large saucepan, saute onion and peppers in oil for 7-8 minutes or until crisp-tender. Add garlic; cook 1 minute longer. Add chicken; cook and stir over medium heat for 8-9 minutes or until no longer pink.

2. Stir in the flour, cocoa and seasonings. Add the tomatoes, lime juice and lime peel. Bring to a boil. Reduce heat; simmer, uncovered, for 20-25 minutes or until thickened, stirring frequently. Stir in beans; heat through.

3. Meanwhile, place tortilla strips on a baking sheet coated with cooking spray. Bake at 400° for 8-10 minutes or until crisp. Serve chili with sour cream and tortilla strips.

ALOHA CHILI

Aloha Chili

Pineapple and brown sugar give this extraordinary chili a tropical flair. Everyone who samples it is pleasantly surprised, and often request a second bowl.

—**DYAN CORNIES** VERNON, BC

START TO FINISH: 30 MIN.
MAKES: 8 SERVINGS (ABOUT 2 QUARTS)

- 2 **pounds ground beef**
- 1 **large onion, finely chopped**
- 1 **can (20 ounces) pineapple chunks, undrained**
- 1 **can (16 ounces) kidney beans, rinsed and drained**
- 1 **can (15¾ ounces) pork and beans**
- 1 **cup ketchup**
- ¼ **cup packed brown sugar**
- ¼ **cup white vinegar**

1. In a Dutch oven, cook beef and onion over medium heat until no meat is no longer pink; drain.

2. Stir in the remaining ingredients. Bring to a boil. Reduce heat; cover and simmer for 20 minutes or until heated through.

LIME CHICKEN CHILI

Hearty Pumpkin Chili with Polenta

You can easily make this healthy chili a day ahead. It reheats nicely, and the polenta keeps for a few days in an airtight container in the fridge.

—**WENDY RUSCH** TREGO, WI

PREP: 30 MIN. • **COOK:** 45 MIN.
MAKES: 6 SERVINGS

- 1 **pound ground beef**
- 2 **celery ribs, finely chopped**
- 1 **medium onion, finely chopped**
- 1 **small sweet red pepper, finely chopped**
- 2 **garlic cloves, minced**
- 1 **can (29 ounces) tomato sauce**
- 1 **can (15 ounces) crushed tomatoes**
- 1 **can (15 ounces) solid-pack pumpkin**
- 1 **tablespoon plus 2 teaspoons sugar, divided**
- 1 **tablespoon chili powder**
- 1½ **teaspoons pumpkin pie spice**
- ½ **teaspoon plus ¾ teaspoon salt, divided**
- ½ **teaspoon pepper**
- 1½ **cups 2% milk**
- ½ **cup heavy whipping cream**
- ¼ **cup butter, cubed**
- ¾ **cup yellow cornmeal**
- 1 **can (15 ounces) black beans, rinsed and drained**

1. In a Dutch oven, cook the first five ingredients over medium heat 8-10 minutes or until beef is no longer pink and vegetables are tender, breaking up beef into crumbles; drain.

2. Stir in tomato sauce, tomatoes, pumpkin, 1 tablespoon sugar, chili powder, pie spice, ½ teaspoon salt and pepper; bring to a boil. Reduce heat; simmer, uncovered, 45 minutes, stirring occasionally.

3. Meanwhile, in a large heavy saucepan, bring milk, cream, butter, and remaining sugar and salt to a boil. Reduce heat to a gentle boil; slowly whisk in cornmeal. Cook and stir with a wooden spoon 2-3 minutes or until polenta is thickened and pulls away cleanly from sides of pan (mixture will be very thick).

4. Pour into a greased 9-in.-square baking pan. Let stand until firm, about 30 minutes.

5. Stir beans into chili; heat through. Cut polenta into six pieces. Serve with chili.

CINCINNATI CHILI

Cincinnati Chili

Cincinnati is famous for chili. Cocoa and cinnamon yield a rich flavor. Top servings with shredded cheddar for authenticity.

—EDITH JOYCE PARKMAN, OH

PREP: 20 MIN. • **COOK:** 1¾ HOURS
MAKES: 8 SERVINGS

- 1 **pound ground beef**
- 1 **pound ground pork**
- 4 **medium onions, chopped**
- 6 **garlic cloves, minced**
- 2 **cans (16 ounces each) kidney beans, rinsed and drained**
- 1 **can (28 ounces) crushed tomatoes**
- ¼ **cup white vinegar**
- ¼ **cup baking cocoa**
- 2 **tablespoons chili powder**
- 2 **tablespoons Worcestershire sauce**
- 4 **teaspoons ground cinnamon**
- 3 **teaspoons dried oregano**
- 2 **teaspoons ground cumin**
- 2 **teaspoons ground allspice**
- 2 **teaspoons hot pepper sauce**
- 3 **bay leaves**
- 1 **teaspoon sugar**
  Salt and pepper to taste
  Hot cooked spaghetti
  Shredded cheddar cheese, sour cream, chopped tomatoes and green onions

1. In a Dutch oven, cook the beef, pork and onions over medium heat until meat is no longer pink. Add garlic; cook 1 minute longer. Drain. Add the beans, tomatoes, vinegar, cocoa and seasonings; bring to a boil. Reduce heat; cover and simmer for 1½ hours or until heated through.
2. Discard bay leaves. Serve with spaghetti. Garnish with cheese, sour cream, tomatoes and onions.

White Chili with a Kick

Store-bought rotisserie chicken helps keep the preparation of this spicy chili easy and quick. We like it with sour cream, green onions, cheese or salsa garnished on top.

—EMMAJEAN ANDERSON
MENDOTA HEIGHTS, MN

PREP: 20 MIN. • **COOK:** 15 MIN.
MAKES: 9 SERVINGS (2¼ QUARTS)

- 1 **large onion, chopped**
- 6 **tablespoons butter, cubed**
- 2 **tablespoons all-purpose flour**
- 2 **cups chicken broth**
- ¾ **cup half-and-half cream**
- 1 **rotisserie chicken, cut up**
- 2 **cans (15 ounces each) white kidney or cannellini beans, rinsed and drained**
- 1 **can (11 ounces) white corn, drained**
- 2 **cans (4 ounces each) chopped green chilies**
- 2 **teaspoons ground cumin**
- 1 **teaspoon chili powder**
- ½ **teaspoon salt**
- ½ **teaspoon white pepper**
- ½ **teaspoon hot pepper sauce**
- 1½ **cups (6 ounces) shredded pepper Jack cheese**
  Salsa and chopped green onions, optional

1. In a Dutch oven, saute onion in butter. Stir in flour until blended; cook and stir for 3 minutes or until golden brown. Gradually add broth and cream. Bring to a boil; cook and stir for 2 minutes or until thickened.
2. Add the chicken, beans, corn, chilies, cumin, chili powder, salt, pepper and pepper sauce; heat through. Stir in cheese until melted.
3. Garnish each serving with salsa and green onions if desired.

WHITE CHILI WITH A KICK

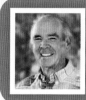

> Perfect for using leftover pork roast, this tasty, easy recipe can be made ahead and reheated—it's even better the second day.
>
> —**PETER HALFERTY** CORPUS CHRISTI, TX

CHUNKY CHIPOTLE PORK CHILI

FREEZE IT Chunky Chipotle Pork Chili

PREP: 15 MIN. • **COOK:** 20 MIN.
MAKES: 4 SERVINGS

- 1 medium green pepper, chopped
- 1 small onion, chopped
- 1 chipotle pepper in adobo sauce, finely chopped
- 1 tablespoon canola oil
- 3 garlic cloves, minced
- 1 can (16 ounces) red beans, rinsed and drained
- 1 cup beef broth
- ½ cup salsa
- 2 teaspoons ground cumin
- 2 teaspoons chili powder
- 2 cups cubed cooked pork
- ¼ cup sour cream

1. In a large saucepan, saute green pepper, onion and chipotle pepper in oil until tender. Add garlic; cook 1 minute longer.

2. Add beans, broth, salsa, cumin and chili powder. Bring to a boil. Reduce heat; simmer, uncovered, for 10 minutes or until thickened. Add pork; heat through. Serve with sour cream.

FREEZE OPTION *Cool chili and transfer to freezer containers. Freeze up to 3 months. To use, thaw in the refrigerator. Transfer to a large saucepan; heat through, adding water to thin if desired. Serve with sour cream.*

TOP TIP

Whenever you have leftover chili, freeze small portions in muffin cups. On busy nights, pull out as many portions as you need and reheat in the microwave or in a saucepan on the stovetop. Serve the chili over rice, mashed potatoes, a baked potato or even a hot dog for an easy chili dog.

General Recipe Index

This handy index lists recipes by food category and major ingredient, so you can easily find recipes to suit your needs.

Alphabetical Recipe Index

This handy index lists every recipe in alphabetical order, so you can easily find your favorite dishes.